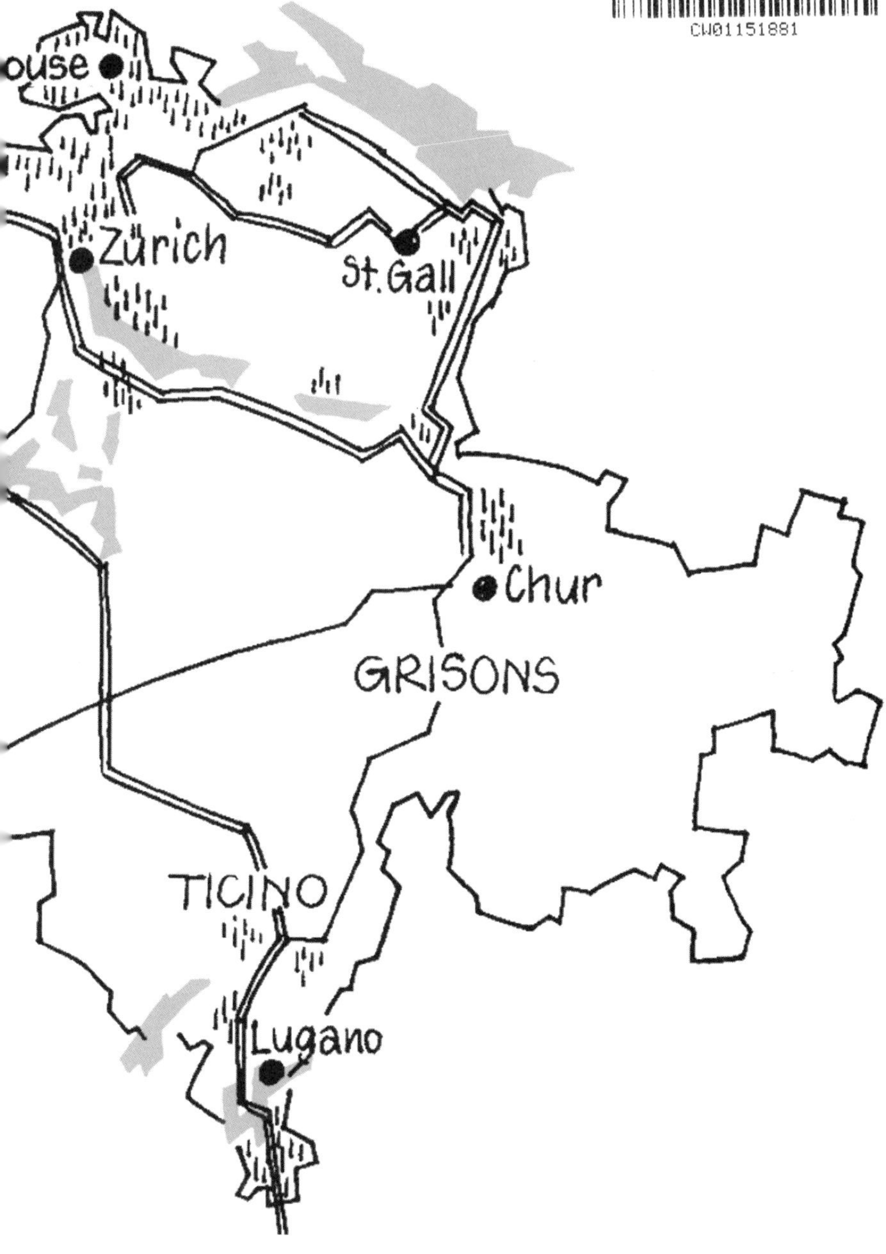

CW01151881

The Surprising Wines
of Switzerland

A Practical Guide to
Switzerland's Best Kept Secret

John C. Sloan

centrepoint
Im Lohnhof 8
CH-4051 Basel

Photographs by Hans-Peter Siffert

Bergli Books
Riehen, Switzerland

The Surprising Wines of Switzerland
A Practical Guide to Switzerland's Best Kept Secret
by John C. Sloan

Photographs copyright © 1996 Hans-Peter Siffert, Zurich
Maps copyright © 1995 Theres Scheiwiller, Gunzwil,

This edition published in 1996 by
Bergli Books Ltd.
Aeuss. Baselstr. 204   Tel: +41 61 601 31 01
CH-4125 Riehen   Fax: +41 61 601 67 01
Switzerland

Text first published in Great Britain in 1995 by
JCS Communications, London.
Text copyright © 1995 and 1996 John C. Sloan

All rights reserved. No part of this publication may be reproduced, stored in a retrieval system, or transmitted, in any form, or by any means, electronic, mechanical, photocopying, recording or otherwise, without the prior permission in writing from Bergli Books Ltd., Riehen, Switzerland.

Printed in Germany by Franz Spiegel Buch GmbH, Ulm
Lithographs, DTP Design, Lörrach
Cover photograph 'Blauburgunder and Elbling'
by Hans-Peter Siffert, Zurich

ISBN 3-9520002-6-4

This book is dedicated to my father, John K. Sloan, and to Martine, Catherine and Stéphanie, who continued to encourage me when a simple project grew into an undertaking much more demanding than expected.

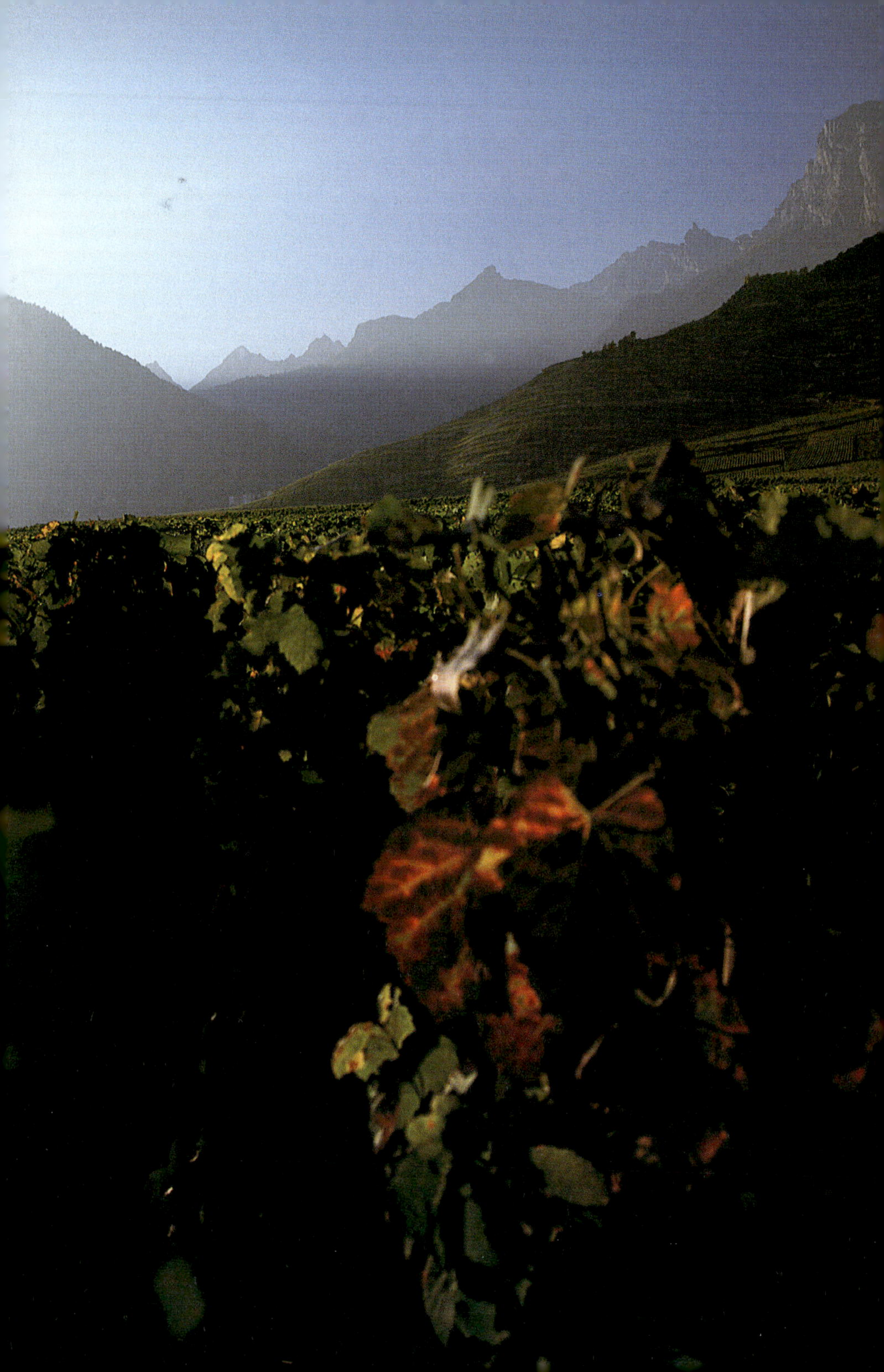

Table of Contents

Maps and Tables		vi
Introduction		vii

I.	Wine in Today's Switzerland	1
II.	The History of Wine in Switzerland	9
III.	Cultivation of the Vine	27
IV.	Grape Types	32
V.	Vinification, Swiss Style	50
VI.	Valais	60
VII.	Vaud, including Fribourg	99
VIII.	Geneva	141
IX.	Neuchâtel, including Berne (Lake Bienne)	163
X.	Ticino	177
XI.	Eastern Switzerland	189
XII.	The Legal Framework and Agricultural Support Systems	220
XIII.	The Fête des Vignerons	228
XIV.	Future Trends	232
XV.	A Final Word On Vintages	235

Measurements	237
Glossary	238
Bibliography	240
Index	243
Acknowledgments	258
About the Author	259

Vineyards at Leytron, Valais

Maps and Tables

Maps

The vineyards of Switzerland	inside cover
The vineyards of Valais	62
The vineyards of Vaud	101
The vineyards of Geneva	143
The vineyards of Neuchâtel	162
The vineyards of Ticino	178
The vineyards of eastern Switzerland	188

Tables

I.	1992 Harvest by Canton	3
II.	Area Cultivated by Canton: 1899 and 1995	25
III.	Comparative Climatic Conditions	28
IV.	Number of Bunches of Grapes per Vine	30
V.	Time Required to Tend Grapes in Valais	31
VI.	Grape Ripening Compared to the Chasselas	33
VII.	Grape Types planted in Valais	64
VIII.	Grape Types planted in Geneva	146
IX.	Eastern Switzerland: Production (1981-1991)	190
X.	Climatic Conditions in eastern Switzerland	191
XI.	A Vintage Chart for Switzerland	236

Introduction

For centuries the Swiss have rested secure in the knowledge that their vineyards produce excellent wines. The late 20th century has not shaken this belief. What is more, a small but influential group of innovative wine-makers is combining modern technical proficiency with age-old traditions to make even better wines with wide appeal.

Swiss wines are generally not well known beyond the borders of Switzerland. They certainly deserve a wider, international appreciation. Wine lovers, in their never-ending search for fine wines which are novel, uncommon or singular can profitably investigate the varied offerings from Switzerland's alpine vineyards. Production may be small and some of the better wines can be difficult to locate, but an exploration of the world of Swiss wines, whose lineage stretches back two millennia, will undeniably pay unexpected and rewarding dividends.

The Swiss themselves would probably be slightly bemused if wine lovers suddenly started beating a path to their door demanding to purchase their wines. Until quite recently very few Swiss vignerons worried about what the rest of the world thought of their wines. Conscientious producers knew that they were making fine wine, and certainly had no problem selling the year's production. If others are finally recognizing this fact, so much the better.

Informed opinion, as reflected in most international wine surveys, affirms that Swiss wines are rarely bad. The reality is more complex and alluring. Intriguing and occasionally sublime wines are made from ancient grape varieties grown today only within Swiss borders. The Chasselas, sometimes disdained by others as a common table grape, is coaxed into producing harmonious and gratifying wines. Conscientious wine makers work wonders with the fickle Pinot Noir when blessed with just a little extra heat in lake-shore vineyards. Swiss wines, at their best, harbour a seductive quality sufficient to entice an interested taster to want to know more. An enthusiast's appreciation for these wines grows with experience and understanding.

At the same time the Swiss are realists. Well aware of their geographic and climatic constraints, they know that their wines will not replace the great classics as the qualitative benchmark against which all others are judged. Nor in fact do Swiss wine makers seek to create another Château Petrus, Mondavi Reserve or Grange Hermitage. They do, however, more than hold their own against the deceptively simple, universal objective of all good wine makers, which is to produce the best possible wine from a particular grape variety within the limitations imposed by geography, climate and economics. Anything less would be unacceptable in a country as focused and technically proficient as Switzerland. Swiss wines, therefore, should be judged on their own merits.

There are problems, of course, and real challenges for the future. These will be identified and reviewed as we proceed. But the overall quality of wine making in Switzerland has benefited greatly from recent technical advances, and today its standards are as high as anywhere in the world. And the story of Switzerland and its wines is even more attractive because such unexpected results have been achieved in an environment which, while stunningly beautiful, can be both physically harsh and economically punishing.

* * *

My objective in writing this book is to provide a brief but comprehensive description of the wines of Switzerland. My approach will be quite personal but, I hope, fair. This text in fact seeks to fill a gap – to produce a book in English telling the rich history of wine making in Switzerland while also offering an introductory guide to contemporary wine makers and their wines for those who wish to explore further.

International knowledge of Swiss wines reflects the very limited amounts of good wine available for export. From the outset, I have been sensitive to the potential problem of obtaining some of the wines mentioned in the text. Accordingly, each chapter on a canton or region ends with a series of useful addresses, including a short, annotated but non-exhaustive list of recommended wine makers, for those wishing to follow-up. My hope is that this text will encourage readers to deepen their understanding of Swiss wines through their own purchases, tastings and vineyards visits.

John C. Sloan

This book is the first attempt to provide a critical and detailed appraisal in English of the wines of Switzerland. This has not made my job as author any easier – in fact, quite the contrary. Nonetheless, I hope that this will not be the last word on the subject and that it will be a useful addition to the many authoritative texts that deal with the world's other important wine regions. In completing this endeavour I have been constantly reminded of a quote from a late 19th century book on Swiss geography, The Scenery of Switzerland, by Sir John Lubbock – *"il n'y a que ceux qui ne font rien qui ne se trompent pas"* (literally: only those who never do anything never make mistakes). If I stimulate a greater interest in and sympathy for the wines of Switzerland, then I will have achieved my purpose.

A Note on the Structure of the Book

The core of this book is structured in the form of a journey around Switzerland. This journey begins by traveling down the Rhône from the point where the glacial run-off becomes a recognizable river. The text then follows the flow of the Rhône past the mountain-enclosed vineyards of Valais, the lakeside terraces of Vaud and leaves the Rhône near Geneva as the river continues its southward journey into France. We cross the natural divide between the Rhône and Rhine river systems into the vineyards of Neuchâtel, and then travel towards the southern sun which blesses the Italian-speaking canton of Ticino. The journey ends in the eastern German-speaking cantons. The circle is virtually completed since the last vineyards described are not far, geographically or in spirit, from the primeval glaciers feeding the waters that emerge as the Rhône and Rhine.

The text is divided into three sections. The first is devoted to the structure, history and technical aspects of the Swiss wine industry. These chapters provide an overview of the development and characteristics of grape growing and wine making in the country. Readers seeking to use this book in its most "practical" sense may wish to turn directly to the second section, beginning with the Chapter on Valais, where we embark on a detailed examination of the individual wine-producing cantons and regions. This section constitutes the core of the book. The third section, encompassing the four last chapters, focuses on other facets of wine making in Switzerland, including past vintages and future trends.

Although the geographical descriptions are fairly straightforward, developing a unified framework for this book proved to be a considerable challenge. Where necessary I have varied slightly my treatment of different cantons and regions to reflect regional peculiarities of the Swiss mosaic. In the end I hope readers will better understand and appreciate both the diversity I encountered throughout the Swiss wine industry and my attempts to give some unity to this account of the wines of Switzerland.

John C. Sloan
London

"Switzerland does not supply more wine than suffices for home consumption. The best is produced in the canton called the Grisons. It is named Chiavenna wine, and is of aromatic flavour, white from the red grape. In Valais they make a Malvasia of good quality; both these are white wines of a luscious kind. The Valais also produces red wine, made at La Marque and Coquempin, in the district of Martigny.

The other wines are for the most part red. Schaffhausen produces them in plenty, and of tolerable quality. At Basle they make the "wine of blood", as it is called from the combat of Birs, in the reign of Louis XI of France, when sixteen hundred Swiss fought thirty thousand French and only sixteen survived, dying more of fatigue of combat than by the power of the enemy. These wines are also known as those of hospital and St. Jacques.

The red wines of Erlach in Berne are good. The red of Neuchâtel is equal to the third class of Burgundy. St. Gall affords tolerable wines. In the Valteline the red wines are remarkable for durability and are of very good quality. They make a wine in that district which much resembles the aromatic wines of the south of France.

A very generous red wine is made also in the Valteline from the red grapes, which is suffered to hang on the vine until the month of November, when the fruit is become very mature. It is then gathered, and carried into a large room or barn, and hung up by the stems for two or three months. The bunches are picked over with great care, and every decayed or injured grape is thrown aside, so that none but sound fruit is submitted to the press. The must is placed to ferment in an open vessel and twice a day it is skimmed. It continues to ferment for a week or fortnight, according to the weather, during which the operation of skimming is constantly repeated. After the fermentation is over it is put into a closed vessel, and set by for a twelvemonth. This wine is remarkably luscious, and will keep well for a century, having great strength and body. The Swiss, when it is a year old, bore a hole two thirds of the way up the head of the cask, drink the wine down to the hole and then renew it annually.

The canton of Vaud produces the largest quantity of wine. Those of Cully and Désalés, near Lausanne, resemble much the dry wines of the Rhine in quality, and are of considerable durability."

                                        Cyrus Redding
                                        The History and Description of
                                        Modern Wine (2nd ed.)
                                        London, 1833

I

Wine in Today's Switzerland

There are 8.5 million hectares of wine grapes growing in the world. Of this amount, the vineyards of Bordeaux occupy 100,000 hectares, those of Switzerland 15,000 hectares while Burgundy has a mere 8,500 hectares. Although Switzerland contains only two percent of Europe's land devoted to the production of wine grapes, this tiny landlocked country provides some four percent of Europe's wine. This translates into just less than one percent of the world's wine.

Given this limited production, it is perhaps not surprising that wines and wine making are not prominent in the world's perceptions of what makes Switzerland uniquely "Swiss". Conventional images of Switzerland are much more closely tied to precision watches, fashionable ski resorts, secretive bankers, exclusive health spas and the mythical Heidi singing across open alpine vistas. Gastronomically, Gruyère cheese and Swiss milk chocolate are recognized and imitated everywhere. But Swiss wines?

The fact is, fine Swiss wines remain among the country's best and undiscovered secrets. One only has to relax at an outdoor café on a summer's day, visit a local supermarket, dine elegantly at one of Switzerland's finer restaurants, or partake of a simple raclette in an inviting *carnotzet* to appreciate that wine is very much an integral part of everyday life in Switzerland. Offering a glass of wine is a natural way to greet friends and visitors. A brief sortie into the hinterlands of Geneva, Lausanne or Neuchâtel will convince even the most jaded tourist that wine is serious business in these parts of Switzerland. While alpine geographic and climatic constraints might at first seem to discourage the production of fine wines, closer investigation reveals that much is possible within the limitations imposed by nature.

At the same time the exceptionally high cost of land and labour are facts of life for Swiss *vignerons*. Producing fine wine, therefore, is either a labour of love or an endeavour which can only be price-competitive if the wine maker maximizes every available advantage. This has emphasized the importance of technical know-how and has increasingly forced the wine industry to concentrate on the upper end of the quality scale. The Swiss have profited greatly from the higher technical skills and improved standards which characterize the remarkable improvement in wine making throughout Europe over the past two decades. They have both the mechanical proficiency and the information networks to make this possible. Refined clonal selection and improved vinification techniques are just two of the changes which have improved the quality of wine production. Efforts to restrict grape growing only to the most appropriate sites have produced more equivocal results. Swiss farmers, like farmers everywhere, are very attached to their land and do not give up their traditions easily. Grim competitive economic reality will, nevertheless, continue to encourage a drive towards quality. Consumers of Swiss wines are the immediate beneficiaries. And as proficiency and standards continue to rise the entire wine industry will gain.

To provide a meaningful context for what follows, the remainder of this chapter will briefly review the basic production, consumption, quality and regulatory aspects of the contemporary Swiss wine industry.

Production

In 1995, according to the Federal Office of Agriculture, Swiss wine makers produced enough wine to fill nearly 170 million bottles. The harvest that year produced 118 million liters of wine from *vinifera* grapes, divided between 65 million liters of white and 53 million liters of red plus a small amount wine from hybrids grapes. Vintages in the early 1990s were slightly more abundant with 1991 producing the equivalent of 200 million bottles and 1992, slightly less, with 180 million bottles.

Traditionally between one-third and one-half of all wines consumed in the country have been Swiss. In several recent years domestic production has satisfied nearly 50% of national demand, although for the period July 1991 to June 1992 it reached only 45%. The majority of Swiss wines have always been white although in recent years the amount of domestic red wine has increased considerably. The national ratio has remained relatively steady in the first half of the 1990s with white wines supplying between 55% and 60% of the domestic total.

Foreign imports, largely reds, are composed of two very different types of red wine: bulk, commodity-style reds for bottling in Switzerland; and top-quality bottled French, Italian and Spanish red wines. Because of the direct effect on the domestic industry, the importation of white wines has been much more closely controlled by import quotas until these were replaced by tariffs on January 1, 1995. The result of these changes is likely to be greater competition from imports, especially at the lower end of the white wine market.

During the 1980s Switzerland ranked 14th in Europe and 21st globally in terms of total land surface dedicated to the cultivation of vines. Throughout the decade, Swiss vineyards averaged 14,000 hectares. During the same period Spain cultivated 1.6 million hectares; the former Soviet Union 1.4 million hectares; Italy 1.3 million hectares; and France 1.1 million hectares. Swiss vineyards, which have slowly been contracting over the 20th century, experienced a modest expansion during the 1980s. By 1992 the land surface devoted to grapes approached 15,000 hectares although in 1995 it was back down slightly to 14,870 hectares. This total is still less than five percent of the country's land surface of approximately 41,000 square kilometers.

Table I: 1995 Harvest by Canton (in hectoliters and hectares)

Canton	Red-hl	White-hl	Total-hl	Area-ha
Zürich	21,990	12,126	34,116	635
Berne-Thun	237	579	816	14
Lucerne	293	650	943	16
Schwyz	932	862	1,794	26
Nidwald	7	4	11	0.2
Glaris	44	12	56	1.2
Zoug	6	23	29	0.5
Soleure	44	37	81	3.1
Basel-Country	3,570	1,702	5,273	93
Basel-City	70	122	192	4
Schaffhouse	22,809	5065	27,874	500
Appenzell-AR	103	49	152	3
Appenzell-AI	0	32	32	0.7
St. Gall	7,898	1,935	9,834	220
Grisons	17,950	2,899	20,849	373
Argovie	12,583	8,398	20,981	390
Thurgovie	10,175	5,496	15,671	272
German-Switz.	**98,712**	**39,992**	**138,705**	**2,551**
Misox	850	37	888	29
Ticino	29,065	1,513	30,578	900
Italian-Switz.	**29,915**	**1,550**	**31,465**	**930**
Berne-Bienne	3,354	9,482	12,836	244
Fribourg	1,742	7,606	9,349	114
Vaud	83,264	279,390	362,654	3,818
Valais	247,842	225,726	473,568	5,259
Neuchâtel	12,575	25,259	37,835	608
Geneva	52,202	62,512	114,714	1,342
Jura	157	110	268	5
French-Switz.	**401,137**	**610,086**	**1,011,224**	**11,389**
Swiss Total	529,764	651,630	1,181,394	14,48?

Production, Canton by Canton

The complexity of the political divisions within Switzerland risks overwhelming the casual reader. Some reference must, however, be made to Swiss production on a canton-by-canton basis. The 1995 breakdown by individual canton of the volumes produced (in hectoliters) and land devoted to grapes (in hectares) is set out on this page and in greater detail in later chapters. The figures in Table I also include the production of table grapes and the limited number of hybrids still being grown, although neither is sufficiently significant to affect the relative balance among cantons.

The visual evidence of the vineyards is immediate to anyone traveling in the French-speaking cantons of the *Suisse romande*. The economic importance of grape growing is also obvious to anyone passing through Ticino to or from Italy. As well, very few cantons in the German-speaking regions cannot boast of at least some parcels of vines producing sound, drinkable wine – even if solely for local consumption. Only in the isolated mountain regions of the Grisons, still inhabited by the indigenous Romansch-speaking minority, is grape production totally absent from traditional farming.

Much of Swiss grape growing is concentrated in the four western francophone cantons of Valais, Vaud, Geneva and Neuchâtel which, with the canton of Jura and parts of Berne and Fribourg, form the region known as the Suisse romande. In 1995, 85% of all wines in Switzerland were produced in the French-speaking cantons which contain only 18% of Switzerland's inhabitants. Just 12% of the country's wine came from the central and eastern German-speaking cantons which contain 65% of the population, while only 3% is from the 10% Italian-speaking Ticino area in the southeast corner of the country. In terms of trends, between the 1992 and 1994 harvests, the acreage devoted to grapes in the Suisse romande dropped slightly while it rose eight percent in the German-speaking cantons and fell a notable 27% in the Italian-speaking region.

Consumption

Per capita consumption of wine in Switzerland averaged 44.5 liters in 1992, sixth in the world after France, Italy, Luxembourg, Portugal and Argentina. Although down from 47.2 liters in 1991, Swiss consumption of wine has not witnessed the dramatic decline evident in other countries of Europe. Compared to French and Italian annual consumption of 64.5 and 60.3 liters per capita respectively in 1992, which are down from earlier averages well over 100 liters per capita, Swiss wine drinking appears to be quite reasonable. National consumption patterns are also better able to support a wine industry than, for example, in the United Kingdom, Canada and the United States where 1992 consumption was 12.4, 8.3 and 7.1 liters per person respectively. The message of these statistics, therefore, is that the Swiss are energetic but wholesome consumers of both domestic and imported wines.

This consumption level confirms that wine is an natural part of the Swiss diet and daily life. These statistics also go a long way to explain why Swiss wines are so rarely encountered outside the country's borders. Since domestic production can, at best, satisfy around 50% of the national demand, virtually everything should be consumed at home. The relatively high consumption per person ensures that, under "normal" conditions, most Swiss wine can be successfully marketed domestically. This does not encourage wine makers to spend additional time and money identifying, developing and servicing markets abroad.

The actual situation, as might be expected, is a little more complicated. Virtually all Swiss whites were traditionally meant to be drunk within two to three years and most reds within five. Freshness and good balance rather than ability to age were the major criteria for quality Swiss wines. If a Swiss wine lover wished to store wines, particularly reds, he or she bought French or Italian wines which fulfill a very different role than the domestic product. This complimentary relationship was reflected in the treatment that high-quality bottled red wines, in particular, received under the import regime (see below and Chapter XII on the legal framework and agricultural support systems). While these common expectations regarding Swiss wines may have been valid for most of this century, they are certainly being challenged today, largely by the younger generation of wine-makers who are producing quality red and even white wines that require time to achieve their best. The established criteria have not been discarded, but new approaches, grape types and fermentation techniques are producing innovative results.

Switzerland has always been largely self-sufficient in white wines. Except for periods when demand and supply were seriously out of balance, the entire harvest of white wine grapes is usually eventually consumed without great difficulty. But in the early 1990s, the specter of a structural surplus, especially for the lower-end, mass-market white wines again appeared, as a result of high yields and the system of import regulations to protect white wines. The shift, beginning in 1995, from the quota system to tariffs for white wines will also put pressure on the low end of the market as the tariffs decline over time.

The domestic production of red wine, however, does not come close to meeting demand. Again, virtually all Swiss reds are consumed within the country. For red wines, a sustained structural surplus is an impossibility. Easy access to the vineyards of France and Italy, in particular, meet the domestic shortfall in red wines. Quality wine from these neighbouring countries also ensures that the market always has competitive products against which the home-grown varieties can be judged.

Quality Considerations

In any country where wine is an integral part of the national diet, wine producers usually satisfy specific sectors of potential demand. This produces a "quality pyramid" with a wide base of wines for everyday drinking, and ascends in increasingly narrow bands until it reaches a pinnacle occupied by unique wines produced for special occasions. Prices rise as one ascends the pyramid, and quality is certainly supposed to rise as well. The situation in Switzerland is skewed, however, as the fixed costs of production raise the floor price to a level considerably higher than that in neighbouring countries. Somewhat surprisingly, wines at the price summit are less expensive than might be expected given the limited availability of the best wines. In part this is due to consumer demand which is basically national and not international. Therefore, while the expected quality/price pyramid certainly exists in Switzerland, it is somewhat squatter than similar structures elsewhere.

Liter bottles of basic, inexpensive wine for immediate consumption can be had for 4-6 Swiss francs (CHF) per bottle in the early/mid 1990s. Prices for a good producer's regular bottling of Chasselas range from CHF 6-9 in Geneva to 8-12 in Valais. Retail prices for the individual estates of Vaud, which are generally the most expensive Chasselas in Switzerland, can rise into the high 20s for the top wines from Dézaley. Bottles of specialty wines such as Chardonnay, Pinot Gris and the

5

indigenous grapes of Valais are usually 2-5 francs more expensive than the Chasselas wines of the same producer. The cost of a standard, widely-produced red wine will largely parallel the price of the basic white, e.g., Genevois Gamay costs approximately the same as a Genevois Chasselas. In Valais, Dôle is usually one or two francs more expensive than Fendant and 100% Pinot Noir several francs over that. Specially selected or oak-aged Pinot Noir, or specialty reds such as Humagne Rouge or Syrah, will cost between CHF 20-35 a bottle.

The above prices are simply indicative of current general costs and there will be considerable variation depending on the producer and where the wine is bought. In addition, in 1995 wine producers began to pay a value added tax of 6.5% which raised ex-cellar prices accordingly. Restaurant prices are usually two to four times the retail prices. Many of the better wines are not bought in stores or even specialty wine shops but rather, as in Burgundy or parts of Germany, directly from the producers. Demand often outstrips supply, and even for long-standing customers, some producers have to ration their best wines.

Given the basic cost of living in Switzerland these prices are definitely not out of line, and in fact some of the reserve bottlings of special wines are good value given the quality of the wines and the care and attention that goes into their production. Where the cost/value relationship breaks down is when the cost of basic generic Chasselas is compared to the everyday wines of other European and new world grape-producing areas. Here the Swiss wines are clearly too expensive to be internationally competitive.

As might be expected, wine production mirrors both national and regional characteristics, the latter adding additional spice and diversity. Despite the relatively small size of Swiss vineyards, the range of wines produced rivals the production of any country. In the Swiss repertoire are everything from light, bone dry aperitif whites to luscious golden dessert wines, and from fruity, purple quaffing wines to substantive, structured tannic reds.

In general Swiss wines are meant to be drunk casually or with food, although certainly there are no strict criteria for their enjoyment. Some of the stronger regional specialties such as Vin des Glaciers or the sweet *flétrie* late-harvest Malvoisie (Pinot Gris) of Valais do require special handling. Soft and only slightly acidic, commodity-Chasselas makes an excellent and enticing café wine, either on its own or with light food. It is often drunk from small unpretentious glasses that reinforce its everyday quality. The same grape, when produced with more structure and intensity, is a wonderful foil to Switzerland's many lake fish and even to some of its aromatic cheeses. An intense Pinot Gris suits fowl perfectly and can even match a smoked duck without wilting. Swiss chefs have made a fine art of pairing special wines with dishes drawn from the culinary traditions of the wine producing cantons. A few of these special combinations will be mentioned when the wines of the specific cantons are reviewed later on.

For the reds, the Goron of Valais, the Gamays of Vaud and Geneva, along with some of the Oeil-de-Perdrix of Neuchâtel and the light Blauburgunders (Pinot Noir) of eastern Switzerland fulfill the same café function as the low-cost Chasselas. The more substantive reds such as a good Merlot del Ticino or a full Dôle blend deserve a more generous partnering with a meat dish. Pinot Noirs usually aim for greater elegance than the above two reds. The finest aged reds should, however, be reserved for the wild game of *la chasse*, an annual Swiss fall ritual in which all the restaurants compete to offer fresh and exotic menus. If a more gentle pairing is needed, the best mature reds are perfect when set beside a fine Appenzell or creamy Vacherin cheese. And in a pinch, they are wonderful just on their own.

Harvesting Pinot Noir grapes at Godi Clavadeltscher's vineyards in Malans, Bündner Herrschaft.

If one can hazard a generalization, most Swiss wines, like the Swiss themselves, are correct, slightly reserved, technically proficient and meticulous to a fault. Rarely does one ever encounter a really bad bottle of Swiss wine. In two words the wines, like the nation that makes them, are "satisfying" and "proper" – and happy to be so. At the same time, even the Swiss would agree that only a few of their wines soar to the greatest heights. But this is not surprising since most wine-producing regions achieve greatness only rarely. However, thanks to the individualistic and stubborn streak found so often in the Swiss countryside, there will be exceptions. The tradition of wine-making under difficult conditions runs too deep for there not to be excellent wine makers around the country who do aspire to and achieve great heights.

A genuine love of the land, combined with local traditions, technical proficiency, and personal integrity guarantee a diversity among the better wine makers which is profound and worth investigating. The problem, as always, is to locate these growers – and, even more importantly, to locate those of their wines which have not already been pledged or reserved in advance. The better producers never have a problem in disposing of their prized and avidly sought output!

Regulatory Environment

Details of relevant legal regulations and governmental responsibilities related to wine production will be given at various points in the text. For the moment the non-Swiss reader need only know that Switzerland's vineyards are the product of a unique historical and economic development, quite different from Switzerland's European neighbours. Behind the enigmatic Swiss facade lies a national culture composed of individual parts as disparate as any in contemporary Europe. Swiss wines reflect the diverse linguistic, social and cultural melange that is Switzerland.

An important element of this mosaic is the system with which the Swiss govern themselves. The country is a confederation with a unique distribution of responsibilities and powers between the federal, cantonal and municipal levels. It is perhaps the last and most sophisticated example of a real direct democracy where the citizens are consulted, frequently and directly, on issues of national importance. These include fiscal, educational, agricultural, defense and foreign policy matters and, not incidentally, the regulations controlling wine sales. Both grape-growing and wine-making are the subject of a historic and subtle division of powers between the federal and cantonal authorities. The introduction in recent years of a system of both national and cantonal *appellation contrôlée* standards has simply added another layer to an already complex but continually evolving relationship between the federal and cantonal interests.

Accordingly, long-standing but fluid governmental, linguistic and cultural arrangements in Switzerland exert a major influence on wine-making developments. While some might argue that it would be closer to contemporary reality to focus immediately on "Valaisan", "Neuchâtelois" or "Malanser" wines, only a comparative and "national" approach provides a complete overview of the Swiss wine experience. The wines and traditions of all the major producing areas reveal the importance of the significant differences among them. At the same time, the tasting, discussion and comparison of Swiss wines often break down linguistic and ethnic barriers and provides an automatic cross-cultural link. Not surprisingly, when confronted with an outsider's interest, the Swiss are genuinely proud of their wines – all of them!

II

The History of Wine in Switzerland

Grape growing and the production of wine have a long and honourable history in Switzerland. Artifacts and records demonstrate that wine has been part of Swiss life from Roman times. Grape growing and wine production have affected the development of Swiss social structure, agriculture, institutions, commerce, trade, legal regulations, politics and even the system of government. Historically, major vineyard owners have enjoyed considerable economic and political influence.

Switzerland is one of the crossroads of Europe and its north-south and east-west corridors have naturally been coveted by aggressive and ambitious empires. More than once in its history, Switzerland has found itself a pawn in other nations' wars, although eventually a national policy of armed neutrality provided a needed element of domestic stability and respite. During times of peace the lakeside slopes and even isolated alpine valleys were transformed into the vineyards which support the Swiss wine industry of today.

This chapter does not attempt to review the complex, heroic and often violent saga of the formation and growth of the Swiss Confederation; but it will identify briefly those moments when the sweep of history intersected with events or people particularly important to the spread of wine and vineyards in Switzerland. A better understanding of the past will help put the present in context.

Many details are lost in time, but the importance of certain developments – the Roman occupation, the spread of the great monasteries, the Napoleonic invasions – on the structure of today's vineyards is too great to ignore. Therefore, while it may initially seem exaggerated to look back to Roman times, the political, social and viticultural links to the present justify such a historical diversion. In fact, the origins of grape cultivation and wine in Switzerland even predate the arrival of the Roman legions.

Helvetii and Romans

Archeologists have found grape seeds while excavating the lake-side communities which existed on the shores of Lakes Geneva, Neuchâtel and Zurich as long ago as 10,000 B.C. At certain sites, the quantities of grape pips suggest that the early inhabitants of today's Switzerland consciously gathered and exploited the indigenous wild vines *(vitis sylvestris)*. Strains of these wild grapes can still can be found in the Jura mountains which protect Lakes Geneva and Neuchâtel to the north. There is, however, no archeological evidence that early lake-dwellers grew grapes for wine.

These early communities were replaced by later invaders, including the Celtic tribes which settled on arable land as far south as Spain and northern Italy. The Helvetii were one such Celtic tribe which, along with the Gaulois, Bretons, Walloons, Welsh and Scotch, occupied much of Europe prior to Rome's northern conquests. These Swiss ancestors were among the most powerful of the Celtic invaders and established themselves in the fertile valleys stretching from Lake Geneva *(Lac Léman)* to Lake Constance. This Helvetii dominion between the Alps and Jura included the relatively arable lands surrounding Lake Geneva, the banks of the Rhône, and the equally fertile lands surrounding Lake Neuchâtel. Celtic tribes also ventured along the Rhône valley as far as Sion in Valais. Independently the Rhaeti, an offshoot of the Etruscans, occupied some of the border regions between northern Italy and the Alps in what is now the Grisons region.

The archeological remains and what we know of the mythological traditions of the Helvetii do not convincingly demonstrate the existence of an indigenous god either of wine or vines, such as Dionysus or Bacchus of Greek and Roman custom. There is also very little archeological evidence that the Helvetii cultivated vines in an organized manner. The alpine environment was generally too harsh, and contact with the outside world too episodic to permit a trade in necessary items such as specialized vineyard tools or root stocks.

The mountain passes through the Alps, and the closely connected river systems which cut through them, ensured that the alpine heartland of the Helvetii inevitably became an influential crossroads for trade and cultural cross-fertilization. Crucial north-south and east-west transportation routes traversed the Swiss landscape and, consequently, the Helvetii communities straddled some of the preferred invasion routes through the Alps.

Through their contact with Greeks, Phoenicians, Carthaginians and Romans, many of the Celtic communities developed ongoing contacts with wine-consuming societies. In particular, the Gaulois established trading links with the Etruscan and Greek merchants working from their base at Massalia, now Marseilles, at the mouth of the Rhône. Eventually an important trading relationship developed to service a growing demand by Celtic communities for wine. There is, however, little evidence that these basically restless tribes deliberately cultivated vines for wine on their march south to the Mediterranean. In the first century B.C., when Julius Caesar subjugated Gaul, his conquering armies discovered no vineyards in the newly occupied territories.

The Celts did, nonetheless, make an inestimable contribution to the expansion of the wine trade. Over time the sturdy Gaulois wooden barrel replaced the elegant but fragile ceramic amphora as the preferred vessel to transport wine and other liquids. This innovation made the trade in wine more reliable, especially with the remote Roman outposts on the Danube or Rhine. The local Celtic communities, including those in the Alps, must also have benefited from improved supply.

For their part the Helvetii lived a considerable distance from the Gaulois tribes of Burgundy and in much different physical surroundings. To the north roamed the troublesome Germanic tribes, the feared Alemanni. When Caesar's legions advanced northwards, the Romans hoped that the Helvetii could act as a buffer between them and the Alemanni. Caught between these two forces, the Helvetii attempted to migrate to Gaul, but Caesar caught and defeated them in 58 B.C. at the Battle of Bribracte near Autun in Burgundy.

Some believe that when the Romans forced the Helvetii to return to their alpine homelands to act as a north-facing shield under Roman protection, they brought with them grape vines that adapted to and survived the harsher mountain climate. In any case, as the Roman legions swept northwards it was only a matter of time before occupying armies and their camp followers insisted on the amenities of southern civilization, including wine and the wine-making techniques suitable for local conditions. Although scholars are therefore reasonably certain that the methodical cultivation of the vine in Switzerland followed closely in the wake of the Roman occupation, the actual manner in which organized grape exploitation was introduced into the Swiss region remains unknown. The Romans demonstrated their ability to adapt their military, road-building and administrative prowess to alpine conditions. In addition, they were also quick to realize the need in this marginal climate to plant vines on south-facing slopes to take full advantage of the sun's warmth. This permitted the successful accommodation of certain Mediterranean grapes to the harsher conditions of the northern reaches of the Empire.

Roman towns flourished in important grape producing regions, such as *Colonia Julia Equestris* (today the Vaudois town of Nyon) and *Octodurum* (Martigny in Valais), encouraging local production on slopes where grapes could survive and fully ripen. Stock selection eventually produced vines that were able to reach maturity on the best exposed slopes. Various historic tools and inscriptions connected with grapes and wine have come to light. One of the oldest is a stele dating between the first and third century A.D. now in the collection of the church museum at St. Maurice in Valais. The inscription reads *"Deo Sedato Vineiius Vegeiinus D S D D"* – a *vigneron* asking his god for blessing.

The long decline and eventual collapse of the Roman Empire isolated frontier posts from central authority. The virtual end of the Empire in the West by the 5th century also produced the linguistic divisions still found today in Switzerland. The Germanic Alemanni crossed the Rhine and Jura mountains to seize the north, while the Christian Burgundians *(Burgondes)* occupied the south. What is now Ticino moved under Italian influence and only the isolated Rhaeti lived in more-or-less peaceful solitude. Thus was the French-German-Italian-Romansch framework for Switzerland put in place.

With the arrival of barbarian invaders from lands beyond the *pax romana*, central authority collapsed and trade diminished. Among the few institutions to occasionally escape destruction were the early Christian abbeys and monasteries which, of necessity, were often transformed into armed protective camps. This concentration of manpower provided the monasteries with a ready and extensive labour force. In times of relative peace, some of those labourers maintained existing and developed new vineyards; they tended and harvested the crop; and finally they managed the fermentation and aging of the wine for both religious and secular consumption. The growth and spread of monastic power slowly transformed the lakeside slopes and alpine valleys into the vineyards still visible today.

Wine and the Spread of Christianity

Common references to "Abbayes" and "Moines" on contemporary wine labels are visible reminders of the importance of the medieval church, the monasteries and the monks in the preservation and development of wine throughout Europe. Switzerland is no exception. While the exact role played by the monastic communities in the preservation of viticulture between the fall of the Roman Empire and the Renaissance is still the subject of historical debate, the importance of the monasteries in the propagation and improvement of vines is readily evident.

The Christian era brought a significant expansion of vineyard production because of the church's role in the preservation of agricultural and viticultural knowledge. From as early as the 3rd century the growth of Christianity with its requirement for sacramental wine, and the spread of monasteries and church institutions, ensured that the amount of land producing grapes steadily increased. In the first half of the 5th century the Burgundians established themselves in Lyon and eventually controlled an area which stretched along Lake Geneva to Martigny. As the outposts of the Roman Empire crumbled, this romanized and Christian tribe occupied the western part of today's Switzerland. The area which is now the *"Suisse romande"* thus became an eastern outpost of Frankish culture facing the Germanic tribes to the north which remained largely beyond Roman hegemony.

The Burgundians established a capital in Geneva and, most importantly, their royal monastery at St. Maurice farther up the Rhône on the border between the modern cantons of Vaud and Valais. This site is appropriately named after a martyred Roman legionnaire who is credited with introducing Christianity into Switzerland. In 502 the Burgundian King Gondebaud enacted the law of Gombette to encourage the planting of "noble" varieties in communal vineyards along the Lake Geneva basin, and to establish strict punishments for anyone stealing grapes or damaging the vineyards.

Benedictines

Virtually all the great medieval monastic orders benefitted from the spiritual and political vacuum which followed the end of the Roman order. In addition to proselytization, they brought with them the knowledge, discipline and organizational skills required to nurture and expand the areas where vines were cultivated for the glory of God – and the comfort of his creatures.

The establishment of the Benedictine order by its namesake, St. Benedict, coincided with the final death throes of the Roman Empire in the west. For 500 years, until losing their monopoly as the only monastic order approved by Rome, the Benedictines exerted an inordinate influence on all walks of life. From their base in the regions of Burgundy and Champagne, the order spread until it numbered several thousand monastic communities, which included abbeys, churches, cloisters, farms, fields and vineyards. The latter counted among them many of the great Burgundy vineyards such as Clos de Bèze and Charlemagne's vineyards in Corton, given to the nearby monastery at Saulieu in 775. The great Benedictine mother-abbey at Cluny, which became the largest land owner in Burgundy, extended the order's influence far beyond Burgundy into all parts of Europe, including Switzerland.

The royal monastery at St. Maurice, Switzerland's oldest monastery, was established by the Burgundian King Sigismund in 515 for a community of Celtic monks. This community eventually adopted Benedictine rules and subsequently prospered. At its peak, the monastery of St. Maurice not only cultivated vineyards in the immediately surrounding fields but also worked better sites farther down the Rhône towards Lake Geneva in the superior Vaudois areas of Aigle and Yvorne. The Benedictine abbey's vines were long ago auctioned off, but the much-altered monastery of St. Maurice still exists and parts are now being used as a school. Regal treasures, once belonging to the Benedictines, include a rare Merovingian bejeweled box and a gold cloisonné ewer reputedly given to the monastery by Charlemagne. Along with the 12th century coffers containing the venerated remains of St. Maurice, these masterpieces are on exhibit in the small treasury, still one of the finest ecclesiastical repositories in Europe. Although Charlemagne is not immediately identified with Switzerland, his administrative division of the country is a legacy which remains the basis for the borders of many of today's cantons.

Ironically, many of the early Christian missionaries to Switzerland came not from the more urbane south but rather from the wilder and more heathen west. From the 6th century onwards, Irish and Scottish monks established monasteries and their supporting structures. The efforts of the renowned Irish monk, Columban, and his followers were particularly productive since they founded the important monasteries of Ursanne in the Jura, St. Gall and Moutier-Grandval. This group, which set out in 610, attacked the "heathen superstitions" of the Alemanni communities around Zurich by throwing their beer drinking vessels into the lake. Needless to say the Alemanni were not amused. Columban eventually led his band of monks south to the relative safety of Italy, leaving behind the fearless monk, Gallus, to found the monastery named after him in 614. Inevitably the community of St. Gall was also taken over by the Benedictines and became one of the great centers of European learning between the 8th and 10th centuries. The monastery of St. Gall was also known for its German vineyards which were often staffed by establishing granges or abbey farms, to which lay brethren were sent.

The Benedictines made a particular point of passing on their accumulated viticultural knowledge as they spread throughout Europe. One example is the founding charter of the abbey of Muri, just outside Zurich, dating from the 11th century. This document established a detailed schedule for tending the abbey's vines – including a timetable for manuring, pruning, hoeing, binding and leaf removal. Other significant Benedictine monasteries in Switzerland include the Caves du Prieuré of Neuchâtel, bequeathed to the abbey of Cluny in 978, and the intact Romanesque San Nicolau church at Giornico near the St. Gottard Pass in Ticino, which dates from the 10th century and is still surrounded by vines grown on old-style stone pergolas.

Cistercians and Carthusians

The black-robed Benedictines were not the only religious order to leave their mark on Swiss wine. The white-robed Cistercians, who emerged from an 11th century reform of the Benedictines, have left perhaps the most enduring legacy.

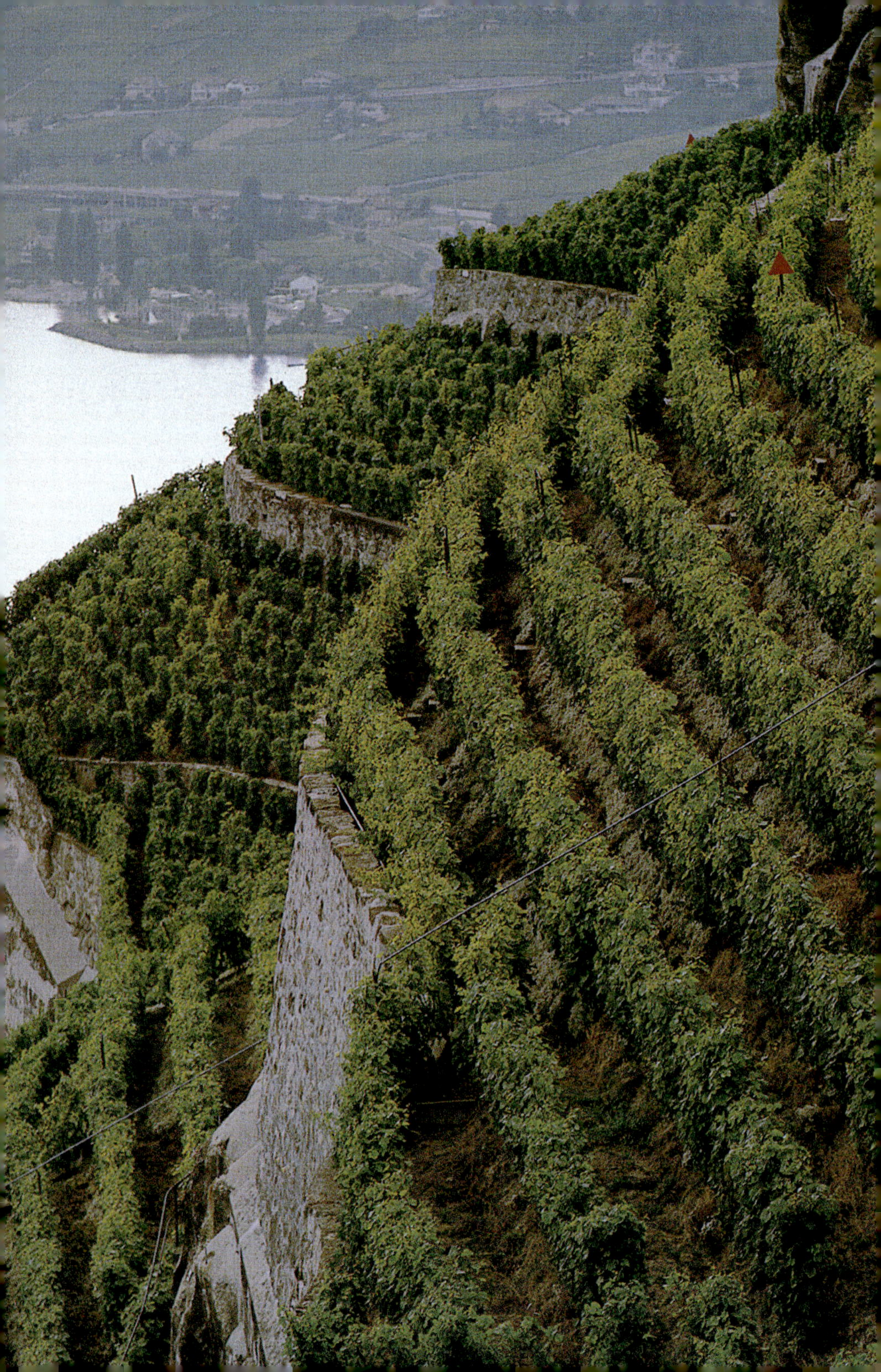

From their base at Cîteaux in Burgundy, the Cistercians not only created the vineyards of Chablis, but through judicious purchases beginning with a piece of land given to the monastery at Cîteaux in 1110, eventually owned the entire 125 acre vineyard at Clos de Vougeot – which they proceeded to surround with a still-standing stone wall. The physical presence of the Cistercians in Switzerland is most prominent at Dézaley in Vaud, where the celebrated Clos des Abbayes and Clos des Moines vineyards both trace their origins back to Cistercian monasteries. Here the monks' remarkable wall-building skills were seriously tested when carving out the narrow terraces that still hold back the steep slopes of Dézaley that rise from Lake Geneva.

The holdings of the church were long ago secularized, and little remains at Dézaley except the monastic connections of the vineyard names to recall the importance of the region's religious past. The high stature of the wines from these two Cistercian vineyards, belonging now to the City of Lausanne, pays homage to the original perspicacity and knowledge of their founders for they remain two of the premier sites in the entire country. In addition, some have credited the Cistercian monks with first introducing the Chasselas grape into Switzerland.

The strict and severe Carthusians had a separate influence in Switzerland and, like the Benedictines, they made their presence felt across the country. The headquarters of this order was established at the end of the 11th century in the French Alps at the Grande Chartreuse, 30 kilometers from Grenoble not far from the Swiss border. A charterhouse was established at La Lance, near Neuchâtel in 1318. The wines from the vineyards were probably made from the "Cortaillod" grape – most likely a strain of Pinot Noir. In the east the red Karthäuser wine from the canton of Thurgovie comes from the vines which once belonged to the charterhouse *(karthaus)* of St. Lorenz, founded in 1458 by Pope Pius II at Ittingen on the banks of the Thur river. The Carthusians also established a charterhouse at Sierre in Valais, along one of the north-south transportation routes. Here, it is claimed, the monks perfected the luscious Muscat dessert wines alongside an equally compelling sweet *vin de paille*. The latter was possibly made from the Païen grape which is related to the Traminer and Savagnin grapes used to produce similar wines at Château Châlon, in the not-too-distant French Jura. The production of these golden sweet wines dates back to the 9th century, and one legend ascribes their perfection to an order of noble-born Benedictine nuns in the Jura region. Itinerant monks or pilgrims may have had a role in transferring successful wine making techniques from one institution to another.

Religious Military Orders

Finally, the activities of the great medieval military religious orders deserve note. The crusades gave birth to orders of knights, including the Templars and Hospitallers, which united companies of armed warriors committed to the liberation of Palestine from the forces of Islam. Although the first objective of such orders was to encourage and protect pilgrims on their way to and from Jerusalem, they amassed considerable property and wealth and established their own abbeys, churches,

Spectacular terraces at Dézaley, Vaud, near the Clos des Abbayes.

hospitals and vineyards. Even after the fall of Jerusalem and the transfer of their headquarters from Palestine to Cyprus, the two rival orders were political and military forces not to be ignored.

Because of jealousies and infighting within the Church the Templars were suppressed in 1307. But the Knights Hospitaller of St. John of Jerusalem, of Rhodes and of Malta, to give them their full title, continued to thrive and to require wine for medicinal and social purposes from their vineyards throughout Europe. The Hospitallers maintained a hospital in Salquenen in the Haut Valais from the 12th to 16th centuries, while on the right bank of Lake Zurich at Küsnacht they established a chapel at the beginning of a fifteen-kilometer stretch of vines, some of which undoubtedly were owned by the Knights Hospitaller. Perhaps it is no coincidence that both regions are known for their red wines, today made from the Pinot Noir, known locally as the Clevner around Lake Zurich. The village of Meilen, half way down the north shore of Lake Zurich where some of the better local vineyards are found, also boasts a restored Hospitaller headquarters which remains a popular tourist destination.

Secular Developments

Although the great monastic houses were a dominant influence throughout the Middle Ages, secular influences on the development of Swiss vineyards cannot be ignored. From the 13th century the St. Gottard Pass grew from a rough path through the Alps to a negotiable and economical transportation route and, therefore, another strategic north-south crossing. As a consequence, previously isolated valleys in the Alps were drawn into broader political and economic movements. In 1291, in a seminal moment of Swiss history, the three alpine forest valleys of Uri, Schwyz and Unterwald clandestinely cemented an earlier *ad hoc* alliance against the expansionist Hapsburg empire. Today this alliance of Rütli, named after the meadow above Lake Lucerne where the pact was sealed, is still commemorated as the founding date of the Swiss Confederation. This struggle with Austria also produced the heroic legend of William Tell as a pillar of honesty and fearlessness in the face of tyranny. More than one wine label still pays homage to the Tell story and these turbulent times.

In fact most historians agree that the allies of Rütli did not intend to establish an independent state in the modern sense, but rather had simply joined forces to preserve their traditional autonomy. The tension between competing concepts of a higher or federal, against a local or cantonal, authority – already evident 700 years ago at Rütli – is a recurrent theme throughout Swiss history. This incipient rivalry between two levels of government has had a defining influence on the establishment and growth of vineyards throughout the country.

A seemingly endless series of despotic rivalries, religious controversy and civil wars dominated the period from the 11th to the 15th centuries. The Swiss, like the Helvetii before them, were most interested in preserving an acceptable margin for manoeuver when they found themselves involved in other peoples' struggles. The martial reputation of the Swiss cantons was established at the Battle of Mortgarten in 1315. This defeat of the Austrian armies was the first recorded instance of a peasant force on foot bettering mounted knights. By the 15th century the Swiss had become a major European military and economic power. This belligerent reputation was fully confirmed when the forces of the Swiss Confederation devastated the forces of Charles the Bold, Duke of Burgundy, in 1476 – a shattering event which led to the demise of the exceedingly rich Dukedom of Burgundy and the rise of France. Because of their proven martial skills, rulers throughout Europe began to employ Swiss mercenaries, a development still recalled today in the Vatican's Swiss Guard recruited from the Catholic canton of Valais. The historians of Chassagne-Montrachet remember the Swiss mercenaries with little affection because their wine-producing village (known then as Chassagne-le-Haut) was destroyed during the struggle between Charles the Bold and Louis XI of France by these very same Swiss mercenaries in the pay of the French!

So lucrative was this trade in mercenaries that the Swiss cantons adopted a firm policy of political neutrality, which allowed them to sell their military services in every major European war between the 15th and 19th centuries.

These developments, perhaps surprisingly, had an important influence on the growth of Swiss vineyards. Returning soldiers sought to maintain the lifestyle they had enjoyed while fighting and living abroad. When they retired to their homeland they brought with them the necessary accoutrements, including new vines and improved growing methods. During these times when drinkable water was scarce, wine was clearly the beverage of choice. In the 15th and 16th centuries the annual consumption of wine per person in certain parts of Switzerland has been calculated at around 200 liters. These would generally have been rather miserable beverages – safer than water but still a rather sour tipple. The alcoholic strength of medieval wine was considerably less than that of today's table wine. They would have been rather bitter and thin drinks, often "improved" with spices and honey to make them more palatable. A 1597 Zurich recipe even suggests that sour wine could be sweetened by adding a mixture of salt and water! Beer was infrequently produced outside southern Germany, and this alternate beverage did not reach the major wine growing areas of Switzerland until the 17th century.

The Reformation

The struggle for Europe's soul during the time of the Reformation and Counter Reformation touched Switzerland intimately. Ulrich Zwingli and John Calvin dominated the Reformation in their respective cities of Zurich and Geneva. Just to show that even great preachers do not live by bread alone, the Geneva *Registre du Conseil* records in 1541 that John Calvin and other notables received two *bossettes* (648 liters) of wine as part of their annual stipend. The Consistory, which dominated all aspects of Genevois life during Calvin's supremacy, passed judgment on all moral and spiritual matters. Not only were ostentatious displays of clothes and food strictly forbidden but the population was forced to consume only local wine. Whether this step was taken as a penance, or simply represents an early example of a restrictive trade practice, remains unclear!

As the wheels of commerce continued to advance, a document from 1692 in the Geneva city archives records that 360 wine makers in the Geneva region marketed wine totaling nearly three million liters produced in excess of their family needs. Over half the production was white wine. Although there is a reference to "Salvagnin" which today refers to a red wine produced next-door in Vaud from Gamay and Pinot Noir grapes, it is unknown whether this historical reference points to a red or white variety. Also included on the list from 1682 are *"clairets"*, *"vin gris"* (grey wine) and *"vin mêlés"* (wine blended with alcohol).

During this period the Swiss must have developed quite a reputation for drinking. In French, to *"boire à la Suisse"*, (literally to drink like a Swiss), came to mean "to drink heavily", a phrase the French author Michel de Montaigne used in his *Essais*. A second traditional phrase linking the Swiss to drink, which may have come from the experiences of Swiss soldiers serving in the armies of France, is *"boire avec son Suisse"* or *"faire suisse"*, both of which mean to drink alone! Later the phrase became modified to *"boire en Suisse"*, but the meaning remained the same – to drink by oneself.

The development of a money-based commerce in wine did not progress unhindered. Even before the 18th century occasional but strenuous efforts were made by local and regional authorities to impede the sale of non-local wines, or importation of foreign wines. The latter, in particular, were a target for governments which sought to protect the livelihood of local producers and prevent the outflow of currency. Various regulatory initiatives throughout the 18th century demonstrated that the problem defied permanent solutions. At the same time there were attempts, at least in Vaud, to limit the cultivation of wine grapes to areas naturally conducive to the production of better wines. By the end of the 18th century and beginning of the 19th century, however, major population increases and economic development contributed to an unprecedented surge in demand for wine, fueling a spectacular expansion of domestic vineyards.

At the end of the 18th century the French Revolution had its predictable and destabilizing impact upon neighbouring Switzerland. Intellectual nourishment for the revolution had been provided by Geneva-born Jean-Jacques Rousseau and part-time Geneva resident Jean François Arouet, better known under his pen name of Voltaire. Inspired by the success of the revolutionary forces in Paris, local upheavals broke out, including the Vaudois Revolution of 1798. Many French nobles, among them the vineyard-owning patrician the Marquis Pradier d'Agrain from Puligny in Burgundy, fled the revolutionary violence in France to the comparative calm of Switzerland.

One of the direct effects of the social revolution on the production of wine was the dissolution of the great monastic orders and the secularization, usually through public auction, of their assets. This dramatic development, which played out across Europe, was more than just an administrative rearrangement. Gone was the social order and technical infrastructure that taught peasants where to plant, how to prune and how much they would receive for their crop. Certainty was replaced by confusion and, in time, independence. This was by no means a completely happy exchange, for the average peasant was accustomed to a high degree of order in his life. With this grudging emancipation, however, began the slow transition towards the modern wine industry. In Switzerland the process may have taken somewhat longer than elsewhere, but even the isolated valleys were not immune to the social movements sweeping the rest of Europe.

The 19th Century

The opening years of the 19th century in Europe were dominated by the rise of Napoleon whose imperial adventures certainly did not leave Switzerland, particularly the *Suisse romande,* untouched. In fact, the physical map of Switzerland's vineyard areas was fundamentally transformed after the Napoleonic invasions. The political order of Switzerland was also overturned as Napoleon's revolutionary armies supported the "Helvetic Republic" and the end of the traditional rule of the "Old Confederation". Eventually the Congress of Vienna in 1815 restored much of the pre-Napoleonic European order and formalized Switzerland's status as an armed but politically neutral confederation. In addition to enlarging Geneva and attaching the canton of Neuchâtel to the Swiss Confederation, the Congress also restored the canton of the Valais to Swiss rule after its brief existence as a French *département*. This post-Napoleonic adjustment, confirming Switzerland's borders as they are today, had an obvious influence on the development of wine in Switzerland, for it is difficult to envisage discussing Swiss wines without a focus on the contributions of these three key wine-producing cantons.

The Napoleonic incursion into Switzerland not unexpectedly reinforced the earlier secularization of the monasteries, continuing the process of dismantling and redistributing the vineyards of the old and formerly wealthy religious orders. Efforts to reduce the land holdings of the remaining monasteries continued throughout the first part of the 19th century, and as late as 1841 and 1849 the dissolution of remaining orders was enforced by legal measures. While driven by deep religious and political differences, this secularization was also undoubtedly supported by ambitious individuals and local authorities who were able to purchase some of the best situated and tended vineyards in the country.

From the mid 19th century Switzerland began to evolve from a rural, predominately pastoral society to a modern, industrialized and service-oriented nation. The political framework of modern Switzerland was established after the 1847 Sonderbund War, a 19th century war of religion, popularly described as a "revolutionary civil war". This domestic clash not only saw Vaudois soldiers occupying Valais, and indirectly spreading the Chasselas grape to a new area, but also hastened the shift from a society of guilds and traditional pastoral and agricultural relationships to one more urban and money-based. The nascent Swiss industrial sector initially focused on textile production, but soon moved into chemicals, machinery and manufacturing. These developments benefited from several specific local advantages, including inexpensive hydro-electric power, (important in a country with few other natural resources); a willing workforce drawn largely from the agricultural sector and foreign migrants; readily available capital; and an evolving transport system. The effect on the countryside was immediate. Whereas 65% of the working population was agricultural 1800, the level dropped to 30% by 1900. (More recently this level has, not surprisingly, fallen to about seven percent). However, even as large numbers of agricultural labourers deserted the countryside for the urban industrial factories, the total volume of rural agricultural production, including wine, continued to rise to meet the urban demand.

Coping with the economic dislocation in rural society during this time was far from easy. Frequently, for example, Switzerland felt compelled to close its borders to traditional wine suppliers from neighbouring regions such as Alsace to shield domestic producers. For example, the closure in 1850 of the Swiss wine markets to imports had a grave effect on Alsacian exporters that had long relied on the Swiss outlet for their production. In addition, the 19th century witnessed an uneasy tension between the Swiss wine and cereal interests, a rivalry that saw producers of both products lobbying separately for tariff protection from less expensive imports.

Between 1853 and 1865 the domestic price of wine rose spectacularly – 84% in the Canton of Geneva alone – and this contributed to an equally spectacular growth in the amount of land allotted nationally to wine grapes. In 1880 the total reached 34,400 hectares, almost two and one-half times the acreage today. One mid-19th century observer of Swiss vineyards was the Hungarian "Count" Agoston Haraszthy, credited by some for introducing the Zinfandel grape into California. Hugh Johnson's book *Vintage: The Story of Wine* quotes Haraszthy's 1861 report where he noted that he "arrived in Geneva (from Neuchâtel) after traveling eight hours continually among vineyards ... Not a spot as large as an ordinary brick-yard was left uncultivated, with the exception of where the old vines have been cut out to give the ground the necessary three years rest". Needless to say, such a rapid expansion of wine grape cultivation did not necessarily improve quality. By the end of the 19th century, production in Switzerland was abundant but, in many places, especially in central and eastern parts of the country, the wines produced were much too acidic and entirely unsuited for long-term commercial exploitation.

In the last quarter of the 19th century, Switzerland did not escape devastation from the small yellow phylloxera louse which so ravaged Europe's vineyards. Undoubtedly carried into Switzerland on diseased vines from nearby France, phylloxera was first confirmed in 1874 on the estate of Baron Rothschild at Prégny, just outside Geneva. As the louse's destruction spread, detection of the insect and the systematic destruction of infected vines became a national obsession. All levels of government participated in the vain efforts to eradicate phylloxera. Initially, infected vineyards were declared temporary state property and the diseased areas were fenced off. The vines were destroyed and the ground doused with carbon bisulphide. Ad hoc compensation to the growers and eventually a government-supported insurance scheme, and a tax on all vine growers, mitigated the direct financial loss. Efforts to control the spread of phylloxera continued well into the 20th century, although in Switzerland as elsewhere, the only workable solution was grubbing up the old vines and replanting with American root-stock. This laborious effort to reconstitute the vineyards was not completed until after World War II.

Switzerland's International Influence

The late 18th century, and in particular the 19th century were times of extensive migration both to and from Switzerland. Immigrant workers played an important role in the development of Swiss industry and agriculture. Equally, the contribution to the development of wine made by migrants from Switzerland, often fleeing the deadening poverty and parochial inwardness of rural Swiss communities, must also be noted. From central Europe and Russia to the early vineyards of California, and elsewhere, Swiss immigrants have played a noteworthy role.

One of the earliest examples of Switzerland's contribution to international vineyard expansion occurred in the United States. In 1806, the Swiss-born J.J. Dufour established the first commercial winery in the United States on the banks of the Ohio River in Indiana. This event took place during the presidency of Thomas Jefferson, also an erstwhile but ultimately unsuccessful *vigneron* on his Monticello estate in Virginia. The grape which Dufour used to plant his vineyard was the hybrid Alexander, a cross between a native *labrusca* grape and an unknown *vinifera* grape, originally discovered in Pennsylvania.

In 1822, at the invitation of the Russian Czar, Alexander I, a hardy group of Swiss *vignerons* set out from Vevey in Vaud for the Black Sea village of Chabag at the mouth of the Dniester River. For over a century these pioneers and their descendants produced wine for the Russian and Bulgarian Czars. The Swiss connection was only broken in 1944 when the remaining Swiss were repatriated during World War II. Separately in eastern Europe, in Hungary, Eder Weber was a pivotal figure in the 19th century revival of the country's vineyards.

Again in the United States, in California, the well-known companies of Italian-Swiss Colony and Sutter Home commemorate early Swiss immigrants to the Golden State. In particular, the remarkable story of Johann August Sutter, the "King of California" and "General Sutter of Sacramento" deserves mention. Born in 1803, Sutter emigrated to the United States and, after an adventurous but precarious existence, he founded the colony of "New Helvetia" on a 200-square kilometer tract of land in the Sacramento River valley. Sutter was the domineering patriarch of this "New Switzerland" until the discovery of gold there in 1848 triggered the California Gold Rush. Unfortunately for Sutter, his immigrant colony could not withstand the invading hordes of rapacious prospectors. Eventually he lost everything he had worked for. Sutter's name, however, lives on through one of the earliest commercial vineyards established in the Napa Valley, "Sutter Home", founded in 1890, and known today particularly for its good-value red Zinfandel and rosé-hued White Zinfandel (alas not Chasselas!).

On the other side of the "new world", in Australia, another Swiss immigrant, Hubert de Castella, was an important contributor to the golden age of wines from the state of Victoria. In the late 1800s, Victoria produced half of Australia's wine and de Castella even suggested, in his book *John Bull's Vineyard,* that Victoria could fulfill Great Britain's entire wine requirement. Unfortunately de Castella's vision did not survive the arrival of the phylloxera louse and other social changes at the end of the century.

Another 19th century Swiss émigré deserving of mention, although only indirectly connected with wine, is César Ritz, the son of peasants from Niederwald and eventually the founder in 1896 of the Hotel Ritz in Paris. One can only wonder how many Swiss wines appeared on the wine list of the Hotel Ritz before his death in 1919. Unfortunately for historical continuity, there are currently no Swiss wines listed on the hotel's *carte des vins.*

Most importantly, for the worlds of both wine and botany, is the work of Professor Doctor Hermann Müller-Thurgau, one of the great practical botanists of the 19th century who first built a reputation in Germany before achieving his ultimate fame in Switzerland. In 1882 Müller-Thurgau created the first successful scientific cross-breeding of *vinifera* grape types at the German research station of

Geisenheim in the Rheingau. In 1891 Müller-Thurgau returned to Switzerland to establish the agricultural research station at Wädenswil on Lake Zurich, where he pursued and perfected his Geisenheim experiments. He brought with him 150 pretested seedlings. The best of these, No. 58, the Riesling x Sylvaner, was further developed. Cuttings were returned to Germany in 1913, when it was named "Müller-Thurgau" in honour of its creator.

Müller-Thurgau was more important than simply a creator of one cross-bred grape variety. As a botanist, he was the first to concentrate on vines. He was among the first to use selected special yeasts for wine production, a practice almost universally followed today. And if this were not sufficient, he was also a student of the physiology of fermentation as well as being a phytopathologist and breeder of grape varieties. The Swiss research center at Wädenswil remains active today and it retains a pre-eminent influence on wine developments in the German speaking parts of Switzerland.

In one sense, the contributions of the creative Dr. Müller-Thurgau remain intriguingly unrecognized in his own country. His useful cross between a Riesling and a Sylvaner is grown successfully from Germany to New Zealand and is still widely planted in the cantons of eastern Switzerland. Almost everywhere it is known as the Müller-Thurgau grape, virtually the only exceptions being Switzerland and Luxembourg. Only in these two countries does the grape continue to recognize its progenitors under the name of Riesling x Sylvaner.

Developments in the 20th Century

The uneven struggle between industrial development and traditional agricultural structures has marked all industrialized countries throughout the 20th century. Attempts to find a balance between industrial and agricultural interests are still with us and are unlikely to end soon. Switzerland has not been spared these controversies and the development of the Swiss wine industry has been conspicuously shaped by the evolution of industrialization.

Since the beginning of this century, and as European transportation systems and marketing channels have grown more efficient, the Swiss wine industry has passed through several periods of relative tranquillity punctuated by occasional major crises. The crises, although economically and socially wrenching, often have acted as catalysts of reform and change.

The origins of the first major crisis of this century are found in the late 19th century. The rapid expansion of the vineyards into areas basically unsuited for grape production had not been well timed, especially in light of the damage from phylloxera, mildew and oïdium, which successively attacked European vineyards in the latter part of the century. In addition, the migration of country labourers to the city produced a rural labour shortage and a rise in agricultural salaries which, in turn, doubled the cost of wine production, and caused a steep rise in wine prices between the mid-19th and early 20th centuries. Because of this, the amount of land growing grapes was reduced between 1880 and 1920 by 50%, and the number of vine owners fell nationally by two-thirds. Prices of domestic wine fluctuated widely and stabilizing measures had to be introduced in 1891 when the Swiss government raised taxes on imported wines.

The years between 1915 and 1933 were relatively stable for the Swiss wine industry. Domestic wine production, however, remained under constant pressure from cheaper imports and, as a result, the government instituted measures to protect producers. These included, in 1922, the first attempt to limit imports by establishing formal import quotas, an initiative quickly abandoned until 1933 because of political and consumer protests. Interestingly, in Switzerland such efforts raised sensitive constitutional questions because the division of powers between the federal government and the cantons prevented the federal authorities from directly intervening to protect the agricultural sector. These defensive initiatives were, however, ultimately justified retroactively under the constitutionally respectable "right of necessity"!

Between the two world wars there was an overall increase in the output of grapes per unit of land. One reason for this was that the control of the three major debilitating grape maladies of the 19th century – phylloxera, oïdium and mildew – produced increased yields. In addition, a rationalization of labour practices, improved soil management, and better grape variety selection all contributed to rising yields.

Switzerland was definitely not isolated from the second major international crisis of the 20th century, the Great Depression. The wine industry throughout Europe was fundamentally shaken by the depression and the protectionist economic and trade policies of the 1930s. To intensify the crisis, the per unit costs of production increased almost 70% between 1931 and 1933 Concurrently, competitive currency devaluations by neighbouring countries drove the price of imports steadily down, which in turn seriously undermined the financial returns possible from domestic wine production. By the mid-1930s real prices had fallen back to the levels of 1910. A franc's worth of wine from Lavaux in Vaud in 1933 was worth no more than 75 centimes in 1934. By 1935 the same wine could be had for 40 centimes. However, as the depression deprived many Swiss of disposable income, there were fewer and fewer buyers even at such reduced prices for wine. The situation was further exacerbated by a series of very poor harvests in the early 1930s, of which 1934 and 1935 were probably the worst.

The growth in harvest yields since 1915 had effectively neutralized the benefits of a reduction of acreage in the first decade of the century. Oversupply and decreasing demand prompted calls for two principal remedies: a further reduction in the amount of land under cultivation; and additional controls over imports. Some reduction of vineyard area occurred naturally as grape growers responded to market pressures. The authorities also encouraged growers to take out of production marginal or clearly unsuitable lands and turn them over to other crops. This was not easy, however, in the economic climate of the 1930s.

Of equal, if not greater, long-term importance were the efforts taken to control imports. In October 1933, the federal government was given the authority to protect the national economy against "foreign threats". Strict limitations were put on wines imported into Switzerland, and a system of quotas was established. These measures established the principles which regulated the import of wines, white wines in particular, into Switzerland until the beginning of 1995. Importers were legally bound to dispose of a certain amount of domestic Swiss production, although, in return, a part of their imported quota could be blended with the domestic wine to produce a saleable product. In addition to controlling imports, the authorities also supported domestic production through subsidies to encourage consumption or to reduce transportation costs. By 1936 the system had evolved into a formalized process which included a tax on imports to assist Swiss growers; the authority to oblige importers to market a certain part of domestic production; and the creation of a consultative commission to "educate" the public and government on the state of the domestic market.

One other practical reaction to the difficulties of the 1930s, and still very much a presence today, was the establishment of cantonal-based caves *cooperatives* (cooperative cellars) by groups of *vignerons* in various parts of the country. The strength of the many was deemed to be greater than the power of a few and, as a result, associations of growers such as Provins in Valais and Vin Union in Geneva were founded to protect the economic and political interests of the grape growers.

The Second World War obviously reduced the pressure from imports on Swiss wine producers as the Swiss economy became largely self-supporting under the strict and watchful eyes of the authorities. Between 1939 and 1945, therefore, there was stability in the Swiss wine industry. The end of hostilities in Europe, however, freed domestic prices from war-time restrictions. Harvests were plentiful and a serious demand for foreign wines reemerged among the Swiss public. These factors, combined with a rise in production costs, led to a recurrence of the traditional cycle of falling domestic prices and a predictable government effort to balance supply and demand. The cumulative results of various state interventions over the years were ratified by a national referendum in 1947 and later reinforced by the adoption of the national legislation governing wine production, including the Law on Agriculture, Federal legislation on Viticulture and the Wine Statute. These actions completed the legal framework.

The 1950s, 1960s and 1970s were decades of technical development and steady improvement for the Swiss wine industry, punctuated by occasional financial crises resulting from overproduction and broader economic cycles. Mechanization was introduced where possible to reduce production costs, and yields were again improved through the increased use of fertilizers and improved vine selection. New vinification technology also markedly improved the quality of the wine in even mediocre years. Switzerland did not escape the economic downturn which affected other wine producers in the early 1970s, but the dislocation was less than that during the crises of earlier in the century.

A significant factor in the improvement of Swiss wines during the 20th century has been the continued, if erratic, reduction of total acreage under cultivation in the ongoing effort to increase quality and bring supply and demand into some broad equilibrium. Table II below, demonstrates just how inexorable the reduction in vineyards has been over almost a century. Only the canton of Valais has defied this trend.

These reductions produced considerable social dislocation and human costs. In addition, the dramatic decrease in the surface area devoted to wine grapes has often been offset by an equally vigorous increase in yields. Most recently, producers have had to address other negative and unforeseen consequences of the increased use of machinery and fertilizers, namely the erosion and gradual impoverishment of

Table II: Area cultivated by canton (in hectares)		
	1899	1995
Vaud	6,630	3,818
Valais	2,584	5,259
Geneva	1,825	1,342
Ticino	6,562	900
Zurich	4,769	634
Neuchâtel	1,177	608

the soil. A growing band of environmentally-minded growers has adopted an "integrated" approach to grape growing which attempts, among other practices, to minimize the use of fertilizers, pesticides and other intrusions in the production of quality grapes. Work on non-chemical controls and disease-resistant clones which require fewer physical interventions have also had a positive influence. The initial results have been sufficiently encouraging that even very traditional growers have taken on integrated vineyard management practices.

Nevertheless, after the remarkable decade of the 1980s, when all Europe enjoyed an unprecedented string of fine vintages, a new structural surplus of unsold white wine again sprang up in Switzerland by the early 1990s. Most, if not all of this excess, was low-quality, bulk wine. The reappearance of a domestic wine surplus, despite continued restrictions on imports under the quota system, does raise a serious question as to whether there is still too much low-quality (white) wine for which there is no ready market. The replacement of quotas by tariffs will only add pressure on cheap domestic white wine. The search continues for an elusive golden mean which will balance the often conflicting interests of consumers, growers, negotiants, importers and other vested interests.

The future prospects for the Swiss wine industry are dealt with separately in a later chapter. This brief historical review is meant only to set the scene for a more detailed consideration of wine production by canton or by region. First, however, short sections on vine cultivation, vinification, and grape types will complete the general description of grape growing in Switzerland.

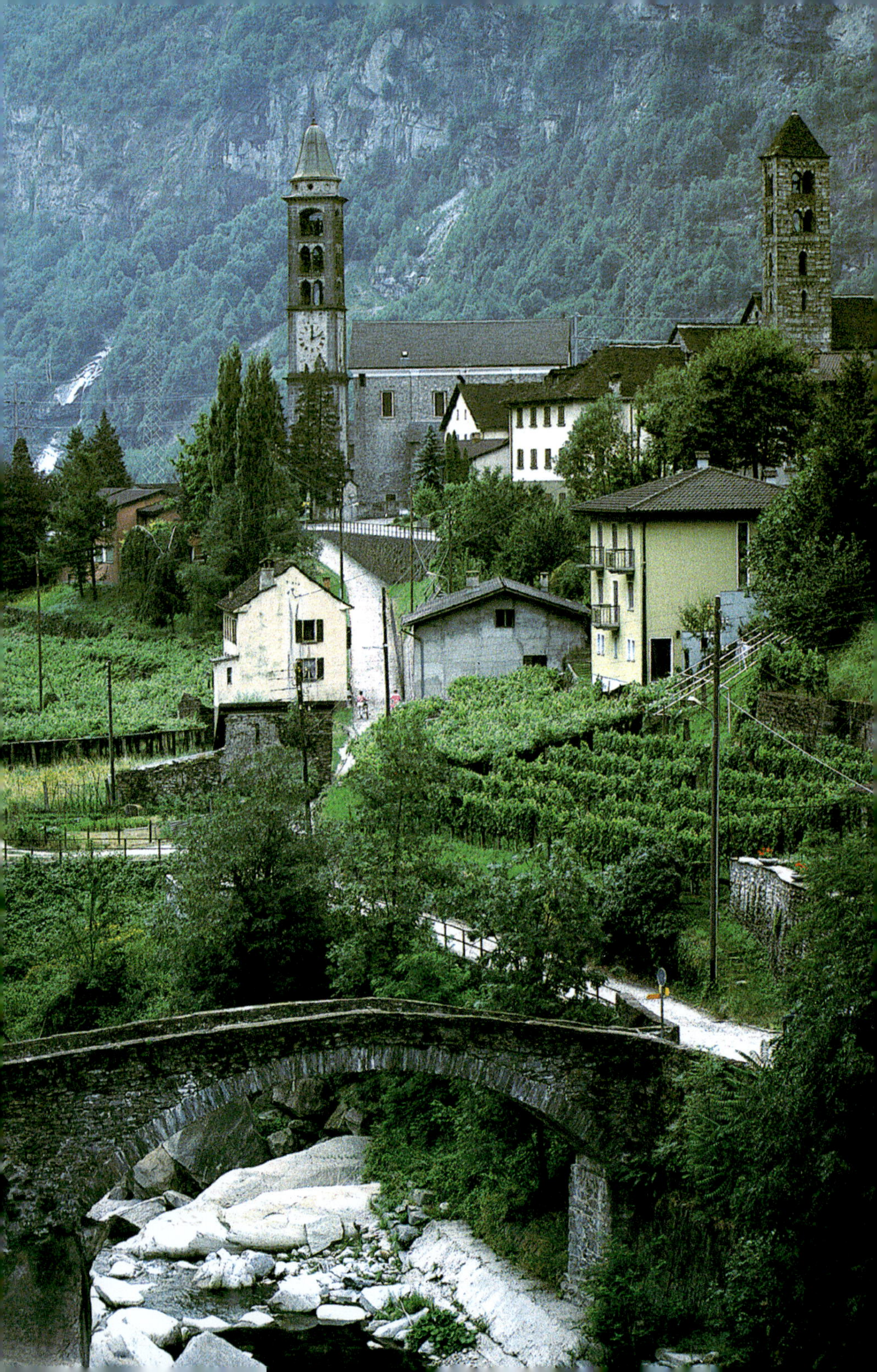

III

Cultivation of the Vine

Climate and the land

In Switzerland, as perhaps nowhere else, geology, climate and geography have dictated land and resource utilization. These factors determine where grapes can and cannot thrive and ripen with acceptable regularity. Every suitable part of the country is used to maximum benefit. A close examination of a map of Switzerland's mountainous and glacial terrain quickly demonstrates the difficulty of identifying those few valley floors, fertile plains and slopes where wine grapes can grow easily. With certain limited exceptions these regions are found on the south-facing slopes rising from the Rhône river, including Lake Geneva; along the basins that are formed by, or drain into, the Rhine; and on the south-facing hills adjacent to the lakes and rivers in Ticino. The first and foremost task for Swiss wine makers is ensuring an exposure and growing environment which permits the grapes to mature fully.

In general, grapes are found in many places where other crops do not grow well, but they only flourish within fairly well-defined climatic conditions. The average annual temperature should be between 11° and 16°C, although ranges as low as 9°C and much higher are not unknown. Each degree of latitude north reduces the average temperature by 0.6°C, which limits European grape culture to the lands below 50° north. A rise in altitude of 100 meters lowers the average temperature by 0.5°C.

These are meaningful statistics in Switzerland where the combination of alpine geography and extremes of climate severely restrict the regions of the country that can successfully support grape growing. Sufficient sunshine is absolutely necessary for growth. For grapes to achieve sufficient maturity, an average July temperature of 18°C is required, and the sum of the daily mean temperatures throughout the growing season should amount to 2,900°C. A minimum of at least 1,500 to 1,600 hours of sunshine annually is needed, of which 1,200 hours should occur during the growing season. This requirement is not, however, an absolute and can be modified, both positively and negatively, by the slope of the ground where the grapes are grown, a particularly important consideration in Switzerland where most vineyards are located on south-facing slopes to capture the maximum possible amount of additional heat. As the Romans discovered two millennia ago, an advantageous heating effect is transmitted to the vine through the warming of the soil on these south-facing slopes.

Giornico in the Leventine is the most northerly wine-growing community in Ticino where grapes grow around the San Nicolau church founded by the Benedictines.

It is also important to note that north-facing slopes, examples of which are found in Valais along the left bank of the Rhône, reheat much less quickly than either the steep south-facing terraced vineyards of Vaud or the flatter plains found in the outskirts of Geneva. The angle of certain Vaudois vineyards can reach an almost absurdly steep slope of 80°. And while the stone retaining wall will certainly radiate heat, such vineyards pose particularly difficult maintenance and erosion problems.

As demonstrated by Table III below drawn from the book *Viticulture,* the general climatic conditions of Switzerland are, however, well within the range of acceptable conditions found in major European wine growing regions.

Table III: Comparative Climatic Conditions

	Latitude	Altitude (m)	Average Temp. (° C)	Average January Temp.	Average July Temp.	Annual Rainfall (mm)	Annual Actual Sunlight
Geneva	46°12'	405	10.1	1.0	19.5	852	2036
Montreux	46°25'	412	10.0	1.0	19.2	1152	1672
Sion	46°15'	549	10.0	–0.2	19.5	599	2094
Neuchâtel	47°	487	9.2	0.0	18.6	994	1699
Lugano	46°	276	11.6	1.9	21.3	1742	2101
Lyon	45°40'	175	11.4	2.2	20.7	813	2018
Bordeaux	44°45'	74	12.5	5.4	19.5	900	2998
Florence	43°45'	73	14.6	5.4	23.9	825	2488
Alicante	38°20'	26	18.0	10.8	25.4	328	3009
Frankfurt	50°05'	104	10.4	0.9	19.6	676	1563

The other factor indispensable for growth is water. Rainfall of 600 millimeters per year is generally considered the minimum, although in some vineyards, (not in Switzerland), annual precipitation as low as 300 mm is possible. Total annual rainfall is generally not a problem except in Valais, where the average annual precipitation is below 600 mm. Certain areas of Valais supplement normal rainfall by using the runoff from traditional *"bisses",* ancient water channels flowing from mountain glaciers, or more modern irrigation or sprinkling systems. In Valais, the vines would normally be sprinkled one to three times a year, with the quantity of water varying each time between 40 mm and 120 mm, depending upon specific soil and climatic conditions.

Irrigation is generally not needed where rainfall exceeds 800 mm per year. The questionable reliance on irrigation to increase yields is, unfortunately, sometimes found in Switzerland, even where the natural rain patterns are normally sufficient. When irrigation is used, the timing, and amount of water additional to natural precipitation must be very carefully controlled to avoid diluting the quality of the grape. Irrigation is, however, rarely justified after the *véraison* (colouring) of the grape, generally in August. On the other hand, precipitation in excess of 900 mm to 1,000 mm can produce other problems such as soil erosion, mildew and gray rot.

Another concern is that vines will freeze at -2.5°C during the growing season. In the destructive freeze of May 1991, lows of -10°C were reached. Damage to unprotected vines during the dormant winter period can begin when the temperature drops below -12°C, although vines can usually withstand temperatures as low as -16°C to -20°C without serious harm. The older the vine, however, the more likely frost damage will occur. At the other end of the scale, temperatures over 42°C can begin to burn the vines, a level certainly not unknown in arid sections of Valais.

Damage from winter frost is difficult to anticipate, but it is fairly unimportant compared to a severe spring frost which can have a devastating impact on the annual harvest. Depending upon the humidity and development of the buds and young shoots, temperatures below -1°C can damage the vines. In areas prone to frosts, several counter measures are possible. The vines can be covered with conical "hats" of straw or plastic, a technique often used in eastern Switzerland. The temperature of the vineyard can also be raised temporarily by burning heating oil or propane, and the grapes protected by sprinkling with water.

Hail, too, is an annual problem in certain areas – particularly in Ticino, the La Côte region of Vaud, some parts of eastern Switzerland, but rarely in Valais. Expensive anti-hail nets constructed with some government financial support can be found where the risk of damage is high. The other alternative is hail insurance, but this adds to the costs of production.

Tending the vines

The selection of site and grape type, which will be discussed later, are only two of the key elements that influence the quality of the fully-ripened grape. Additional critical factors include root-stock selection, growing method, plant density and protection from disease. In all these aspects of viticulture, Swiss *vignerons* have developed solutions appropriate to their individual situations by adopting or modifying standard techniques employed elsewhere. The government-sponsored agricultural research stations have been particularly important in ensuring that information on new techniques and experimental results reach the growers.

Virtually all Swiss vines are grown on phylloxera-resistant American root-stocks which have been adapted over time to meet Swiss climatic conditions. Several isolated plots of pre-phylloxera vines are still reported in both the upper Valais and parts of German Switzerland, but these are of limited production and commercial value. Legally, any such pre-phylloxera vines should have been replaced. Most American root-stocks originally were imported from other European countries, although some have been propagated in Swiss nurseries.

Two critical decisions to be made when establishing a new vineyard are the growing method and density of planting. These two factors must be treated together since one will clearly influence the other. The geographical limitations affect which option is most appropriate, as do the alternatives available for cultivation and harvesting (i.e., manual or mechanical). Traditionally, the most common method for training the vines in the French-speaking areas of Switzerland was the *gobelet sur échalas* (a single staked vine) which has the advantage of keeping the vines close to the soil for heat, allows sufficient aeration, is well suited for the verdant Chasselas, and permits dense planting and hence potentially large harvests.

Mechanization has transformed vineyard layout where machinery can be effectively used. As a result various systems for training the vines can now be found throughout Switzerland, including the *gobelet* (a single, unstaked vine); the commonly found *guyot* (single, double or "arched" branches trained on wire from a single stem); and *cordon de royat* (similar in some ways to the *guyot* system and used for particularly fertile vines such as the Chasselas and the Gamay). Local variations can be found, for example, in Ticino where a single branch *guyot* system is used almost exclusively, but with 8-12 shoots instead of the usual 6-8 shoots common in French-speaking Switzerland. Both the *guyot* and *cordon de royat* systems are well adapted to mechanization. They have the advantage of easy care and minimal labour intensity, but they are only suitable for certain soils. They need good ripening conditions and can be susceptible to rot if air circulation is not sufficient. In planting a vineyard, the *gobelet* needs 0.7-1.0 square meters per plant, the cordon de royat 0.8-1.1 square meters per plant and the double guyot 1.9-2.4 square meters per plant. Finally, where spring frosts are a particular problem, such as in parts of eastern Switzerland, stakes are used to allow the vines to be covered easily and quickly with protective straw "hats".

The inverse relationship between the quantity of grapes harvested and quality of wine is well recognized in Switzerland, even if past practice sometimes neglected its importance. The size of the harvest may only be just one of the factors influencing the eventual quality of the wine. But everything else being equal, large yields will result in an inferior wine. The Swiss *vigneron* is therefore faced with the age-old dilemma of whether to adjust his crop for quality or quantity. A superior quality requires a severe pruning, usually in July, to ensure that only a limited number of grape bunches are encouraged. Such cutting back will reduce the final harvest and certainly runs counter to the traditional farming mentality which equates quantity with prosperity. These ingrained attitudes, which are well-rooted in the painful experience of bad harvests and a system of compensation that is usually based on straight grape weight, are difficult, if not impossible, to change overnight. Economic incentives or disincentives will, however, have a telling influence on how growers tend their crops. If the better quality grapes fetch a higher price, or if poorer producers cannot find a market for their harvest, attitudes will quickly change.

Table IV: Number of bunches of grapes per vine

Bunches		4	8	12	16	20
Production	kg/m2	1.18	2.05	2.64	3.07	3.42
Sugar levels	° Oechsle	82.1	78.8	72.6	66.9	63.5
Total acidity	gram/liter	12.3	12.8	12.5	13.1	13.3

Tests to encourage smaller yields conducted by the Federal Station for Agronomic Research in Changins, located between Geneva and Lausanne, produced over a nine-year period the telling results shown below in Table IV. This research clearly demonstrates the direct, negative relationship between overproduction and sugar levels as measured by degrees Oechsle (see Chapter V for details). As the number of grape bunches per vine rises and overall production increases, the sugar content per grape drops notably while overall acidity rises slightly.

Overproduction of grapes results in many problems, not least of which is the increased susceptibility of the vines to frost and parasite damage. Switzerland is also by no means free of the diseases that afflict other vineyards world-wide. Although the use of American root-stock has controlled the damage from the phylloxera louse, other parasitic diseases such as mildew, oïdium, *rougeot* and gray rot, along with various fungi and parasitic animals (red and yellow spiders) and insects (caterpillars, worms and wasps) must be taken into account and thwarted. Treatments have traditionally been dominated by fairly standard chemical-based applications. Although the use of chemicals has certainly not disappeared, growing environmental consciousness has encouraged prophylactic rather than treatment-based approaches. The current "integrated" approach incorporates economic, toxicological and ecological factors in ways to improve the overall health of the vineyard. Human and chemical interventions are limited to those situations where they are indispensable. Otherwise a naturally healthy vine is the goal.

Mechanization and new technologies have introduced major changes into the techniques used and time required to tend vineyards. One slightly dated study, reproduced in Table V, demonstrated that between 1961 and 1975 the amount of human labour required to tend one hectare in Valais fell by almost 40%. Given the basic cost of labour in Switzerland, such a drop is not inconsequential. The trend continues today, reinforced by the increased use of mechanical cultivation and harvesting where appropriate.

Table V: Time required (hours/ha.) to tend grapes in Valais

	1961	1975
Care of the vines	1051	752
Care of the soil	583	217
Anti-parasites	164	83
Anti-frost, sprinkling	70	33
Surveillance	–	5
Harvest	413	293
Total	**2281**	**1413**

In general Swiss *vignerons* remain on the leading edge of proficient vineyard care, if only because of the fragile nature of many of their vineyards. Even when human interventions are restricted to an absolute minimum, this overriding concern for the health of the vines underscores a methodical approach to vineyard care. Changes, such as the introduction of mechanization or the spread of integrated viticultural procedures, come slowly – too slowly for some – and only after considerable study and testing.

IV

Grape Types

The diversity of wines produced in Switzerland is one of the country's great strengths. Despite the fact that six varieties (Chasselas, Riesling x Sylvaner, Sylvaner, Gamay, Merlot and Pinot Noir) produce almost 90% of all domestic wines, the Swiss contribution to the "world of wine" is only fully understood by considering the diverse and unique varieties of grapes found in the country. The range, vitality and appeal of Swiss wines is predicated on a combination of wines obtained from internationally recognized "noble" grapes and, quite separately, wines made from indigenous grapes rarely found outside certain cantons. Indeed, some of the uniquely Swiss grapes claim an ancient lineage, while one *vinifera* variety, the Chasselas, achieves its international apogee only on Swiss slopes. Over 35 different grape varieties are grown in Valais, more if experimental vineyards are counted, while in Vaud the corresponding number of authorized varieties was increased in 1993 from seven to twenty seven.

In the following chapters on individual cantons or regions, detailed observations will be made on which grapes are grown, where, and why. A short introduction to both the variety and uniqueness of the national mixture of grape varieties found in Switzerland will set the scene. The country's mountainous terrain and the climatic conditions define which grapes are even potential candidates for producing fine wine, and where they can be grown. However, within these overall confines, the Swiss have pushed to the limits the boundaries constricting the development of certain grape varieties. In addition, through the propagation of new clones, the Swiss have continued to improve the adaptation of various grape types more commonly found elsewhere in very different circumstances.

In one category are those vines now found nowhere else, whose lineage (according to local tradition) sometimes stretches back to medieval, if not earlier, times. This group includes the Petite Arvine, Amigne, Rèze, Heida (Païen), Humagne Rouge, Humagne Blanc, Cornalin and Bondola. In the second group are grapes grown elsewhere but adapted to Swiss conditions; the Chasselas, Pinot Noir and Gamay, and secondary varieties such as Merlot, Pinot Gris, Syrah, Sylvaner, Marsanne, Aligoté and Muscat. This second group of grapes also includes the internationally popular Chardonnay and, in small but growing quantities, Cabernet Sauvignon. Initially these latter two varieties were grown more as experimental vines than as commercially important crops, but the trend towards producing wines for aging has increased their importance in regions where they can achieve maturity.

The Chasselas, Pinot Noir and Gamay remain the three most important varietals found, to a greater or lesser degree, throughout almost all parts of Switzerland. The wines produced from these grapes, however, vary considerably. In addition, particular circumstances resulted in the adoption of specific grapes, for example, when early in this century, the Merlot grape of the St. Emilion and Pomerol was consciously introduced into Italian-speaking Ticino during the post-phylloxera replanting. Over time it has become the grape of choice in the entire canton

The "arbiter" of all grape types in Switzerland, however, remains the Chasselas. As a result, the Swiss have developed a general classification comparing the time of ripening of the Chasselas to other varieties. The table below is reproduced from the book *Cépages du Valais*, and is particularly useful for Swiss *vignerons* in determining which grape type is appropriate for a particular microclimate or slope:

Table VI: Grape Ripening Compared to the Chasselas

Early: – 7 to 10 days before Chasselas	Riesling, Riesling x Sylvaner, Aligoté
1st Group: – same maturity as Chasselas	Pinot Noir, Gris & Blanc, Gamay, Chardonnay
2nd Group: – 7 to 10 days after Chasselas	Sylvaner, Muscat, Humagne Blanc, Merlot. Cabernet Sauvignon
3rd Group: – 14 to 20 days after Chasselas	Amigne, Arvine, Ermitage, Humagne Rouge, Syrah, Cornalin

White Wine Grape Varieties

Chasselas (Fendant, Perlan, Gutedel)

Although wine made from the Chasselas grape is by no means synonymous with all Swiss wine, this variety is most often identified as producing the "typical" Swiss wine. While overall plantings have fallen in recent years in response to the increased demand for red wines, 40% of all Swiss wine is still made from the Chasselas. It is found virtually throughout the entire country, with the exception of some parts of the German-speaking region. The Chasselas still dominates the French-speaking cantons. In Geneva and Valais, it provides between 50% and 85% of the harvest and is marketed under the trade names of Perlan and Fendant respectively. For a while the Vaudois *vignerons* also attempted to distinguish their Chasselas by calling it "Dorin". Chasselas may produce 99% of Vaud's white wine, but the name "Dorin" never caught on and it is now no longer used.

As one of the earliest *vinifera* varieties to ripen, the Chasselas is as well-suited as any grape to the vagaries of the Swiss climate. In Switzerland, as elsewhere, it is grown as both a wine grape and a table grape. The Chasselas is arguably one of the oldest grape varieties cultivated by man, and the vast majority of the world's Chasselas vineyards are now found in Switzerland. Today it is rarely found in France with the exception of wines labelled Pouilly-sur-Loire, the Chasselas equivalent of the better known Sauvignon Blanc-based Pouilly Fumé wines. It also appears in certain vineyards in the Haute Savoie such as Crépy, notably at Château de Ripaille on the south shore of Lake Geneva at Thonon. Small pockets are found in Alsace, from where some stylish versions have been released in the early 1990s, Nièvre and the southern German region of Baden. The variety has also migrated across the Atlantic to the vineyards of the Okanagan Valley of British Colombia, Canada where the cold winters and short growing season perfectly fit the Chasselas profile. One British Colombia winery, Mission Hill, produces a very respectable facsimile of an acceptable Swiss wine. As might be expected, the winery employed a Swiss wine maker.

In total, the Chasselas provides almost half of all wines in the French-speaking regions of Switzerland. More than 5,000 hectares (13,200 acres) are planted in the *Suisse romande* cantons alone, compared with just over 1,000 hectares (2,200 acres) in France and 1,300 hectares (2,860 acres) in Germany's Baden Württemberg.

The Chasselas produces a neutral must, usually with reasonable but not high sugar levels, and not too much acid. These attributes seem particularly suited to the majority of Swiss palates which enjoy smooth white wines, often outside of meal times. Given its soft nature, it is not a successful blending wine; nor does the must produce a particularly complex wine, although when carefully grown and correctly vinified, the result is anything but one-dimensional.

The fundamentally neutral character of the grape reflects particularly well the nature of the soils and micro-climate where it is grown. It is not a grape suitable for cooler vineyard sites, and because it suffers from *coulure* (failure of the raisins to set properly), it must be given some protection from the direct effect of strong winds.

The origins of the Chasselas are still a matter of some dispute. Three separate theories on its development in western Europe are usually put forward, although it is generally conceded that the grape is at least as old as any of the following accounts. The first suggests the grape originated in the vineyards around the Burgundian town of Chasselas, near Mâcon. Here the grape was initially known as the Mornant. Renamed Chasselas, it spread out from there. It is, however, generally conceded that the grape gave its name to the village, and not the other way around. The second theory traces the origins of the Chasselas to Asia Minor or even farther east. According to this theory the Chasselas was grown in the environs of Constantinople as a table grape. An ambassador of French King François I to the Ottoman court sent some cuttings back to France, and from these the vine was propagated. The final hypothesis also involves François I, but instead of importing the cuttings from Asia Minor, the origin of the vines is placed in the Midi region of France. From here François I selected certain shoots which were transported to the royal gardens and became the origin of the *"treille du roi"* or "King's vine" still found in the park of Château de Fontainbleau outside Paris. Efforts begun in 1985 to reintroduce the Chasselas into the Midi as a wine grape were not successful, however, and with the limited exceptions noted above, the Chasselas remains a table grape in the minds of the French.

The Chasselas is best known as a high-yielding variety. It can be pushed to provide a remarkable 150 hectoliters per hectare, although no serious *vigneron* would come close to that figure for his fine wine. Normal production should be closer to 50 hectoliters per hectare or less, and therefore the vine's natural temptation to overproduce must be controlled. Only the severest of timely pruning will bring out the best in the grape. If harvested and produced under rigorous conditions, the Chasselas is capable of producing elegant and interesting wines notable for a "smoky" bouquet and a certain flinty, "gunpowder" taste. In addition, many Chasselas wines are produced *petillant,* with a slight spritz, which gives the wine a particularly refreshing characteristic. When pushed to overproduction or grown on inferior slopes, however, it produces a wine which is either heavy and boring from lack of acidity, or herbaceous and "common".

Given the neutrality of the grape and the fact that it reflects the soil in which it is grown, the regional distinctions found within Switzerland are surprisingly important. If one can hazard some simple generalizations, the best Chasselas from Valais are full, rounded wines with attractive fruit and balance, and complemented by slightly "tangy" character. The counterpart wines from Vaud, in particular the Lavaux area, have a more "velvet" and smooth countenance with overtones of flint. Genevois wines are generally lighter and have a pleasant refreshing acidity, while those from Neuchâtel more often than not have a slight spritz which makes them a particularly good aperitif.

Perhaps surprisingly, the Chasselas can also be used to produce a fine dessert wine. These rare qualities only develop over time in wines from the finest sites with the concentration and backbone to last. After ten years of bottle age, and lasting well into their fourth decade, fine Chasselas can take on a lovely deep honeyed and aromatic nose. These wines are not sweet in a conventional sense, but can stand up to any but the most overpowering desserts.The different geographic and climatic conditions of the arid, "heat-trap" environment of Valais, the rolling fields around Geneva or Neuchâtel, or the famous lake-reflected vineyards of Vaud ensure that an endless variety of wine will be produced from the Chasselas. While the wines share the important commonality of the same grape stock, other elements such as the soil, climate and differences in growing techniques guarantee that the variations between cantons, or between communes within single cantons, can be genuinely striking.

Riesling x Sylvaner (Müller-Thurgau)

In the Swiss context, particularly for the central and eastern cantons, the Riesling x Sylvaner grape precedes both of its generally recognized parents in importance. In fact, although the paternity of the Riesling is accepted, questions have recently been raised about the role of the second parent, the Sylvaner, in the initial cross-breed. Such detailed debates among specialists need not delay us here.

Suffice to note that the Riesling is rarely planted in Switzerland, presumably because of ripening difficulties, while the Sylvaner is widely found (see below).

The Riesling x Sylvaner is the second most planted white grape variety, producing five percent of all Swiss wines. Although found in most regions of the country including Geneva and the upper Valais valley, the majority of Riesling x Sylvaner vineyards are confined to the German-speaking areas of eastern Switzerland where it has replaced the traditional Räuschling as the most planted grape. Its current popularity reflects the commercial success of this high-yield varietal in both Germany and Switzerland in the 1960s and 1970s. An additional attraction for Swiss *vignerons* is the Swiss heritage of this grape's "creator," Hermann Müller-Thurgau, who first developed this cross at the German research station in Geisenheim in the 1880s. As mentioned above, it is surprising that only in Switzerland and Luxembourg is this variety known as the Riesling x Sylvaner and not as the more generally accepted name of Müller-Thurgau.

The Riesling x Sylvaner produces early ripening grapes and large jagged leaves. Currently, Switzerland has about 500 hectares (1,250 acres) of the variety planted. The grape is a generous producer of gentle medium-sweet musts that are perfumed but low in acid. Over the years its international popularity has spread. It is now grown successfully in the Franken area of Germany, although recently its plantings there have declined somewhat, as well as in eastern Europe, England, New Zealand, upstate New York and Canada. Recent efforts to severely limit the yields of Müller-Thurgau grapes (to as low as 33 hectoliters per hectare) by certain German wine makers have successfully demonstrated a more refined side to this grape.

Given the characteristics noted above, the Riesling x Sylvaner is clearly a "northern" grape which needs a fresh, temperate climate to bring out its fine but restrained bouquet. Like the Sylvaner, it can suffer from winter frosts. If grown in areas which are too warm, the resulting wine can be heavy and uninteresting. The grapes have not thrived on the normally favoured south-facing exposures of central Valais or in certain areas around Lake Geneva where its planting was once much more extensive. The best examples come from the German-speaking areas of eastern Switzerland, although a few of the Genevois wines are fairly attractive. Much of the wine produced from the Riesling x Sylvaner in eastern Switzerland is lightly *petillant* and some is even late-harvested. The Riesling x Sylvaner can produce fresh and elegant wines, but efforts to blend this grape with the Chasselas have not been successful as both wines lose their better characteristics.

Johannisberg (Sylvaner, Grüner, Gros Rhin)

The Johannisberg or, to use its more international name, the Sylvaner, originated from the area surrounding the Danube and is still found extensively in the vineyards of eastern and central Europe. It is often called the "Rhin" or "Gros Rhin" grape to distinguish it from the "Petit Rhin" or Riesling. The acreage dedicated to this variety has been shrinking of late, although it still remains the second most important white varietal in the canton of Valais where it is exclusively called "Johannisberg". Today it produces two percent of all wines in Switzerland. The characteristic must has both good sugar and acid levels and can produce a full and elegant wine. The Sylvaner, however, is yet another varietal that must be grown on slopes with good exposure. It is particularly sensitive to oïdium but resistant to *coulure*. If grown on less well-placed slopes it produces too much foliage and a wine that is thin and herbaceous. The Sylvaner is also prone to winter frost damage.

Compared to the Chasselas, a well-made Sylvaner produces a richer wine with a higher degree of alcohol (11.5° to 12.5°). They should be drunk cool. The nose is generally less floral than the equivalent German varietal, and the Sylvaner-based wines generally are best drunk young. The vines need a light, gravely soil.

The Sylvaner is also found in limited quantities outside Valais in some other areas of French-speaking Switzerland where occasionally it is grown on trellises or against stone walls. The clones used in Switzerland are selected to balance good production with superior quality. Many other clones are found in Alsace and Germany. Under current European Union legislation, a wine labeled "Johannisberg" cannot be exported to the EU. Several export-minded producers have therefore changed the label back to Sylvaner.

Chardonnay

In recent years there has been a notable increase in the cultivation of the fashionable Chardonnay in Valais and Geneva. Some very limited plantings have also produced quite promising results in Vaud and Neuchâtel. While some examples of better, limited-production wines made from Chardonnay are showing positive varietal characteristics, this grape has generally been less successful in Switzerland than its transplanted cousins in the newer wine worlds of California, New South Wales, New Zealand and Chile. Early efforts to introduce this grape into Switzerland suffered additionally from difficulties in obtaining virus-free stock.

The Chardonnay grape produces a finely-scented must with good levels of acidity. The wine should have a fine but characteristic bouquet. If the vines are grown in the wrong or marginal soils, the wines can become heavy – as can also happen if the grapes are left on the vine beyond maturity. The vines are fast growers but also delicate and prone to both oïdium and gray rot. Chardonnay ripens later than Chasselas, but its higher acid levels contribute to a longer aging potential. In areas that are too hot, the refined bouquet can intensify to the point of vulgarity, although this is not normally a concern in Switzerland except for parts of Valais. Even in Switzerland the Chardonnay is used for both still and sparkling wines. To the extent possible, Swiss *vignerons* attempt to find micro-climates that resemble those of Burgundy or Champagne for their plantings of Chardonnay. The results are often interesting, although the amount of wine produced usually falls short of commercial viability. This is a prestige varietal produced as a labour of love by some of Switzerland's best wine makers, more an intellectual and technical challenge than a core product of their business. With so many good, price-competitive Chardonnays available internationally, how much effort should be put commercially into this popular grape, at the expense of existing varieties, is an open question.

Chardonnays can be found from Geneva to Salquenen in Valais, and some minuscule patches are even found in the steep terraces of Lavaux in Vaud, although such wines are seldom found on the open market. The *cave communale* in the

Lavaux village of Chexbres is known occasionally to stock some local Chardonnay. In Valais, Chardonnay has been blended with an indigenous grape, Petite Arvine, with considerable success.

Pinot Gris (Malvoisie, Grauburgunder, Ruländer)

The Pinot Gris is an important grape in Valais and is found in varying quantities in most other wine-growing regions of Switzerland. The Pinot Gris is in fact descended from the Pinot Noir and there are examples of Pinot Noir mutating into one or the other of its related variations – the Pinot Gris or Pinot Blanc.

The neutral must, with good levels of both sugar and acidity, produces a quality wine. If the grapes are left on the vines to overripen, the resulting wines, which still contain residual sugar after fermentation, can be excellent. The ability of the grape to produce temptingly rich, sweet wine with a touch of *botrytis cinerea* (*pourriture noble* or noble rot) is one of the reasons why the grape is known as the Tokay in Alsace, and the Malvoisie in Valais. The Pinot Gris is in fact a finer and more versatile grape than many observers acknowledge, although it appears to have found a welcome home in Switzerland.

The style and quality of Pinot Gris wines, therefore, greatly depend on the maturity of the grapes at harvest. The Pinot Gris vine produces vigorous foliage and, consequently, the *vigneron* must be very attentive to pruning to discipline the vine.

In addition to the Pinot Gris wines of Valais, the variety is also successfully grown on the northern shore of Lake Neuchâtel, in several cantons of eastern Switzerland and on the outskirts of Geneva, in particular by the independent producers clustered around the village of Dardagny. Earlier efforts to blend Pinot Gris with Chasselas to provide additional backbone to the latter have not proved successful because the wines, especially in bad years, suffered from excess acidity and lack of balance.

Pinot Blanc (Weissburgunder)

This grape type is most often found in the Valais where, depending upon sugar levels at harvest time, it can produce either a well-balanced, fresh, tasty wine, enjoyable when young, or a rich and full drink that more closely resembles a Pinot Gris. It is used for both still and sparkling wines in Valais, and is also grown in Geneva by the growers on the hills around Dardagny. Again, individual producers in eastern Switzerland, for example in Grisons, have successfully introduced the Pinot Blanc. In Alsace, the Pinot Blanc has virtually replaced the earlier plantings Chasselas.

The regular fertility and adequate richness and sugar levels of the must have encouraged its adoption in suitable growing areas in Switzerland. Pinot Blanc wines generally have slightly more acidity than wines made from the Chasselas grape and, therefore, have somewhat more aging potential. In several areas of Valais previously dedicated to growing Chasselas, the Pinot Blanc has taken over because the Chasselas wines from these particular slopes lacked sufficient acidity.

(H)Ermitage (Marsanne Blanche)

This varietal, known as Marsanne Blanche in France, is believed to have been introduced into Switzerland in the 19th century from vineyards in the Hermitage area of the Rhône valley – hence its Swiss name. Found throughout the central Valais valley, above all around the commune of Fully, it produces large grape clusters with small, sun-coloured copper-green grapes. Because it is a very late ripening variety, the Ermitage can only be grown successfully in Valais and on slopes with excellent exposure. It is resistant to *coulure* and therefore is sometimes grown on less well-exposed slopes with the unfortunate result that the wines are mediocre, green and lacking in interest.

If the soils are too rich, or the vines are pushed to overproduction, the wines will be thin, green and ordinary. For this reason it is often necessary to remove excess clusters of grapes to produce the best possible wines. When allowed to ripen fully, the must is quite sugared, and in exceptional years the grapes can be left on the vine to overripen producing a wine containing residual sugar. In such cases the wine should be rich and contain a correspondingly high level of alcohol. However, the late ripening of the Marsanne poses particular problems as certain climatic conditions will cause the skins to disintegrate if the grapes are left too long on the vine. The grapes then turn brown and rapidly oxidize. Once the skins begin to deteriorate it is crucial to pick immediately.

Given the difficulties encountered in growing the Marsanne, there are years when the return is hardly worth the effort. In less than good years, the under-sugared must can be used as the basis for a sharper aperitif wine, or even for a sparkling wine. However, in years which are warm and dry enough to allow for a touch of residual sugar, the wine will be well balanced; smell like forest berries; and taste like liquid velvet.

Gewürztraminer (and Traminer)

The aromatic Gewürztraminer (sometimes known in some French-speaking areas as the Savagnin Rosé Aromatique) is occasionally found in Switzerland, although it is certainly of less commercial importance there than it is in Alsace or Germany.

Efforts to introduce it in several parts of Switzerland, have had mixed results. If grown in areas where it adapts well, the grape produces a must which is sugared, fairly low in acid and with its characteristic spicy taste. The wine is perfumed and aromatic, with a hint of roses. If growing conditions are less than ideal, the wines are heavy, unbalanced, and lack finesse.

The Gewürztraminer only develops its characteristic bouquet during the process of alcoholic fermentation. Prior to fermentation the musts of the Gewürztraminer and its less floral and less appreciated relative, the Traminer (Savagnin Rosé), are virtually indistinguishable. This grape type is also related to the Savagnin Blanc which produces the sought-after *vin jaune d'Arbois* of the neighbouring Jura and the rare Château Châlon. One other Traminer-related grape is the Heida (Païen) of Valais (described later in this chapter).

Räuschling

The Räuschling is mainly found in the vineyards rising from the shores of Lake Zurich and on the banks of the Limmat river in eastern Switzerland. It is also found in southern Germany but rarely, if at all, in the French-speaking *Suisse romande*. Although common in earlier days, the Räuschling lost considerable ground to the Riesling x Sylvaner because of the latter's greater fertility, yields and early ripening. In the right situation, however, the wine produced from Räuschling grapes is very fresh and attractive. Consequently it has undergone something of a renaissance and the grape has recently regained some lost acreage.

"Specialty" White Grape Varieties of Valais

It is common to group the *"spécialité"* varietals of Valais together when discussing Swiss wines. These include both indigenous grapes, unique to the canton, such as the Petite Arvine, Amigne, Humagne Blanc and Rèze as well as grapes of lesser commercial importance found in other parts of Switzerland, such as the Muscat and Heida (Païen). Additional details will be provided about their growing conditions in the chapter on Valais. In general, however, they are late (or later) ripening varieties that cannot reach full maturity in those parts of Switzerland which lack the torrid summers of Valais.

Petite Arvine

The Petite Arvine is a long-established indigenous Valaisan grape variety. The Petite Arvine and the Amigne (see below) are the two most important white grapes unique to Valais. Some believe that the Arvine originated near the town of Martigny, the ancient Roman post-town which marks the end of the St. Bernard Pass through the Alps. There are, however, no early references to this grape type in historical manuscripts, and although the name "Arvine" might indicate that it came from the Haute Savoie or Lake Geneva region, there is no comparable grape from which it might be descended. The conclusion, therefore, first put forward in 1878 after scientific examination, is that the Petite Arvine is an indigenous grape of "unknown" origin.

The Petite Arvine is now grown over a much wider area than the Amigne, with plantings stretching from Sion to Martigny. The grape bunches are elongated but compact, and the grapes are small and round. The variety ripens late and, therefore, can only be grown on slopes with good exposure. It is rarely found outside Valais and, within the canton, most plantings are concentrated around the villages of Fully, Chamoson, Conthey and Sion.

The Petite Arvine grows quickly but, as a consequence, the shoots can break easily if not properly supported. The vines are frost-sensitive and experience has warned growers not to use too much herbicide. Nor do they grow well on soils which are either too dry or too rich. The vine, if grown on accommodating ground, produces a must which is well-sugared and balanced by good acid levels. The alcohol level in the final wine is usually between 12%-13%. The full but somewhat aggressive bouquet, and slight residual sweetness of the Petite Arvine make it suitable as both an aperitif or dessert wine. If the grapes are allowed to ripen fully, the wine can be full, well-rounded and, according to the Swiss palate, slightly salty. A scent of violets can be detected in better versions.

Wines made from the Arvine grape have good aging potential. When vinified dry, the wine has both good structure and relatively high acidity. When the grapes are left on the vines for extra (over) maturity, the residual sugar of these wines also contributes to successful development over time. Depending upon how long the grapes are left on the vine, and how shriveled they have become, the wine will be labeled *mi(half)-flétrie* or *flétrie* (withered). These wines should be rich and full, but never cloying. Overall, the Petite Arvine is considered by many to be the finest of the uniquely indigenous Swiss *vinifera* grapes.

Just to confuse matters, both a "Petite" Arvine and an occasionally-found "Grande" Arvine exist. The Grande Arvine, distinguishable by its larger berries, may have been the result of a selection over time made from the Petite Arvine. Unfortunately the wine from the larger variety is marked by a certain heaviness which does not disappear. Plantings of the Grand Arvine are being phased out. The wine of quality comes from the "Petite" variety, often labeled just "Arvine", and in fact, the two grapes are now not related morphologically.

Amigne

The Amigne grape is the second uniquely Swiss white *vinifera* varietal from Valais with excellent possibilities for producing attractive and balanced wines. The Amigne is one of the oldest varietals grown in the canton and is only grown in a limited zone concentrated around the slopes of the village of Vétroz. It can produce a charming wine, marked by a restrained nose, but backed by a full and generous taste.

If the Amigne is allowed to achieve its full potential, it produces a wine which is not overly tannic but one which will benefit from some cellaring. Some Amigne is also sold for immediate consumption.

The origins of this varietal are obscure, especially as it does not bear immediate resemblance to any other vine type found in Swiss vineyards. Efforts to introduce the Amigne elsewhere in the country have not met with notable success. The Amigne thrives on sunny, wind-blown slopes exposed to the warm breezes from the south. The vine is characterized by large, shaggy leaves and long bunches.

The grapes can be picked at maturity for a full fragrant wine or left on the vine to shrivel and develop greater sugar concentration and additional character. This adds an extra roundness and depth without detracting from the basic characteristics of the grape.

The alcohol levels, varying between 12° and 13°, and the acid levels are sufficient to balance the additional concentration of sugar and to provide a structure necessary for improvement through aging. The wine from grapes picked at normal maturity can be fine, alcoholic and slightly tannic, and may even retain a slight touch of residual sugar.

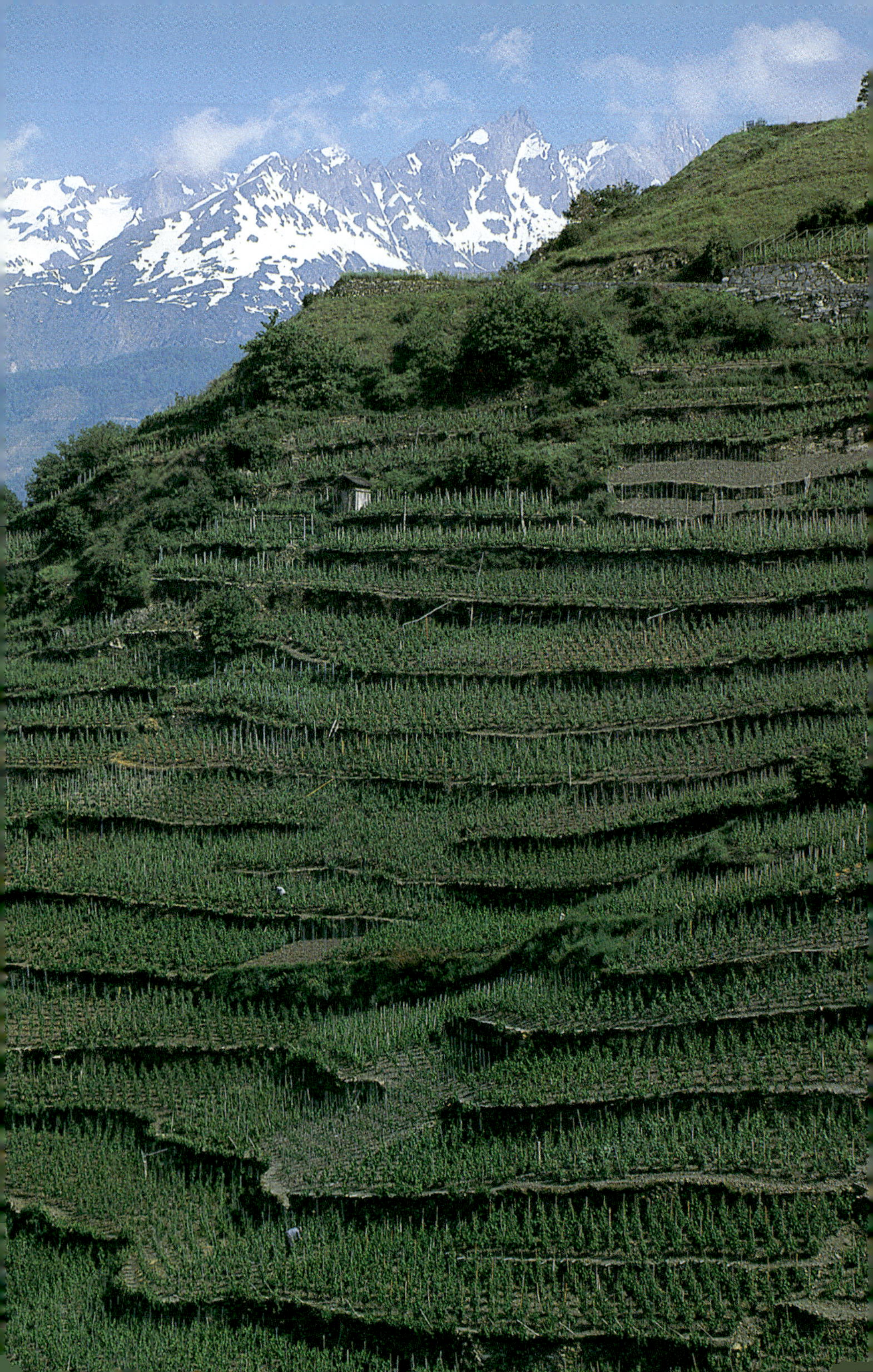

Muscat (du Valais)

This ancient perfumed grape of Greek origin goes by many names – Muscat blanc à petits grains; Muscat de Frontignan; Muscat d'Alsace; Muscat de Canelli (Asti); and, in Switzerland, Muscat du Valais. Originally largely grown around the town of Sierre in Valais, the Muscat is now increasingly found farther afield in the canton, although because of its need for heat, it is still only rarely grown outside Valais.

An early ripening and vigorous vine, it must be pruned to prevent uneven ripening of the grapes, which happens if the Muscat is pushed to overproduction. The vines require attentive care as they are also susceptible to attack by numerous blights and various parasites, insects and animals, including the occasional greedy chamois or passing tourist, undoubtedly attracted by the powerful smell of the grapes. Depending upon the year and the length of time the grapes are left on the vine, the wine will have an alcohol level that varies between 10.5% and 12%.

The Swiss Muscats maintain the characteristically aromatic nose and distinctive taste for which the grape is known. The ripened grapes take on a bronze hue and the leaves have sharp edges. Harvesting is complicated by the fact that the grapes ripen at irregular intervals. The vines need good sun exposure but even this does not guarantee that the wine will achieve notable body. Given its unique bouquet, Swiss Muscats are best when drunk fairly young and are not considered wines for laying down.

Heida (Païen, Savagnin Blanc, Traminer)

According to legend, the Heida, (or Païen to the French-speaking Valaisan), is of Hungarian origin and arrived in Switzerland some time in the 13th century. An indigenous origin is not, however, totally excluded. The Heida certainly shares a familial connection with the Formentin of Hungary; the Grumin of Bohemia; the Traminer of Germany; and the Savagnin Blanc of the French Jura.

On the slopes around the village of Vispertermin, cultivation of this grape is possible even above 1,000 meters, the highest vineyards in Europe. The grapes ripen early, virtually at the same time as the Chasselas, and under normal conditions they will produce between 800-900 grams of fruit per square meter. The sugar level averages around 99° Oechsle producing wines with alcohol levels between 12.5% and 13% without chaptalization. In exceptional years, the Oechsle degree has been known to reach 126°. The grapes are small and, like the Rèze, it is considered by growers to be a difficult producer. The wine from the Heida should be light, crisp and quite refreshing.

The highest vineyards in Europe at Vispertermin where the Heida is cultivated.

Humagne Blanc

Both Humagne Rouge and Humagne Blanc are grown in the Valais, but morphologically the two grapes are not related. Of the two, the Humagne Rouge is commercially the more important. The Humagne Blanc is exclusively found in Valais and the bottle labels use both "Humagne Blanc" and "Humagne Blanche" to identify the grape, depending on the producer.

The Humagne Blanc grapes mature some 7-10 days after the Chasselas and it is neither a prolific producer nor has notably high sugar levels. The resulting wine is dry and moderately alcoholic (10° to 12°). Fresh when young, it evolves slowly, and properly vinified and cared-for bottles have good aging potential. The wine maintains fairly high acid levels and is known for its distinctive taste, faintly reminiscent of resin. The Humagne Blanc naturally contains three times more iron than other wines, which undoubtedly accounts for its reputed traditional medicinal reputation.

Rèze

The Rèze, traditionally concentrated around the town of Sierre, often produces a rather thin, acidic wine, although it can be pleasantly refreshing. The Rèze has two distinct styles. First, it can be picked at normal maturity and made into a straightforward, fresh but somewhat uninspiring wine. Second, it provides virtually all the wine that is still transported annually from the banks of the Rhône up the Anniviers valley where, after aging, the wine eventually develops a sherry like *flor* to become the famous Vin des Glaciers, one of the highly sought after rarities of Swiss wines. This alone, however, is not sufficient to protect the commercial future of the grape and its cultivation has virtually ceased except to produce the base wine for Vin des Glaciers. Only around 7,200 square meters (a mere 0.72 hectares) were in production in 1994.

Less Commonly Found White Wine Grapes

Other vinifera grapes, including cross-breeds

The second white grape of Burgundy, the Aligoté, has shown considerable success in the vineyards around Geneva. In particular, the quality of the Aligotés from the villages of Lully and Satigny, in addition to Dardagny has encouraged increased plantings of this grape. Small plots are also found in Valais.

Rarely found in Switzerland today, the Semillon and Sauvignon Blanc of Bordeaux are most often encountered in the white blends of Ticino. Chasselas is usually the third element in blend. Occasionally bottles of unblended Semillon or Sauvignon can be found, but these are not common. A very small amount of Sauvignon Blanc is grown in Valais and in Geneva. Other *vinifera* grapes found rarely in Switzerland include the Chenin Blanc from the Loire and the Altesse, more commonly known as the "Roussette", from the neighbouring vineyards of Savoie.

Active research continues to develop vines suited to the Swiss environment and some of the crosses and clones nurtured in Swiss research stations hold considerable promise. These include the Charmont and Doral (two Chasselas x Chardonnay crosses), the Nobling (Sylvaner x Chasselas) and Freisamer (Sylvaner x Pinot Gris).

In addition, the Kerner, an uncommon but successful crossing of a red (Trollinger) and white (Riesling) grape has been imported from Germany. This variety produces better must weight than the more popular Müller-Thurgau and planted acreage has increased dramatically in Germany since its registration in 1969. Today it is found in eastern Switzerland along with small plantings in Ticino and Geneva. The Findling, a Müller-Thurgau clone, is sometimes found in Geneva and elsewhere.

Red Wine Grape Varieties

Pinot Noir (Blauburgunder, Spätburgunder, Clevner)

Throughout Switzerland, the Pinot Noir is grown in the most unlikely places – often isolated against the heat-reflecting walls of steep terraced vineyards surrounded by a sea of Chasselas, or stretched out on the flat valley floors with Chasselas dominating the higher slopes.

The variety of local names for the Pinot Noir demonstrates that it is grown in both French- and German-speaking cantons. It produces just over one-quarter of all wines in Switzerland. Even in the premier vineyards of Vaud, more specifically in the famous plots in Dézaley, St. Saphorin and Epesses, one finds rare, frequently individually-tended, Pinot Noir vines.

The Pinot Noir is the only red grape officially approved for planting in Neuchâtel and is planted throughout eastern Switzerland. It is, however, grown most widely and successfully in the canton of Valais, although pockets of fine Pinot Noir can be found in both Vaud and along the shores of Lake Bienne to the east of Neuchâtel. It forms the backbone of the traditional Dôle du Valais but is also increasingly marketed on its own. Dôle legally must now contain a minimum of 51% Pinot Noir, although the composition can, in fact, be 100% Pinot Noir. Many of the better producers limit the percentage of Gamay to just five percent to provide an attractive hint of fresh berry fruit on the nose.

In Vaud, Pinot Noir is also combined with Gamay to create the wine known as Salvagnin. Given its exclusive status in the canton of Neuchâtel, it is the sole grape used to produce the well-known rosé Oeil-de-Perdrix.

The national research station at Wädenswil has done considerable work developing cold-climate strains of Pinot Noir. This research has produced a general improvement in quality and fostered the introduction of better strains in certain non-traditional Pinot Noir areas. This work has also received international recognition by wine makers in cool regions of the United States, such as the Pacific northwest states of Oregon and Washington, which have been able to put to good use some of the Swiss-developed Pinot Noir clones.

Gamay

The bountiful Gamay of Beaujolais is a popular grape in Switzerland where it captures some 14% of all wines. Gamay grapes have the advantage of good performance at high altitudes. It is generally a regular producer but buds early and therefore is sensitive to spring frosts.

In Vaud and Valais, the Gamay is often grown alongside the Pinot Noir, although usually on the heavier, less preferred slopes. It is the minor partner in Valaisan Dôle providing from five percent to 49% of the combination depending on the quality and desired weight of the wine. It is also part of the blend used to produce the Salvagnin red wines of Vaud, and it is possible, though not common, to find bottles of 100% Gamay for sale in both cantons.

The Gamay is susceptible to attacks of gray rot even when the grapes are still green. If over-sugared (chaptalized), the wine can become heavy and uninteresting. Because of the variety of clones, growers can select a vine suited to their particular needs or micro-climate although some clones tend to overcrop and at best produce a mediocre wine. These vines must either be severely pruned or replaced with less generous, but superior clones.

In Geneva, the Gamay has become the preferred red varietal. There is even a Beaujolais nouveau type "Gamay nouveau" which competes on price with the just-fermented French wine. Surprisingly, some of the better made Gamays from older vines can be quite good and, occasionally, even fuller "oak-aged" Gamays are found. These wines are quite attractive, even if the style contradicts our usual conception of a Beaujolais-style Gamay. Responding to the growing popularity of this grape in the Geneva region, the amount of land producing Gamay continues to increase.

Merlot

Merlot in Switzerland is found almost exclusively, and certainly most successfully, in the Italian-speaking region of the country, the canton of Ticino. Its near total domination of the red wines of Ticino means that Merlot produces 6% of all Swiss wines.

The grape was introduced systematically into the Ticino and the nearby Misox valley early in the 20th century when the vineyards were being reconstructed after the damage done by the phylloxera louse. The Merlot has thrived when planted in the right soil conditions on well-exposed slopes, although it can produce flaccid wines if pushed to overproduction. Patches of Merlot are also found in the cantons of Valais, Vaud and Geneva. In the latter, in particular, Merlot is viewed as a grape with good potential for aging.

The Merlot is a vigorous grower which ripens later than both the Pinot Noir and Gamay which explains its suitability to the more southern, Mediterranean region of Ticino. The leaves are a deep green and very jagged. The grapes are small, with a unique taste; the wines have good body and colour which, with aging, can acquire a round fullness.

Merlot grapes

Syrah

Pockets of Syrah are found in Valais and Vaud. It is, in general, a more demanding and less successful grape than the other import from the lower Rhône valley, the Marsanne Blanche (Ermitage). There are, however, notable exceptions in both cantons. The late-ripening Syrah does not respond well to a climate which is too cool and, therefore, can only be really successful on the best, well-exposed slopes in summers that have been particularly hot. Certain very skillful growers in Valais have been very successful in developing fine, ruby, deep Syrah from experimental plots and increasingly the variety is found in commercial production. The Syrah is also one of the grapes in the blend used to produce the rare but excellent red wine from the Clos des Abbayes vineyard in the Lavaux region of Vaud. Its contribution of a peppery nose adds another level of texture to this complex wine.

Cabernet Sauvignon

The backbone grape of the Medoc region of Bordeaux is increasingly finding a home in Switzerland. As good producers from Valais to Geneva attempt to produce wines with aging potential, it was perhaps inevitable that plantings of Cabernet Sauvignon would increase in Switzerland. The plantings are generally quite recent and the wines are only just beginning to achieve the recognition bestowed on the Syrah of Valais. But more and more Cabernet Sauvignon is found on the lists of quality producers. Similar to the comments on Chardonnay above, given the intense international competition between Cabernet Sauvignon producers, the Swiss will be hard-pressed to produce a distinctive and price competitive wine from this grape. That challenge will not, however, prevent the better producers from trying.

Indigenous Red Wine Grapes of Switzerland

Bondola

The Bondola is the traditional *vinifera* grape of the Italian-speaking Ticino region. It has, however, been completely eclipsed by the Merlot as the grape of choice. It is still found in the northern Sopraceneri region, but areas planted with Bondola continue to disappear and now produce just 2.5% of Ticino's wines. The vine produces loose bunches of spherical grapes, considerably larger than the Merlot. The must is fairly acid and somewhat bitter, but lacks a distinguishing taste. When the Bondola is combined with other local *vinifera* varieties, it is sold under the name "Nostrano".

Humagne Rouge

This grape originates from the Aosta valley in Italy. In Switzerland plantings are almost completely restricted to Valais. For most of the 20th century it has only been grown in small quantities. The British wine writer Jancis Robinson, who once described the wine from the Humagne Rouge as a "declining old faithful", also noted Hugh Johnson's description of the Humagne Rouge as a "simple, pleasantly tannic and appetizing country wine." "Rustic" is a word used frequently to describe Humagne Rouge wines.

The Humagne Rouge produces a must which is low in acid, and if the grapes are not allowed to ripen fully, the wine can be green and herbaceous. The grapes require slopes with good exposure to achieve full maturity. Despite its low acidity levels, well-produced Humagne Rouge can be a very attractive, and even long-lasting wine. Several of the more adventurous wine makers of the Valais are now producing richer oak-aged Humagne Rouge to lay down. The renaissance of this late-ripening variety reflects a recognition that the Humagne Rouge is potentially one of the most interesting indigenous varietals of Valais. Often the grapes are not harvested until November and, if vinified with care, the wines can exhibit a pronounced "savage" character, but one not without finesse and style. The best Humagne Rouge wines are quite remarkable and the area devoted to this grape is increasing.

Cornalin (Vin Rouge du Pays)

Cornalin is another old Swiss variety which is also grown across the Italian border in the Aosta valley, but in Switzerland is mainly found in Valais. It is a very late ripening variety and the grape must is very dark and intense. The wine is fruity, a bit rough when drunk young but smoother with age. Today it is grown successfully in Valais between Sion and Sierre and around Fully, near Martigny. Several small patches also appear in the Chablais region of Vaud, although increasingly the Cornalin is a grape of limited commercial significance.

Other vinifera grapes, including cross-breeds and clones

The Swiss have been particularly adept at cloning the Pinot Noir, selecting for both climatic and productive qualities. Sometimes, however, the short-term gains from more fecund varieties have been carried too far, and the use of temporarily popular strains had to be banned or discontinued because the wines were not acceptable. Selection and experimentation, often at government research stations, continue in an effort to isolate and propagate characteristics particularly suited to an alpine environment.

Other *vinifera* vines found in greater or lesser quantities include the Nebbiolo and the Ancellota from Italy, of which the latter is grown for its rich colouring capability. Important cross-breedings include the Valaisan Diolinoir (a cross between "rouge de Diolly" and Pinot Noir) and the Gamaret and Granoir (two Gamay x Reichensteiner crosses). Certain Genevois and eastern Swiss growers have successfully experimented with the Granoir.

Red Hybrids

Hybrids were born out of the experimentation which followed the damage done by the phylloxera louse. The objective was to combine the best qualities of the fine wine European grape *(vitis vinifera)* with the phylloxera-resistant American grape *(vitis labrusca)*. Unfortunately, the results rarely lived up to expectations. Banned most elsewhere in Europe, red hybrids are less and less grown commercially in Switzerland. Some are reportedly still found in Geneva, (in a "Cru" vineyard, no less), and they are occasionally still grown in Ticino. The main hybrids are Seibel 5455 (Planet), Seibel 7053, Landot 244 (Landal) as well as some early ripening varieties such as Maréchal Foch, etc. As is the case with the white hybrids, their use is diminishing for both economic and quality reasons.

In addition, small quantities of *vitis labrusca* grapes such as Isabella and Clinton are found in Ticino where they are used to produce the unique beverage "Americano". These North American vines were imported as part of the response to the damage caused by the phylloxera louse in the 19th century.

V

Vinification, Swiss Style

The quality of the vinification is the indispensable link between the growing of grapes and the character of the final wine. The vinification of the grapes is the point in the wine-making process where the skill of the wine maker comes to the fore. Given the Swiss penchant for technical precision, it is not surprising that vinification is approached with a high degree of technical proficiency and sensitivity. First one must consider the raw material – i.e., the quality and health of the grapes. Only then can the more technical process of fermentation begin. One advantage for the Swiss wine maker is that the site of vinification in Switzerland is rarely far from the vineyard. Immediate access to freshly-picked grapes can therefore be assumed.

The two crucial determinants of grape quality at the time of harvest are sugar levels and the production yields. The disciplined grape grower will limit yields to produce the higher concentration and sugar levels which ideally will achieve higher prices for the crop. Sugar levels in the grape must are usually expressed in degrees Oechsle, while output is calculated in Switzerland on the basis of (kilo)grams of grapes, or liters of must, per square meter. The use of such small units reflects the tiny size of many Swiss vineyards compared to the French, where calculations of hectoliters per hectare are the norm.

The better producers throughout Switzerland have always exercised a fairly rigorous control over production to ensure as ripe and concentrated grapes as possible to produce the best possible wine. The introduction in recent years of federal and cantonal regulations governing *appellation contrôlée* classifications has also improved the minimum sugar levels for many wines. While the top *vignerons* are concerned that minimal appellation standards have been set too low by some cantonal authorities, the net effect of the new regulations should be an improvement of overall quality, especially at the lower end of the scale. The better producers will continue to exceed any basic requirements.

Sugar Levels

The standard Swiss system for measuring grape sugar levels is degrees Oechsle (°Oe), a method of calculation commonly found in Germany but rarely elsewhere. The Oechsle reading provides a ratio of the weight of the must to the weight of an equal volume of water at the same temperature, or in other words, the "specific gravity" of the must. (See *Modern Winemaking* by Philip Jackisch for a

Vineyard of Tourbillon at Sion, Valais. Oenologist Madeleine Gay, from the Provins cooperative, is measuring the Oechsle degrees of the Ermitage grapes.

more detailed comparison of different systems used by wine makers). For purposes of rough calculations, the eventual percentage (by volume) of alcohol in the wine is approximately equal to the degrees Oechsle divided by eight. Therefore, a must with a reading of 70°Oe would provide a wine with about 8.8° of potential alcohol from natural grape sugar, i.e., without chaptalization. Wine makers using different systems elsewhere would say that the same 70°Oe must had a specific gravity of 1.070 or readings of 9.4 or 17.0 under the Baumé and Brix systems respectively. A 95°Oe must has a specific gravity of 1.095 and Baumé and Brix readings of 12.5 and 22.5 and a potential alcohol percentage of 11.9%.

More specifically, the formula for determining the amount of sugar contained in a grape must is a follows:

$$\text{Sugar} = \frac{°\text{Oechsle} \times 8}{3} - 30$$

For example, with a must of 84° Oechsle:

$$\text{Sugar} = \frac{84 \times 8}{3} - 30 = 194 \text{ grams/liter}$$

Determining the eventual percentage of alcohol for white wines and for vat-fermented reds varies slightly. For white wines the formula is as follows:

$$\text{Alcohol} = \frac{°\text{Oechsle} - 15}{6}; \quad \text{again using a must with } 84°\text{Oe:}$$

$$\text{Alcohol} = \frac{84 - 15}{6} = 11.5°;$$

whereas for a red wine the denominator increases slightly to 6.5; hence:

$$\text{Alcohol} = \frac{84 - 15}{6.5} = 10.6°.$$

As °Oechsle is referred to throughout the text, reference to German guidelines might be useful. Under the 1971 German wine law, table wine only requires a Oechsle reading of 44° to 51°, somewhat lower than the minimum required for Swiss table wine (see below).

For German Qualitätswein (QbA) the minimum sugar reading rises to 51° to 72°, while for Kabinett, the lightest QmP wine, the standard is between 67° and 85°. For Spätlese, Auslese, Beerenauslese and Trockenbeerenauslese the ranges are 76°-95°, 83°-105°, 110°-128° and 150°-154° respectively. The Swiss *flétrie* wines rarely reach the degree of concentration of the Trockenbeerenauslese wines, but sugar levels above 100 are quite common among the specialty wines, particularly in Valais and in the eastern Swiss cantons.

Grape Classifications

Immediately following the harvest the grapes are weighed and checked for sugar content. The 1992 federal viticulture regulations established three separate categories for musts depending upon the grape sugar levels. Category 1, which includes all musts destined for *appellation d'origine* wines, requires a minimum natural sugar level of 60°Oe (14% Brix) for whites, and 65°Oe (15.8% Brix) for reds. Category 2 wines can identify the provenance of the wine, but without the *appellation* cachet, while Category 3 wines are not allowed to refer to either an *appellation* name or provenance on the bottle label. The respective minimum natural sugar levels are 58°Oe for white and 62°Oe for reds in Category 2, and 55°Oe for white and 58°Oe for reds in Category 3.

It is important to note that these are minimum natural sugar levels applied to all Swiss wines under federal legislation. The individual cantons have established separate and stricter criteria, of which minimum sugar levels are only one element for wines which aspire to the higher canton-regulated *appellations*. For example, in order to be labeled a Fendant du Valais, the must requires a minimal reading of 71°Oe. Other cantons have established similar minimum requirements. There is nothing, however, to stop good wineries from exceeding, often considerably, these minimums, especially in sunny, dry years. Even the large-scale cooperatives have been known commonly to exceed the basic requirements; the standard Fendant du Valais from the Provins cooperative often has an average Oechsle reading well above the cantonal minimum.

Other production elements regulated by the cantonal authorities as part of an *appellation* system include zones of production, grape types, growing techniques, production levels, vinification processes and a requirement to submit the wine to analysis and tasting. Various cantons have established their own standards depending upon the specifics of local circumstances. These regulations are dealt with in greater detail in Chapter XII.

White Wine Fermentation

Once the grapes have been weighed and checked for health, ripeness and sugar levels, they are brought to the cellar for crushing and eventual fermentation. As might be expected, the basic process of fermentation in Switzerland does not vary widely from that employed elsewhere. There are, however, some local differences in addition to the standard variations between the fermentation of white, rosé and red wines.

Most often the grapes are first gently broken to extract the maximum amount of juice without breaking the stocks or seeds. Usually, only the red grape varieties are destalked *(égrappage),* although the white grape producers in the eastern part of Switzerland also commonly destalk. Often some of the juice is strained as it passes onto the grape press. In addition, the broken grapes can be macerated for four to six hours before pressing for certain aromatic varieties such as Muscat and Gewürztraminer which gain extra extraction from being left with the skins.

Today, gentle but efficient horizontal pneumatic presses have all but replaced the great wooden basket presses which once dominated every wine cellar. As the interior of the press is inflated, the grapes are pressed against the inner walls of the cylinder. The free run is reserved for wine, while later pressings, at higher pressure levels, are reserved for eventual distillation into *marc* (brandy).

It is standard practice for the must of varieties such as Chasselas to be sulfured (maximum dose of 100 mg per liter of SO_2) to kill any wild yeasts, although some wine makers now delete this step, especially in good years where the risk of diseased grapes in minimal. The must settles for 12 to 48 hours in a cool environment (10°C to 12°C) to precipitate out the various solids which remain suspended in the juice. The must is then racked or filtered to leave behind any undesirable solids, although many of the larger operations use centrifugal presses to separate the juice from the solids.

The clear must is composed of the following: water 73%-83%; sugar 15%-25%; and other elements (tartaric acid, malic acid, tannin, colouring material, pectins) 2%. If sugar is to be added (see chaptalization below), it is introduced at this point.

Once the must has time to settle, the selected yeasts are added. Alcoholic fermentation follows, transforming the grape sugars into alcohol, and raising the temperature of the must to between 16°C and 25°C as carbon dioxide is released. By the end of the alcoholic fermentation other precipitates, i.e., the lees, are deposited at the bottom of the fermentation vats as the yeasts perform their duty and die off with the sugar decreasing and alcohol levels rising. The lees are eventually removed by the first racking, and the tanks are filled to the brim to prevent oxidization. The fermentation for Swiss white wines can last up to two weeks, but rarely longer.

In general, the alcoholic fermentation is followed by a secondary, malo-lactic fermentation. The transformation of the malic acids into their lactic equivalents softens and stabilizes the wine. During the secondary fermentation the temperature of the wine can rise to between 18°C and 20°C. At the end of the malo-lactic fermentation, the wine has completed its biological evolution and must now be stabilized to prevent oxidization. To achieve this a dose of sulfur dioxide is introduced which is follow by a period of cold stabilization near 0° for up to 8 weeks.

For Chasselas, as for all wines, this natural cold stabilization will cause the tartaric acid to precipitate and the wine to clarify. Any remaining carbon dioxide will be preserved, giving the wine its final *petillant* character. In German Switzerland, an additional filtering step is often added before the cold stabilization. Towards the end of January a light fining prepares the wine for bottling. A final check usually accompanies the last filtration before bottling. The bottled wines are then rested for some time before being released for sale.

Rosé and Red Wine Vinification

The vinification of rosés is, in general, very close to that of whites. The difference is that the grapes are left to macerate on their red skins for several hours after destalking. For the Gamay and Merlot, this usually takes six to eight hours; for Pinot Noir the average maceration is around 12-18 hours. Following this maceration, the fermentation of one to three days is similar to that of Swiss white wines. Virtually all Swiss rosés are made from red-skinned grapes, e.g., Pinot Noir for Oeil-de-Perdrix or Federweiss, although the Schiller wine of eastern Switzerland is produced from both red and white grapes grown in the same vineyard.

For reds the process is slightly different and generally more delicate and subtle. The quality and health of the raw grapes is particularly important in the production of good red wine because so much of the red's colour and quality is extracted from the vulnerable grape skins.

Following their arrival for pressing, the grapes are destalked and usually sulfured to kill wild yeasts. Again, if sugar is to be added, it is introduced at this point. Red grapes, including the skins and seeds, are now often macerated after crushing and prior to fermentation to increase the extraction of colour and tannins.

Temperatures during the alcoholic fermentation of red wines can rise considerably above those found for white wines – up to 30°C to 32°C – which contributes to both the extraction of colour and tannin, and in turn provides the structure and backbone of good red wines. The length of fermentation depends upon the grape type, the regional style and the type of wine desired. Fermentation for fuller and more concentrated wines can continue for up to three weeks.

After the alcoholic fermentation is finished, the wine is racked to separate it from the lees. The higher temperature of the red fermentation eliminates any residual carbon dioxide in the must. After the alcoholic fermentation the wine is left to stabilize at a low temperature for between six to eight weeks, again at near 0°C. Eventually the wine is fined, usually with egg whites or gelatin, and then bottled. Swiss reds that are destined for early consumption spend their time in vats before being bottled during the following spring. Some of the fuller reds will be left in vats for several additional months prior to bottling. Increasingly, however, finer wines, in particular better Pinot Noir from all over Switzerland, Humagne Rouge and Syrah from Valais, Merlot and even some Gamay in Geneva, spend from four to eighteen months in small new or used 225 or 228 liter oak barrels for an extra layer of texture before being bottled.

Two other fermentation techniques are used for Swiss red wines, namely thermovinification and *macération carbonique*. The former, used mainly in German Switzerland, employs heat to speed the release of colour from the skins into the juice prior to fermentation. Imitating the success of the producers in nearby Beaujolais, some growers, especially around Geneva, are encouraging fermentation of uncrushed grapes under a blanket of carbon dioxide. The natural enzymes inside the grapes produce an internal fermentation along with increased extraction of colour and flavour from the inner skin of the grape. Although slower than normal fermentation, *maceration carbonique* has the advantage of obtaining more intense aromas which well support a fruity, fresh wine.

Sparkling Wine Fermentation

Swiss sparkling wine is not produced in abundance. That which is, however – the best known is from the Valais – is produced using the traditional *méthode champegnoise* or the closed cuvée method. The former, in which secondary fermentation occurs in the bottle after the addition of a *dosage* of sugar and yeast, is reserved for the better wines. The closed cuvée method, on the other hand, provokes the second alcoholic fermentation in large vats under pressure. The wine is then bottled, again under pressure, to prevent the carbon dioxide from dissipating. The traditional method is much more labour intensive and, consequently, that much more expensive.

Chaptalization Debate

Three issues remain unresolved among Swiss wine producers. The first concerns the addition of sugar to "improve" the must; the second focuses on the desirability of the secondary malo-lactic fermentation for white wine; and the third, although not strictly a part of the fermentation process, is the value of blending or "cutting" *(coupage)* the just-fermented wine with other wines to improve colour, taste or marketability. The addition of sugar, or *chaptalization,* is a complex and sometimes emotive issue. The practice is certainly as prevalent, if not more prevalent, in Switzerland than is the case elsewhere. The amount of sugar which can legally be added to the grape must is regulated under the Food Products Ordinance *(Ordinance sur les denrées alimentaires (ODA))*. It explicitly states that the quantity added must produce a wine of average alcoholic strength which demonstrates the same characteristics as a wine from the same region produced from ripe grapes.

It is, however, accepted by many better wine makers and the oenological research stations that some sugar should be added to the musts of the Chasselas and Pinot Noir in all but the finest years to raise the fermentable sugars to an acceptable level. In the best years, such as 1989 and 1990, the natural Oechsle readings should be high enough to make the addition of sugar unnecessary. In more normal years, one reliable Vaudois producer believes that it is not unreasonable to add 1.5-2 kilograms per hectoliter for whites (Chasselas); 1 kilogram for reds (in his case Pinot Noir); and 0.5 kilogram per hectoliter for richer *"specialités"* (Muscat and Gewürztraminer). The amount of sugar should, however, never exceed 3% of total volume, i.e. an amount which would raise the alcohol level by a maximum of 1.5%. If used in a judicious and disciplined fashion, sugar may be one of the adaptations demanded by the marginal climate and geological circumstances affecting Swiss vineyards.

The addition of sugar is, however, obviously open to abuse. Since it recently became possible to distinguish between natural grape and artificially added sugar using nuclear magnetic resonance spectrometers, some startling results have come to light, including the possibility that up to one-quarter of the alcohol level of certain Swiss wines (i.e., three degrees in a 12% wine) was produced by supplementary sugar! In the excessive use of chaptalization, Switzerland is clearly not alone. The temptation, especially for *vignerons* searching for quantity rather than quality, is to compensate for undisciplined vine growth and lack of pruning by adding additional amounts of sugar to a thin must. Increasingly, the establishment of minimum natural sugar levels as part of cantonal *appellation* standards will ensure that the basic raw material is of sufficient quality to produce an honest and reasonable wine. And if anything, the standards will be tightened over time.

Any conscientious *vigneron* will attempt to maximize the natural sugar in his grapes. While it is conceivable that the disciplined addition of sugar can assist fermentation – a practice certainly not unknown across the border in Burgundy – the excessive addition of sugar will only mask, and not eliminate, the faults of a thin, acidic juice from vines pushed to overproduction. The move towards lighter, cleaner wines, especially for whites, may also reduce the use of sugar to cover up poor grape quality.

Malo-lactic Fermentation Debate

In recent years a second debate has developed over whether or not white wines, in particular Chasselas and Riesling x Sylvaner, should undergo the secondary malo-lactic fermentation following the primary alcoholic fermentation. In general the better specialty wines such as Chardonnay, Pinot Gris, Aligoté, etc. do not undergo a secondary fermentation but this process has traditionally been accepted as basic for Swiss Chasselas. Now, however, a small band of wine makers firmly believe the fermentation process should be stopped after the primary, alcoholic cycle is complete, and the secondary fermentation prevented. Those using this new approach argue that while the malo-lactic conversion may produce a "safer", softer white wine, the final result is insipid. A few serious *vignerons*, including some of the most respected producers in Valais and the large Valaisan cooperative Provins, have flirted with this "new style" wine making at various sites. According to enthusiasts, the initial results are encouraging and, for some, convincing.

Many traditional growers, backed by the weight and authority of the Swiss national research stations, argue with equal fervour that the secondary fermentation is what imparts those characteristics most attractive in Swiss wines – soft fruits, balance and a harmonious and attractive nose. The malo-lactic fermentation also provides a biological de-acidification of the raw wine. For the traditionalists, a wine that has not gone through the malo-lactic fermentation risks undermining the overall harmony of the wine by emphasizing the natural herbaceousness of the Chasselas grape.

The vast majority of Swiss wines will continue to undergo a secondary fermentation. There is unlikely to be a rapid conversion to a style which stops the fermentation process before malo-lactic fermentation begins; the fact that such a debate is taking place at all demonstrates the experimentation that is stimulating some parts of the traditionally insular Swiss wine world.

"Cutting" Debate

The act of blending or "cutting" *(coupage)* a wine with another without changing the nature or label designation of the initial wine is one of those admittedly time-honoured practices that every now and then drags the wine industry into disrepute. Traditionally Swiss merchants cut the thin, acidic domestic wines with fuller imports to make the domestic product more marketable, some of which they had been forced by regulation to buy. The usual objective in cutting a wine is to improve its overall colour, taste or quality. The improvement of vine growing and vinification technology should, in fact, make the practice virtually unnecessary. It is still done, however, and cutting remains legal under regulations set out in the Food Products Ordinance (ODA). Limited amounts of supposedly "superior" foreign or domestic red wines can be added to certain Swiss wines without the final product losing its legal identity. With white wines, however, only other indigenous wines may be added.

Better *vignerons* recognize that cutting hinders the development of recognizable and marketable categories of fine wines in Switzerland. Fortunately, the practice is decreasing, although it will be some time before it dies out completely. The introduction of the *appellation d'origine contrôlée* regimes in recent years by several cantons has given the authorities the opportunity to ban the use of coupage for higher quality wines. This trend will continue.

A related problem is the question of *ouillage,* or ullage, which in this case is the amount of wine that evaporates or is lost during the fermentation process.

Traditionally *vignerons* have been able to compensate up to a set limit (8%) for losses with wines of the same provenance. The control over the added wine has not been especially strict and wines of varying quality have been used. In 1993 the canton of Valais became the first canton to outlaw for its higher quality wines the addition of different wine to make up the loses due to *ouillage*. Other cantons may follow suit as regulations are tightened, especially for premium wines.

Bottles and Stoppers

Interestingly, most standard-sized Swiss bottles are still only 70 centiliters, rather than the more common 75 centiliters (26 ounces) found in Europe and elsewhere. This smaller bottle size allows the harvest to be stretched a little farther, but inroads are increasingly being made by the 75 centiliter size bottle. In addition, slight physical variations are found between the bottles used in different cantons. Although bottle design is often based on popular and recognizable shapes borrowed from France, one can, with practice, immediately identify the standard bottles from several cantons, Vaud being the most obvious. As the movement towards *appellations* gathers steam, the use of standardized bottle shapes for particular wines will become more the rule, although the range of wines produced by some producers could pose logistical problems.

One final issue deserves to be raised in the context of vinification and aging of wines in Switzerland. This is the growing use of screw-tops instead of corks. Initially these devices were found only on the less expensive wines. Increasingly, however, the use of screw-tops has expanded beyond the lower end of the wine spectrum. A few firms even promote on the back labels of wine bottles the benefits, economic and otherwise, of these stoppers.

The debate is very real among Swiss wine makers, and the questions raised by the advocates of screw-tops are being seriously deliberated by *vignerons* and in the market place. The arguments favouring screw-tops are threefold. First, corks are increasingly scarce and expensive, and the quality is often not what it used to be. Second, the use of a screw-top will reduce the price of the wine to the consumer and insure a certain quality. And third, those who fear a deterioration in the quality of the wine should have no concern. Screw-tops, especially for white wines intended for consumption within two years of bottling, will preserve the freshness of the wine which is one of its most appealing qualities.

The counter arguments are basically twofold. First, aesthetically, screw-tops leave much to be desired; and second they prevent the wine from breathing and developing in the bottle by denying access to minute amounts of oxygen which contribute to the chemical breakdown, complexity and attraction of a properly aged wine. In addition, screw tops are known not to support heat well – although one could argue that wines should never be stored in circumstances where this defect comes into play.

The cork-versus-screw-top debate regarding quality wines is not just limited to Switzerland. Similar concerns have been voiced by recognized wine makers in California and Australia. And even in France, wines from the Tavel region have recently been marketed with a screw-top instead of a cork. Of all the European wine producers, however, the Swiss seem to have traveled farther along the screw-top path, and higher up the quality scale.

While there are few, if any, advocates of screw-tops for quality red wines meant for aging, increasingly there is no simple answer to whether they are appropriate for white wines meant to be drunk young. Experiments have identified two years aging as something of a cut-off point. There is a strong preference for a cork for any wine over two years old but for younger wines, there is no clear winner. As the pressure increases on a finite supply of quality natural corks, the use of screw-tops will undoubtedly increase. Whether their acceptability also grows, and whether their use exerts a subtly negative effect on the wine in the bottle, remains to be seen.

The Valaisan wine 'channe' made of pewter and used for serving wine at the Ratsstube of Grimentz, famous for the legendary Vin des Glaciers.

VI

Valais

The Region

Today the canton of Valais is the pre-eminent wine region in Switzerland. Over the last century the canton's vineyards have grown steadily both qualitatively and quantitatively, and by the mid-20th century Valais had become the largest wine-producing canton. This glacial valley is also Switzerland's most diverse wine-growing region, in which is cultivated an astonishing range of quality grape types. It is the driest region in the country, with the greatest extremes of summer and winter temperatures. Spring and fall are, however, moderated by the warm dry *foehn* wind from the south which can dramatically change the character of the vintage. Valais is home to many of the new breed of wine-makers who are producing some of the most exciting wines in Switzerland.

Consequently, the canton is very much on the leading edge of the challenges and changes that confront the contemporary Swiss wine industry. Tradition and innovation co-exist creatively and naturally, but at times uneasily, among the canton's wine makers. The *Valaisan* inhabitants of the canton are often considered by the French-speaking Swiss to be particularly independent and insular. Valais, however, also contains some of the most experimental vineyards in Switzerland, run by perceptive wine makers who are well aware of the competitive pressures Switzerland faces from an increasingly integrated European market in the 1990s. Here, newer approaches to wine-making, and particularly marketing, exist alongside the decidedly more "traditional" attitudes of well-established wine firms.

Most of the Valais' vineyards lack the 1000 years of historical prestige and exalted prices of the wines of the most famous sites in the Lavaux region of Vaud. The better wine producers in Valais have attempted to overcome this lack of status by concentrating on improved production through low yields, refined vinification, and close identification with markets. Even the Valais cooperative, Provins, which produces one-third of all wines in the canton, is known for the overall high standard of its products, its innovative search for improved quality, and its willingness to experiment with new techniques and grape types to meet market demands. While the problems of overproduction, excessive irrigation, chaptalization and nature's unpredictability are by no means absent from Valais, the region is proving that it has as much potential to produce top-class wines as any part of Switzerland.

The northern starting points for the Simplon and St. Bernard Passes are located in Valais. These two well-traveled routes through the Alps have always been critical to the movement of goods and people between northern and southern Europe. Despite its rich history as a commercial and military crossroads, Valais remained a rural backwater until the construction of the railroads and alpine tunnels in the 19th century which irrevocably breached physical and psychological isolation of the region.

During the 19th century, grape growing in the canton began changing its focus from production of traditional grapes for immediate consumption to more commercially-oriented vineyards. This process built upon the rapid expansion of land dedicated to vines and the introduction of new grape species such as the Chasselas and Pinot Noir from outside the canton. Isolation had insured that indigenous grape types such as the Humagne, both red and white, Rèze, Petite Arvine, Amigne and Cornalin continued in commercial production. But the success of the vigorous new grape types virtually decimated traditional varieties. Only with experience did growers and wine makers realize that even if produced in limited quantities, these "local" grapes provide unusual and occasionally glorious wines. These unique grapes are certainly well worth preserving in our increasingly homogenized world of international Cabernet Sauvignons and Chardonnays.

The heart of the Valais vineyards is a narrow eighty kilometer strip of valley floor running from east to west and dominated by the two central features of the region, the Alps and the Rhône river. The Rhône begins its path to the Mediterranean high in the Alps on the Rhône Glacier at 2,200 meters above sea level. The river is hardly more than a mountain torrent until it reaches the town of Brig. But at Brig the addition of glacial waters flowing from the ice-capped peaks looming on both sides of the valley floor doubles its size. A cross-cut of the topography of Valais would show a rather symmetrical "U" gouged out by glaciers which descended from the Alps as far as Lyon. The retreating glaciers left a considerable moraine deposit which contributes to the good drainage of the light, non-clay soils. Chalky outcrops are found particularly in the upper Valais, but by the time the river reaches Fully, there is very little chalk in the soil. The "cones" formed by debris deposited by alpine streams as well as from avalanches torn away from the steep cliffs have proven to be particularly hospitable to grape cultivation.

Wine grapes grow along both banks of the upper Rhône River from the towns of Brig to Martigny. The most favoured sites are the right bank, south-facing hillsides rising from the valley, although in some places vines are also found on the north-facing left bank, and even extend well up the mountain sides to the village of Vispertermin, where the highest commercial vineyards in Europe are located.

The climate of Valais has been compared to that of the steppes of eastern Europe, or parts of California. The Valais valley is one of the driest in all the Alps because the surrounding mountains prevent moisture-laden clouds from dropping their precipitation in the valley. The average annual rainfall in Sion is only 599 millimeters, compared to 832 millimeters in Geneva, 1152 millimeters in Montreux or 813 millimeters in Dijon and 900 millimeters in Bordeaux. The arid conditions, at times, border on drought.

Hot, dry summers give way to warm, late falls, critical for the full ripening of late-maturing grapes such as the Syrah and Humagne Rouge. The harshness of winter and early spring can be softened by the warm, Mediterranean *foehn*. Without

The vineyards of Valais

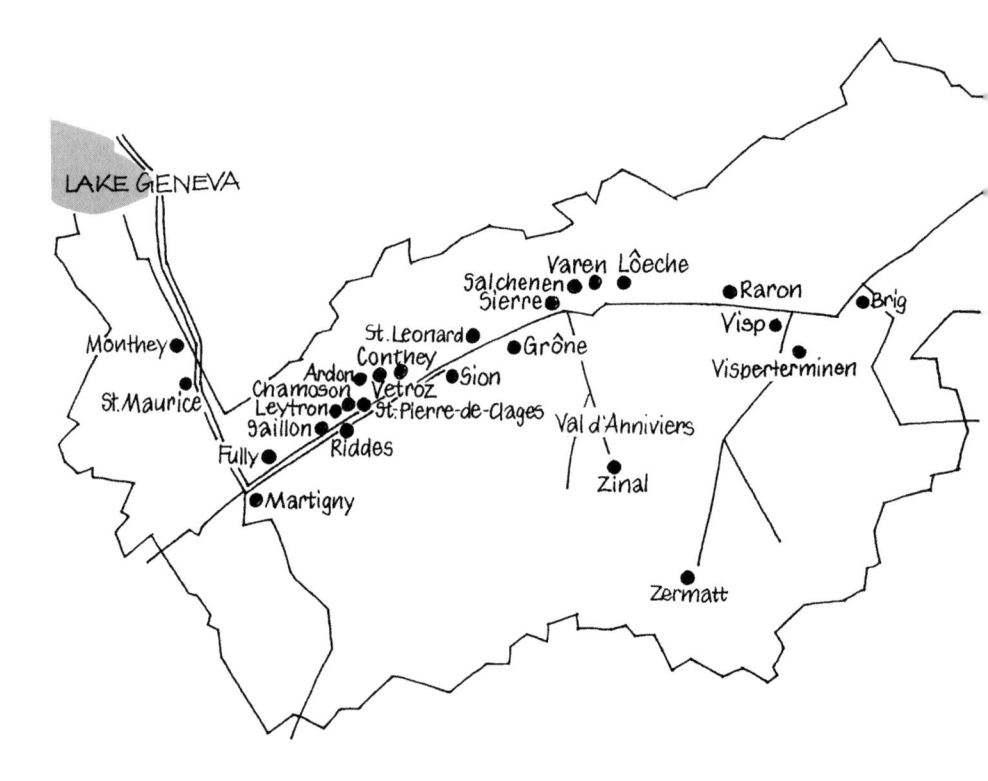

the *foehn*, grape growing on the north-facing left bank of the Rhône would be virtually impossible. In addition, especially for the late harvested *flétrie* wines, a medium quality vintage such as 1993 can be transformed for the better by a beneficial *foehn*. In 1994 record sugar levels of 200° Oe were reported at Mont d'Or near Sion as a result of a long fall enhanced by the *foehn*.

At the same time, the vineyards are subject to spring frosts in April and May, which occur perhaps twice a decade. Relatively effective but expensive anti-frost systems have been deployed, yet an early warming followed by a severe frost, such as happened in 1991, is always a very real threat to the size and quality of the harvest.

Although fully one-fifth of the canton of Valais consists of glaciers, the locked-in water does little to alleviate the arid conditions. Spring and summer glacial run-offs disappear quickly into deep and fast running torrents. Although the construction of *"bisses"*, or wooden canals, helps to catch some of the run-off, irrigation by hoses or jet sprinklers is often unavoidable for the nourishment of the vines. Judicious use of irrigation may be necessary, especially in light of the expansion of Valaisan vineyards in recent years. The use of additional water, however, remains unfortunately open to abuse. More positively, low rainfall and a glacial moraine base provide excellent heat reflection during the hot summer months.

The slopes of the vineyards in Valais can be as steep as 60° to 70°. Construction, maintenance and extension of the Valaisan walled vineyards are therefore extremely labour-intensive. The valley floor and lower mountain slopes have literally been transformed by manual labour to produce *"tablars"*, as these uniquely Valaisan vineyard terraces are called. Most wine production in the valley occurs in bands between 450 and 800 meters above sea level with the south-facing slopes commonly divided into three zones. This particularly applies for white wine production, as the majority of red Pinot Noir and Gamay grapes is grown on flatter land at the base of the slopes. Zone 1 includes anything up to 650 meters above sea level, i.e., approximately 150 meters above the valley floor depending on the location. Zone 2 is between 650 and 750 meters, while Zone 3 is anything above 750 meters. (For reference, the altitude of the major towns in Valais, Sion, Sierre and Martigny, is 512 meters, 534 meters and 476 meters respectively).

The highest quality grapes are grown in Zones 1 and 2 and certain grapes – for example the Sylvaner of the Provins cooperative – will be labeled as "Sylvaner" in Zone 1 but "vin blanc" in Zones 2 and 3. The growers of Vispertermin, where the vines thrive well above 1000 meters, would argue that the altitude of a vineyard is not an infallible guide to the overall grape quality. Over 80% of the wine grapes are grown on the favoured right bank of the Rhône. In addition, over 90% of grape production comes from the western, French-speaking regions of Valais.

The fact that the Valaisan vineyards have steadily expanded since the 19th century, in comparison to all other cantons, is exceptional. From 1877 to 1957, the area in Valais almost doubled, from 2,350 to 4,200 hectares, although the land in Switzerland devoted to vines decreased in those same years from 32,500 to 13,200 hectares. Over the last 100 years, Valais has become the leading canton in terms of different varieties grown as well as production, providing today some 40% of the total national output. This increase has continued in recent decades with total acreage of wine grapes rising nearly 50% since 1950. In the same period the production of red wines has increased from 9.5% to over 50% of the total production. Output in 1991 was 497,000 hectoliters while 1992 produced only 454,300 hectoliters of wine. The 1995 harvest produced somewhat more, 473,588 hectoliters from 5,259 hectares of vineyards. The division in 1995 between red and white wine was 247,842 hectoliters of red versus 225,726 hectoliters of white.

This harvest is produced by over 20,000 individual *vignerons* scattered throughout the canton, the majority of whom are part-time farmers. The most immediate impact of the traditional system of land inheritance, reinforced by the Napoleonic system of succession, is on the size of vineyards. Over one-fifth of the properties are less than 500 square meters and another one-fifth are between 500 and 1,000 square meters. The majority fall between 500 and 2,000 square meters, while almost half the properties (8,000) are between 1,000 and 5,000 square meters (a mere 0.5 hectare). Only 1,500 *vignerons* own between 5,000 and 10,000 square meters and a considerably smaller group of 800 owners, less than 5% of the total, have over 1 hectare (10,000 square meters) devoted to wine grapes. By comparison, Burgundy's Clos de Vougeot, a vineyard often used as an example of the complicated subdivision resulting from French inheritance law, is 50 hectares (125 acres), divided into various sized plots among 80 owners. While most Swiss vineyards are small by French standards, they are not so out-of-line with other European countries such as Germany and Italy where respectively 72% and 77% of the vineyards are less than one hectare, and under one percent are over 10 hectares.

Grape varieties

Valais is an ampelographers dream for the variety of different grapes planted. This comes not from a lack of focus, but rather reflects a rich

Table VII: Grape Types planted in Valais (In hectares planted)1994

White	hectares
Aligoté	0.95
Altesse	0.20
Amigne	19.56
Petite Arvine	46.04
Bernarde	0.04
Chardonnay	56.98
Charmont	0.37
Chasselas-Fendant	1,793.08
Chenin Blanc	0.67
Ermitage	34.08
Freisamer	0.15
Gewürztraminer	2.3
Gwäss	1.35
Himbertscha	0.17
Humagne	7.02
Lafnetscha	1.29
Muscat	43.4
Nobling	0.07
Païen (Heida)	15.19
Pinot Blanc	16.16
Pinot Gris	51.12
Rèze	0.72
Rhin/Sylvaner	227.45
Riesling	17.01
Riesl. x Sylvaner	13.68
Sauvignon Blanc	1.38
Traminer	0.15

Red	hectares
Ancelotta	0.91
Cabernet Franc	2.58
Cab. Sauvignon	9.47
Cornalin	22.21
Diolinor	11.12
Durize	0.59
Gamaret	1.47
Gamay	981.32
Humagne rouge	52.63
Merlot	2.24
Nebbiolo	0.21
Pinot Noir	1,788.59
Syrah	34.01

viticultural past integrated into a varying topography and a vibrant oenological present. A 1991 publication, *Cepages du Valais,* examines 15 major grape varieties and another 25 types of lesser importance, all currently used for commercial wine production in Valais. Of these, 27 are white varieties and the remaining 13 are red. Table VII, drawn from the national statistics, shows the 1994 plantings in hectares for each variety.

Responding to the growing demand for recognizable quality standards, and to gain some control over the diversity of wines being produced under a Valaisan label, the cantonal authorities followed the example of Geneva and, in 1990, introduced cantonal criteria for a system of *appellation contrôlée.* The new production limits were not introduced without controversy and it will be some time before there is a definitive answer as to whether the objectives of higher quality and greater consumer acceptance have been achieved. In fact, some of the better producers argued that the maximum yield norms were set too high in order to benefit large vineyard owners. Others argued that the canton-wide standards ignore recognized micro-climates and the changing growing conditions found throughout Valais in an attempt to introduce an artificial standardization. Concern was also voiced over the time frame for the implementation of the new regulations as some high-volume producers could be forced, albeit for their own long-term benefit, to change long-standing viticultural habits.

The maximum production limits for the Valais, which are slightly more severe than the equivalent federal regulations, are now as follows:

Fendant (Chasselas):	1.3 kilograms per square meter
Pinot Noir/Syrah:	1.1 kilograms per square meter
Gamay:	1.2 kilograms per square meter
Sylvaner:	1.35 kilograms per square meter
Specialties:	1.2 kilograms per square meter

Translated into the more commonly understood French system, these maximum harvests provide yields of approximately 104 hectoliters per hectare for Fendant, 82.5 hectoliters per hectare for Pinot Noir/Syrah, and 90 hectoliters per hectare for Gamay, and specialty wines. Once fully implemented, the appellation limits are supposed to reduce the amount of wine on the market by restricting the production of the lower grade, low sugar, thinner wines.

The immediate effect on the higher quality wines will be minimal as their producers are already harvesting well below the maximum. Unfortunately, the upper limits are still too high for, as serious wine makers argue, the maximum yield from which a good Chasselas or Gamay can be produced is around 75 hectoliters per hectare, while for the specialty wines the limit is closer to 60! In 1994, average production in Valais was 72 hectoliters per hectare for red wines and 87 hectoliters per hectare for white. This is, however, an improvement over 1991 when the average production per hectare of red wines was 89 hectoliters and for whites an incredible 102 hectoliters! Similar production limits, which admittedly can be adjusted depending on the conditions prevailing in any particular year, for a

Beaujolais Villages are 50 to 55 hectoliters per hectare. For a communal Burgundy such as Gevrey-Chambertin they are 40 hectoliters per hectare.

Once again, it is necessary to stress that these are average results which lump together the most disciplined and conscientious producers with the most profligate. The better growers will severely restrict their output, especially for varieties whose quality quickly falls off when production surpasses a certain limit.

The Major Grape Varieties:

Fendant (Chasselas)

"Fendant," as noted above, is the widely used Valais name for quality Chasselas. The name derives from the fact that if the golden Chasselas *(doré)* is pressed between the thumb and the index finger it splits *(fendre)* rather than squishes.

The Chasselas grape was introduced into Valais from the Lake Geneva region only at the end of the 18th century. It quickly took root although it did not begin to dominate production until the mid-late 19th century. The occupation of Valais by troops from the Chasselas-drinking regions of Vaud and Neuchâtel following the Sonderbund War of 1847 brought in its wake a rapid expansion of Chasselas-growing vineyards.

In the decade from 1982 to 1991 Chasselas accounted for somewhat less than 50% of the canton's total annual wine output. In 1994, 1,793 hectares of Valais were planted with Chasselas compared with almost 1,788 hectares for Pinot Noir, the next most widely planted variety. Much of the canton's Chasselas is localized in a triangle between the right bank villages of St. Léonard, Savièse and Sion, and along two additional strips of land from Conthey to Vétroz and Chamoson to Saillon.

Together with the Pinot Noir and Gamay for the reds, the Chasselas is the basic everyday grape of the canton. The Chasselas grape is best found on the arable mid-level south-facing slopes on the right bank of the Rhône. The higher and usually very much steeper slopes are mostly devoted to indigenous specialty grapes although plots of Chasselas are often found alternating with other varieties. All Fendants in Valais share the same grape stock and basic climatic conditions but they vary considerably in both their style and character even within the canton. As elsewhere, the guiding hand, experience, discipline and expertise of both the grower and wine maker (often the same) remains critical in the production of memorable Valaisan Chasselas.

Every producing area in Valais, however, traditionally claims particular strengths for its version of Fendant. According to one *amateur* these include: Sierre for its "exquisite" bitterness; Sion for the freshness and richness; Ardon and Vétroz for the stimulating dryness; Leytron and Saillon for the smell of the fruit; and, finally Martigny for the bouquet. Poetic distinctions perhaps, but they are real enough to influence the itinerary of the wine taster who travels across the canton.

Chasselas grapes.

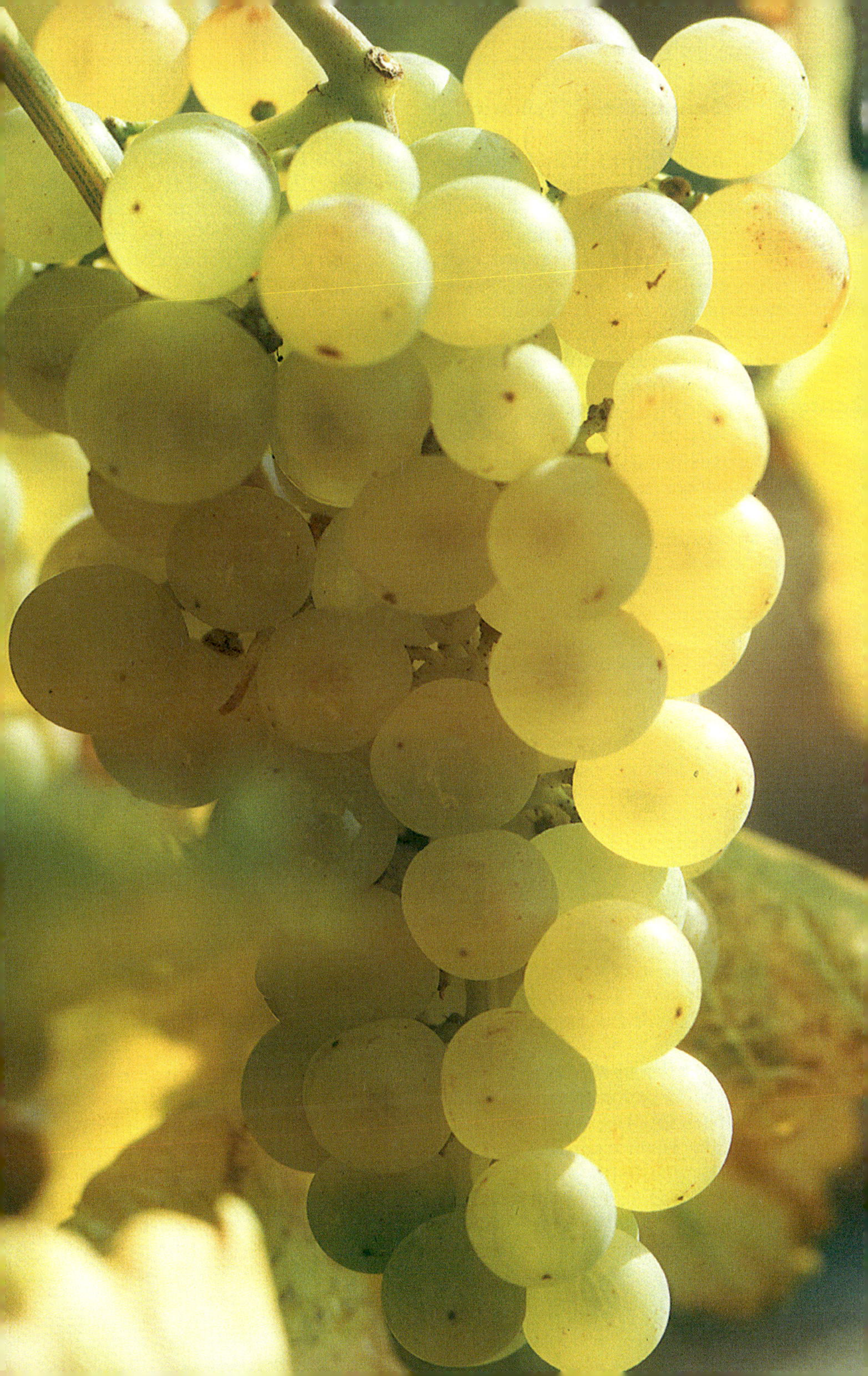

Johannisberg (Sylvaner or Rhin)

"Johannisberg" is the name used in Valais for wine from the Sylvaner grape. This intriguing designation alludes to the great Rheingau estate of Schloss Johannisberg. Following the final dissolution of the Benedictine priory at Schloss Johannisberg in 1801, the title to the ancient German vineyard was given in 1816 by the Austro-Hungarian Emperor to Prince Metternich, his Foreign Minister and Chancellor, whose descendants still own the estate. Ironically, at least in terms of the use of the vineyard name in Switzerland, Metternich is perceived by the Swiss as having assiduously worked against their national interests in his diplomatic maneuverings, despite the fact that his crowning achievement, the post-Napoleon Congress of Vienna, returned Valais to Swiss rule in 1815.

The Sylvaner was apparently introduced into Valais sometime around the 1840s, and the first written references to a "Johannisberg" wine are found in documents dating from the late 1860s and early 1870s. The existence of an 1880 Johannisberg wine label from the prestigious Mont d'Or vineyard outside Sion demonstrates the acceptance of this grape as an appropriate varietal for better sites, while other documents show the increasing popularity of the grape throughout the canton in the 1880s. During this period there was a certain confusion as to whether Riesling or Sylvaner was being bottled under the name "Johannisberg", a confusion compounded by the existence of an 1885 Mont-d'Or label which reads "Johannisberg 1885 – Riesling". However, contemporary analysis of the acid level of the wines seems to confirm that the wine being sold as Johannisberg was the less acidic Sylvaner, or at most a *mélange* of Sylvaner and Riesling grapes.

Reflecting the different adaptation of the two varieties to the specific conditions of Valais, the Riesling harvest has diminished over time while the acreage of the Sylvaner has increased. Legislation eventually restricted use of the title "Johannisberg" solely to wines produced from the Sylvaner grape.

With the increase of vineyards in Valais in the 1960s, the Sylvaner was often planted on the higher slopes of south-facing right-bank vineyards and on the better exposed portions of the less attractive north-facing left bank. Some of these new plantings turned out to be less than a complete success, in part because the vines on the higher reaches of the right bank were exposed to a level of cold that the Sylvaner does not tolerate well. In the latter part of the 1970s some of these plantings were replaced with other varieties, and the Sylvaner was confined to mid-level, but less fertile, vineyards. Total annual production is slightly in excess of five million liters (eight percent of the canton's wines) from almost 290 hectares planted with this variety.

The region to which the Sylvaner has adapted most successfully is around the village of Chamoson. If the grapes are grown on well-exposed, dry, gravely, mid-level slopes, the wine will exhibit a certain warmth, enhanced by both fruitiness and depth. The better examples will have a hint of almonds. Many larger Valaisan producers who bottle a range of wines from different grapes will also have a Johannisberg in their repertoire. In general, a good producer of Fendant is likely to release a good Johannisberg. There are exceptions, however, and the only sure way of confirming this is to sample the complete range of a particular producer's wines.

A true Valaisan native will suggest nothing but a Johannisberg to complement the local asparagus, traditionally served during the season in everything from a soufflé to a gratin or a quiche.

(H)Ermitage (Marsanne Blanche)

Contrary to the situation of the Malvoisie where both the Swiss name, Malvoisie, and the more common French grape name, Pinot Gris, are both found on labels (see below), the name "Marsanne" never appears on bottles of Swiss wine made from the Marsanne Blanche. This grape, like several others, worked its way up the Rhône valley finally to take root in Valais around the mid-19th century. Instead of keeping the grape name, the Valaisans began calling their wine by the name of the most famous slopes upon which it is planted in France, those of Tain l'Hermitage. Both "Ermitage" and "Hermitage" are seen on labels.

The Marsanne is a fairly late-ripening grape and therefore must be grown on gravely, warm soils, which most often means at the mid-levels of the right bank of the Rhône. It can thrive on slopes that are generally too arid for other varieties. Concentrated around the village of Fully, the best examples of Ermitage display a velvety, at times almost sweet, texture. Around Sion, particularly on the terraces of the Mont d'Or, are found slopes to which it has taken well. It is now the third most popular white grape in the canton, producing an average of 3,570 hectoliters annually.

Malvoisie (Pinot Gris)

The French Pinot Gris or German Ruländer *or* Grauburgunder, is known in the Valais as the Malvoisie. An early ripener, the Pinot Gris is used in Valais to produce both full, structured, dry wines, as well as quite different, late-harvested sweet nectars. The latter wine is particularly renowned and usually carries the notation *"flétrie"* (shriveled) on the label. At their best, these wines exude a hint of chamomile on the nose. For the late-harvested variety, the grapes are left on the vine as long as possible, often until December, at which time some berries will have shriveled while others may also have been attacked by *botrytis cinerea*, the famous noble rot. The concentrated must is thick and very high in sugar – sometimes over 135°Oe. The wine is fermented slowly over the winter and produces a final product with considerable residual sugar and between 12° and 14° alcohol.

The Pinot Gris was first introduced into the Valais in the 19th century. It is a grape that seems to thrive in arid areas and is often planted successfully in the poorest of soils. The yields, especially for the *flétrie* wines, are less than most, averaging between 0.5 and 0.7 liters per square meter. The most important centers of production are around Sierre and Leytron. Just over 50 hectares of Pinot Gris are currently planted. Average production is around 3,300 hectoliters and the Pinot Gris is the fourth most popular white variety after the Chasselas, Johannisberg (Sylvaner) and Ermitage (Marsanne).

While the dry Malvoisie can be found without great difficulty, the better *flétrie* versions are not easy to track down because of their rarity due to very low yields.

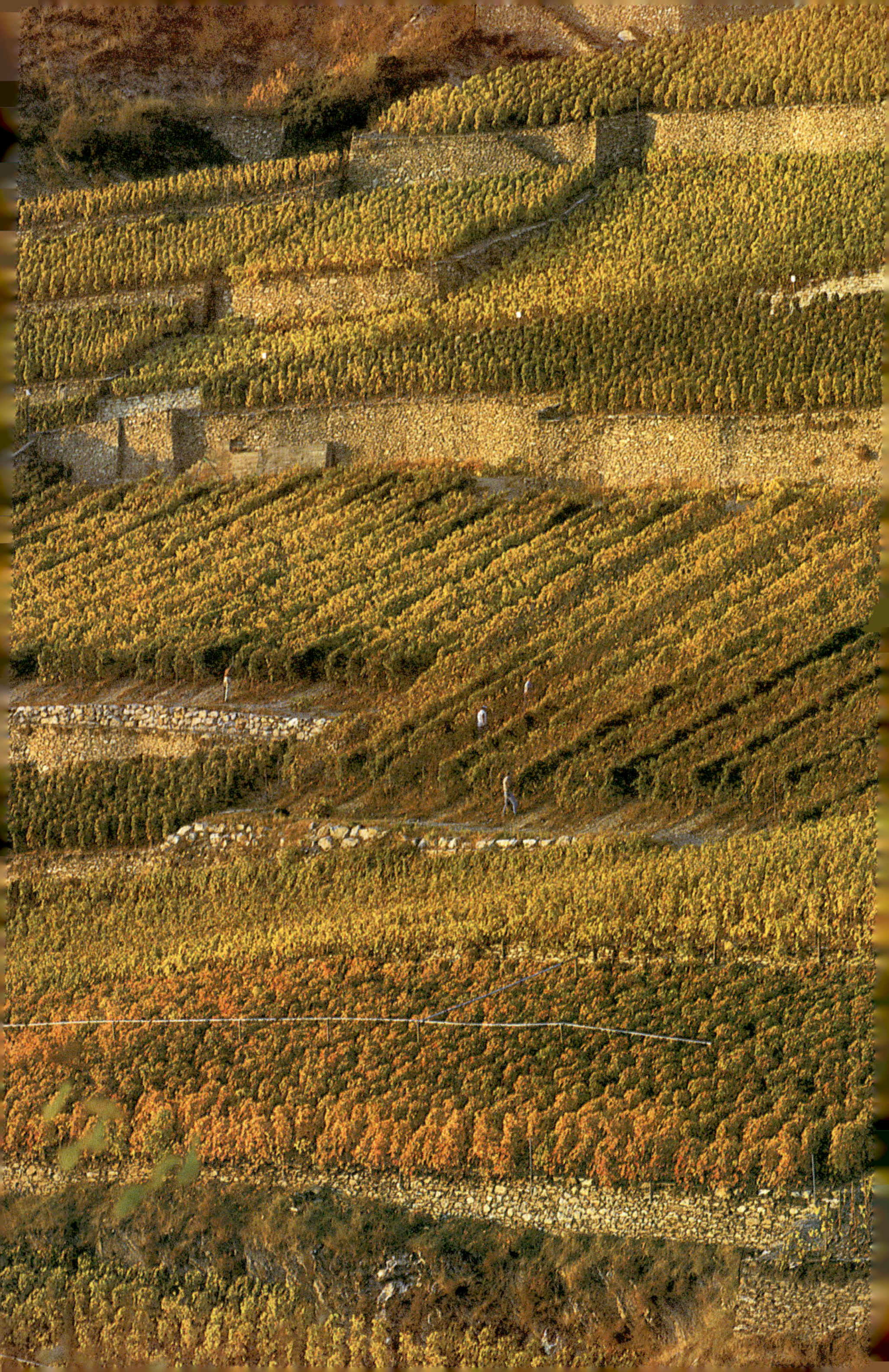

Chardonnay

Although the Chardonnay is not in the traditional pantheon of Valaisan wines, growers here have also caught the international fever for this varietal that has swept across both new and old world vineyards. The Chardonnay grape was first introduced in the 1920s, and the land dedicated to this variety has grown considerably in recent years. Today, with almost 45 hectares planted in Chardonnay, only the Chasselas, Sylvaner, Marsanne Blanche (Ermitage) and Pinot Gris (Malvoisie) are cultivated on more acreage. Production in the Valais has jumped remarkably from just 700 hectoliters in 1986 to over 2,500 hectoliters.

A relatively precocious grape, the Chardonnay can suffer from spring frosts. Placement of the vines is therefore quite important. On well-exposed slopes, Chardonnay can achieve a sugar level of 90°Oe to 100°Oe, producing a full, rich wine. At times it is not fermented perfectly dry and therefore provides a slight touch of residual sugar to increase the richness. Several producers even market an incongruous Chardonnay "Spätlese". As is the case with wine makers in other areas, Valais producers are eschewing the over-ripe, super-rich Chardonnays for a leaner, more elegant style with, as might be expected, just a light touch of oak aging. The grapes are planted in sites that are only moderately hot to prevent too rapid maturation, and they are usually picked at around 85°Oe. In addition to the still, dry versions, some Valais growers are beginning to produce an all-Chardonnay *blanc de blancs* sparkling wine, using *methode champenoise* techniques. The grapes for these wines are picked at even lower sugar levels to preserve sufficient acidity.

Given the immense international popularity of the Chardonnay grape, the acreage devoted to it in Valais will continue to increase. Over time, however, the Valaisan growers will have to develop their own style of Chardonnay or risk becoming lost in the growing ocean of less expensive, correct Chardonnay wines. In fact, given the stiff international competition, the Valaisan efforts with this grape are not entirely convincing. Although there is certainly nothing wrong with Chardonnay from Valais, the Valaisan growers and wine makers may eventually have to decide how far they wish to join the global rush rather than maintaining a greater degree of independence by producing wine that is commercially less immediately attractive, but more distinguishable and attuned to the canton's traditions.

Muscat du Valais

In common with the Chasselas grape, various varieties of Muscat are cultivated for both table and wine grapes. This ancient Mediterranean grape had certainly found its way to Valais by the mid-19th century, although subsequently the acreage devoted to the Muscats dropped as vineyards were replanted at the end of the last century. Its popularity has only revived over the last several decades, and it remains a popular white wine grape with just over 40 hectares planted producing an average of 2,650 hectoliters of wine annually.

Autumn colours distinguish the various types of grapes on Sion's Mont d'Or.

As is the case with the Malvoisie (Pinot Gris), there is a range of distinct styles of Valaisan Muscat, all of which attempt to preserve the distinctive luscious "muscaty" bouquet for which this grape is famous (or infamous). The Muscat is often served as an aperitif wine because of the slight residual richness, and various growers produce good typical examples of the Muscat.

Petit Arvine

The Petite Arvine, and its possible relative, the Amigne, are two of the *"spécialité"* white grapes that make this region particularly interesting. The Petite Arvine is, in fact, considered to be the quintessential indigenous Valaisan grape and, perhaps even more than the Humagne Rouge, a grape that can hold its own with the classic noble *vinifera* varieties. If imitation is the greatest praise, the producers of Petite Arvine can rest content – a one hectare experimental site was planted in the early 1990s much farther down the Rhône valley in France!

Similar to the Pinot Gris, the Petite Arvine comes in two distinct styles, dry and *flétrie*. The former has good backbone, acid balance and fruit and will develop with age. It is, however, the late-harvest version that can be really exceptional. Often picked a week before the Malvoisie in mid-November, the Petite Arvine produces an even rounder and fuller wine. In unusual years, sugar levels of 190°Oe. have been registered (around 160°Oe is common for Sauternes), although readings in the region of 130°Oe are fairly typical for good sites.

Because of the uniqueness of this grape and its ability to produce quality *"vin de garde"* wines, parcels of Petite Arvine have been planted over the last century in various sites down river from Sion. The slopes around Martigny and, in particular, the area of Octodure with its Marque and Coquempey vineyards, are sites to which it has adapted as well as anywhere else. This grape, however, is found throughout the canton, and some 46 hectares are currently planted, producing over 2,000 hectoliters annually. In the past it was, confusingly, often inter-mingled with other varieties in the vineyards and, as a result, it was difficult to judge with any accuracy how much Petite Arvine was actually planted.

The need for water has traditionally limited plantings in Valais to areas which were serviced by water-carrying *bisses*. Yields are generally quite low, with only 0.5-0.7 liters per square meter.

Amigne

After the Petite Arvine, the Amigne is the second of the two fine indigenous white grapes of Valais. The variety may in fact be descended from an ancient Roman vine. While there are some similarities with the Trebbiano grape of Tuscany and the Ugni Blanc of Provence, the differences in growing cycle, and the qualities of the wine, identify the Amigne as another unique varietal, indigenous to Valais. The special status of this vine did not prevent its virtual disappearance when confronted at the end of the 19th century by more remunerative varieties such as the Chasselas. However, after a bottle of Amigne was judged the best wine of the 1903 Swiss

National Exhibition, the variety was able to hold its ground and is today grown on just over 19 hectares in the canton, producing an average of 1,300 hectoliters of wine annually. The Amigne has adapted particularly well to the slopes around the village of Vétroz.

Heida, (Païen, Savagnin Blanc, Traminer)

The Heida grape is found almost exclusively in the "Valley of the Virgin," from Visp leading to Vispertermin on the way to Zermatt and the Matterhorn. Its local French name is the Païen and the grape is closely related to the Savagnin Blanc of the French Jura.

The Heida is clearly a grape long grown in Valais as there are written references to "Heyda" as early as 1586. In the local patois "Heida" is usually translated as "ancient" or "from an earlier time", although it may also mean "unusual" or "foreign". The French name Païen also descends from "pagan", i.e., before Christianity, another testament to the age of this particular vine. After World War II, many Heida vineyards were found to be suffering badly from phylloxera and they were uprooted and replaced by other varieties. It was only in the late 1950s and early 1960s that grafted plants were again replanted in the traditional Heida vineyards. The varietal suffered a second major crisis when, some years later, the replanted vines visibly began to deteriorate. In the late 1960s the problem was identified as a virus which caused *bois ridé* (wrinkled vines) and steps were taken to develop virus-resistant stock. The variety is making a comeback and has developed a loyal following. Total plantings are still fairly limited with only 15 hectares giving an average annual production of just over 700 hectoliters (around 8,000 cases).

Vineyards planted with Heida are found almost exclusively in the largely German-speaking regions of the Haut-Valais, from Raron to Vispertermin and the neighboring villages. It thrives on slopes that benefit from the warming *foehn*. The Heida is grown on the upper reaches of the Vispertermin vineyards to an altitude of almost 1,100 meters, making these the highest commercial vineyards in Europe, a fact well advertised on the Heida labels of the St. Jodern-Kellerei cooperative of Vispertermin.

Humagne Blanc

The oldest surviving document in Valais, dated 1313, records the sale of a vineyard in Sion. Reference is made not only to the vineyards but also to particular grapes grown: *"de Neyrum, de humagny"* and *"de Regy"*. The first is a black grape, while the latter two are undoubtedly the white Humagne and the Rèze. Earlier manuscripts also talk about *"Vinum Humanum"* and *"Vinum Rezium"*. It appears that the Humagne Blanc has no familial relationship with any other variety growing in Valais or elsewhere, including somewhat confusingly, the Humagne Rouge.

Age alone, however, does not guarantee continued viability, and by the beginning of this century the acreage devoted to the Humagne Blanc was steadily reduced. In contrast to the recent popularity of the Humagne Rouge, few have actively promoted the merits of the white Humagne, no doubt contributing to its increasing rarity. As an ancient, indigenous iron-rich grape it is, however, of historical interest because of its traditional reputation as a tonic for the ill, women in labour, monks and bishops! In the hands of a skilled *vigneron,* it can be coaxed to produce a scented, rich, full-bodied, well-balanced wine.

The Humagne Blanc is now an increasingly rare wine and, in 1994, there were just over seven hectares planted.

Rèze (Resi)

Together with the Heida and the Humagne Blanc, the Rèze is one of the oldest but increasingly rare specialty wines of the Valais. The name Rèze comes from "Rhétie", a word used to describe the wines from the region of Verona. While the Païen seems to be undergoing a revival because of the inherent qualities of the mature grapes, the same cannot be said for the Rèze. Not long from now it may disappear from commercial production. Even as late as the 19th century, the Rèze was the vine most planted in the Valais. Its limited yields, however, have meant that the Rèze has rapidly been replaced by the more vigorous Chasselas and other varieties. Traditionally it was widely planted in the lateral valleys to the north and south of the Rhône. Today less than a hectare remains in production, mainly around Sierre, where it is still used as the foundation for the sherry-like Vin des Glaciers. Some Rèze is also still grown in the alpine vineyards leading to Vispertermin.

Other white grapes of the Valais

Although numerous other white grape varietals in the Valais are grown more extensively than either the Humagne Blanche or the Rèze, they are of relatively limited historical or commercial interest. Some are particularly well-suited to certain micro-climates; others are the result of *vignerons'* propensity to experiment.

Commercially the most important by far of these other varieties are the Pinot Blanc, the Riesling and the Riesling x Sylvaner (Müller-Thurgau) with plantings of each exceeding 10 hectares. The Pinot Blanc is used as a workhorse grape in the Valais, since the variety is fertile and easy to grow. It can be treated similarly to its relative, the Malvoisie, to produce two different styles of wine. If picked before full maturity the grapes will produce a balanced, pleasant wine; if they are left on the vine to ripen further, the result is rich, full and velvety.

As mentioned above, the Riesling, the great varietal of Rheingau, is known in the Valais as the "Petit" Rhin to distinguish it from the more common "Gros" Rhin (Johannisberg) or Sylvaner. Today it is not widely grown in the canton although, in some cooler sites which allow the grapes to mature slowly, its characteristic tightly-knit floral quality has been known to show through. In addition, some late-harvested, sweet, *flétrie* Riesling is produced on the slopes of Mont-d'Or outside Sion.

Finally, there is Professor Müller-Thurgau's successful cross-breed, the Müller-Thurgau or, to give it its Swiss name, Riesling x Sylvaner. Compared to the true Sylvaner (Johannisberg), the Riesling x Sylvaner, perhaps surprisingly, is not widely planted in the Valais. The parched summer temperatures of the canton do not permit the slow ripening season needed for this variety to achieve its best. Generally, the Valais version of this grape is heavy and lacking in elegance.

Other varietals worthy of note include the Aligoté; the Altesse, (Roussette of Savoie); the Chenin Blanc; the Gwäss or Gouais, (one of the oldest varieties from the Haute Savoie); the Gewürztraminer; the Lafnetscha (the Blanchier or Completer of eastern Switzerland, although considered to be an indigenous grape of the Haut Valais); and the Himbertscha. There are even others including such *vinifera* cross-breedings as the Charmont (the Swiss Chasselas x Chardonnay cross) and Nobling (a similar Chasselas x Sylvaner cross). The wines of these grapes are, however, unlikely to be found outside their immediate areas of production.

Red Wine Grapes

Pinot Noir

It is well recognized that the Pinot Noir is a temperamental grape. Although it has been exported far from its Burgundian origins, there are very few transplanted examples that have captured the "essence" of this noble grape. Has Switzerland succeeded where others, better known, have failed? Yes and no. No, because that ethereal quality which makes Burgundian wines "Burgundian" remains elusive in Switzerland, as elsewhere. But yes, because the Pinot Noir, supported by the range of clones that it has spawned, can produce an excellent, complex and sophisticated wine in Valais and a few other choice sites scattered throughout the country, if it is grown with care, discipline and intelligence.

The Pinot Noir is not an old vine in Valais. It was first formally introduced in 1848 from Burgundy into the state-owned "Plata d'en-Bas" vineyard near Sion, a former monastic property. Then the varietal was known as the "Cortaillod", the traditional name for the Pinot Noir in the canton of Neuchâtel. Initially very little Pinot Noir was grown in the Haut-Valais, and there was understandable confusion between the Gamay (called then the "Grosse Dôle"), a Pinot Noir-Savagnin cross (the "Petite Dôle"), and the Pinot Noir proper, known as the "Petit-bourgogne". Until 1942 all Pinot Noir had to be bottled under the label of Dôle. In that year, however, the innovative Valaisan wine pioneer, Dr. Henry Wuilloud, obtained permission from the national authorities to bottle and sell a Pinot Noir without the appellation "Dôle".

Somewhat ironically perhaps, much of the Valais production of Pinot Noir is still subsumed in the production of Dôle where it is, to a greater or lesser extent, combined with Gamay (see below). Quality red wine makers in Valais are increasingly bottling both a Dôle and a 100% Pinot Noir and today, after the Chasselas, the Pinot Noir is the second most widely planted grape in the canton. Almost 1,800 hectares are under cultivation, producing an average of 150,000 hectoliters of wine a year which is 27% of the canton's total production. The Pinot Noir is very sensitive to both soil and climatic conditions and, over the years, several important clones have been selected to meet the specific circumstances of Valais. The varieties know as the Pinot Noir du Valais, Bourgogne and Cortaillod dominate although other strains are known as the Wädenswil and Oberlin. Some clones have been less successful, usually because they are overproducers with particularly large grapes. Such is the case with the "Marienfeld" clone which was banished from the Valais in 1981. By far the greatest part of the Pinot Noir in the Valais is grown in the Haut-Valais, particularly around the village of Salquenen. However, the terrain available for vines in the area immediately around Salquenen is extremely limited, and it is a hard-pressed producer, especially with any volume, who can produce a true "Pinot Noir de Salquenen". Much more common and honest are the bottles of "Pinot Noir du Valais" which, if properly selected and assembled, can be a fine wine indeed.

The standard and potential of 100% Pinot Noir wines from Valais, must increasingly be assessed separately from the question of the consistency and soundness of the traditional Dôle blend. Pinot Noir output is much affected by the well-known fickleness of this grape, intensified by variations found in Valais due to micro-climates, grape selection or vinification techniques. If a generalization can be made, most Valaisan producers search for a certain refinement and elegance in their Pinot Noirs, while the Dôle designation is reserved for richer, more full bodied wines. Valaisan Pinot Noirs run the full gauntlet from the sublime to the sadly unsatisfactory. As is the case in Burgundy itself, finding a superior Pinot Noir is a classic case of caveat emptor, or better yet, know your producer!

Gamay

Similar to the Pinot Noir, various clones of Gamay are grown in Valais. These include the Arcenant, Caudoz, Chaudenay and Sainte-Foix. Again, as was the case with the Pinot Noir, the Gamay grape was introduced into Valais in the 19th century. Indeed, it was the importation of some Gamay stocks which produced the name of the best known red in the canton. In the mid-19th century a Valaisan exile, Alexis Joris, sent some cuttings to his brother-in-law from the "Dole" vineyards in Franche-Comté. At the 1857 Agricultural Exhibition in Berne the brother-in-law, François Bovier, exhibited some bottles of 1854 "Dôle" to widespread acclaim. From that time onward, plantings of both the Pinot Noir and Gamay have risen appreciably.

The Gamay is most frequently used in the blend to produce Dôle, including Dôle Blanche, or Goron rather than being bottled on its own. Although some selected Gamay is bottled separately as Gamay du Valais, the amount is considerably less than bottlings of 100% Pinot Noir. Gamay can also be sold as Gamay *primeur,* reflecting the commercial success of Beaujolais nouveau-type wines. A small amount of Rosé de Gamay is produced.

The region around the town of Fully at the lower end of the Rhône Valley, just before the river turns north towards Lake Geneva, is the center of Gamay production. As one moves up the valley in the direction of the Haut Valais and Salquenen, the plantings of Gamay retreat in favour of Pinot Noir. The Gamay is second only to Pinot Noir among red wine grapes in terms of acreage planted, with nearly 1,000 hectares producing 15% of the canton's total wine output with an annual average of 84,000 hectoliters.

Dôle and Goron

The well-known Valaisan wine, Dôle, is not a "grape type" and hence is probably best considered following discussion of its constituent grapes, the Pinot Noir and Gamay. Superficially, the Dôle blend recalls the generally lower-quality Passetoutgrains wines of Burgundy made from a similar blend.

Dôle is perhaps THE conundrum of Valaisan, and perhaps of all Swiss wines. There are Dôles and Dôles – a point that Jancis Robinson emphasized in her book *Vines, Grapes and Wine,* when she referred to this unique *"melange"* as the "ubiquitous" Dôle. This blend can be an insipid, flat, heavy, over-sugared confection. Dôle can, equally, be a deep, long-lasting and complex creation. The greatest "problem" is that the legally-mandated ratio has traditionally varied from 51% Pinot Noir/49% Gamay to 100% Pinot Noir. The Provins cooperative alone markets five different Dôles which range from 55% to 85% Pinot Noir. There is no clear rule of thumb, although as one moves down-river from east to west along the Rhône valley from Salquenen to Martigny, the concentration of Pinot Noir generally decreases and that of Gamay increases until Gamay is virtually the only red wine grape variety grown around the village of Fully at the end of the right-bank vineyards. Producers with access to vineyards in the upper reaches of the Rhône valley will emphasize Pinot Noir; those further downstream will rely to a greater degree on the fruitier, more forward Gamay. Consequently, the character of Dôle produced between Salquenen and Fully can vary considerably.

In Valais, the provenance of the two parts of the blend is, within limits, probably as important as their actual proportions. A Dôle with a somewhat greater portion of Gamay from the right areas will be a better wine than one with a higher portion of Pinot Noir, but from less favoured or less severely tended slopes. Given the potential for quality variation, wherever possible the consumer should taste before purchasing or, at a minimum, rely on the reputation of the producer rather than be seduced by a fancy label.

Just to add a further complexity, as of the 1993 harvest, producers of Dôle are allowed to add 10% of another grape which is neither Pinot Noir nor Gamay to the blend. Some speculate that many of the better producers will use this change of the regulations as an opportunity to add a touch of Syrah to their Dôle. Whether this revision to the allowed blend helps establish a more accepted "type" for Dôle will only become clear in time. The results will be closely watched.

To be labeled Dôle the sugar levels of the grape must have to exceed a defined Oechsle level which is set each year depending upon the characteristics of the vintage. If the wine cannot meet this standard, it is declassified and sold as Goron. There is, however, no legally defined maximum percentage of Gamay grapes permitted in a Goron blend, and therefore the Gamay often dominates. Goron is generally a light, rustic, quaffing wine – refreshing, but short. Many restaurants will carry both a Dôle and a Goron among their "open" wines, with the Goron several francs a liter cheaper.

Humagne Rouge

Without doubt the Humagne Rouge is the quality indigenous red grape grown in Valais. The vine is old but not ancient; its origins are unknown. It has been long grown across the Italian border in the nearby Aosta Valley from where it was imported into the Valais in the 19th century. As mentioned in the section on Humagne Blanc, there is no varietal connection between the two Humagnes – Rouge and Blanc – the white variety being one of the oldest grapes still found in production in Valais. The name Humagne Rouge is of much more recent origin and is applied to the wine from a grape formerly known as the Oriou, but today is rarely referred to as such.

The Humagne Rouge is a vigorous grower which regularly produces a good harvest. It is resistant to *coulure* and rot. It matures late and therefore grows best on the better exposed slopes that catch the maximum amount of autumn sun. In some years it is necessary to cut back the number of grape bunches lest the vine overproduce, resulting in a mediocre, herbaceous wine. The must is dark, and although the young wine can be heady and almost rustic, a good Humagne Rouge will develop both finesse and smoothness with age. The young Humagne Rouge wine generally has more tannin than a Pinot Noir, but slightly less than a Syrah from the same vintage. There is a hint of black current *(cassis)* in the better wines. Well made Humagne Rouges can command a premium price and the grape is increasing in popularity. It is the third most widely planted red variety in the Valais, with 52 hectares planted in 1994.

Cornalin (Vin Rouge du Pays)

The acreage devoted to the Cornalin, perhaps the oldest grape variety in the entire canton, had been steadily diminishing until several years ago. The grape is now undergoing something of a revival.

It is probable that all the red wine referred to in documents and manuscripts going back to the 9th century was produced from what is now referred to as Cornalin. In the 19th and early 20th centuries the *"Rouge du pays"*, as it was often called, was an increasingly popular trade name for wine produced from the Cornalin. The acreage planted with this variety was, however, already beginning to decrease. By 1952 the Cornalin was grown in only two communes. The reasons behind this decrease in production are fairly straightforward – the Cornalin is a very late maturing grape, some 20 to 25 days after the Chasselas, and often is not fully mature until November 1. It therefore requires planting on the best exposed slopes. Its late maturity also exposes the vine to grape worms and certain diseases (mildew and oïdium). In addition, it is also an uneven producer, the traditional harvest being acceptable only once every two years. However, researchers at the State vineyard, Grand-Brûlé in Leytron, developed a revised pruning program which has largely solved the uneven harvest problem and hence contributed to the come-back of the variety. The key to producing successful Cornalin is proper pruning to remove all but the lowest bunch of grapes on the branch three weeks after flowering. If treated in this way the grape can produce an acceptable harvest, although its output remains of much less commercial value than the canton's production of Humagne Rouge.

Just over 22 hectares of Cornalin are grown today, making it the fifth most popular red grape variety after the Pinot Noir, Gamay, Humagne Rouge and Syrah.

Syrah

Like the Cornalin, the Syrah is a late ripener. A hot climate grape introduced from the lower Rhône valley, the Syrah can adjust well to the hot summers that inflict Valais. The vine was first introduced into the canton at Diolly in 1926 by Dr. Wuilloud, then an agricultural engineer and later head of the cantonal viticultural services. After several years of experimentation, the plantings of the grape gradually increased.

The Syrah is usually grown on low trellises. The vegetal growth and amount of grapes produced by the vigorous vines must be attentively controlled to prevent overproduction. As the vines mature, the grapes develop in complexity and a must from 12 year old plants is considerably more spicy, deep and peppery than a must from vines only six years old. At harvest the sugar levels of the juice should reach at least 95°Oe. The wine is purplish when young, deep and well-structured. With age, it balances out and develops a spiciness with a hint of raspberries. Some producers are beginning to vinify and age their Syrah in oak to add another layer of texture to their already complex wines. When successful, which is by no means every year, this difficult grape can produce magnificent wines which are cassis-scented, tannic and peppery. If good progress continues on adapting this variety to the conditions of Valais, the Syrah has a very bright future in the canton. As noted above, the Syrah may also become a minor, but important, element in the allowable grape blend used to produce Valaisan Dôle.

Rosé Wines

There are several types of rosés made in the Valais, including the Dôle Blanche. Based on a standard Dôle blend of Pinot Noir and Gamay, this wine is really a very light rosé rather than the white wine its name suggests. There also exists a somewhat darker Rosé de Dôle, fermented longer on the skins than the Dôle Blanche, as well as an Oeil-de-Perdrix, made from 100% Pinot Noir grapes. A third style is from the small amount of rosé made from the Gamay grape. Late-harvested Pinot Gris grapes have also produced rosé-hued wines, although technically these should not be counted as rosés.

Basically the standard Valais rosé should be a light, pleasant wine for summer drinking. Many, unfortunately, are too thin or anemic. Rosés are therefore not the ultimate test of the skills of the Valaisan wine maker. On the other hand some of the more carefully vinified 100% Pinot Noir Oeil-de-Perdrix, a designation cribbed from Neuchâtel, can show good balance, fruitiness and even some structure. They are especially enjoyable when drunk quite cool.

The Vineyards

The Haut Valais

Traveling in Valais from east to west, down the Rhône from its source, the first real vineyards are encountered just beyond the town of Brig near villages such as Eyholz and Brigerbad. Here several ancient grape varieties such as the Lafnetscha (Blanchier or Completer of Grisons), Hafnätscha and Himbertscha are still grown *à l'Italienne,* that is on trellises or "pergolas". Some sources say that on occasion pre-phylloxera root stocks are used, although given current national regulations this seems improbable. Locally produced wines from these grapes are, however, of little commercial importance. The courageous wine maker Josef-Marie Chanton of the firm Oskar Chanton in Visp produces a fascinating range of wines unlikely to be equaled anywhere else. These include a Heida, Himbertscha, Lafnetscha, Gwäss (a true sharp workingman's wine) and Hibou.

A short detour away from the main Rhône valley to the south at the town of Visp takes one up towards the village of Vispertermin and Europe's highest vineyards. Three hundred *vignerons* around this community who cultivate grapes on the steep hillside up to 1,100 meters above sea level have formed the St. Jodern-Kellerei Winery. The annual output of around 250,000 liters a year is usually two-thirds white, including the increasingly rare Rèze (Resi) and the Heida (Païen), with the remainder red, made from the Gamay and Pinot Noir grapes. The cooperative accounts for most, but not all, of the wine produced around Vispertermin. They process some 40 tonnes of grapes annually. For virtually all producers, growing grapes is a secondary profession, and demand outpaces supply because of the limited amount of land on these steep slopes suitable for grapes. The wines of Vispertermin are rarely exported. But a visit to the winery, a short and winding diversion from the road to Zermatt and the Matterhorn, is a rewarding and particularly scenic journey.

The Heida from the St. Jodern-Kellerei cooperative is a remarkable wine by any standard. The final result is not nearly as thin as one might expect from such an elevated site, and in years when the sun provides sufficient warmth, the wine preserves the bouquet and freshness that typify the best of Swiss wines. On the other hand the cooperative's Rèze is quite forward, with an attractive floral nose and a straightforward taste. It is not a wine with great finesse, but rather an honest and refreshing wine with reasonable length.

The Pinot Noirs from the St. Jodern-Kellerei show good fruit, a surprisingly forward nose and well-balanced acids. The wines generally contain very little tannin, but overall they are very pleasant. Given the altitude at which the grapes are grown, it is not difficult to accept the difference between this lighter, refreshing style of Pinot Noir and its more serious valley-based counterparts. The St. Jodern Pinot Noirs share an affinity with certain fruity Alsacian Pinot Noirs and should probably be served slightly chilled for maximum enjoyment.

Returning again to the main Rhône valley, scattered patches of vines are found on the right bank of the river until the medieval market town of Leuk (Loèche in French), architecturally renowned for its impressive Episcopal palace. Here the major vineyards of the Valais begin. Here, too, is first manifest the fruit of human efforts over the centuries to transform the natural geography of the Rhône valley into land amenable to grape production. With eight hectares, the Domaine de Lichen is the first significant large unified holding. Already between the towns of Leuk and Salquenen, and surrounding the intermediate village of Varen (Varonne), are the Pinot Noir vineyards that provide the foundation for the Dôle du Valais and produce many of the finer red wines of the canton.

Salquenen

Salquenen (or Salgesch in German) and its environs is one of the premier sites for Pinot Noir in all of Switzerland. Perched slightly above the arid plain, the village has a celebrated history, not least because of the hospice founded by the Knights of Malta which was active from the 12th to 16th centuries. Today, Salquenen is the headquarters for important growers such as Mathier-Kuchler, producers of the well-regarded "Vins des Chevaliers"; Gregor Kuonen et Fils of Caveau de Salquenen; Adrian Mathier; and René Mathier, a producer of a comparatively rare Salgesch Chardonnay. The Pinot Noir has adapted particularly well to the pebbly and chalky soil around Salquenen. Along with a little Chasselas and Sylvaner, the Pinot Noir dominates the 192 hectares of vines in the commune. The area did, however, encounter problems some years ago because of accusations that some wines bottled as Pinot Noir de Salquenen included a healthy dose of imported wine. The region's reputation went into a tailspin. Clearly there was a problem, but steps were taken to stop serious abuses. Controls are generally tighter today, although there is still too much wine sold claiming to come exclusively from the very limited vineyards of Salquenen.

Like many other larger Valaisan producers, the firm of Mathier-Kuchler does not have direct control over its entire production. The firm owns only a small part of their total output from their vineyards, mainly around Salquenen. The company has 14 hectares of its own vines, virtually all Pinot Noir (along with limited amounts of Chasselas and Johannisberg (Sylvaner)) which provide between 15% and 20% of the total output of 500,000 to 600,000 liters per year. They complete their production by purchasing grapes which meet their standards from other established producers. Quality is maintained through close attention to restricted grape production and, for example, by ensuring a very high percentage of quality Pinot Noir in the company's Dôle, a practice repeated by other producers of quality Dôle. In the 1930s the company Mathier-Kuchler was the first to start bottling its wine rather than just selling *en fût* (in bulk). Since 1952, it has continuously supplied wines to Swissair, most particularly for the first class service, the only Swiss wine producer to have such a record.

Mathier-Kuchler's top wines are their Réserve des Chevaliers trio, Dôle, Pinot Noir and Oeil-de-Perdrix. In good years, such as the excellent vintages between 1988 and 1990, these wines are well-structured with good levels of tannin (for the reds) and fruit. The Dôle and Pinot Noir, in particular, exude both style and power and are worth cellaring for several years, if not longer, until reaching full maturity. Yields are limited to 800 grams per square meter and chemical interventions, whether via fertilizers or sprayings, are kept to the absolute minimum. Produced in very limited quantities and quickly sold, these are Valais wines worth searching out. Mathier-Kuchler's *réserve* Dôle should be mandatory for those who say that they have never tasted a good Dôle.

The Mathier-Kuchler non-reserve selections, labeled Vins des Chevaliers, usually are young and fruity with good balance; basically, very pleasant wines. As might be expected, the blend for the Dôle of the Vins des Chevaliers is 95% Pinot Noir and five percent Gamay from some of the best sites in the canton. Whether from good or difficult harvests, the firm's Pinot Noir du Valais exhibits a similar forward, fruity and light nose. The wine also carries the more honest reference to the wider "Valais", rather than more prestigious but limited "Salquenen" designation. These wines will improve with some age but are not for long keeping. The firm also produces non-reserve Fendant, Johannisberg and Rosé de Dôle. The non-reserve Mathier-Kuchler wines are fairly easy to find throughout Switzerland, although they are not necessarily inexpensive.

There are many wine producers in Salquenen, although most would agree that Mathier-Kuchler leads the list. The Caveau de Salquenen of Gregor Kuonen offers an extensive list, including a "Spätlese" Chardonnay and an exclusive oak-aged Pinot Noir Granmaître. Adrian Mathier is another Salquenen firm known particularly for its Pinot Noir. They also produce wines from parts of the Valais better suited to growing other varieties. One example is white Chasselas from the "Terre Promise" vineyard of Chamoson. Other experimental growers of the Chardonnay include René Mathier whose bright, clean and well-balanced Chardonnay von Salgesch (from Salquenen) shows acceptable character.

Sierre

Leaving Salquenen, the vineyard route passes below the hill-side villages of Miège, Venthône and Veyras before arriving at the important town of Sierre, the traditional dividing point between the German-speaking upper (Haut) Valais and the remaining French-speaking part of the canton.

Sierre, an ancient bishopric, is a city with a rich and tumultuous past. It is the second wine town of Valais after Sion, with 324 hectares of vineyards providing some 12% of the entire canton's production. The area around Sierre is the driest in Switzerland, with minimal rainfall and an average of almost seven and one-half hours of sunshine daily from May to the end of October. All the major Valais grape varieties are grown in and around Sierre, although the Chasselas for Fendant maintains a particular importance.

In the north section of Sierre is found the 16th century Château de Villa, originally built for the de Platea family. Today it is the site of the canton's wine museum which opened in 1991, the *Musée de la vigne et du vin*. A pleasant restaurant inside the château, with an excellent Valaisan wine list, operates daily. The museum concentrates on the wine-making activities which take place in the *chai* while a sister institution in Salquenen, the Zumofen House, displays items related to viticulture. A well-marked wine path connects the two sites, winding in and out of the vineyards.

The Château is also home to *L'Ordre de la Channe* (Order of the Channe) founded in 1965 at the Château de Villa as the Valais version of the wine Confréries established in other regions of Switzerland. A "channe" is a distinctive and typically Swiss – some would say Valaisan – carafe or mug often made from pewter and it is used for serving wine (see photo on page 59.) The aims of the Order of the Channe are the same as those of similar groups, namely the promotion of a greater understanding of the wines of Valais through historical research, dinners and tastings. By the late 1980s the Order had a diverse membership of close to 2,000.

Any list of fine wine-makers from the Sierre area would certainly include near the top both Maurice Zufferey at Muraz and Bernard Rouvinez et Fils, the latter slightly separated from the city on the rock outcrop of Colline de Géronde. Others close behind would be Gérald Clavien at Miège, Simon Favre and Jacques Clavien at Venthône, Michel Savioz at Château Ravire, Joseph Vocat at Nöes, and even the larger firm of Caves Imesch in Sierre.

Anita and Dominique Rouvinez in their cellars at the Colline de Géronde near Sierre.

Maurice Zufferey is a particularly meticulous vinifier of his grapes. Zufferey is descended from a family originating in the nearby Val d'Anniviers and is known for his attachment to that region. His production of 40,000 bottles includes good wines made from the Cornalin, Chasselas, Pinot Noir (Clos de la Combettaz) and a Chardonnay (Les Glariers). Zufferey's Humagne Rouge de Sierre is an exceedingly dark wine. It is initially closed, but if given some air the wine opens up to reveal pronounced fruit on the nose. Zufferey's better wines need time but, with care, they will become rich, full and very pleasant with good length and concentration

The cellars of Bernard Rouvinez et fils are found several hundred meters from the old Bernadine monastery of Géronde, just south of the town of Sierre at a point where the Rhône River flows around the Colline de Géronde. Jean-Bernard and Dominique Rouvinez are especially well-regarded for their innovative Pinot Noir/Syrah/Humagne Rouge/Cornalin "super-blend" called Tourmentin, and their Chardonnay/Petite Arvine combination, Trémaille. Although these are certainly "created" wines, to call them designer wines would undervalue the Rouvinez's commitment to solid wine making practices and a high quality product. The 1992 blend for the Tourmentin is 70% Pinot Noir and 10% each of the other three varieties while the Trémaille is 50% each of both white grapes. The Trémaille, in particular, is a stellar wine with a concentrated, almost haunting, nose supported by citrus undertones. Unfortunately such quality only comes at a premium price.

The Pinot Noir here is often picked earlier than other Valais Pinot Noirs to avoid overripening. Other wines, including a Johannisberg and a full-flavoured Chasselas, are produced from the vineyards at their Colline de Géronde site. Although almost on the south side of the Rhône valley, at least some of the Rouvinez vineyards at Colline de Géronde have a south facing slope because of an accident of geography.

To the north of Sierre is the Cave des Deux Crêtes winery of Gérald Clavien at Miège. Clavien's Humagne Blanc du Valais is everything that one could hope for from this varietal – fresh but already full and well-balanced with enough structure to last for several more years. On the other hand, his Pinot Noir du Valais, Cave Les Deux Crêtes is an unusually austere wine that needs time to come around. A good late 1980s vintage had a lightish colour and initially seemed to lack concentration. The 1990 Pinot Noir packed a great deal of tannin but only developed a fuller presence after some time in the glass. These wines are made in a particular style and appreciation grows with increased familiarity. Given the balanced structure of Clavien's wines, they will improve considerably if given sufficient time to develop.

Simon Favre of Cave d'Anchettes near Venthône is one of the wine makers known for his Malvoisie "Flétrie de Sierre". This producer is also a nurseryman and fruit grower who cultivates grapes at a series of sites from the Géronde alluvial cone to high up the slopes behind Venthône, each with varying levels of limestone in the soil. He is also the President of the Confrérie de St. Théodule, a group of professional vigneron-oenologists dedicated to improving the quality of Valais wines. The organization is named after the first bishop of the Valais who was appointed in 350 A.D.

An intense Malvoisie (Pinot Gris) wine is made by Michel Savioz at Château Ravire in Sierre. Another fine example of a characteristic wine is found in the

Château Ravire Ermitage (Marsanne) which can be well-balanced, full and perfumed, smelling of apricots. This vineyard also markets a Glacier d'Anniviers, Caves d'Ayer, which displayed a slightly oxidized, sherry-like nose holding some promise. The taste, however, lacked some of the fruit and balance needed to give the wine substance.

Sierre is also headquarters to the large firm of Caves Imesch managed by Marie-Hélène Siegrist. Imesch specializes in Malvoisie (Pinot Gris) and their expensive, concentrated barrel-aged Pinot Gris is truly a superb wine. Their Petite Arvine and Ermitage are also well-regarded, but the firm's bread and butter is their Chasselas, Soleil de Sierre, which receives fairly wide distribution. This somewhat aggressive and straight-forward wine is one of the few Swiss listings carried by the Liquor Control Board of Ontario, the wine and spirits monopoly in Canada's largest province. The broader horizons of this company are evident in their use of the label "Sylvaner" in preference to the more traditional "Johnnisberg" in order to meet European Union import regulations.

Vin des Glaciers

From Sierre one can also travel up the Val d'Anniviers, the summer home to the nomadic mountain people who, as late as several decades ago, still moved annually with the seasons from the valley floor into the Alps. This valley is home to the rare Vin des Glaciers, once described in 1951 by the British wine writer H. Warren Allen as "all salt and metal, like unblended centenarian sherry, and had that extreme dryness and bitterness, though perfectly sound, which Pliny attributes to the wines of the Opimian vintage of 121 B.C." A noted Swiss poet had a somewhat different, but perhaps not contradictory, view:

Glacier d'Anniviers

Pour trouver ce nectar, il faut quitter la plaine
Et s'engager bien loin dans le Val d'Anniviers
Il vous faut arriver sur la montagne hautaine
Car ce n'est pas en vain qu'on l'appel' le glacier.
Et c'est du vieux tonneau, tout couvert de poussière,
Que l'on tire ce vin au parfum délicat.
De rudes paysans en sont propriétaires,
On ne le trouve point chez Monsieur l'avocat.

(To find this nectar, one must leave the plain
And travel far up the Valley of Anniviers
To arrive on the mountain high
For it's not for nothing, we call it "the glacier".
From the ancient barrel, covered in dust,
We draw this wine with its delicate perfume.
It's the property of these rough peasants,
Something never found in the offices of lawyers.)

This poem was written, probably in 1930, by Jean Savioz. The verse has been turned into a song but unfortunately it loses its vitality and humour in translation. It celebrates a wine which occupies a unique spot in both Swiss folklore and Swiss wine making.

The real Vin des Glaciers was born out of necessity as the wine of the herders who moved in summer from the valley floor to the mountain pastures. The base for this wine is the once-common, but increasingly rare, Rèze grape. The wine is made from pure Rèze grown in the vineyards around Sierre belonging to the herders, or from a *mélange* including Rèze, Ermitage (Marsanne) and Malvoisie (Pinot Gris). It is only labeled Vin des Glaciers or Glacier d'Anniviers after it has gone through a unique maturation process. It is the product of a quasi-solera system where the wine is aged many years, often well over a decade, in small 37-liter larch barrels. Stored in the high pasture shelters, it is preserved almost in a state of suspended animation at low temperatures throughout the long winter. Every year the wine is topped up with the succeeding vintage, carried up at great effort from the valley below. In the days before motorized travel the wine was transported slowly from the valley via a series of postal stations to its alpine resting place.

The final product is a deep shade of rosé. Jean-Jacques Rousseau, during his time as a political refugee in Switzerland, once sung its praises as the "glory of the Anniviard!". The modern version, although certainly floral, can unfortunately suffer from excess oxidation unless drunk directly from the barrel. It is a wine that requires some time and experience to get used to, especially for those not brought up on a diet of Swiss traditions. It is perhaps best celebrated for its rarity, rather than its intrinsic value. One of the most readily obtainable versions is the one noted above, the Glacier d'Anniviers Caves d'Ayer, from Château Ravire of Sierre.

Sion

Between Sierre and the Valaisan capital of Sion is a string of important and lesser wine villages on the right bank of the Rhône. Ollon, St. Léonard and Uvrier are pleasing well-ordered villages known for producing top-quality Fendant. Here, for the first time on the journey down the Rhône, on the north-exposed left bank of the river, a group of significant wine-producing villages, including Chalais, Grône and Granges, provides cross-river balance. Chasselas remains the most important varietal, although certain Valais *"specialités"*, such as the strong and aromatic Muscats of Granges and Lens, have established strong local reputations.

Good producers such as Jules Duc in Ollon, known for his Malvoisie and Cornalin, and the Cave St. Matthieu in Chalais, which releases a noteworthy Vertiges, Amigne de Vétroz, are sprinkled throughout this area. Laurent Hug of Caves des Places in Champlan just to the north-east of Sion, also produces a very passable Fendant.

Further down river, dominated by the two church/châteaux-topped hills of Valère and Tourbillon, is Sion, the political and vinous capital of the Valais with 370 hectares planted with vines. The importance of wine to the region is perhaps symbolized by the vineyard found on the ridge which straddles the two hills dominating the city below.

The area around Sion has been inhabited since Neolithic times and, in the Iron Age, Sion was the Celtic town of Sedunum. At various times this strategic site has been occupied by the Celts, Romans, Burgundians and Franks, as well as troops loyal to both the Holy Roman and Napoleonic empires. A bishopric was founded in the 4th century and Sion has been the political and ecclesiastical capital of Valais since the 6th century. The town has played an important spiritual and temporal role throughout the Middle Ages, particularly after Rudolphe III, the last Burgundian king to hold lands across the Jura, donated the Comté of Valais and its vineyards to the church of Sion. Religious influence was severely curtailed in 1630 when the Bishops of Sion, controllers of both the Upper and Lower Valais, were forced to renounce their temporal holdings during the religious wars that plagued this region in the 17th century.

One-quarter of all Valais wines is produced in and around Sion. Within its boundaries are found some of the canton's largest and most important producers such as Robert Gilliard, Charles Bonvin Fils and Varone Vins. The firm of Gilliard produces the Fendant Les Murettes and Dôle des Monts from their 38 hectares of vines, two of the most successful and internationally distributed wines of Valais. Les Murettes is one of the more straightforward but better Fendants with good balance and concentration. It is more stylish than most, and its quality is evident.

The Dôle des Monts, one of the Dôles found most often outside of Switzerland, has contributed much to people's impression of this Swiss blend. The wine is 80% Pinot Noir and 20% Gamay and is consciously not oak-aged. Here, however, the author must confess a stylistic preference. While certainly an acceptable wine, on repeated tastings, the Dôle des Monts has always seemed less successful than Gilliard's Fendant. This traditional style wine appears almost stolid when compared to the offerings of other producers although successful exports since the 1940s attests to the widespread demand for this wine. The firm also bottles a full range of other Valaisan wines, including a very good single domaine Chasselas, Domaine de la Cotzette, as well as Amigne, Petite Arvine, Marsanne, Malvoisie, Muscat, Dôle Blanche and a 100% Pinot Noir, Vendémiare. A good selection of these wines is available from the New York fine wine shop, Morrell's.

The well-established firm of Charles Bonvin also produces a wide selection of wines, including three single-vineyard Fendants, from their 22 hectares. Their Domaine Plan Loggier, Fendant de St. Léonard, can be a good wine even in off years. The other two Chasselas-based wines are Domaine Brûlefer and Domaine Château. Of the two, Domaine Brûlefer from the firms south-facing 4.5 hectare estate above Sion, is considered to be the firm's top white wine. Johannisberg and Pinot Noir are also harvested from their property in St. Léonard. Bonvin's signature Dôle is harvested along a rocky ridge 720 meters above sea level from the large 8.5 hectare Domaine Clos du Château vineyard. The blend contains between 75% and 80 % Pinot Noir and the wine is not without complexity. In recent years, under the direction of André Darbellay, Bonvin has restructured its product line and introduced several new wines with more immediate appeal including a Fendant Sans Culottes, a Dôle Grand Carré and a crisp Pinot Blanc.

One of Bonvin's specialty wines is the Arvine Vieux Cepage du Valais which displays a straw colour and a floral nose but without real intensity. The taste is pleasant and fresh, although the wine unfortunately can lack the distinctive style of the Arvine. The firm also produces an Amigne de Vétroz with a surprising level of residual sugar. Most sweeter Swiss wines, such as a Malvoisie where the grapes have been left on the vine to gather additional sweetness, are labeled *"flétrie"* to identify their overripe nature. This is not the case for Bonvin's Amigne. When first tasted, the unusual golden colour was, for a Swiss wine, an obvious clue that this was not a dry wine. It had a refined floral bouquet, good concentration on the nose and a sweet, full, but not completely rounded, taste. The finish was dry. This offering from Bonvin is an interesting but ultimately perplexing wine since, in the end it is neither a table nor a dessert wine, but presented itself as an aperitif wine with positive characteristics of both styles.

The firm of Varone, founded in 1900, manages to balance large output with superior standards. Their vinification methods and wines are quite traditional with the Dôle and Pinot Noir remaining for several months in 10,000 liter barrels before bottling. The firm's signature wines are Fendant Soleil du Valais and Dôle Valeria and a Petite Arvine du Valais.

One of the relatively small but growing number of top-class female wine makers in Switzerland is Hanny Favre whose firm's slogan is *"La Petite Maison des Grands Vins"* (The Small House of Great Wines). Her Johannisberg des Coteaux de Sion, produced in the admittedly good year of 1990, had a deep colour and a reticent nose but a smooth, almost velvet texture. While not a wine for laying down, it will drink well for some time. Her cellar both owns vineyards and buys grapes for its extensive range. Their particular specialty is Petite Arvine. Another respected Sion firm with the name Favre is Les Fils de Charles Favre. They also bottle a good Petite Arvine, Réserve Tous-Vents.

In Pont de la Morge, on the western outskirts of Sion is the headquarters of the company run by the enterprising Michel Clavien, whose Domaine de Chatroz "Fin Bec" wines have been gaining a serious following among enthusiasts in recent years. Much of the credit for the move towards higher standards and quality for the wines in Valais can be attributed to a number of influential and successful "boutique" wineries which have realized that a viable future can only be secured if Valais delivers a quality product that meets a specific demand. Clavien, a very special *vigneron* with an artistic touch, is clearly one of the "new breed" wine makers. His goal is to create a special niche for his wines in a more open and competitive Europe. Current annual production runs around 300,000 bottles.

One senses immediately that Clavien's horizons extend well beyond even Europe's frontiers. Realizing that Swiss wines will never be able to compete on price alone, Clavien, like others of the new generation, is working assiduously to promote and fill a stable demand for high quality wine. He has consciously set out to create well-made, "constructed," wines that, while carrying a gastronomic cachet, are at the same time immediately approachable. Not surprisingly, his role model is Angelo Gaja of Italy's Barbaresco region. His prices, though, are much more reasonable. Clavien seeks to make a high quality product that is somehow different, but attractively so. His white Fin Bec Mer from Sion, a *mélange* of five grapes – Chasselas, Altesse (Roussette), Hermitage, Petite Arvine and Pinot Blanc – is a flinty, almost austere, atypical Swiss wine that superbly compliments sea food and crustaceans. As the ultimate accolade it is featured on the wine list of Fredy Girardet's famous three-star restaurant at Crissier outside Lausanne. His range of other *grand vins blancs* made from the Chasselas includes four Ville de Sion selections, including two from Lentine and Gravelone, as well as a more straightforward Fendant du Sion.

Clavien's rich, complex Pinot Noirs and Dôles are wines for laying down. Certainly the standard set by his La Follie, Pinot Noir de Sion, is very hard to challenge. Ideally, a Dôle should combine the intensity of a Pinot Noir with the forward fruitiness of a Gamay. The combination might be anathema to a traditional Burgundian *vigneron,* but in the hands of a skilled and disciplined wine maker the marriage can certainly be made to work. Clavien's Dôle de Sion, Tête de Cuvée is also an example of what the blend should be – intense, complex and layered, but immediately attractive. From a good year it is a wine that will continue to develop well for years after the vintage. In 1994 Clavien began to market a Cabernet Sauvignon, one of the first Valaisan producers to release this grape commercially.

To the north-east of Sion in Clavoz is one of Switzerland's most famous *"bisses"*, or water channels, built in the Middle Ages to capture at least some of the glacial run-off to irrigate vineyards suffering from the traditional Valais drought. This particular *bisse* extends for seven kilometers up the valleys behind Clavoz. As long ago as the 13th century, it was already providing water for 200 hectares of agricultural land. The dry-stone walls which climb the hills behind Clavoz are also a marvel. They rise five meters or more, strikingly reminiscent of a castle's ramparts, to provide a narrow terrace for seven or fewer rows of vines.

To the south-east of Sion, on the left bank of the Rhône, is the village of Bramois which leads to the Val d'Hérens where several isolated patches of vines can be found. More importantly, up the hill to the north-west of Sion is the village of Savièse which is headquarters for the producers Stéphane Reynard and Dany Varone whose "Buteo" and "Cornulus" wines from nearby vineyards in Lentine, Sion, Uvrier and more distant Chamoson are well-regarded. Their cave stands out somewhat incongruously on the Sion-Savièse road immediately behind the Mont d'Orge. The Lentine Cornulus, made from Chasselas, and Hermitage Lentine, are wines that generally benefit from some aging. These wine makers also have a holding in Mont d'Orge and produce a rare oak-aged "Reserve" 1er Cru Humagne Rouge in very limited quantities which, although expensive, is a remarkably full and complex wine for laying down. Their Savièse Dôle is composed of 70% Pinot Noir and 30% Gamay. Total production of this partnership, which owns some 12 hectares, is approximately 100,000 bottles.

Mont d'Orge

From Sion the main *"route de vignoble"* continues to follow the path of the Rhône towards the next major wine town, Vétroz. Walled vineyards partition the gravelly plains, overwhelmed in turn by the alpine peaks that permanently guard the Valais valley. Most often Chasselas and other white grape varieties command the terraced hillsides, while Gamay spreads out on the flatter vineyards at the base of the slopes. On the western outskirts of Sion, in the direction of Vétroz, stands the steep rock outcrop rising abruptly from the valley floor, the Montorge (Barley Mountain). This is the site of the Mont d'Or vineyard, one of the best exposed locations in Valais. It produces musts with some of the highest Oechsle readings in all of Switzerland. Not an ancient vineyard, this 21 hectare site was formally established only in 1847 after the Sonderbund Civil War by a prescient sergeant-major from Lavaux whose company of soldiers happened to be stationed at the foot of the Montorge hill. His vineyards were consciously modeled after the rocky, sun-drenched hillside of the ancient terraced plots of Dézaley. Today the Mont d'Or vineyard is known for the quality and variety of its production, including Malvoisie, Petite Arvine, Johannisberg and even Riesling in addition to Chasselas. Different bottlings of various grapes are released.

Even the basic Chasselas, Fendant Mont d'Or La Perle du Valais, is everything a good Chasselas should be – taut, smoky peach, fragrant with good body and extract, and reasonable length. The red equivalent is Perle Noire. The Mont d'Or wines such as the Perle du Valais demonstrate that special quality upon which rests the superior reputation of the vineyards. Other grapes that thrive in different parts of this vineyard are Malvoisie, Ermitage and Riesling. Two consistent favourites are the Johannisberg St. Martin, which is not harvested until St. Martin's day, November 11, and the Petite Arvine Sous l'escalier. Another exclusive wine is their Ermitage *flétrie,* bottled under the name La Morle des Roches.

In less sun-blessed years, however, some of the regular bottlings of Mont d'Or Johannisberg have been inconsistent. Although they showed an initially attractive nose, closer examination revealed surprisingly acidic and thin wines, with even a touch of excess sulfur. In these cases, however, the wines often reflect more the vintage than the vineyard.

From the Mont d'Or, the wine trail traverses the vineyards of Sensine, Premploz and Erde which surround the town of Conthey, center of a commune with 381 hectares in vines. The 4.2 hectare Clos d'Anzier vineyard in Conthey, owned by Gabrielle Michelet-Escher, produces the usual selection of grapes, plus some Cabernet Sauvignon, up the south-facing mountain slope hard against a deep gorge. Their Dôle shows a strong Gamay nose, although some underlying Pinot Noir is evident.

Also in Conthey is Jacques Germanier, the best-known producer of the sparkling version of Chardonnay.

Nearer Vétroz begins a region where some of the highest-regarded Amigne, the fine indigenous white wine grape, is produced. As is the case in virtually every other part of the canton, much Chasselas is also grown in the proximity of Vétroz, some of it rivaling the best of Sion. But the Amigne seems to have taken particularly well to Vétroz's gravelly, sunny soils. Vineyards cover 180 hectares in the commune around Vétroz, and the town is headquarters for producers such as Jean-Luc Putallaz and Marc Roh, both known for their Amigne; Les Fils de François Moren, producers of a solid Fendant at the Prieuré de Vétroz; Edmund Desfayes-Crettenand, whose scrupulously tended 3.5 hectare vineyard produces excellent Pinot Noir along with Humagne Blanc, Petite Arvine, Cornalin and Syrah; and Urbain Germanier of Bon Père Germanier, a firm actually better known for its popular fragrant *eau de vie Poire William* (pear brandy) than for its reputable range of wines. Germanier manages a very large holding of 180 hectares spread around the canton, including a good selection – Chasselas, Chardonnay, Malvoisie, Dôle Blanche, Dôle and Pinot Noir – from the highly regarded Balavaud vineyard just outside the village of Ardon. Their dry Amigne de Vétroz is pleasingly well-rounded and full.

Chamoson to Saillon

Following the route *du vignoble* from Vétroz to the town of Saillon, the road passes through a string of communes which produce some of the best known Chasselas-based Fendant wines of Valais. These include the communes of Ardon, Chamoson, Leytron and Saillon with, respectively, 135 hectares, 417 hectares, 259 hectares and 187 hectares of communal land planted with grapes. To give a sense of the quantity produced, the commune of Chamoson has as much land devoted to grapes as the entire canton of Neuchâtel. In Saillon, archeological evidence has uncovered grape cultivation dating back to Roman times, an historically important fact partially confirmed by the discovery of the oldest glass drinking vessel unearthed to date in the canton.

This length of the route is also home to many respected Valaisan producers such as Vincent Favre-Carruzzo and Maurice Favre in Chamoson; Simon Maye, René Favre and Albert Biollaz in St. Pierre-de-Clages; and Marc Raymond in Saillon. As one passes through these wine villages, the cellars of the local *vignerons-encaveurs* are immediately recognizable by the helpful and bright red and white signposts pointing the way.

Chamoson is a village thick with Favres. Vincent Favre-Carruzzo is certainly one of the better wine makers with this surname. Many of his wines, such as the Fendant de Chamoson, Chardonnay, Humagne Blanc, Humagne Rouge are sold under the name La Tornale. The Fendant is more than acceptable – spicy, forward and floral. A Humagne Rouge de Chamoson La Tornale, on the other hand, was fruity and forward but lacked a degree of the concentration that is one of the most attractive qualities of the Humagne Rouge. Total production from Favre-Carruzzo's 12-hectare estate is around 70,000 bottles.

From another Favre, this time Maurice, a Malvoisie, Selection Excelsus Chamoson has an enticing herbal nose. The complexity and texture come through on the taste, and the wine finishes dry, with good length. This Favre wine convincingly displays the dry, intense style that Malvoisie can produce. Favre's Petite Arvine de Chamoson is quite a mouthful – an alcoholic, almost aggressive, fruity, acidic, highly perfumed and ultimately memorable wine. His Cornalin is fruity, rustic and attractively simple. A third Favre, René, is recommended for Chardonnay and Johannisberg.

A fourth Chamoson wine producer with Favre in his surname is Jean-Claude Favre-Philippoz. His oak-aged Dôle demonstrates quite clearly what a wine from the lower Valaisan reaches of the Rhône can achieve. With a good colour, a forward strawberry nose, a touch of tannin and a hint of oak, this wine revels in the special attention it received.

A Chamoson wine maker marching to the beat of a different drummer is the more traditional François-Emmanuel Comby who still vinifies in large wooden barriques and bottles his Fendant under the label Domaine du Crêtacombe. Comby's oak-aged Muscat "La Pierre du Crêt" is an ideal aperitif. This fruity, almost sweet wine is well-balanced, enjoying a dry finish and good length.

The area below the village of Chamoson is the site of the Haut-de-Cry, an alluvial cone which forms a natural rock barrier to the passage of commerce along the banks of the Rhône river. The stone outcrop has, however, excellent exposure and consequently progressively has been planted with grapes. Just south of Chamoson is St. Pierre-de-Clages, site of one of the finest Romanesque buildings in the Valais, a 12th century church, whose vines were once the property of a now disappeared Benedictine priory. The nave of the church used to be set on a platform but the accumulation of debris over the years is such that one now descends down a set of steps to reach the church floor.

St. Pierre-de-Clages is also the headquarters for one of Switzerland's most highly respected *vignerons,* Simon Maye, one of three Maye families in St. Pierre. Simon Maye has been labeled the "Girardet of Valaisan viticulture" – a very complimentary pairing with Switzerland's famous chef, Fredy Girardet, also referred to above. There is no doubt whatsoever about the quality of the wines Simon Maye produces with his two sons Axel (responsible for the cellars) and Jean-François (responsible for the vines) from their eight hectares of vineyards. His annual production is 80,000 bottles spread across an entire range of wines. His output includes at least three Chasselas (Fauconnier, Trémazière and Moette – the latter a *"vin du côteau"* from the steep slopes near the Clos Balavaud); full bodied Johannisberg de Chamoson; superb dry and *mi-flétrie* Petite Arvine; rich Malvoisie *flétrie;* classic Valaisan Pinot Noir; full-bodied Humagne Rouge; and first-rate wines from Syrah. The Syrah are offered in both a regular and barrel-fermented versions, the latter from vines at least twelve years old. In some years the regular inox fermentation has such a depth of fruit and flavour from the Syrah that the additional complexities imparted by barrel fermentation almost seem superfluous. Maye's wines are always in very high demand, and some of the more limited bottlings are difficult, if not impossible, to obtain without directly contacting the winery. Every year the cellar must resort to quotas for some wines to ensure that even long-standing customers get a fair share of the output.

In 1990, the Swiss-German wine magazine *Vinum* organized the first "Swiss Cup" for Chasselas from the excellent 1989 vintage. Much to the delight of the Valaisans and to the undoubted horror of their Vaudois neighbours and competitors, extensive tastings awarded five of the eight finalist positions to wines from the Valais. The eventual winning wine was Maye's "Fauconnier", confirming what most *vignerons* already believed about the quality of wines produced by this outstanding cellar. Many would also consider Maye to be Switzerland's best producer of Syrah, even if quantities are still quite limited.

Other firms located in St. Pierre-de-Clages are Albert Biollaz and Daniel Magliocco, another producer of respectable Syrah, in addition to Johannisberg. Biollaz's Pinot Noir du Valais, Saint Empire Le Grand Schiner at first shows a light colour and agreeable nose with good fruit. The wine is more concentrated than its colour would suggest, and it exhibits both a clean taste and good length. Annual production of 140,000 bottles includes a full range of Valaisan varieties from

Fendant to Humagne Rouge. The cellars of the firm Maurice Gay and the Cave St. Pierre, whose wines have managed to carve out a niche in some international markets, are located just outside the village. Both these producers are controlled by the important wine concern Schenk, based in Vaud.

Nearby, in the vicinity of Leytron, is the 12-hectare nursery, Le Domaine du Grand-Brûlé. Established by the cantonal government after World War I, this vineyard has been home to many experiments beginning with the propagation of American root stocks to replace vines destroyed by the phylloxera louse. Other notable wine-makers in Leytron include Ulrich Devayes, a daring producer of the capricious Syrah.

Marc Raymond stands out as the exemplary vigneron of Saillon. With his son Gérard he cultivates a 3.5 hectare estate which produces just 40,000 bottles annually. His Fendant and Dôle Vieux Saillon are considered models of the wine makers' art and regional character. Needless to say, both sell out very quickly. Other wines from this superb estate include a Petite Arvine, Malvoisie, 100% Pinot Noir and, perhaps surprisingly, a Nebbiolo du Valais. Marc Raymond was one of the founding members of the Confrérie St. Théodule and was instrumental in developing the Pinot Valais strain of Pinot Noir which has shown itself to be particularly well-suited to the Valais.

Paul Briguet of Cave au Clos, and Jean-Luc Cheseaux, are other Saillon producers worth searching out. The former sells 50,000 bottles a year across a full range, while the latter is known especially for his Humagne Rouge.

The World's Smallest Vineyard

One of Saillon's claims to fame besides the Bayard Tower, and some of the best-known Fendant in Valais, is title to the smallest officially recognized and registered vineyard in Switzerland, and probably the world – three vines, one plant each of Chasselas, Pinot Noir and Petit Arvine, on exactly 1.67 square meters. The selection represents the *crème de la crème* of the vines of Valais. This vineyard was presented in 1984 by the authorities of Saillon to the respected French actor Jean-Louis Barrault and his wife, Madeleine Renaud, who co-starred in the 1945 classic French movie, *"Les Enfants du Paradis"* (The Children of Paradise). The vineyard may be small, but it attracts a lot of press attention which blankets the gathering of the harvest.

Riddes

Across the river from Leytron is Riddes, headquarters for the firm Les Fils Maye, a traditional and typical Valaisan producer whose best holdings are the steep, gravely slopes back across the Rhône on the right bank at Clos de Balavaud. In many ways, the development of this firm demonstrates the growth of a traditional Valaisan wine company. Founded in 1889 by Léonide Maye immediately after the phylloxera debacle, the company headquarters was located in Riddes to take advantage of the rail line on the south side of the Rhône. The tracks for the railway, unfortunately, did not extend to the north side of the river as far as the vineyards of Saillon or Ardon. But Maye realized earlier than most the importance of access to transportation routes. Today the firm of Maye purchases much of its wines from smaller producers throughout the canton, which it ages in its cellars prior to bottling or selling in bulk. Unlike many firms of its size in Switzerland, it is not a wine importer. In days past, 70% of production used to be sold directly to restaurants, but today that figure has fallen to 30% with the rest now bottled for retail sale. Although exports are small, some of Maye's wine does find its way to Germany. 1989 was the first year that Maye produced more red wine than white, again reflecting the wine makers' response to changing consumer demand. Some of the grapes are still fermented in wood, although the majority of wines are now vinified in lined cement vats. Throughout the bountiful decade of the 1980s, harvests were generally good; if sugar levels were high enough, chaptalization was not used to strengthen the firm's Fendant. Grapes are pressed using a centrifuge to avoid the effects of gray rot. The traditional standard yield for Fendant at Maye is 1.4 kilograms of grapes per square meter. When sugar levels are not high enough, the wine can be declassified to "Chasselas de Romandie," and production can rise to 1.6 kilos per square meter, although the introduction of the revised cantonal AOC regulations is likely eventually to change these informal production limitations.

Maye's excellently-situated Clos de Balavaud vineyard has a layout that is anything but simple. This vineyard is located near the village of Ardon on the right bank. Moving up the slope it reads like a viticultural map of Valais: Pinot Noir, followed by Chasselas; Petite Arvine, superseded by Ermitage (Marsanne); Amigne and Chasselas, followed by Païen, Petite Arvine, topped again by Chasselas, followed again by Petite Arvine, Amigne and Chasselas. And at the top is a plot of Malvoisie. Every usable level of the slope is cultivated to the best advantage, but the layout does not necessarily produce logical and easily identifiable groupings of different vines.

Maye's standard Fendant is bottled under the label "Grandgousier". Wines from this producer are generally straight forward, clean and fresh. Their basic Chasselas is well-made, although rarely exciting. However, at times, certain of Maye's wines can be surprisingly unstructured, displaying a good nose but lacking concentration. This is unfortunate because all the ingredients of a superior wine are evident but not brought together.

Fully

The region from Saillon to Branson, passing through the village of Fully, includes the last series of vineyards on the right bank of the Rhône before the river is forced by the surrounding mountains to turn almost ninety degrees at Martigny, on its way towards Lake Geneva. Branson is the end of the *route du vignoble* on the right bank in Valais. Between Saillon and the end of the Valais vineyards, Fully is the most important wine-producing village and headquarters for firms such as Eloi and Gérard Roduit and Adrian Bender. The town of Fully, at the base of the towering *massif* Grand Chavalard, is surrounded by a virtual sea of vines. Chasselas, in particular, dominates the terraced slopes, while well-regarded Gamay lower down is blended with up-river Pinot Noir to produce Dôle. 345 hectares of land in the commune of Fully produce wines.

Eloi and Gérard Roduit at Cave de Liandaz in Fully are known as careful and conscientious wine makers. Their Petite Arvine and Humagne Blanc are particularly well-regarded. Interestingly, they occasionally produce two different versions of their successful Ermitage: one with the standard Marsanne Blanche grape and the other using the Roussanne (Altesse) grape. Another Fully star is Marie-Thérèse Chappaz known for her Gamay de Saillon, and for her Fendant, Ermitage, Petite Arvine and Pinot Noir under the label Président Troillet from the Domaine des Claives. She cultivates 3.5 hectares in total.

Returning briefly to the left bank of the Rhône, isolated patches of vines continue to be found after Riddes on the route towards Saxon, one of the few Valaisan villages still physically able to expand its vineyard area in recent years. Unfortunately, the wines are generally less rich than their right bank counterparts. At Charrat, at the base of the Pierre-à-Voir, a small holding of Gamay is intermingled with apricot orchards.

Martigny

The *route des vins* of Valais virtually ends at the left-bank city of Martigny, a town more important as a commercial and transportation center than for its grape production. This is the ancient Roman city of Octodurum and the site of some of Switzerland's most impressive Roman ruins which today are partly enclosed within the manicured grounds of the contemporary art and automobile museum, *"Fondation Pierre Gianadda"*. Martigny is the northern starting point for passage across the St. Bernard Pass into Italy. This fact alone ensured its historical importance. It remains the headquarters of several large wine companies such as Caves Orsat and Cave de la Bâtiaz. Grape-growing terraces are found to the west of the city in the hamlets of la Combe and Plan-Cressier. La Combe is headquarters to Gérald Besse who produces some of the best Gamay in the canton, while Plan-Cerisier borders the south-facing slopes that line the winding road westward towards the Forclaz Pass and eventually on to France and Chamonix.

Most of the standard bottlings of Caves Orsat, a company that has had its financial ups and downs over the years, are unlikely to leave much of an impression. Such a wine is the mass-market oriented Eden Rose, Rosé du Valais. The wine can be thin, a touch acidic and lacking in fruit. Happily this is not the case for the company's premier line, Primus Classicus. Their dry-style Malvoisie du Valais Primus Classicus displays both good body and weight, accompanied by a floral nose. Other wines in this series have received similarly positive reviews.

The wines from the Cave de la Bâtiaz outside Martigny are generally straightforward and scented with limited depth, but enjoy reasonable balance and length.

Beyond Martigny, minor holdings can be found in the towns between the city and the eastern end of Lake Geneva, such as near the ancient abbey at St. Maurice as well as in Monthey, Vionnaz and Vouvry. The production of these wines, however refreshing they may be, is almost exclusively for local consumption.

Provins

The cooperative Provins merits a separate entry because of the group's influential role in the wine production of Valais. Provins produces almost one in three bottles from Valais and an amazing one of every seven bottles in Switzerland. As might be expected from a large cooperative, Provins produces its fair share of forgettable wines, much of it ending up in crown-capped liter bottles and half-liter "pots" meant for immediate consumption. But Provins is, thankfully, more than just a volume producer and merits this added attention because of its reputation as the most quality-conscious of the major cantonal-based wine cooperatives in Switzerland.

This Valais cooperative was founded during the difficult years of the depression of the 1930s. Today its four production centers group together some 5,400 grape growers from throughout the canton. Provins is not only the marketing arm for the Valais cooperative, it is also responsible for important education and training programs for growers (including soil analysis and technology updates); for signing and supervising growing contracts *(contracts de culture);* and for managing an experimental plot for its own research purposes. 70% of the cooperative's total production is bottled while the other 30% is sold in bulk.

Although some of the more independent individual producer/bottlers criticize Provins for being too big to hope to achieve more than the lowest common denominator, there is a commendable emphasis on quality. This can be traced back to initiatives such as the *"capsule dorée"* program began in 1945 and copied from the German system of different capsules and bands for higher grades. This program rewards producers of better quality grapes for Fendant, Johannisberg and Dôle, with not only a visible recognition but also a higher price for the raw grapes based on both weight and maturity.

Such commendations can be won only by consistent attention to quality. And they can also be lost. Moreover, Provins has nurtured a full range of Valaisan *specialités,* vital symbols of the canton's unique viticultural history. More recently, responding to continuing consumer pressures for prestige bottlings, the company has begun to market several different series of limited-production wines including, Vins des Celliers de l'Evêché de Sion, Le Maître de Chais and their top-line Sélection du Grand Métral which reflect the supreme skills of the Provins wine makers.

Provins also enjoys a distribution of their wines well beyond the Swiss borders. For example, the most common Fendants outside Switzerland are probably Provins' Pierrafeu and Robert Gilliard's Fendant de Sion, Les Murettes. The standard Provins wine is usually very straightforward – a solid and at times almost stolid wine, slightly acidic but well and cleanly made, and certainly refreshing to drink. Among the specialty wines, probably the most readily obtainable Malvoisies are Provins' ordinary bottling or the more exclusive Malvoisie du Valais, Roxane. The equivalent Muscat is their specially-selected La Treille des Césars which, when young, demonstrates a characteristic floral nose with a typically rich Muscat taste. Although basically clean and well-made, a Provins Muscat tasted two years after harvest was beginning to loose its freshness, if not its unique Muscat nose.

The higher-quality *capsule dorée* series Marsanne is labeled Les Chapelles, Ermitage du Valais. It does not have as full a nose as some other Valaisan wines made from the Marsanne, but it shows fruit and concentration, although without much length.

Given its restricted production, it is particularly difficult to find the Humagne Blanc outside of the Valais. Again, probably the most accessible is the Provins selection, the Humagne Blanche du Valais, Chandeleur.

Provins will also bottle for other concerns. When the national grocery chain Co-op launched a series of Swiss wines to celebrate the 700th anniversary of Swiss confederation in 1991, at least two of these wines, a 1990 Oeil-de-Perdrix du Valais Rosé de Pinot Noir and a 1990 Gamay d'Ardon Coteaux du Valais, were from Provins. The rosé has a light but pleasing pink colour, with some fruit on the nose, but not great depth. It would serve admirably as a refreshing afternoon drink, exactly what one would want and expect from a wine in which the Pinot Noir grapes have been macerated for twenty-four hours and then pressed before being transferred to vats for fermentation. On the other hand, the comparatively rare 100% Gamay displayed a fruity, Gamay character, although it lacks some of the balance and freshness found in a good Beaujolais.

In addition to Provins' numerous different bottlings of red Dôle, a white Dôle Blanche, "Angeline" is sold. It is a light, almost *oeil-de-perdrix* colour, with a restrained nose and a sharp, but pleasant taste. Not unreasonably, it can be compared to a Beaujolais blanc, although the acid level of the Beaujolais is usually higher.

Not to be outdone by the other Valaisan producers, Provins also has its Humagne Rouge du Valais, L'Aubépine, a somewhat more straightforward uni-dimensional wine than the Humagne Rouge of some of the other specialized producers. It does have the definite advantage that it is relatively easy to find.

For a cooperative cellar, Provins produces a remarkable range of wines reflecting the full diversity of grapes grown in the canton. The above is just a small sampling of the wines marketed by the cooperative. Its full range would take the better part of a separate book to review. Even though its output may not always be as exciting or as individualistic as the boutique wineries or specialty producers, with the exception of the low-end bulk wines, it is rare to find a truly bad bottle of wine from Provins. In fact some of Provins offerings, although harder to find because of limited production, can be quite exceptional.

Useful addresses in the Valais:

Office de promotion des produits de l'agriculture valaisanne (OPAV), Avenue de la Gare 5, 1950 Sion; (027) 322 22 47

Wine Museum

Musée valaisan de la vigne et du vin, Château de Villa, 4 rue Sainte-Catherine, Sierre (027) 455 85 35.

Recommended Wine makers:

Gérald Besse, Les Rappes, 1921 Martigny-Combe (026) 722 78 81: Known particularly for his excellent Gamays.

Charles Bonvin Fils, Grand-Champsec 30, 1951 Sion (027) 203 41 31: Producer of interesting specialty wines, as well as holder of recognized important vineyards.

Oskar Chanton SA, Kantonsstrasse 2, 3930 Visp (027) 946 21 53: The specialist in the ancient varieties of the Haut Valais.

Gérald Clavien, Cave Les Deux Crêtes, 3972 Miège, Sierre (027) 455 57 13: A well-regarded producer of solid if austere wines.

Michel Clavien, Domaine de Chatroz, 1962 Pont de la Morge (027) 346 20 17: Certainly one of the most stylish and influential producers of Valais. Excellent quality.

Robert Gilliard SA, Rue du Dent-Blanche, 1951 Sion (027) 323 39 21: Producers of some of the best-known and widely-available wines from Valais. Fendant Les Murettes is particularly good.

Mathier-Kuchler, 3970 Salquenen (027) 455 14 34: Pinot Noir specialists. Their Reserve des Chevaliers wines are especially fine.

Simon Maye et Fils, Route de Collombey 3, 1956 St. Pierre-de-Clages (027) 306 41 81: Recognized as one of the finest producers in all of Switzerland. Maye's best wines are difficult to obtain without direct contact with the cellar.

Domaine du Mont d'Or SA, Route de Savoie, 1962 Pont-de-la-Morge (027) 346 20 32: Sion: Producers of a wide range of quality wines from well-exposed terraces. Top wines are great; lower quality can be uneven.

Château Ravire, 3960 Sierre (027) 455 01 54: Vigneron-Châtelain Michel Savioz produces some of the more exotic wines of Valais. Inconsistent at times, but definitely worth trying.

Marc Raymond & Fils, 1913 Saillon (026) 744 21 96: Excellent producer of a range of typical Valais wines from his Vieux Saillon vineyard.

Bernard Rouvinez, Colline de Géronde, 3960 Sierre (027) 455 66 61: One of the finer producers of the Sion region. Good, deep wines from his Géronde vineyards complement superb blended creations.

St. Jodern-Kellerei, 3932 Vispertermin (027) 946 46 41 46: A cooperative whose wines are worth searching out for their uniqueness and quality under difficult conditions.

Reynard & Varone, Vins Fins, 1965 Ormône-Savièse (027) 395 25 45: Very interesting wines with lots of local flavour. Try the Reserve Humagne Rouge if it ever presents itself.

Maurice Zufferey Chemin des Moulins 52, 3964 Sierre/Muraz (027) 455 47 16: One of the most respected vignerons in all Switzerland. Elegant wines with presence.

Cooperative

Provins, Rue de l'Industrie 22, 1951 Sion (027) 321 21 41: Producers of a truly remarkable range of wines. Lower end is easily avoidable. Better wines can be very good and true to type.

VII

Vaud, including Fribourg

The Region and its Wines

The canton of Vaud contains some of the world's most scenic wine villages. This region is also home to some of Switzerland's historically famous vineyards whose wines are among the most sought after in the country. Vaud is almost the geographical center of the French-speaking *Suisse romande,* and is surrounded by the cantons of Valais, Fribourg, Geneva and Neuchâtel. Its vineyards radiate to the east, west and north from Lausanne, the terraced capital of the canton. To the east, Vaud stretches beyond Montreux and the eastern end of Lake Geneva *(Lac Léman)* to the communes of Aigle, Ollon and Bex; to the west, its borders end at the canton and city of Geneva. And to the north, the canton spills across the major European watershed which divides the Rhine and Rhône river drainage systems, to the shores of the Lakes of Neuchâtel and Morat.

Until the mid-20th century, Vaud was the largest wine-producing canton of Switzerland. Today it is second only to Valais. Three-quarters of its total production is white; most of the remainder is red with some limited amounts of rosé. Total output of wine in 1995 was 279,390 hectolitres of white wine; 83,240 hectolitres of red wine; and 24 hectolitres from the remaining hybrids for a total of 362,654 hectolitres (36 million litres). This volume is produced from the 3,818 grape-producing hectares of land in the canton. Production in 1990 and 1992 was slightly higher with 44.8 million litres and 39.3 million litres respectively. The ten-year average from 1981 to 1990 was 41 million litres. As was generally the case in Switzerland, 1988, 1989, 1990, 1992, 1994 and 1995 have been the most successful vintages of recent years.

Of equal note, however, is that Vaud has the highest average production per given acreage by a considerable margin. In 1991, the average yield for whites was 117 hectolitres per hectare and a remarkable 134 hectolitres per hectare for red. In 1994 the average for whites fell back to 109 hectolitres per hectare and the red average dropped even more to 84 hectolitres per hectare but such elevated production figures point to a potential problem – Swiss industriousness is a mixed blessing if overproduction leads to a decrease in quality.

If the wines of Valais are a virtual symphony of different varieties, the output of Vaud more closely resembles "variations upon a single theme", with occasional supporting harmonies. The overriding theme is a neutral one, but very Swiss – the

Chasselas. This grape provides, on average, 99% of the canton's white wine and nearly 80% of the total output. The canton's geology provides the raw material, in particular a soil attuned to the grape's qualities, which allows disciplined growers and skilled wine makers to encourage the Chasselas to achieve its best. As one experienced Vaudois authority observed: "if the Valais is marked by the sun, temperature and choice of grape, the Vaud is marked by the soil".

A good Vaudois Chasselas is the quintessential Swiss wine. At its best, Vaudois white wine is as good as any produced in Switzerland. It is fresh, perhaps slightly *petillant* with hints of smoke, flint and gunpowder over underlying fruit; slightly acidic but still well-balanced; not great length but with a clean, dry finish. It is wine meant to be drunk for pleasure and to be enjoyed usually within a year or two after harvest. Some Vaudois wines, however, are capable of sustaining greater aging while others, unfortunately, suffer from the pitfall of overproduction.

The Lavaux area of Vaud is the historical center of Swiss wine-making and in the first rank in terms of quality. Here the history of the great ecclesiastical estates stretches back over a millennium. Although certain wine makers in Valais might quibble, the producers in the most prized sites of Lavaux and Chablais remain very secure in their belief that they consistently produce the world's finest wine made from the Chasselas grape. The neutrality of the grape seems particularly well-suited to the gravely, terraced soils of the better exposed slopes. When produced with care, the wines will reflect the slightly burnt, flinty, velvety, concentrated fruit characteristics for which this grape is known.

While the leading Vaudois vineyards have a national reputation, the same cannot be said for much of the more mundane Chasselas-based wine produced throughout the canton. In a marketing effort to create a Vaudois version of the successful "Fendant" of the Valais, Vaudois Chasselas was for a while called the "Dorin". This was an attempt to give greater consumer appeal to well-made wines which, although they did not have the right to a particular *appellation,* were better than *vin de table.* The name, however, never really took hold and the designation Dorin has ceased to be used.

Other white wine grapes such as Chardonnay, Pinot Gris and Pinot Blanc produce the remaining one percent of white wine. In addition, some Riesling x Sylvaner is grown in cooler Bonvillars, Côtes de l'Orbe and Vully areas. The basic grapes for the Vaudois red wines are the Gamay (14% of total production) and the Pinot Noir (five percent). They are often combined to make the Vaud's signature red wine, the Salvagnin. In the 18th century the Salvagnin existed as a separate, native grape variety. Over time, the original grape has disappeared but the name remained in use for Vaudois red wines. In 1960 the name "Salvagnin" was reserved by cantonal decree for a wine made from Gamay and Pinot Noir grapes, grown separately but vinified together. In order to be labeled as "Salvagnin" the wine must pass a cantonal taste test. The equivalent quality designation for white wines is "Terravin" which must also undergo a taste test. This mark of quality is being promoted by the Vaudois Federation of Vignerons, but it is not yet widely seen.

The canton is divided into four major wine regions. Beginning in the east, first is the Chablais (not to be confused with the Chablis), which starts at the border with Valais and follows the north-west direction of the Rhône until the river expands into

The vineyards of Vaud

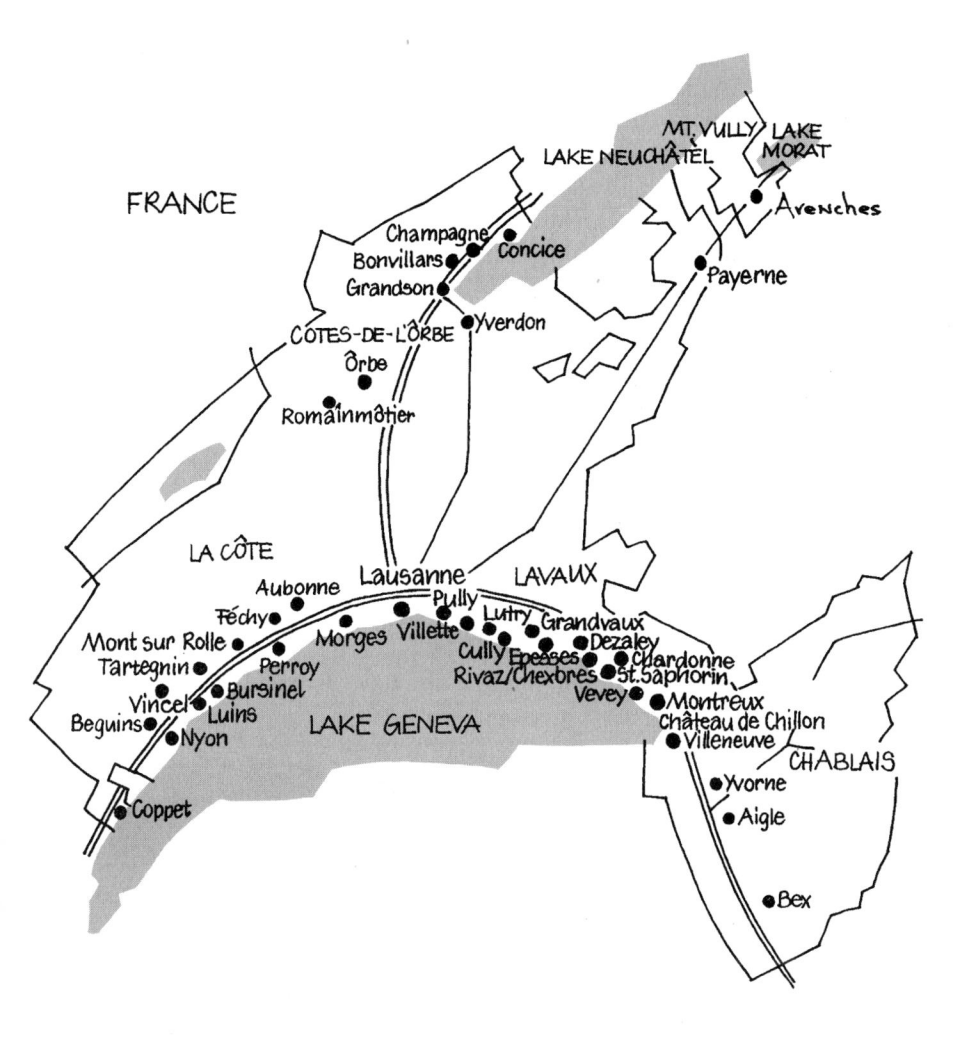

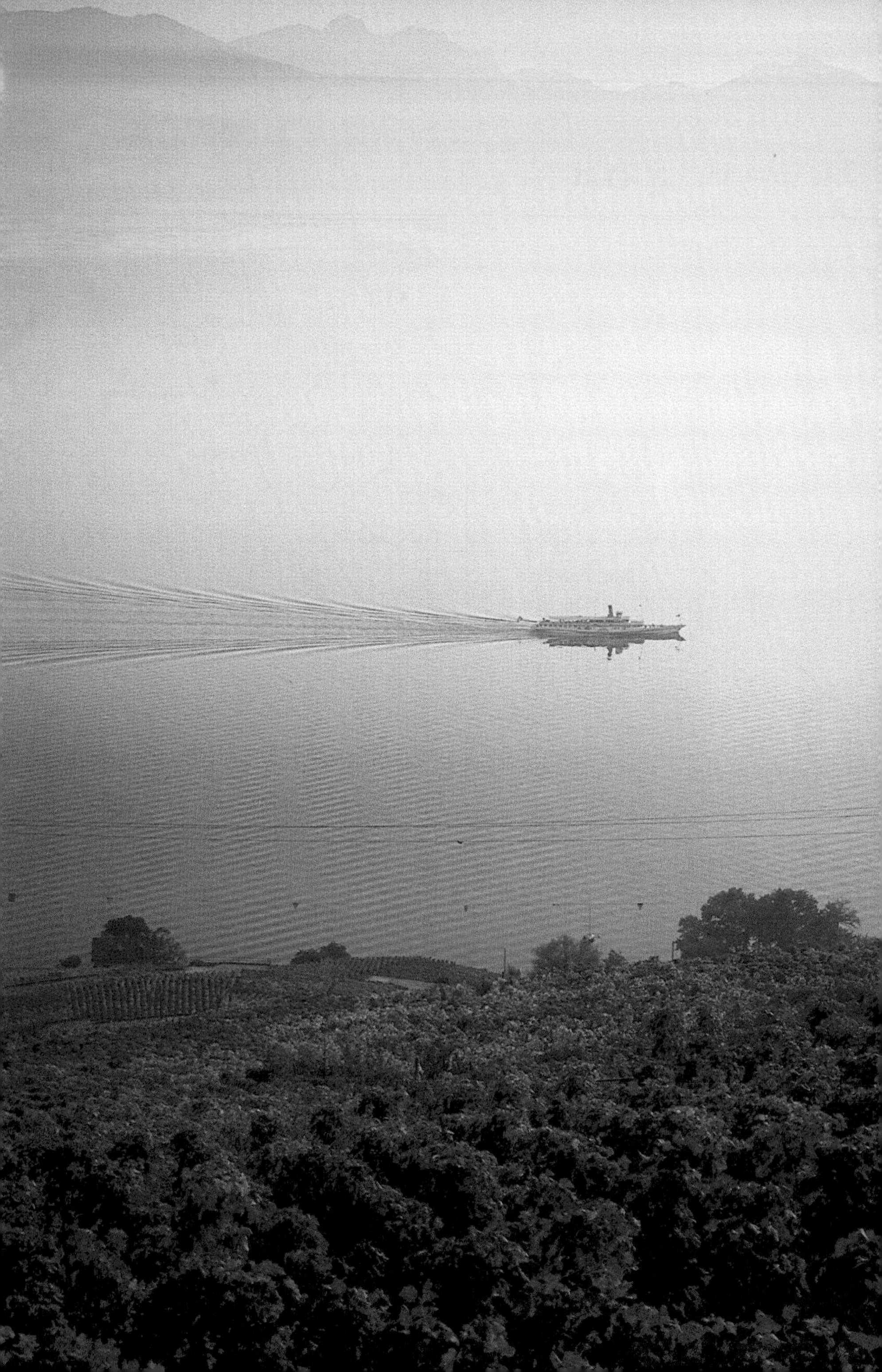

Lake Geneva near the town of Villeneuve. Around 550 hectares, producing 15% of the canton's wine, are planted with grapes across five separate *appellations* (Bex, Ollon, Aigle, Yvorne, and Villeneuve).

The second area stretches from Montreux, a city famous both for its jazz festival and Mediterranean micro-climate, to the eastern limits of Lausanne. This is the Lavaux which is for many the pinnacle of the Vaud hierarchy and home to some of the most highly-prized vineyards in the country. Lavaux boasts six separate *appellations* (Vevey-Montreux, Chardonne, St. Saphorin, Epesses, Villette, Lutry), along with two special "crus" (Dézaley and Calamin), and almost 800 hectares devoted to growing wine grapes. Average production is one-fifth of the canton's total.

The third area is La Côte which begins at the western limits of the city of Lausanne and stretches to the border between the cantons of Vaud and Geneva. It is physically the largest of the Vaud wine regions with over 1900 hectares of grapes and 12 separate appellations (in more or less geographical order from east to west: Morges, Aubonne, Perroy, Féchy, Mont-sur-Rolle, Tartegnin, Côteau de Vincy, Vinzel, Bursinel, Luins, Begnins and Nyon). La Côte produces just under 55% of all Vaudois wine. Together the three Vaudois regions that border the Rhône and Lake Geneva produce 90% of the canton's total.

The fourth wine-producing region is the most northern and smallest, and includes vineyards located at the western end of Lake Neuchâtel as well as those around Lake Morat. It contains only 300 hectares of vines and three *appellations*: Côtes de l'Orbe, Bonvillars and Vully. Although Vully is usually lumped together with the other two for convenience sake, its 35 hectares of vines are situated between Lakes Neuchâtel and Morat, physically quite separate. Only six districts in the Vaud grow no grapes at all. The special characteristics of the commune include a climate averaging around 10°C in most of the vine growing areas. Vaud is affected by all three of the major European weather systems; the Atlantic, the Mediterranean and the eastern steppes. It also has the fewest days of frost and fog in all Switzerland. Lake Geneva provides a permanent moderating influence on the climate, softening any extremes and providing the reflected heat which is so important for achieving full grape maturity. However, the visual impression left by the vineyards changes dramatically as one moves from the mountain-backed slopes of Chablais to the precipitous terraces of Lavaux, and then to the softer, rolling hills of La Côte.

The Grand Council of the canton has defined where vines may be planted in Vaud, and new plantings of vines are prohibited outside of the area designated appropriate for wine grapes. The current *appellation d'origine* system is moving towards a stricter *appellation d'origine contrôlée* regime. Currently there are three levels of appellation: regional, such as Lavaux, La Côte or Chablais; communal, if the wine all comes from a particular commune such as Yvorne, Epesses or Mont-sur-Rolle; and finally a name denoting a group of communes, such as St.-Saphorin or Villette, if the communes are contiguous and produce a similar wine. Place names such as Dézaley, or designations such as "cru", can only be used if they are

Twilight in the Lavaux vineyards at Cully.

registered as such in the communal land registry *(cadastre)* and the wine comes exclusively from the named area. As is the case elsewhere in Switzerland, the use of "cru" or "grand cru" on a label is not necessarily a denotation of quality *per se*, and can lead to some confusion.

The Vaudois wine industry includes 30-40 medium to large négociants (55%-60% of total production), 17 associations and cooperatives (30%), and around 1,500 individual growers and producers (10%-15%).

The Vineyards

The Chablais Region

At the heart of the Chablais area are the great vineyards in the communes of Yvorne and Aigle. Beginning, however, at the border between the Valais and the Vaud, the first vineyards encountered are those of Bex, a village known for its ancient salt mine as much as for its wines. The historical Chablais covered a much greater area, stretching from the thermal town of Thonon, now in France on the south side of Lake Geneva, to the city of Vevey, now part of the Lavaux. Today the Chablais is concentrated around the district of Aigle where the Rhône valley, guarded on both the French and Swiss sides of the river by imposing alpine peaks, eventually expands to form Lake Geneva. The name Chablais is derived from the Latin *"caput laci"* or "head of the lake".

In general, the wines of the Chablais are known for their bouquet, structure and balance. The climate throughout the region is temperate, characterized by little fog, few frosts, early springs and long summers. In the fall, the Swiss sporting and gastronomic passion for hunting comes to the fore. The season of *la Chasse* often occurs simultaneously with the grape harvest. It is not uncommon here to see hunters scouring the fields for rabbits attracted by the sweet ripe grapes left behind by the pickers.

Bex and Ollon

The wines of Bex are largely consumed locally and do not often find their way to outside markets. They are known for a flowery bouquet, and those from south-facing terraces take much of their structure from the limestone and gypsum found in the soils. A slightly bitter finish marks the better whites, while the reds, both Pinot Noir and Gamay, will keep for a while without deteriorating. The nearby picturesque village of Chêne is also known for producing agreeable, local wines with some degree of subtlety. Here vines grow up to 700 meters, among the highest in the canton.

Bex is home to the Domaine des Caillettes of Jean-Louis Ambresin whose solid Philos wines are sold in stylish elegant bottles. His whites show a good Chasselas nose, slight acidity and moderate length. The reds, Gamay and Pinot

Winter near Bex in the Chablais region.

Noir bottled separately, are both quite light but show good characteristics of the grapes from which they are produced. A second, and perhaps even better known wine maker in Bex is Pierre-Alain Indermühle who produces a full range of wines from his five hectare Cave de Cimes vineyard. In addition to two distinct Chasselas, Indermühle bottles several different Pinot Noirs, one of which, Le Solitaire, is oak-aged.

The district of Ollon is a more important wine-growing area. For some the wines of Ollon recall roses and resin. At times they demonstrate a "chewy" character. They are comparatively well-structured and solid. The village of Antagnes, perched on the hillside overlooking its vines and the Rhône valley, marks the dividing line between Bex and Ollon. Below Antagnes, at the foot of the hill, is the ancient Abbey of Salaz, originally founded in 1014 A.D. by the Burgundian king Rudolphe III, and known particularly for its red wines. The village of Ollon is surrounded by vines which rise in the shape of an amphitheater from the plain below until they can climb no more. Several plots of Sylvaner are grown here, producing wines which are notable for the aroma of nuts. The Chasselas, however, remains the *cépage* of choice for the whites. More recently Pinot Noir and Gamay have been introduced into the district with some success. Vers-Chiez on the hillside and St. Triphon on the plain are two other towns known for wines produced in the surrounding vineyards.

The wines of Ollon often carry the notation "District d'Aigle" on their labels. It is an area where a considerable amount of generic Chasselas is made for the restaurant trade. One of the more common wines is L'Oisemont, bottled by Jean-

Michel Conne of Chexbres, a firm more known for its wines from the region of Lavaux. In addition, Henri Badoux of Aigle (see below) bottles a single-vineyard Chasselas and Pinot Noir from their five-hectare estate, the Domaine Grange Volet. The slope of this terraced vineyard reaches 46°.

Aigle

The striking Château d'Aigle is an ancient stronghold built on a rocky outcrop, well situated to control the movement of peoples and commerce on the Rhône plain which spreads out immediately below the Château's ramparts. Today its task is much more prosaic, for its thick walls enclose and protect the informative wine museum for the canton of Vaud. The Château is the heart of today's Chablais region. The current castle was begun by the Dukes of Savoie in the 12th century, and there are traces of earlier habitations on the same site which date back another two thousand years, including a Ligurian bronze smelter, Celtic place names, a Roman aqueduct and a Burgundian cemetery. In the 13th century the "Savoyard" court, enclosed by four imposing towers, was added to the original fortress. The Château used to be the property of the House of Savoie, a family which reached its zenith in the 15th century. But following the Convention of Fribourg in 1476 the Château and the district of Aigle became the property of the government of Berne which

Chateau d'Aigle, home to the Museum of the Vine and Wine.

governed Aigle until the Vaudois Revolution of 1798. The Château itself was burned and rebuilt during the period of domination by the "foreign" Bernois.

Immediately prior to its transformation into a museum, the Château served as a communal prison. In 1976 the fortress opened its doors as the "Musée de la vigne et du vin" (Museum of the Vine and Wine), the most complete wine museum in Switzerland. Visible from the freeway by cars rushing towards the Alpine ski resorts of Verbier, Zermatt and Crans-Montana, the Château and its collection are well worth a visit. The museum holds some 5,000 items connected with the development of wine in Switzerland, although the accent is very much on Vaud.

The collection includes impressive 400-year old wooden grape presses and fermentation casks; numerous religious sculptures and delicate glass decanters; historic wine labels and everyday measuring and drinking vessels demonstrating the extent to which wine is an integral part of traditional Swiss culture. A visit to the Château, stoically anchored in the midst of a sea of vines, is almost indispensable to a complete appreciation of the importance of wine in Swiss life.

Together with the wines of Yvorne, those of Aigle are the best wines of the Chablais. The gravelly, clay-soil vineyards of these two communes produce wines which are remarkably similar in weight and style and are recognized immediately throughout Switzerland. The best examples are well-concentrated, fruity, spicy with a good acid balance and, in good years, can be laid down beneficially for a year or two. In fact, at their best, the wines of Aigle and Yvorne are among the very top Swiss wines – their reputation in Vaud only equalled or exceeded by the very finest of Lavaux vineyards.

The white Aigle wines should show good berry fruit on the nose and have a sufficiently acidic backbone. At times a touch of caramel can be detected on the nose. The better wines demonstrate a certain restrained elegance. The more poetic have evoked "burnt stone" to describe Aigle wines. In general, it is difficult to find a bad white Aigle, although variations between producers can be very evident, and it is possible to pay too much for the cachet that comes with a particular name. The red wines of Aigle, as those more recently introduced in Ollon, are developing a reasonable reputation.

The quaint town of Aigle is headquarters for the well-regarded firm of Henri Badoux. Its widely-marketed white wine, Les Murailles, with its quirky salamander on the label, comes from the steeply terraced vineyards that climb the hills behind the village and Château. This is a well-structured, rounded wine with a pleasant bitterness on the taste. In total the firm owns some fifty hectares of land and produces around one of every five bottles of wine from the Chablais region. In addition to Aigle, Badoux vineyards are located in some of the best sites of Yvorne, Ollon and Villeneuve. The firm also owns the Domaine de Charmigny in St. Saphorin in Lavaux and purchases wines from other areas to complete its product line. The firm's signature red, also from Aigle, Pourpre Monseigneur, is grown in a well-exposed vineyard that is in fact an extension of the slopes of Yvorne. The wine is 100% Pinot Noir and presents a harmonious nose, good fruit and weight, some tannin and reasonable length. The Monseigneur will continue to improve and therefore will benefit from some cellaring.

Although the winery doesn't explicitly follow the "integrated production" approach promoted by certain grape growers, Badoux interferes as little as possible with natural processes. The firm attempts to let the vines concentrate their energy in the grapes through the use of low gobelet pruning. Output is restrained, particularly on the better slopes, although the firm's Chasselas on the flat plains has been allowed to produce up to 1.5 kilograms per square meter.

Similar to the more far-sighted wine makers of Valais, the firm of Badoux is very much concerned about the prospects of the Swiss wine industry. Badoux is fully aware that the future of Swiss wines can only be secured if the wine makers and, in their case, wine-marketers, can identify and sustain a demand for a certain quality of particular Swiss wines. The introduction of the *appellation* system will help, especially as it increasingly takes hold at the commune and village levels.

Nonetheless, Badoux is pessimistic about the future of the Vaudois Pinot Noir/Gamay blend, the Salvagnin, partly because it has not successfully established a solid and individual niche. Like many of the other better-situated producers in the Vaud, the firm does not lament the demise of the "Dorin" classification for generic Chasselas. From their perspective, lumping together under a single name the best wines of the Chablais and Lavaux with some of the less disciplined or outlying regions, was only inviting confusion and trouble. Badoux is one of the few Swiss wine firms to begin consciously marketing their wines in North America. Results to date are limited, but educational efforts have been made along the eastern American seaboard. As a result, it is possible to find some of their wines in Boston, New York and elsewhere.

Among the smaller growers, the Crosex Grillé "Grand Cru" from Paul Tille has an extremely good reputation. This wine demonstrates a fine complex nose with scents of flowers and spices, and has a good acid balance. It finishes well with excellent length. Other wine makers in Aigle who enjoy a good reputation are Henri Lagnaz and Pierre-André Baud. Both concentrate mainly on Chasselas and Pinot Noir, and produce a more limited range of wines totaling 25,000-30,000 bottles annually.

Many other the large producers and bottlers in Vaud either purchase or own some production in Aigle. The Aigle selection from the Hammel firm of Rolle in La Côte is bottled under the name Erminette and generally provides reasonable fruit and complexity. The Cuvée du Comte Pierre from the large firm of Fonjallaz in Epesses can unfortunately be less spicy than one would hope from an Aigle, and it perhaps suffers from overproduction. The firm Obrist in Vevey, a subsidiary of Schenk in Rolle, bottles its Aigle under the name Les Délices, with the intriguing sub-title "Le Jardin de Délices"! The wine can certainly be pleasant, although perhaps at times not quite concentrated enough to entice the Eve on the label. It shows a good bite, a touch of smoke and good quality. Finally, the Association Vinicole of Aigle produces a well-structured wine with good fruit and some depth which goes under the name of Les Plantailles.

Yvorne

The vineyards of Aigle merge naturally into those of the neighbouring village of Yvorne. On the route from Aigle through Yvorne the road passes the site of the famous 1584 Ovaille landslide, the debris of which, in the shape of a vast cone, is still evident. The landslide turned the entire surrounding countryside of villages and vines into a virtual moonscape. It was not until 1609 that the village was re-established and the vines replanted on the manganese-rich soil which now extends outside the commune proper. The nearby commune of Corbeyrier, where these new vines were planted nearly 400 years ago, produces its "grand vin d'Yvorne" under the name of "Ovaille" to commemorate the landslide.

Yvorne, not surprisingly, is known for its Chasselas, enhanced by the *goût du terroir* provided by the high manganese content of the soil. The vineyards face due south towards the Rhône and, consequently, have a particularly good sun exposure and can reap maximum benefit from the warm foehn winds. Yvorne, like Aigle, produces full-bodied and "masculine" wines which are among the best-regarded in the entire country. Attributes of the wines of Yvorne include the scent of hazelnuts, peaches and apricots.

Not everyone, however, has remarked on the masculine attributes of the wines from Yvorne. In a charming post-war description, again from H. Warren Allen in 1952, he observed:

> "Longevity and splendor, however, are not to be expected from the vineyards planted within sight of the glacier source of the river before it has become French. Aigle in the upper valley of the Rhône gave me my first revelation of mountains and I remembered its Yvorne wine so light and deliciously flower-scented as the best Swiss wine that ever came my way, until only the other day when André Simon introduced me at the Connaught Hotel to a white Neuchâtel, a most charming master of ceremonies to introduce a fine Château Pavie from 1924 .... Yvorne in my boyhood stood for the ne plus ultra of refreshing and pleasurable sensations at the end of a long day's walking and climbing."

Although there may be other contenders for the best vineyard of the commune, the Domaine de l'Ovaille belonging to the firm of Deladoey et Fils is certainly considered to be one of the pre-eminent sites of Yvorne. The walled and terraced vineyard to the northeast of the town is located on the lower remains of the 16th century avalanche. The engaging Jacques Deladoey produces 50,000 bottles annually from the 4.5 hectare site. Ninety-five percent of the production is Chasselas while the remaining five percent is Auxerrois which produces a sweet wine from the vines at the very top of the vineyard, bottled under the name Les Brulons. When young, the Domaine de l'Ovaille is a vivacious, sometimes *petillant* and forward wine. Best drunk within several years of the vintage, it has the concentration and structure to age respectably. It is not surprising that Deladoey is another contentious wine maker who believes that the lower limits for the Vaudois AOC should be set sufficiently high to discourage low-sugar, overproduced grapes.

The Auxerrois, on the other hand, needs time to come into its own. In 1986 the Les Brulons wine was 13.8% alcohol and even after six years the sweet nose was still evolving. For Jacques Deladoey, this is a wine for rich *fois gras* or Roquefort cheese – high praise indeed.

Other highly regarded producers include Claude Isoz at Domaine de la Commune, who markets some 60,000-80,000 bottles from his six hectares. He is known for his three Chasselas (Clos de l'Abbaye, Trechêne and L'Ombren) and his domaine Pinot Noir. Phillippe Gex, on the other hand, produces a mere 10,000 bottles of Burgundy-inspired Pinot Noir from his small 1.5 hectares estate.

Among the larger, more widely distributed vineyards, Clos du Rocher and Gros Caillou are well-known. The former is marketed by the firm of Obrist in Vevey. It maintains a good reputation as a "Grand Cru Suisse" (a somewhat confusing "cru" designation). A Clos du Rocher steeply priced at 47 Swiss francs a bottle for the 1989 vintage (in 1991) at the charming Relais de Chambésy just outside Geneva was among the most expensive and best screw top bottles of wine that one might hope to drink. The wine was rich, well focused with both a good nose and length. The vineyard is on the south-facing terraces which rise above Yvorne where the gravelly soil is well-suited for Chasselas. The Clos du Rocher is actually owned by the Very Venerable Confrérie of Vignerons of Vevey, an institution with a history of over three hundred years. Recent vintages maintain a good level of concentration. The wine is stylish and full, with a good smoky texture.

The reputation of the wines of Yvorne also shows well with the Gros Caillou which displays such a solid structure, balance and smoky taste that it can be mistaken for an even more exalted Dézaley. The 7.5 hectare estate, Château Maison Blanche, is one of the stars owned by the firm of Schenk. It is one of the few vineyards in this area to have a real "Château". Eighty-five percent of the vineyard is Chasselas while the remainder is Gamay and Pinot Noir. The wines are well-structured and flavourful.

Petit Vignoble is Henri Badoux's well-regarded white wine vineyard in Yvorne and is located at the foot of the ancient avalanche. The firm also produces an Yvorne Pinot Noir, Bel-Honneur. Compared to Badoux's Pourpre Monseigneur red from Aigle, the Yvorne wine shows a lighter but equally harmonious nose, with very little tannin but considerable elegance. It is not, however, a wine for laying down for long.

The Clos de la George estate is located just outside the town of Yvorne to the north-west. Here are found the rock-hewn cellars of the vineyard whose heat-reflected wines are supposed to enjoy almost Mediterranean qualities. The white *grand vin* of the eight-hectare, terraced vineyard Clos de la George, "Grand Cru d'Yvorne" can be refreshingly acidic and slightly citric on the taste. The red Clos de la George, on the other hand, is a wine that definitely needs some time to achieve its best. Even after five years in the bottle the wine still has a forward nose, with good fruit, and it preserves sufficient tannin to provide the "stuffing" for several more years aging.

Also worth mentioning is the one-hectare vineyard, Vers-Les-Ecots, owned by Clos de la George and whose wine is marketed by the firm of Hammel of Rolle. While not as powerful as many Yvorne wines, the Vers-Les-Ecots wines are pleasant, fresh and almost charming.

Château Maison Blanche of Yvorne, Chablais.

Villeneuve

From Yvorne, the next important wines are found around Villeneuve, the town nearest the point where the Rhône enters Lake Geneva. The town includes the site of one of the most important medieval hospitals in Switzerland. Founded in 1236 A.D. by Aymon of Savoie, the *Maison Dieu* (House of God) of Villeneuve was placed under the control of the nearby Royal Abbaye of St. Maurice in 1375. In 1536, the institution passed over to "Their Excellencies of Berne", where it remained, generating funds for the poor and sick until the hospital was closed during the Vaudois Revolution of 1798. The lands and vineyards were subsequently expropriated and sold.

The wines of Villeneuve are the first of the Chablais to benefit from the heat-reflecting qualities of Lake Geneva and the absence of fog, limited rainfall and lots of sun. The climate hovers between that of the Valais and the other regions of Lake Geneva. In the 19th century the wines of Villeneuve gained international recognition when they became famous, or infamous, for their medicinal ability to dissolve the gall stones of France's Napoleon III! In the early part of the twentieth century, the establishment of a local cooperative cellar produced both a rationalization of existing vineyards of Villeneuve into larger units, and an important overall qualitative improvement of the vines and wine.

The wines from Villeneuve do not have the intensity or strength of the offerings from Yvorne and Aigle but they are certainly not without their attractions. The white wines are known for their bouquet, presence, vigour and longevity. The reds have a certain sweetness and a loyal local following. As is the case in the communes of Ollon and Bex, a considerable amount of wine from Villeneuve is sold directly to restaurants for immediate consumption.

One of the better known and central vineyards is Sous les Hospices belonging to the Lehmann family and owned, coincidentally, by a distant relative-by-marriage of the author. Even in off-years their Chasselas can display good colour and acid balance with a floral nose. From better years the wine is fuller and more concentrated, reminiscent of peaches and fruit. The family's Pinot Noir shows good balance, extraction and weight, although at times a touch too much acid. It is not a heavy wine, but is pleasant rather than overwhelming. With some time the wine develops a good varietal character. The Lehmanns also produce a rosé which is excellent for summer quaffing.

Other wines of note include the Cave du Crépon, from Anita and Jean Schenk. It has a slightly alcoholic, but not unpleasant, nose. The taste of fruit is evident. Sur La Tour is another wine marketed by the firm of Hammel which follows the trend in Switzerland towards screwtops. In this case, however, Hammel explicitly defends the practice on the back label. Certainly Sur La Tour is not a bad wine; light, overly neutral, but cleanly made. And because it is produced for early consumption, perhaps it really doesn't need a cork.

The Lavaux Region

A day spent wandering through the steep, terraced Lavaux vineyards that cascade down the hill from Chexbres towards Rivaz, Dézaley and St. Saphorin is an inspiring and invigorating experience. It is also more than sufficient to convince even the most skeptical observer of the Swiss commitment to overcome all obstacles to the production of good wines. One wonders how such well-tended, postage-stamp vineyards can ever be economically viable? As they tumble down the hillside towards the north shore of Lake Geneva, the terraces at times are only three to five vines deep. And yet they receive the best care and attention. Even the use of specially-adapted agricultural machinery is impossible on many of the best-exposed slopes, so cultivation, harvest and maintenance remain classically labour-intensive.

The Lavaux is no ordinary area. It is the historical heart of the Vaud and hence at the center of the complex and rich traditions of wine growing in Switzerland. The better wines of Dézaley, Epesses and St. Saphorin compete for the pinnacle of quality and price. Sixty percent of the production is bought by Swiss-German wine lovers – "the only ones who can afford them", a cynic might say! These wines are challenged only by the finest producers of Yvorne, Aigle and Valais for the title of the most sought-after white wines of the country. The vineyards of the Lavaux are steeped in history, their origins directly traceable to the founding of the great Cistercian abbeys of the Middle Ages. Drawing from the wisdom of the ages, the abbots established their vineyards on the south-facing slopes rising from Lake Geneva to take full advantage of the "three suns" that nurture the vines: namely, the direct light of the sun, the reflected sun of the lake and the stored sun of the stone terraces.

The Chasselas reigns over the Lavaux as nowhere else. This grape reflects and resonates the composition of the soil in which it is grown. Consequently, more than one *vigneron* in the area undoubtedly echoes the sentiments of the wine makers of the Clos des Abbayes who firmly believe that the chalky limestone, in combination with the underlying alkaline earth, makes the Lavaux, and the sub-region of Dézaley in particular, "the best soil in the world for the Chasselas".

The traditions of this region which for centuries have sought to coax the very best from the Chasselas grape have not, however, prevented the *vignerons* of Lavaux from branching out and occasionally experimenting with new plantings of Chardonnay and Pinot Gris. Many growers have also taken advantage of the extra radiant heat from terrace walls to produce very limited quantities of fine red wines, usually concentrating on the Pinot Noir or Gamay grapes, but also including traces of Merlot and Syrah for complexity and depth.

The region of Lavaux stretches 30 kilometers from the Château de Chillon to the eastern edge of the city of Lausanne. In total it produces an average of 6.5 million litres of white wine, almost entirely made from the Chasselas, and half a million litres of red. The mean temperature is the mildest in Switzerland, as witnessed by the palm trees on the lakeside paths of Montreux. The region is strongly influenced by the moderating effects and reflected heat of Lake Geneva, and is protected by the surrounding mountains from the cold northern bise wind. The area rarely suffers the effects of cool fogs. The apparently contradictory reference to Lavaux, and Montreux in particular, as "the Riviera of Switzerland", is therefore not as strange as it may first sound.

Ville de Lausanne

Special mention must be made of the unique position of the Ville de Lausanne (City of Lausanne) as a major vineyard owner and, more notably, the producer of some of the finest quality wines in Vaud. The holdings of the city are spread across the region and include vineyards in both Lavaux (to the east of Lausanne) and La Côte (to the west). In terms of quality, the immediately recognizable red and white crest of the city between two standing lions is, if not a guarantee, at least a solid indication of a superior wine.

The collection of vineyards belonging to the city was acquired over a period of time. Today they form perhaps the finest grouping of quality sites in the country. Major individual vineyards (from east to west) include the six-hectare Domaine du Burignon in St. Saphorin; the two exemplary Swiss vineyards of Clos des Moines and Clos des Abbayes in Dézaley; and the 13.5-hectare vineyard Abbaye de Mont near Mont-sur-Rolle and Château Rochefort in Allaman, both in the La Côte region.

Château de Chillon, Montreux and Vevey

The first vines of the Lavaux begin near the starkly romantic Château de Chillon, built by the Dukes of Savoie when the entire region, including the Chablais to the south, was part of their dominion. Already by the 13th century the lakeside castle had developed its distinctive "floating" profile. Even when the House of Savoie was forced to retire to the Château de Ripaille, across the lake in Thonon on the south (French) side, records show that they still continued to drink the wines of nearby Aigle and Yvorne. In 1536 ownership of the Château was assumed by the rulers of Berne who possessed it until the revolution of 1798 when ownership was handed over to the Vaudois. From Chillon to the city of Vevey, vineyards can be found along the arch that passes through the towns of Montreux, Clarens, Blonay (famed for its castle), St.-Légier (equally famed for its Chiésaz church) and the Tour-de-Peilz with its small port on the lake.

The wines from the vines growing around the Château de Chillon are often served at the various ceremonial functions which still take place in the Château. These include the meetings of the "Confrérie du Guillon", a wine fraternity founded in 1954 in order to promote the wines of Vaud. The organization now has over 3,500 members. The Confrérie is modeled on the Confrérie du Tastevin of Burgundy. Instead of the Burgundian's Clos de Vougeot, the Confrérie's activities are centered on the equally impressive Château de Chillon where the group holds ten to twelve *"ressats"* (traditional Vaudois meals) to celebrate the end of the harvest and to recognize the efforts of all who contributed towards a successful vintage. The atmosphere at such events, which are held in the wood-paneled halls of the historic Château overlooking the lake, is almost otherworldly.

Lord Byron and Vaud

> Chillon! thy prison is a holy place,
> And thy sad floor an altar—for't was trod,
> Until his very steps have left a trade
> Worn, as if thy cold pavement were a sod,
> By Bonnivard! May none those marks efface!
> For they appeal from tyranny to God.

Although somewhat off the vinous trail, a slight digression on Lord Byron and his most popular poem, *The Prisoner of Chillon,* is perhaps appropriate. In June 1816, Byron established himself at the Villa Diodati, "a very pretty villa in a vineyard – with the Alps behind – & Mt. Jura and the Lake before ...". From this base, and using Rousseau's *La Nouvelle Héloïse* as a surprisingly reliable guide, Byron and Shelley toured Lake Geneva, including the wine areas of Clarens and Vevey. From this sojourn came not only *The Prisoner of Chillon,* actually written at Ouchy, the lakeside terminus below Lausanne, but also the third canto of *Childe Harold* with its references to Rousseau. Here too are found the origins of Mary Shelley's *Frankenstein,* a tale which grew out of the ghost stories exchanged between Byron and the Shelleys at Villa Diodati. Poor Mr. Frankenstein was the German consul in Geneva! Byron also used the opportunity to visit Mme de Staël, then ensconced at the Château de Coppet farther down the lake, as well as Voltaire's Château just across the border from Geneva in Ferney. A greater concentration of the intellectual giants of the late 18th and early 19th centuries is difficult to imagine. One can only speculate as to the influence on Byron's writings of the stark contrast between the idyllic cottage, set among the Vaudois vineyards, and the cold, dark reality of Chillon's infamous dungeons.

Montreux

The nearby wines of Montreux are perhaps not the most sought after of the Lavaux but, as always, some surprises can be found. They were of sufficient renown to merit a description of the grape harvest in Jean-Jacques Rousseau's 18th century romantic bestseller, *La Nouvelle Héloïse.* From a purely viticultural perspective, Rousseau's chronicle of the 1744 vintage at Clarens, above Montreux, is most notable for recording how late the harvest took place, i.e., after the first frosts, which implies that the *vignerons* of that time may already have been looking for the greater sweetness and concentration of a *vendage tardive.*

Among the vineyards that encircle Montreux, one of the most impressive is that of the Château de Châtelard which enjoys a magnificent view over the town of Montreux and Lake Geneva. The vineyards, which date from at least the 15th century, surround the ruins of the ancient dungeon – the only remaining part of the original Château which was constructed on the foundation of an even earlier fortress. The vines, however, are now managed separately from the Château proper. The 9.9-hectare vineyard is only planted with Chasselas and annually produces an average of 80,000 bottles of Château-labeled wine. The wine operation is managed and marketed by the firm of Fonjallaz from Epesses, next door in Lavaux. The wine usually has a good floral nose which is fresh and concentrated with a faint hint of smokiness and reasonable length. The vaulted cellars of the Château still contain an 18th century wooden barrel, "La Barone", which holds almost 13,000 litres. The cellars are no longer used for commercial wine making.

Another Chasselas producer from the Montreux suburb of Blonay is the Domaine des Châbles. Here André Sager produces a pleasant white along with three separate reds from his three hectares: a Pinot Noir/Gamay; a Gamay/Pinot Noir; and a straight Pinot Noir. These are among the good straightforward reds which are especially enjoyable when sipped on the porch of one of the quaint wooden Swiss chalets clinging to the hills which rise behind Montreux. From here there is a stunning view over Lake Geneva with the Jura mountains to the north and the French Alps to the south, a view which can only contribute to the pleasure of the wine. A good deal of Montreux's production goes to the restaurant and hotel trade, upon which a large part of the local economy is based.

Passing through the lakeside village of Tour-de-Peilz, one soon reaches the city of Vevey, well-known as the headquarters of the international food giant Nestlé. This town, with its well-preserved core, is also the home of the *Confrérie des vignerons de Vevey* who sponsor Switzerland's oldest, and the world's largest wine festival held only once every twenty-five years. The last full presentation was in 1977 and the next is not scheduled until after the year 2000 (see Chapter XIII). Vevey itself is no longer a major producer of wines, but behind the town can be found the Coteaux du Châtelard, anchored by the villages of Pallens, Mottex, Sottex, and Sully which stretch back to the hinterland of Montreux. Here limited quantities of fairly modest red and white wines are produced. They are agreeable and adequate, but without great structure or richness. Vevey does, however, remain headquarters to a number of wine firms, including the company Obrist, which has important holdings throughout Vaud.

Vevey to Dézaley

The western outskirts of Vevey mark the beginning of one of the most beautiful and concentrated areas of vineyards in all of Switzerland. The two villages of Corsier and Corseaux announce a procession of wine hamlets that stretches, virtually unbroken, to the city of Lausanne. Between these two villages and their better-known neighbour, Chardonne, lies the community of Jongny, not a well-known wine producer but capable of pleasant well-made wines. Although most of the small villages on the slope to the west of Vevey have their local wines, the first area of real consequence is Chardonne. Here is found the consistently delightful Cure d'Attalens, coincidentally from the firm of Obrist in Vevey which since 1896 has owned this vineyard, first founded in the 12th century. The wine exhibits a very floral nose with a good acid balance and a fresh taste reminiscent of tree fruit. In better years the Cure d'Attalens can develop into a smoky, intense and elegant wine.

The old town of Chardonne, perched on the hill rising from the lakeshore to the forest line, marks the real beginning of the core area of the Lavaux. The vineyards of Chardonne spread out below the town. Obrist also bottles a straight Chardonne which, although it lacks the concentration of the single vineyard Cure d'Attalens, it is still a pleasant, balanced wine. The wines of Obrist are generally easily found in Switzerland as the firm falls under the umbrella of the large Rolle negotiant Schenk. Another Chardonne wine maker with a reputation for well-made wines is Marius Ducret et fils.

St. Saphorin

At the base of the terraced slopes of Lavaux, the village of St. Saphorin guards the entry into the heart of the region. Hugging the lakeshore, the vineyards are separated from the lake by only a road and a railway track. The vines start immediately at the boundary of this tiny but meticulous village and work their way uphill towards Chexbres on the corniche. Virtually all vineyard sites here enjoy an excellent southern exposure, the benefits of which are further amplified by the reflective warmth of Lake Geneva. The three villages of St. Saphorin, Chexbres on the corniche and Rivaz further to the west, encircle the separate *"cru"* of Dézaley which is discussed below. St. Saphorin, sympathetically named after a 2nd century saint martyred near Beaune for refusing to venerate the idol Cybele, boasts some of the best known sites of the whole region.

The vineyard of Faverges was first planted by the Cistercian monks of the Abbey of Hauterive shortly after the abbey was established in 1138. Since that time the vineyard of Faverges has had but two formal owners, the Abbey of Hauterive from 1138 to 1848 and the City of Fribourg from 1848 until the present. In 1580, however, the property was placed under the supervision of the Jesuits of St. Michael College who, in turn, lost everything when the Jesuits were expelled from Switzerland in 1847. The Faverges vineyard continues to produce one of the most sought-after wines of the Lavaux.

The six-hectare Domaine du Burignon property, immediately overlooking the village roofs of St. Saphorin, is also very well regarded, although perhaps not as highly as the two Dézaley vineyards of the Ville de Lausanne, the Clos des Abbayes and Clos des Moines. The Burignon vineyard has existed as a recognized property since the middle of the 12th century. Before secularization it belonged to the Cistercian Convent of Haut Crêt. It was acquired by Lausanne in 1803. The hill slope is 30° while the soil is a combination of chalk (10%-15%), sand, clay, sandstone and marl. Around 15% of the production is red, made from Pinot Noir and Gamay, although the vineyard is best known for its fruity, well-balanced white.

The distinctive crested label of the "Ville de Lausanne" designates Burignon a "Grand Cru". When young, the wine displays a restrained bouquet with a notable touch of flint. It should be well-structured with good weight and acid balance. From a good year the wine will be very fine and finish long. In addition it is reasonably priced compared to its more prestigious Dézaley neighbours.

Other well-known St. Saphorin vineyards include Clos O(r)goz, also belonging to the City of Fribourg, and Les Fosses, one of the properties of Jean-Michel Conne of Chexbres (see photograph on the next page), an important wine maker who controls 12 hectares of vineyards around St. Saphorin and elsewhere. Some recent vintages of Conne's wines have adopted the contentious screw top. Tasting the wine, nonetheless, reveals true Chasselas characteristics, including a flinty character and reasonable length. Conne's wines can often be found downstairs in the local chalet-style *caveau* in Chexbres. His other wines from Lavaux include a Dézaley Plan Perdu and a St. Saphorin-labeled Le Semillant *"muri sur lies"* which provides that extra character with a good scent of smoke on a tight nose. The wine is well-structured and balanced, a first rate Chasselas. Conne also has a red Gamay/Pinot Noir blend, Champ de Clos, and a surprising St. Saphorin Pinot Noir with quite a remarkable cherry nose. The fruit of the Pinot Noir is not as evident on the palate, but for an elegant light-style Pinot Noir the result was more than acceptable. In addition to his Lavaux wines, Conne has holdings at Ollon and Aigle in the Chablais region.

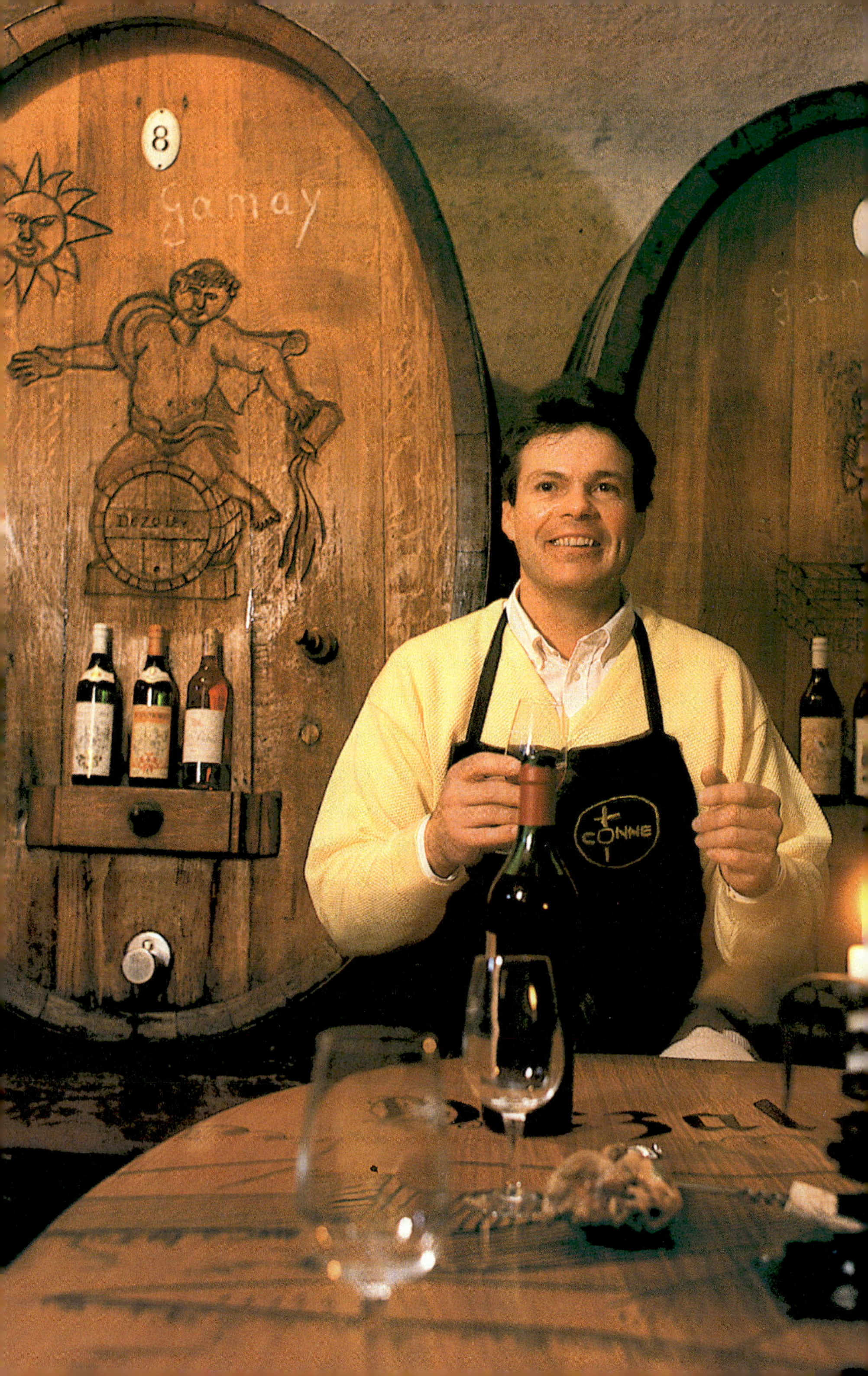
8
Gamay
CONNE

Not to be confused with the Domaine du Burignon of the Ville de Lausanne is the "Burignon" of the Barbey family in Chexbres who claim a vinous descent reaching back to 1394. The Burignon from Roger Barbey, also available at the Chexbres *caveau,* shows good, if somewhat restrained fruit, a slight smoky bouquet and a solid structure. This is not a flashy wine, but is rather well-made and properly characteristic. Maurice Cossy produces a third recognized wine from the Burignon area of St. Saphorin.

In the nearby village of Rivaz is the firm of Alexandre Chappuis whose holding of four hectares includes several labels from St. Saphorin. In fact Chappuis, who also runs a nursery, is considered something of a specialist in the wines of St. Saphorin. In addition to wines made from Chasselas coming from Rivaz, St. Saphorin and a Grand Cru Dézaley, Chappuis also bottles a rare St. Saphorin Plant du Rhin (Sylvaner)/Pinot Gris combination. Chappuis' reds are both from St. Saphorin: a regular bottling of Pinot Noir/Gamay; and, somewhat unusually, the same blend rather than a straight Pinot Noir, in a "reserve" selection. The Château attached to the vineyard les Rueyres now serves as the headquarters for the *vignerons* of Rivaz.

Reflecting the importance of the terraced vineyards which surround St. Saphorin, rocks and rock walls figure prominently in names and labels. These include such sites as Roches Brûlées, La Roche aux Vignes, Roche Ronde and Mur Blanc. The 1990 Roches Brûlées is sparkling but lightish coloured, with a somewhat unfocused nose. The taste was also on the light side when this wine was consumed after a spring morning of scrambling up the stone walls which climb the hill behind the village of St. Saphorin. However, the atmosphere couldn't have been more pleasant at the rustic Auberge de l'Onde, located at the old St. Saphorin crossroads in the shadow of the 16th century church (itself built over a 2nd century Roman building). After a healthy ramble over the rather daunting terraces, the Roches Brûlées provided a harmonious accompaniment to a lunch of local perch. It is not, however, a wine for keeping.

The La Roche aux Vignes, from Bernard Bovy of Chexbres is a well-structured wine whose well-knit bouquet provides hints of smoke and grass. The wine is complex and enjoys good length. The 1989 vintage was particularly memorable, and over the years Bovy has developed a reputation as one of the best producers with a full range of wines in the St. Saphorin/Dézaley area. The firm is also known for the uniquely-painted barrels found in its cellars. Roche Ronde belongs to the firm of Jean and Pierre Testuz of Cully and is a forward wine with some structure. The Mur Blanc of Jean-Louis Jomini, also of Chexbres, is styled as a "Grand Cru". This wine lacks some of the concentration that one might have expected. However, a second St. Saphorin wine from the same producer, but without the Grand Cru designation, is actually better, with a forward, almost peppermint nose. The well-balanced taste combines both spice and smoke. The wine is not deep, but might benefit from a year of aging.

Every visitor to the area will come away with his or her own favourites. Other St. Saphorin wines worth searching out are Les Molettes from Olivier Simon and the

Jean Michel Conne, Chexbres, in the Lavaux region of Vaud.

Les Médailles from Henri Contesse of nearby Cully. The latter displays a floral nose over a well-concentrated base and the wine holds together well as a result of the good structure of balanced acids. A Les Blassinges of Pierre Leyvraz from Chexbres tasted in the inviting albeit smoke-filled Caveau de Chexbres, had a straw colour with a touch of sulfur on the nose which disappeared shortly after the top was unscrewed. The wine was fresh and had reasonable length.

One of the most commonly found St. Saphorin communal selections is from the large, respected shipper, Louis Bovard, of Cully. Usually Bovard's are reliable, although, occasionally, as happens with many larger concerns, some wines may not be as concentrated as they should be. Bovard also markets a superior St. Saphorin vineyard, L'Archeveque. Another large producer is the Epesses-based firm of Fonjallaz which markets its St. Saphorin under the name of La Rionde. Although not bad, some of the Fonjallaz wines can at times need an additional touch of concentration without which they appear one-dimensional. One final offering comes from the local community, De la Commune, which is generally clean and straightforward.

Dézaley

Approaching the region of Dézaley from the corniche crowning the cliff-like slopes which rise ever-more-abruptly from the lake, one soon arrives at Chexbres. This village, with its stunning view over Lake Geneva and the French Alps in the distance, is among the most picturesquely-placed wine villages in Switzerland, if not in the world. Directly below Chexbres is found Dézaley, the center of the Lavaux and a specially designated "cru" found entirely within the commune of Puidoux. Even farther below are the wine villages of Rivaz and carefully-restored St. Saphorin.

Bound on the west by the neighboring commune of Epesses and on the east by the stream of the Rivaz mill, the sixty-five-hectare area of Dézaley rises straight up from the shores of Lake Geneva to the corniche road above. In places the slope is so steep that the height of the walls holding back the cliffs, some still dependent upon the original thousand-year-old Cistercian terraces, is far greater than the width of the terraces growing vines. This hillside is entirely a man-made creation, dedicated solely to vines and the production of wine. The angle of the slopes perfectly captures the reflected light from the lake and, as a result, the wines of Dézaley are known variously for their strength, depth, warmth and generosity. They display the perfumed nose of flint or gunpowder for which the Chasselas is celebrated. The grape musts are required to have a minimum natural sugar level of 70° Oe. before they are entitled to the Dézaley *appellation*.

The vineyards descend, suspended between heaven and earth, like a staircase for giants from stone terrace to stone terrace, all hewn and preserved from erosion by human efforts over the centuries (see photograph on page 14). The soil, a compacted pebbly molasse commonly referred to as "pudding stone", has been shaped into thin arable strips called *charmus*. The vineyards are, without exception, extremely well-tended which in part explains the stiff prices commanded by the wines from this region. Production and maintenance costs are, according to the cantonal authorities, at least twice the cost for wines produced at Morges in the La Côte region.

The backbreaking effort to sculpt the most favoured sites of the Lavaux hillside dates from the late Middle Ages, when the Church was pursuing its liturgical and economic interest in wine. Monks sent from the medieval Abbey of Montheron created the famous Clos des Abbayes in Dézaley, while the Cistercians of the Abbey of Haut Crêt, nearby, were responsible for planting vines which would become the equally famous vineyards d'Oron and Clos des Moines in Dézaley and Burignon in St. Saphorin. The Tour de Marsens, a local landmark, is also of ecclesiastical origins. It was built in 1160 by the Bishop of Lausanne, and its ruin is still very visible atop the steep slopes above Dézaley, presiding over vineyards such as Marsens and Ogoz first carved out by the Premontagne monks of Abbey of Joux. History runs very deep through these slopes.

When the German-speaking Bernois gained control of Vaud in the 16th century, ownership of the single most famous Dézaley vineyard, the Clos des Abbayes, passed to the City of Lausanne. The Clos des Moines in Dézaley and the Burignon in St. Saphorin, however, remained under the control of the Berne authorities who encouraged the consumption of these wines through their monopoly over the wine sales in Berne, much to the disadvantage of the other Vaudois producers. The Bernois also ensured the continued financial success of their vineyards by restricting new plantings and controlling the transport, importation, and sale of wine. They were, however, unable to retard the growing reputation of the Clos des Abbayes. In the aftermath of the upheavals of the late 18th century, the Bernois were forced to turn over their properties to the Vaudois "République lémanique" (Léman Republic), one result of which was that the Burignon and Clos des Moines vineyards, over nine hectares in total, came under the control of the Lausanne city government in 1803.

Clos des Moines and Clos des Abbayes

The wines from these two Ville de Lausanne vineyards impressed the venerable wine writer André Simon in times past. Certainly they are two of the very few Swiss wines with established international reputations. The first vineyard is the Clos des Moines, one of the impressive vineyards the Cistercians carved out of the rock face in the heart of Vaud. This four-hectare vineyard has a south-west exposure which is excellent for catching the afternoon sun, with an average slope of 33°. The soil is clay over molasse with a considerable mixture of chalk. In good years the Chasselas of Clos des Moines assumes the restrained "honeyed-velvet" power that characterizes the best of Swiss wines.

These wines will vary more than most with the character of the vintage. Concentrated and powerful in great years, the Clos des Moines does not necessarily perform so well in off years. However, in excellent vintages the wines of Clos des Moines demonstrate finesse and fine aging potential. They are wines worth cellaring for at least a year or two, and will live much longer under the right conditions. In fact, the wines from Clos des Moines are slower to develop than those from neighbouring vineyards because of the greater amount of chalk in the soil which gives the young wine a slightly higher acidity level. Rare bottles from the 1950s are just reaching their best. Originally bottles from the very best vintages were sealed with wax rather than a capsule to see them through a long and slow aging. The practice seems, however, to have disappeared. There is also a good red, although produced in very limited quantities, made from Gamay and Pinot Noir grapes grown on trellises located next to the heat-reflecting stone walls.

The second of the two domains, the Clos des Abbayes, is believed by many to be the finest single vineyard in Switzerland. Since the vineyard came into the possession of the City of Lausanne in 1536, it has remained the core of the city's holdings. The care and attention lavished on this vineyard epitomizes all that is good about Swiss wine-making. No expense is spared, and the wines, responding to the additional attention they receive, have a reputation for complexity and depth.

The terraced vineyard covers an area just over 4.5 hectares, with an average incline of 33° and an excellent south south-west exposure. Clos des Abbayes can be one of the longest-lasting wines in Switzerland, drawing strength to survive for decades from a solid but balanced structure and greater concentration. After their first decade the wines from sites such as Clos des Abbayes begin to show the complexity and floral undertones that the Chasselas can achieve. Certainly wines from the 1955 and 1957 vintages tasted in the early 1990s showed no sign of rapid demise and admirably countered the myth that Swiss wines can't age – although admittedly they had been stored in perfect conditions in the vineyard's cellars. The wines were elegant, floral and still almost young although they had taken on the honeyed texture which can turn the great Chasselas of Vaud into fine dessert wines. Minute quantities of Chardonnay are also produced. For the small amount of excellent red produced here, the *cépage,* in addition to the usual Gamay and Pinot Noir, includes both Merlot and Syrah, again grown against the heat-reflecting stone walls. The wine is one of the deepest of all Swiss reds with an intriguing, almost chocolate/toffee nose, and an excellent length.

The Other Wines of Dézaley

There is, however, much more to Dézaley than just the fine vineyards of the Ville de Lausanne. Depending upon the year, the most famous sites can be challenged or even outshone by some of their nearby rivals. In terms of acreage, the Ville de Lausanne leads the pack with a total of just under nine hectares. Next in line are the two major firms, Jean and Pierre Testuz and Louis Bovard, both of Cully and both with approximately six hectares each. The vast majority of Testuz's vines in Dézaley are located on the slopes to the east of Clos des Abbayes while the core of Bovard's Dézaley holdings are to the west of the Ville de Lausanne sites in the Treytorrens region. The remainder of Dézaley's 65 core hectares is divided between some 100 different owners.

L'Arbalete is Testuz's well-known Dézaley vineyard. The name means "crossbow", the emblem of the firm and, not unnaturally, a prominent feature on the label. Testuz also has a second highly-regarded but smaller Dézaley vineyard, La Borne. Wines such as L'Arbalete should have staying power for a decade, even if the usual inclination would be to drink it earlier. L'Arbalete is a wine that can be found outside Switzerland. It shows good fruit and concentration even when harvested in difficult circumstances.

Médinette is Louis Bovard's fine Dézaley offering. The wine is classic Chasselas, a steely combination of flint and flowers, which needs time to display its charms. Bovard's unique label for Médinette commemorates a 1905 picture of Bacchus designed for the great Vevey Fêtes des Vignerons of that year. Since the beginning of this century Médinette has been one of the most immediately recognizable of all Swiss wines.

In total the Bovard firm owns 16 hectares in Lavaux and the clutch of higher-quality vineyards controlled by Bovard is quite impressive: La Médinette in Dézaley; L'Archeveque in St. Saphorin; as well as Terre à Boire in Epesses. Their reds include the Dézaley Grande Cuvée, a judicious blend of Merlot, Syrah, Pinot Noir and Gamay, and the Cuvée Louis from St. Saphorin, which remarkably substitutes the usual Syrah grape with the Humagne Rouge from Valais! The firm's annual production is around 17,000 cases. Bovard's elegant labels are immediately recognizable and the firm's wines are widely distributed, some internationally.

Generally, one of the best overall wines from Dézaley is the Dézaley Renard from Gérard Pinget of Rivaz. Fresh, but with stylish depth and a very nice flinty nose, this "Grand Cru" led a list of 37 Dézaley wines from the 1988 vintage tasted by the gastronomic magazine Gault Millau. More recent vintages of Pinget's wines have continued this fine tradition. Interestingly, some of the more famous Dézaley names did not do as well as their reputations might suggest in the Gault Millau comparison.

From another "Grand Cru" vineyard comes Dézaley, Chemin de Fer, produced by the Massy family of Epesses. At its best the wine demonstrates a classic structure, good concentrated Chasselas fruit, and reasonable length. While not outstanding every year, Chemin de Fer is certainly a well-made wine from one of the best-known and sought-after vineyards of Vaud. Even in less stellar years, Chemin de Fer is a wine with structure and presence. The same producers have a Dézaley-Marsens, also labeled as "Grand Cru". This wine showed backbone and depth, but was not stamped with a great individual character.

Recent years have seen a major effort by the owners of vineyards in Dézaley to reverse the effects of erosion through impressive and expensive engineering works. At the same time, the vineyards surrounding the Tour de Marsens have been expanded into areas which, because of differences of soil and micro-climate, are not of the same caliber as the other vineyards of Dézaley. The vineyards in the immediate vicinity of the Marsens tower, including the better sites of Sous-Marsens and Dézaley-Marsens, are some of the best of the region. Expansion up the hill, however, is pushing the limits too far. It is almost as if the *vignerons* of Corton replanted the woods above the existing vineyards with vines and tried to pass off the product as authentic Corton.

Other fine vineyards in the Dézaley region include the well-known L'Anneau d'Or, Pavois (fourth out of 38 in the Gault Millau tasting of 1988s); Les Côtes-Dessus; L'Ermite of Michel Fonjallaz; La Gruyre from André Rouge of Epesses;, Dézaley-Marsens de la Tour of Les Frères Dubois of Cully and Sur Les Abbayes, from Marc Leyvraz of Rivaz. Dézaley, Domaine de l'Hôpital, a well-structured wine, is owned by the Hôpital des Bourgeois of the City of Fribourg. Among other recognized wines in Dézaley is Grottes des Moines which exhibits good smoky characteristics and a quality finish. Dézaley Notre Dame on the other hand shows reasonable Chasselas traits, but unfortunately lacks great presence. The vineyard list could go on at length but in the end each enthusiast will have to search out his or her favourite single vineyard wines.

In addition, certain shippers such as Bovard, Fonjallaz and others produce generic Dézaleys which, if well-made, such as the selection from Bovard, should be more than acceptable, although none of them is likely to be inexpensive. Fonjallaz bottles two wines from Dézaley; a regular wine under the names l'Eperon and a Grand Cru l'Evêque. The former can be refreshingly acidic while the latter usually needs some time to evolve properly.

Epesses

Moving west from Tour de Marsens and beyond the steep rocky outcrops of Dézaley, the landscape expands and softens somewhat as one passes through the quaint village of Epesses, home to over 30 separate *vignerons,*. Here the exposure turns slightly from south to south-south-west. From the village of Chexbres above Dézaley to the city of Lausanne, the string of tidy wine villages (Epesses, Rieux, Grandvaux, Aran and Châtelard) pass in succession along the *route de corniche* for seven kilometers across the communes of Epesses, Villette and Lutry. The traditional villages that dot the hills and shores between Epesses and Lausanne preserve both an aesthetic harmony and compactness, the latter trait undoubtedly to give as much as possible of the valuable slopes to grape production. These are very much villages of wine families. Epesses, for examples, boasts seven Fonjallaz, four Duboux, two Bovard, two Massy and two Rouge on the list of local wine makers. Particularly important among them are the firms of Fonjallaz and Jean-François and Luc Massy, the latter owners of the Chemin de Fer vineyard in Dézaley.

The best wines of Epesses are only ever-so-slightly below the levels in the pantheon of Swiss wines occupied by those of Dézaley. It is also often easier to find the wines of Epesses outside Switzerland, since several of the larger estates with sufficient production have found export niches as far away as London or New York.

Among the better sites of Epesses are the Clos des Treize-Vents, Roches, Barberonnes, Montaux, Chapotannaz, Côtes des Courseboux, Clos des Burnettes, Clos de la République, Crêt-Dessous, Boux d'Epesses, Clos de la Béguine, Clos de St.-Amour among others. Just as the "cru" Dézaley lies completely within the commune of Puidoux, the region of Calamin is located within the boundaries of the commune of Epesses. It is contiguous with Dézaley and is entitled to its own separate "cru" status (see below).

In this area are also found the anomalous vines belonging to the communes of Corcelles and Payerne. Beginning in the 16th century when these two vineless Vaudois communes still formed a single political entity, their governments began making small purchases in areas such as Grandvaux and Calamin. The wine produced from these vineyards was transported to specially designated cellars in

Payerne where it was aged and sold as a "communal wine" under the watchful eye of a special magistrate. In 1806 the two communes split apart and, in a classic case of Swiss obstinacy, took 16 years to settle which commune got which vines! Payerne ended up with the lion's share of almost 16 hectares, while Corcelles received just over four hectares. The annual sale by auction of the wines of Payerne was the local equivalent to the price-setting sales of Burgundy at the Hospices de Beaune, or the now-discontinued annual pre-Christmas auctions of the wines of the City of Lausanne. Perhaps in an effort to catch up with the times, however, the auctions have been replaced more recently by negotiated direct sales *(vente de gré à gré)* to interested buyers.

Certainly one of the best-known and most easily-recognized wines of Epesses is La République. This popularity is reinforced by a large billboard at the top of the vineyard, clearly visible from the corniche autoroute between Lausanne and Vevey. The evocative label with its revolutionary symbolism celebrates the allegiance of François Fonjallaz to the *Republique lémanique* which emerged in 1798 from the Vaudois Revolution. Patrick Fonjallaz continues the family tradition at the firm. Recent tastings of La République have been mixed, at times showing an unfocused wine not living up to its excellent reputation. Some vintages in the late 1980s were not very successful as the wines were sharp and without grace. Others, however, were fuller and showed more fruit – the difference undoubtedly can be attributed to stricter contol over yields. Another Fonjallaz in Epesses is Jean-Daniel Fonjallaz, who produces wines from the sought after areas of Calamin and Dézaley. His wines (see under Calamin below) are available in the UK.

Farther down the hill, another fairly common and usually dependable wine is the Domaine de la Maison Blanche, owned by Hoirie Palaz but marketed through the firm of Henri Contesse of nearby Cully. The wine is known for a good, forward floral nose and a well-balanced taste with some acid providing the required structure and backbone. The wine has a good length.

Both Louis Hegg and Claude Massy et Fils, two well-regarded wine makers whose headquarters are in Epesses, also produce attractive Calamin among their range of wines. Hegg controls four hectares spread around the region producing 40,000 bottles, while Massy has three hectares and an annual production of approximately 35,000 bottles. Hegg's selection also includes Epesses La Boursière, Epesses Pinot Noir Les Mariages and the Dézaley Grand Cru La Gruyre. Massy's range is even more adventurous and includes a Merlot/Syrah/Pinot Noir blend La Bouquetin, along with a St. Saphorin Gamay, La Rueyre, a rosé blanche (made from a Gamay x Reichenstiener cross), and Chasselas-based wines from Calamin, St. Saphorin and Dézaley.

The intriguingly-named Terre à Boire (Earth to Drink) is from the Louis Bovard whose headquarters are down the slope from Epesses at La Maison Rouge which looks out over Lake Geneva from the waterfront of Cully. This wine is always very pleasant, although certain vintages require greater fruit intensity to justify fully its high reputation and price. It should show good length, and in good years will have the the concentrated smoky fruit nose that marks a fine Vaudois wine. Bovard's standard Epesses is generally a good and dependable wine. Those visitors lucky enough to visit Bovard in Cully should plan to complete their stay with a meal at the

The harvesting team for the firm of Philip Bovard in Cully, Vaud.

authentic and excellent nearby Auberge au Raisin whose wine list is as impressive as its food.

Antoine Bovard, based in nearby Treytorrens, is also developing a separate but well-deserved reputation for the wines from his three hectares of vines, particularly those from Epesses and Dézaley. Jean & Pierre Testuz of also have their selection from Epesses, the vineyard Coup de l'Etrier. The wine is clean, well-made, and shows off the better characteristics of the Chasselas to good effect. Less easily found will be the wines from Groset Grilli, although they are on the list at Fredy Girardet's restaurant Crissier, just the other side of Lausanne. A late 1980s vintage tasted two years after the harvest was enjoyably forward but somewhat flowery and lacked the required acidic backbone. It was almost a touch breezy, and although by no means a poor wine, it lacked a bit of structure.

A third Cully producer with vineyards in Epesses is Les Frères Dubois et Fils, located at Le Petit Versailles. The firm claims 800 years of history and tradition. Their best wine from Epesses is enticingly labeled La Braise d'Enfer. It complements the well-situated Dubois holdings at Tour de Marsens in Dézaley, St. Saphorin, Villette and elsewhere. Dubois wines are beginning to get wider distribution and they are now on the UK market.

Calamin

The wines of Calamin, the separate "cru" entirely enclosed by the commune of Epesses, also deserve mention. The entire area is only seven hectares, spreading in a triangular shape below the village of Epesses. If one considers the vineyards of Epesses to form a natural south-facing amphitheater, the location of Calamin is front-row centre. The exposure is excellent.

Here the wines have a reputation for strength, although they certainly don't lack a degree of elegance. Production, however, is quite limited and they are not easy to find. In addition to the producers of Calamin mentionned above, the Swiss wine club, Divo, did locate a very good 1990 Grand Cru Calamin from Vincent and Blaise Duboux of Epesses which combines good structure and style with a velvety smoothness. It is a restrained, almost tight wine, with good aging potential. The Calamin of Jean-Daniel Fonjallaz is a full, well-balanced and concentrated wine, certainly more striking than the elegant Dézaley La Gruyre from the same producer. Other growers who market the wines from this area include the firms Chevalley and Antoine Bovard.

Villette, Grandvaux, Lutry and Pully

From Epesses one gradually enters the suburbs of Lausanne, the expansion of which has encroached on nearby vineyards over the years. Good wines are produced around the villages of Villette, Grandvaux and Lutry, although often in modest quantities that deter extensive marketing. At Grandvaux, Jean Vogel produces his relatively rare "Fleurettes de Grandvaux aux 4 Plants", a blend of four different grapes. The wine comes in both dry and late-harvested versions. His late-harvested *Crème de Tête* release is a rich, luscious wine, clearly owing much of its floral nose at least to some Riesling or Sylvaner in the blend. This most interesting wine is available only in half bottles. Vogel also produces a range of other wines including Chasselas from Villette, Epesses and distant Ollon in the Chablais region, as well as a Chardonnay from Ollon and an unusual Oeil de Perdrix from the northern Vaud village of Champagne. He cultivates 19 hectares and produces 170,000 bottles annually. At Domaine de la Grille in Grandvaux, Alain Parisod, who also teaches oenology at the agricultural school in Changins, produces highly appreciated wines.

The next commune of Lutry is still one of the larger wine communes in the canton. Although most of the noted "cru" vineyards are situated elsewhere, there are fine wines made in the commune, including at the rather good Crêt de Plan vineyard from Paul Coderey et Fils. This winery produces well-structured wines with some grip which might be worth putting down for a year or two. Coderey produces approximately 10,000 cases annually. Finally, another of the Ville de Lausanne vineyards is in Lutry. As a consequence of the purchase of land for a water pumping station in the 1930s, the city acquired an adjoining vineyard. The land devoted to vines has been reduced over the years to less than a hectare, and no one claims that the results can rival the output of Clos des Abbayes. But Clos de la Pompe still produces up to 6,500 bottles of reasonable Chasselas and Gamay a year.

Closer to Lausanne, the growth of the city has been achieved only at the expense of land formerly devoted to wine grapes. The area of Pully, the commune directly east of Lausanne, is rapidly losing the last of its commercial vines, although the Federal agricultural station at Caudaux continues to grow experimental varieties on ancient ecclesiastical lands.

The La Côte Region

Lausanne stands as an impenetrable barrier to the unbroken progression of vines from the regions of Lavaux in the east to La Côte in the west. It also marks an important change in topography from the precipitous, terraced, tightly bunched vineyards of Lavaux, to gentler, rolling, less intense and more pastoral slopes of La Côte. The wines reflect this change of terrain as the softer, generally less-focused output from La Côte rarely matches the best from Lavaux. Overproduction in the La Côte region also appears to be a continuing problem. There are, however, some clear exceptions. The better wines complement the inviting pastoral scenery and make this a very pleasant region to visit.

Visiting the vineyards of La Côte is distinctly reminiscent of traveling along the Côte d'Or in Burgundy. A long band of hillside vines runs parallel to the plain, and is in turn topped with a cluster of trees. What is different, however, is the series of well-ordered villages interspersed among the neat and walled plots of vines. Especially in the early autumn after the leaves have turned and the ground haze begins to soften the light, La Côte can be an enchanting vineyard area, even when speeding along the autoroute from Geneva to Lausanne.

The region of La Côte stretches continuously for forty kilometers from the western suburbs of Lausanne to the border with the canton of Geneva. The vineyards are divided into three distinct zones: the Côte de Morges, Bonne Côte and Côte de Nyon, which encompass 12 separate wine-producing communes – Morges, Aubonne, Perroy, Féchy, Mont-sur-Rolle, Tartegnin, Côteau de Vincy, Bursinel, Vinzel, Luins, Begnins and Nyon. The middle area, the Bonne Côte, comprising virtually all the lands between Morges and Nyon, is the most important both in terms of quality and quantity.

The vines of La Côte very rarely extend as far down as the lakeshore. Instead they are almost all concentrated on the lower and mid-slopes of the Jura hills which rise above the flatter, agricultural plain where orchards, grain and other crops dominate. The 1,900 hectares of La Côte provide just over fifty percent of the total production of the Vaud. Annual production hovers around ten million liters of white wine and three million of red.

There are a great number of individual producers in La Côte. The mission of many local producers, however, remains to provide generic, pleasing "open" wines for immediate consumption in the restaurants and cafés of Geneva, Lausanne and elsewhere. This they do quite successfully. How these wines will adjust to greater low-end competition in the future and a growing necessity for Swiss wines to create identifiable marketing niches, remains to be seen. In addition, consumers seem to have trouble identifying with the proliferation of *appellation* names found throughout the La Côte region. The future may bring some rationalization around the more easily identifiable villages such as Mont-sur-Rolle. It will, however, not be easy for current producers to give up the name under which they identify themselves.

The Côte de Morges Region

The old market-town of Morges, with its squat round-towered "savoyard-style" 13th century Château, has long been an important center for the sale of wine. The prices set in Morges often establish a standard for the entire canton. The area produces elegant red and white wines which are usually drunk young. The estates here are relatively large, unlike those of Lavaux. Among the better known are the Clos des Abbesses at the village of Echandens; the Clos des Berles; the Clos de Jérusalem at Vufflens-le-Château; and the Clos des Truites d'Avaux at Tolochenaz. In addition, there are the large cooperatives Villars-sous-Yens and Clos des Vallaires at Morges, as well as the Domaine de la Commune, which shares the village of Marcelin with the cantonal agricultural station and school. Finally there is a series of small villages sprinkled across the commune such as Bremblens, Lonay, Colombier, Echichens, St. Saphorin, Lully, Lussy, Gollion and Chigny all of which produce simple, straightforward whites which, if the vines are not pushed to overproduce, can be pleasant and refreshing. One of the best producers in the Morges region is the Cave du Signal, run by the Cruchon-Muller family in Echichens. The firm of Henri Cruchon at the Cave du Village, in Echichens, has developed a national reputation. They sell some 25,000 cases annually, the best known of which are two "Grand Cru" vineyards, Les Pétoleyres and Les Lugrines, the former Chasselas and the latter Gamay.

Many vineyards around Morges are not bottled separately or, if so, they are not widely marketed outside the region. J & P Testuz of Cully does promote its Clos des Abbesses from La Côte Morges. Other producers have similar offerings.

Parallel with Morges, but farther back from the shores of Lake Geneva, are found the wines of Vufflens-le-Château. This is an area of mixed farming, and grapes do not dominate as they do on the slopes which lead down to the lake. The wines, however, can be quite attractive. Although the Clos de Jerusalem is the best known wine in the immediate vicinity, the Chasselas from Château de Vufflens is also one of the more impressive offerings of La Côte. The wine of the Château is designated as (again somewhat confusingly) "Grand Cru de la Côte". It can be a concentrated, well-knit drink. The flint evident on the nose combines harmoniously with the fruit on the palate. The vineyards are owned by Claude de Saussure, but the wine is marketed exclusively by the fairly large firm of Bolle in Morges.

Another influential Château in the region is Château de Denens of the village of the same name. This Château, which has a history of at least 600 years, is certainly not stuck in tradition. In 1985 a portion of grapes in the gently sloping vineyards was picked by machine, under the watchful eyes of the oenologists at the nearby federal agricultural station. This was the first use of mechanical harvesting in the Vaud. After separate vinifications of hand and machine-picked grapes, the mechanical selection was declared acceptable. The reputation of the Château, which produces some 22,000 bottles from just over seven hectares of vines of Chasselas, Riesling x Sylvaner and Pinot Noir, has continued to grow.

This is also a region where the production of red wine is fairly prominent. The ancient town of St. Prex is most commonly associated with the traditional red wine of the Vaud, the "Salvagnin", originally an indigenous grape type similar to the Humagne Rouge in the Valais or the Bondola in the Ticino. The historical vine, however, has disappeared and now the name is used within the Vaud for a wine which can be made from Vaudois Pinot Noir, Gamay or a combination of the two. To be awarded the "Salvagnin" appellation, the wine must receive a minimum of 17 out of 20 points in an official canton-controlled tasting. The large Morges cooperative,

Unavins, produces acceptable fruity and forward Salvagnin with a hint of cherries on the nose.

The Bonne Côte Region

The wines from the Bonne Côte should be fragrant, well-balanced and structured, slightly *petillant,* leaving an impression of both delicateness and finesse. The best take some time to develop their potential. Spring frosts can be a problem here, as was evident in April 1991. Summer hail is also not unknown. In general, however, the Bonne Côte is a rich, pastoral land. The southern exposure and drainage provided by the slopes of the Jura make the area suitable for growing grapes. The most important factor, therefore, is to ensure that the natural fecundity of the Chasselas remains under control to allow the strength of the vine to be concentrated in a limited number of grape bunches. This requires a constant discipline from the *vignerons* if the vines are to produce their best.

Aubonne, Allaman and Perroy

Moving west from the Côte de Morges, one soon enters the Bonne Côte which stretches from the charming hill-side town of Aubonne, built around its unique baroque-style Château, to the village of Begnins. This region is the heart of La Côte, and produces some of the best wines in the area. Aubonne is particularly known for the Curzille vineyard. The Association Viticole Aubonne produces a charming Château d'Es Bons (note the unique spelling) in addition to its more standard wines.

Farther down the hill, Allaman enjoys an attractive 15th century Château surrounded by vineyards. The Château grounds now house a collection of up-scale antique shops complemented by a well-stocked wine bar in the ancient cellar. The commune of Allaman includes among its better wine producers the vineyards of Château Rochefort, Chantemerle, Sarraux, Chatagnéréaz, Jordils and St. Vincent. Neighbouring Perroy, also separated from hillside Aubonne by the autoroute, is known for the vineyards of the Clos de Bolombert, la Dame, la Donery, Pérosel, les Renaudes, Malessert and the Crêt du Bérolon.

The vineyards of the Château d'Allaman, owned by the Société Vinicole de Perroy, are in fact fairly close to Lake Geneva. This wine is quite typical of most Côte wines: light, pleasant, especially appropriate for summer drinking, but without great depth and focus, and a fairly short finish. It is well worth trying though, especially in the vinoteque in the cellar of the Château after browsing among the boutiques above.

Allaman is equally well-known as the site of the Château Rochefort, another of the vineyards belonging to the Ville de Lausanne. The vineyards of Château Rochefort were willed in 1838 to Lausanne for the benefit of its poor. From 1979 the area of this vineyard has been increased from 2.64 to 4.28 hectares in four separate parcels to the west of the town of Allaman. Of all the Ville de Lausanne vineyards, the 15th century Château Rochefort has the most impressive Château, including distinctive red and white shutters and an unusual round tower with an octagonal roof. The cellar has been expanded to hold some 90,000 liters of wine. The neutral soil is less chalky than others, and ranges from light to heavy with good fertility depending on the deposits from glacial remains. Two-thirds of the production is made from Chasselas which is quite light and floral on the nose and often *petillant*. The red, made from Gamay and several Pinot Noir clones, is also fruity and fresh, with some tannin, almost showing more Gamay than Pinot Noir. The average production is 100 hectoliters per hectare giving some 30,000 liters of white and 15,000-18,000 liters of red. These wines are comparatively inexpensive and offer reasonable value.

Féchy

Farther up the hill the gravely, poor, chalky soil of Féchy is suited to the Chasselas, although parcels of both Chardonnay and Sylvaner are also found. Féchy produces some of the better wines of La Côte. In particular, the wines from Jacques Pelichet, including the widely-distributed Mon Pichet, are recognized as among the best of the area. Pelichet's three hectares of vineyards are well-cared for and he keeps the yields down. The wine has a typical Chasselas nose and is refreshing and a bit less acidic, but fuller, than most La Côte wines. Pelichet also produces a range of other white wines from Féchy, including a Pinot Gris, Chardonnay and strong Gewürztraminer. In addition, the vineyards of the Clos des Barrettes, Bayelles and Martheray are known for their well-structured, relatively long-lasting wines. Other medium-sized Féchy producers with solid reputations include Willy Kursner and Raymond Paccot.

Féchy Les Martines, from the firm of Hammel, can also be a considerable success. The wine is light but well-balanced with a slightly flowery nose and medium length. Generic "Féchy" is very popular as an "open" wine for immediate consumption in the restaurants of eastern Switzerland. As a result, many larger producers also bottle a Féchy, although the quality can be mixed.

Bougy-Villars, Mont-sur-Rolle and Tartegnin

The restored village of Bougy-Villars, situated on the first slopes of the hill which gives the name to La Côte, is known for its well-exposed slopes which produce wines with good finesse and balance. The "Grand Cru de la Côte", Domaine de Fischer, from Bougy-Villars is an exclusive reserve of Hammel in Rolle. It is another wine that must be considered among the best of the wines of La Côte. It occupies an excellent south-west exposure at the base of the hill which rises from the flat plains west from Morges. Domaine de Fischer should be a full, fruity wine, better balanced and longer than the normal wines of La Côte. The Bougy-Villars Les Vaulangines from Phillipe Cretegny shows both a good nose and reasonable concentration.

The picturesque village of Mont-sur-Rolle is the site of some of the best-known vineyards of the region. Among these, pride of place is usually given to the most western of the Ville de Lausanne vineyards, Abbaye de Mont, not to be confused with the Clos des Abbayes wine of Dézaley. The Abbaye de Mont has better concentration and extract than most La Côte wines. The vineyard is just outside the village of Mont-sur-Rolle and, at 13.5 hectares, is the largest of the City of Lausanne vineyards.

The vineyard dates from the end of the 10th century and, like several others, became the property of the city at the beginning of the 19th century after which it was extensively reworked. The gently-sloping vineyards are composed of chalk and medium-to-heavy clay. Chasselas is grown on the clay soil, Gamay on the moraine and Pinot Noir on the chalkier soils. The whites are characterized by fullness and concentration, with production limited to 80 hectoliters per hectare. The reds are fruity and forward with some tannin. The wines, especially the whites, show good length, but are still relatively expensive when bought retail. Interestingly, the responsibility for production is now split in three – 1.5 hectares jointly run by Albert Chevalley and François Gaillard, and six hectares managed separately by each of the pair.

The vineyards of Haute-Cour and Biborne in Mont-sur-Rolle are also well-regarded. The wines from this area are prized by local consumers for a slight, but distinguishable, salinity on the taste. Farther down the hill the Bougy vineyard in Rolle recalls a history of changing rule in this region. The Bernois, who once were rulers over the entire area, have never completely left.

Auguste Chevalley, Fernand Blanchard and Edmond and Jean-Daniel Gallay are three other important producers at Mont-sur-Rolle. Of the three, Chevalley is the largest with some 200,000 bottles of his own wine on the market annually. His local white wines include two Chasselas; La Montoise, sometimes a touch unstructured, and Domaine de Famolens, as well as a Pinot Gris. Chevalley's reds are a Mont-sur-Rolle Gamay and a Vaudois Pinot Noir, Souche Ardente. Blanchard produces just over 4,000 cases from vineyards in Mont-sur-Rolle and Tartegnin, while the Gallays release some 3,300 cases of Chasselas, Chardonnay and Pinot Noir from their Cave de la Muscadelle in Mont-sur-Rolle. Other wines of Mont-sur-Rolle include a Château de Mont from François Naef. The Château de Mont a reasonably priced screw top; fresh, light, and pleasant, but without any great depth or weight. It finishes fairly short.

Down the hill from Mont-sur-Rolle, in Rolle next to the Geneva-Lausanne freeway, are the headquarters for the large shippers Schenk and Hammel. The former, founded in 1893, is the largest wine concern in Switzerland and controls important estates such as the Château de Châtagnéréaz in Mont-sur-Rolle, Domaine de Martheray in Féchy and Château Maison Blanche in Yvorne. They also own the firms of Obrist in Vevey, Maurice Gay and Cave St. Pierre in Valais and are major importers of French, Italian and Spanish wines into Switzerland. Schenk is one of the stronger Swiss exporters and their wines can be found in markets in London and North America. Hammel is equally both an importer of non-Swiss wines and a Swiss grower with important estates concentrated in the La Côte region. In addition to Domaine de Fischer mentioned above, wines distributed by Hammel include Château de Luins in Luins, Domaine de Riencourt in Féchy and Domaine des Caillattes in Tartegnin.

Slightly to the west of Mont-sur-Rolle, the village of Tartegnin is known particularly for its red wines, many of which end up in Vaudois "Salvagnin". One rather good example, however, is Salvagnin-Rocvigne in its striking gold-lettered, paint-on-glass bottle. The wine was surprisingly good and racy, showing the Pinot Noir/Gamay blend to best effect and, in fact, is a wine worth putting down for a year or two.

Côteau de Vincy and Vinzel

Continuing west from Tartegnin, the next region on the slope is the Côteau de Vincy. The region is best known for the Château de Vincy whose rich soils actually produce a slightly bitter, citric wine. To some the wines of Vincy are reminiscent of grapefruit and peach. Another wine from Vincy is the Domaine Les Creuses, Côteau de Vincy, which is pleasant and light but leaves little impression,

Next door to the Côteau de Vincy is found another "V" – this time the commune of Vinzel. The first vines in this area were planted almost 1,000 years ago by monks from the monastery of Romainmôtier, renowned for its isolated but lovely abbey found between the Vaudois villages of Orbe and Valorbe, and Bonmont. The village of Vinzel is surrounded by vines and stretches up the slope from the flat agricultural fields below, eventually ending at the lower limit of the forest which caps the top of the hill overlooking the vineyards.

In good years the wines of Vinzel are said, with slight exaggeration, to resemble the highly regarded Chablais wines from Yvorne. They can be strong and fragrant with intense smoky fruit. The best known vineyard is the Château de la Bâtie, "Grand Cru de La Côte". In addition to ten hectares of vines, the Château de la Bâtie is renowned for its beautiful cellars which can hold 200,000 liters of aging wine. The Château is one of the landmarks of La Côte. The wines are clean and forward, often with a slight spritz, a typical Chasselas nose, and reasonable weight.

Another Vinzel producer with a solid reputation is Philippe Straub of the Domaine de la Tuilière. From 2.2 hectares he produces just over 1,000 cases of Chasselas, Chardonnay and a Gamay/Pinot Noir blend. The Chasselas is bottled under the label Clos des Chaponnières.

Bursinel, Luins and Begnins

With Vinzel ends the best-known section of La Côte. Although still part of the central Bonne Côte, the terrain of the western communes of Bursinel, Luins and Begnins flattens out as one approaches Nyon. The region of Bursinel is another wine-growing area that borders Lake Geneva. The known vineyards are Bourdouzans, the Clos du Château, En Corneau, la Curtillode and the Château du Rosey. The wines of Luins are usually light, fresh and comparatively inexpensive, making them good aperitif or reception wines. Wine from the Château de Luins is fairly common in Geneva, but unless the wines are from an extremely creative wine maker, there are only minor nuances to distinguish between them. Finally, further to the west, Begnins produces a well-regarded Pinot Noir from a soil whose composition, it is claimed, resembles that of a Burgundian vineyard more closely than any of its neighbouring lands.

The Côte de Nyon Region

The transition from the Bonne Côte to the Côte de Nyon is virtually instantaneous. Nyon, site of the ancient Roman city of Colonia Julia Equestris, boasts a Roman vine cutter *(serpe)* in the local museum which provides evidence of the cultivation of vines in the region for almost 2,000 years. The topography of the Côte de Nyon is softer still than the Bonne Côte and, consequently, the wines are generally agreeable, delicate, soft and slightly thinner than the wines further to the east. The expansion of Nyon and the development of nearby satellite villages surrounding Geneva has removed some land from grape production in recent years. But national and cantonal legislation encouraging continued agricultural production, and the collapse of the late 1980s speculative land bubble, will protect vineyards at least for some years to come.

The soil throughout this region is sandstone covered by glacial deposits with pockets of sand and gravel. The Château at Coinsins is the center of the viticultural portion of the Côte de Nyon. The reds of the Château are well-regarded, as are the wines of the Clos de la Colombière. Towards Geneva, the Château at Crans is known for its whites, while in Commugny, the whites from the vineyards Clos de la Fontaine, Muret, Charrue and l'Eglise have good local reputations. These are all reasonably priced wines which can be picked up during an easy drive from Geneva. They are honest wines without pretensions to great depth or complexity. Most of the small towns which encircle Nyon have their own vineyards catering to the immediate population, the city dwellers on a Sunday drive, or the very occasional tourist from farther afield.

The 18th Century château of the lakeside village of Coppet is best-known historically as the seat of the glittering artistic society that gathered around Madame de Staël, the French woman of letters who passed part of her exile in the 1790s from France on the shores of Lake Geneva. Not incidentally, the Château also has its own vines. So too does the village of Duillier on the other side of the autoroute. The quaint bedroom village is located on top of a small glacial outcrop, and is known for the Clos des Verchères whose wine press and cellars are located in the basement of the 12th century Château around which the village has grown.

Arnex is known for both red and white from the Clos de Villars and the Clos du Bochet. Genollier has the En Barin, En Chaton, La Cure and Sous-la-Ville vineyards. In the Geneva dormitory suburb of Founex are found the wines of Jean-Jacques Dutruy, sold under the name of Domaine de la Treille. In addition to normal Chasselas, a range of reds and whites is grown, including a particularly pleasant Rosé de Pinot Noir, a light, refreshingly simple, well-made wine. In Founex are also found the vineyards of Châtaingneriaz, Clos de la Châtaigneraie, and Clos des Repingonnes. By now one is almost in the western suburbs of the next major wine-producing region, Geneva. There are quite a few commuters in Geneva who, upon returning home in the evening, unwind with a glass of the local wine from the *cave* just down the road.

Finally, reference must be made to Changins, just north of Nyon, where the federal agricultural research station and the Higher School for Viticulture, Oenology and Arboriculture have been established inside the Domaine of the Château de Changins. This institution, along with its sister station for German Switzerland in

Wädenswil on Lake Zürich, have had as great an influence on the development of grape growing and wine production in Switzerland as any other organization. Some in the Swiss wine industry have criticized the work of Changins and Wädenswil by claiming that their influence has been directed more towards a "leveling" of the interesting differences among Swiss wines. Practical experience does not seem to bear this out. The efforts of the federal research stations are heavily based on continuous scientific inquiry to improve the care of vines and grapes, the vinification processes, and the overall quality of Swiss wine. In the end it is for the *vignerons* themselves to apply appropriately and selectively the results achieved by the research stations, and thereby raise the basic standard for all Swiss wines.

Côtes de l'Orbe, Bonvillars and Vully

The passage from the vineyards of the southern Vaud to those of the north of the canton is more than a simple journey. The areas surrounding Lake Geneva are an integral part of the Rhône valley river system, just as the lake itself is an expansion of the river. With the exception of a few vines that line the corridor between Morges and Yverdon, the vineyards in the north of the Vaud are all part of the drainage system that feeds into the second of Europe's great rivers, the Rhine. The vines of this area, therefore, share more in common in terms of topography and climate with the neighbouring vineyards of Neuchâtel and eastern Switzerland than with the more southern vineyards of the same canton.

Without the moderating influence of Lake Geneva, the temperature becomes more harsh. The average annual temperature in the Morges-Yverdon corridor rarely exceeds nine degrees centigrade.

Vineyards in this region total slightly over 300 hectares and produce only 10% of the canton's wine total. Most of the plots are quite small and the wine, more often than not, is consumed in the region. Although many of the wines are honest and straightforward, the entire region is as marginal as any in Switzerland. Greater competition from imports will place pressure on this region to rationalize and reduce planting of grapes. The long term economic viability of wine production here is in some doubt.

Côtes de l'Orbe

The climate of the Côtes de l'Orbe is drier than that of Geneva and, with a harsher winter, wine production has evolved more towards the production of cold-resistant red vines and the Riesling x Sylvaner at the expense of the Chasselas. As one moves away from Lake Geneva northwards along the valleys that connect Lausanne with Yverdon, the first vines are located near Gollion, still very much influenced by Lake Geneva. Farther north, Eclépens marks the dividing line between the Rhine and Rhône river systems. The region between Eclépens and the neighbouring villages of La Sarraz and Pompaples is collectively called *"le milieu du monde"* (the middle of the world) because it straddles the dividing line between the Mediterranean and North Sea river systems. The wines begin to show the higher acids that mark the more northerly wines. Even further north is the town of Arnex. Here the monks from the Abbey of St. Peter and St. Paul of Romainmôtier, founded in the 10th century by the mother Church of Cluny, played an important role in the development of the vineyards throughout Vaud. The surviving abbey buildings are among the oldest and most important in Switzerland.

The city of Orbe, in ancient times the prosperous Roman town of Urba, is the center of the commune of the same name. Orbe once boasted the largest amount of land devoted to grapes in the entire canton of Vaud. It now has no vineyards. Worth visiting at La Boscéaz to the north of the town of Orbe are the finest Roman mosaics in Switzerland, dating from the 3rd century A.D.

Traveling still north, the village of Montcherand is known for several vineyards; the Clos Dufour, Clos des Grillières, and the Clos des Mangones. A short distance away, the picturesque village of Valeyres-sous-Rances has developed a following for its reds, both Gamay and Pinot Noir, which are legacies of earlier contacts with Burgundy. The Riesling x Sylvaner wines of Valeyres-sous-Rances have also developed a strong local reputation. Finally, the village of Mathod, known for its well-preserved 13th century Château, produces wines of some local note from the Clos de la Combaz and Champvert vineyards.

In general, the better wines from the Côtes de l'Orbe are balanced and refined with a bouquet which, although full and floral, can border on faintly bitter. Straightforward, honest and refreshing, these wines are difficult to find outside of the area of production because of the small quantities produced.

Bonvillars

The vineyards of Bonvillars, which hug the north shore of Lake Neuchâtel, are visually reminiscent of those that cover the north slopes of Lake Geneva. The region produces just five percent of the Vaud's wine on 170 hectares. North of the city of Yverdon, the area of Bonvillars begins with the village of Montagny with its Clos des Secrétaires vineyard. The neighbouring villages of Giez and Valeyres-sous-Montagny have their vines; the latter particularly known for its Clos des Crusilles and Grand-Vignes. Grandson is the site of one of the most famous battles of Swiss history. There in 1476, Charles the Bold of Burgundy was defeated by the Swiss Confederation, led by Fribourg and Berne. The town retains its imposing 13th century Château along with the vineyards of Clos des Combes, Clos des Pierres, Revelins and Clos des Murets, which mainly produce white wine.

The village of Bonvillars, from which the region takes its name, is set slightly back from Lake Neuchâtel. Here is found the headquarters of the wine cooperative which produces a good proportion of the wines from this region – once again generally lively and pleasing whites, but also some red and sparkling wine. In particular, the Vin des Croisés Pinot Noir from the Cave des Viticulteurs de Bonvillars has done quite well in national and international comparisons of Pinot Noir wines. The known crus of Bonvillars are Boulaz, Clos des Epinettes, as well as Clos de l'Eglise. Nearby is Champagne, a village reputed as much for the production of elegant pastries which are consumed, naturally, with French champagne, as for its production of Swiss wine of the same name. Most wine is drunk young, within a year or at most two of the vintage. Typical of the area, and bought by some as much for the name as for the wine, is the 1991 Champagne, Appellation Bonvillars d'Origine, a light, slightly acidic but not unpleasant wine with a short finish. There is also a fair amount of Oeil-de-Perdrix produced around Champagne.

Stretching from west to east along the scenic lakeshore are Onnens and Corcelles, once connected to the Benedictine order at Cluny through its ancient church, and Concise, all of which maintain their local vineyards. The soil of the region alternates between chalk around Grandson and Concise, and the red clay and silica of Bonvillars. In addition at the base of the Jura there are stony soils resembling those of Burgundy. Here Chasselas is most often grown with both Gamay and Pinot Noir, at times on trellises higher than those usually found throughout Vaud.

Vully (of Vaud)

The region of Vully is located quite separately from Bonvillars and Côte de l'Orbe between the north shore of Lake Morat and the south shore of Lake Neuchâtel. Vully is divided between two cantons; one-fourth is Vaudois while the majority falls within the borders of the neighbouring canton of Fribourg. On the Vaudois side, less than forty hectares of vines are split between six Vaudois communes. The dominant influences are the lake, the sandstone, and the sandy soil of the south-facing plateau. The area has a long history, stretching back to Roman times when the region was governed from the walled Roman city of Aventicum, now Avenches. Aventicum once boasted 20,000 inhabitants and was the prosperous capital of Roman Helvetica. Records show that in 971 A.D. Berthe de Bourgogne bequeathed all the vineyards of the area to the Abbey at Payerne.

The most important wine-producing villages of the Vaudois Vully are Vallamand, Cudrefin, Bellerive, Chabrey, Constantine and Montmagny. The vineyard of Vallamand-Dessous produces approximately one-third of the total production. The Chasselas grape dominates, although pockets of Pinot Gris and Riesling x Sylvaner are also found. In general, the white wines of this area are light, fragrant, often *petillant* and refreshing. Both Pinot Noir and Gamay are also grown in small quantities with some success. Other vineyards include Clos des Avaris, des Rintzes, Vermon, Gruppes and Château de Cotterd.

Vully (of Fribourg)

The Vully wines belonging to the canton of Fribourg are best dealt with as a natural extension of their neighbouring Vaudois vineyards. The French- and German-speaking canton of Fribourg remains an important holder of vineyards in the Lavaux region of Vaud. Within the canton there are also just over 100 hectares of vines. The most important part is in the commune of Vully, while the remainder lies on the southern shore of Lake Neuchâtel. There is no physical distinction between Vully Vaudois and Vully Fribourgois; the vineyards are a continuum from one canton to the other moving from west to east along the north shore of Lake Morat.

The Caveau des vignerons at Grandvaux in the Lavaux region, similar to the many communal cellars that can be found in the wine-growing villages of Vaud.

Vully is astride the historical and linguistic divide between German- and French-speaking Switzerland. It is at the same time the border between three very different Swiss cantons: Vaud, Berne and Fribourg. The history of the region is, accordingly, complex, and the villages reflect and remain proud of their varied traditions. In the 15th century the vineyards of Fribourg were much more extensive than today, reaching as far as the cheese-making center of Gruyère. The gradual cooling of the climate over the last 500 years forced a reduction of vines on marginal lands, although through various diplomatic alliances with Berne, Fribourg was able to compensate for the loss of "domestic" vineyards by purchasing useful sites in the Lavaux area, most importantly the vineyard Les Faverges.

Today the total production of Vully in Fribourg is around 500,000 liters, of which 90% is white. Most is drunk locally or by the residents of the Swiss capital of Berne. Production is fairly concentrated, and 12 larger producers own over half the vineyards. Some of the best sites are owned by the city of Morat and the canton of Fribourg. In addition to Vully, there are some 12 hectares of vineyards at Cheyres and Font in the district of Broye on the south-east shore of Lake Neuchâtel, where the wines, while rare, are scented and *petillant*.

In addition to the dominant Chasselas, Gewürztraminer was also successfully introduced from Alsace in the 1950s and is producing a well-structured perfumed wine, albeit in minute quantities. An indigenous grape, the Freiburger, similar to the Räuschling of Zurich, is still found in very small quantities. Finally, the Pinot Noir produces a wine somewhat between the fuller reds of Vaud and Valais and the lighter wines usually found in German-speaking Switzerland.

Fribourg has also recently created a wine fraternity to preserve local traditions and promote the quality and wider knowledge of Fribourgois wines. The *Confrérie des Vignolans,* similar to other such groups, concentrates its efforts on a combination of educational and promotional activities – largely focused in and around the region of the three lakes (Neuchâtel, Morat and Bienne).

Confrérie de Guillon

The name *"guillon"* comes from *"guille"* or *"quille"* in French, a wooden plug which was used as a stopper in a barrel. This Confrérie was founded in part to defend the economic interests of the Vaudois wine makers confronted by a flood of imports in the early 1950s. One of the organization's chief aims was to prod the Swiss federal government into action. Starting as a political protest movement, the organization soon developed the more positive ambition of promoting the wines of Vaud. The fraternity played an important role in the realization of the wine museum at the Château d'Aigle. The Confrérie de Guillon also works closely with the Office des Vins Vaudois (OVV) to encourage a better appreciation of Vaudois wines.

Useful Addresses in Vaud:

Office des Vins Vaudois (OVV), Chemin de la Vuachère 6, Case postale 158, 1005 Lausanne (021) 729 55 26.

Wine Museum

Musée du vin et de la vigne, Château d'Aigle, Aigle (024) 466 21 30.

Wine Fraternity

Confrérie du Guillon, 58 avenue Tivoli, P.O. Box 58, 1000 Lausanne 20 (021) 724 48 15.

Recommended Wine makers:

Chablais

Henri Badoux, 1860 Aigle (024) 466 20 02: A very extensive selection from some of the best sites in the Chablais. Top quality but not cheap.

Clos de la George, 1852 Roche (025) 466 37 69: A large estate near Yvorne whose wines get good distribution throughout Switzerland.

Jacques Deladoey, 1853 Yvorne (024) 466 35 48: Domaine de l'Ovaille represents the best of Yvorne. Worth searching out.

Paul Tille, Caves de Prieuré S.A. 1869 Aigle (024) 466 51 32: Well-made concentrated wines.

Lavaux

Roger Barbey, 1605 Chexbres (021) 946 12 56: A smaller producer specializing in the wines of St. Saphorin.

Louis Bovard SA, Place d'Armes 2, 1096 Cully; (021) 799 21 25: A large producer of first-rate wines. A company to look for internationally.

Jean-Michel Conne, Cave de Champ de Clos, Rue Bourg de Plaît, 1605 Chexbres; (021) 946 26 86: Good selection of wines from the Lavaux and even farther afield. A quality producer.

Dubois Frères et Fils, Le Petit Versailles, 1096 Cully (021) 799 22 22: A broad selection from well-located sites in Lavaux.

Fonjallaz SA, 1098 Epesses (021) 799 14 44: An uneven producer but with the potential to produce better wines from its well-exposed vineyards.

Jean-Louis Jomini, 1605 Chexbres (021 946 24 46: One of the Chexbres specialists. Good wines showing typical characteristics.

Claude Massy et Fils, La Place, 1098 Epesses (021) 799 15 58: A superior Lavaux producer with wines from Calamin, Dézaley and St. Saphorin.

Jean-François & Luc Massy, Clos du Boux, 1098 Epesses (021) 799 21 47: A well-established firm which manages excellent vineyards in Dézaley and Epesses.

Obrist SA, 26, avenue Reller 1800 Vevey (021) 921 12 62: Selections from throughout the canton. Single vineyards wines can be very good.

J & P Testuz SA, 1096 Treytorrens/Cully (021) 799 20 21: A widely-distributed négociant with excellent sites throughout the canton.

Ville de Lausanne, c/o Service des forêts, domaines et vignobles de la Ville, Au Boscal, C.P. 27, 1000 Lausanne 25 (021) 784 39 19: The best overall producer in the canton. The wines are not inexpensive but the quality cannot be denied.

Jean Vogel, La Croix Duplex, Route de Chenaux, 1603 Grandvaux (021) 799 15 31: Produces a range of interesting, different wines. A creative wine maker.

La Côte

Cave Auguste Chevalley SA, 1185 Mont-sur-Rolle (021) 825 26 41: A large producer of typical well-made La Côte wines. Good Mont-sur-Rolle.

Henri Cruchon SA, Cave du Village, 1112 Echichens (021) 801 17 92: Considered by most to be the best producer in the Morges area.

Hammel SA, 1180 Rolle (021) 825 11 41: A large *négociant* with a wide but uneven selection of wines from across the canton. Some very good wines.

Jacques Pelichet, 1173 Féchy (021) 808 51 41: Pelichet's Mon Pichet is among the best known wines of Féchy.

VIII

Geneva

The Region

The canton of Geneva is Switzerland's third wine region in terms of quantity. Its topography is an extension of the soft rolling hills of the La Côte region of Vaud. It lacks the dramatic steep slopes of Lavaux or the spectacular mountain scenery that guards the vineyards of Valais. This lack of geological drama does not, however, inhibit the production of some very pleasing wines and, what's more, the wines of Geneva often provide good value for money compared to similar wines from the Vaud and Valais.

Historically wine production in this canton has had its successes and problems and recently the canton has gone through some wrenching structural changes. In the mid-19th century, grape growing was a widespread occupation in and around Geneva and the vineyards were economically important. The crisis sparked by the phylloxera infestation of the 1860s and 1870s, and compounded by the replanting of the vineyards with high-yielding hybrid varieties, fundamentally changed the quality equation and the wines of Geneva went into a serious decline.

The establishment of the Vin Union cooperative in 1933 probably marked the nadir for the fortunes of Geneva's wines. Established to protect the interests of the grape growers, the cooperative's concentration on relatively easy to grow Chasselas and Gamay meant that improvements, while notable, were slow and intermittent. The gulf between grape growing and wine making continued to widen. As a result, for much of its recent history, the Genevois have been known as volume producers of pleasant but usually undistinguished Chasselas, known locally as "Perlan", and "useful" reds.

In 1970s this situation began to change with the rise of the independent *vignerons-encaveurs* and since then there has been a steady but genuine improvement of the Genevois wines and wine-making skills. Previously, oenological developments were overwhelmingly influenced by the dominant commercial position of Vin Union. As late as 1975 the Vin Union cooperative still controlled 80% of the canton's production; there were only 19 independent wine producers. It was, however, these independent growers that provided the catalyst for greater experimentation, rising standards and commercial success for Geneva's wines. By 1994 the share of canton's production produced by La Cave de Genève (the cooperative's successor organization) fell below 50% while the number of

141

vignerons-encaveurs rose to 53, many them members of the Association genevoise des vignerons et encaveurs independants (AGVEI). The independent producers, together with Geneva's 100 grape growers who sell their grape harvest mainly to négotiants, now control over one-half the canton's grape production – a remarkable shift in economic influence.

The Genevois vineyards largely follow the contours of the western end of Lake Geneva *(Lac Léman)* and, in the shape of a pointed triangle, thrust into France. They are protected by the Jura mountains to the north and the Salève range to the south. There are important variations among the soils, exposures and, consequently, the wines from the tidy but vibrant villages which dot the countryside behind Geneva. Much of the difference among the wines is due, however, to the skill and discipline of the wine maker rather than marked differences in the physical environment – although the latter certainly do play a role.

Geneva sits at the confluence of two rivers that rise in the Alps; the Rhône which departs Lake Geneva in the middle of the city before continuing its journey to the Mediterranean, and the Arve which passes through Chamonix before merging with the Rhône one kilometer beyond the west end of Lake Geneva. This river system determines the geographical division of the Genevois hinterland and, in turn, sets the boundaries for the major vineyard areas in the canton.

With 1,478 hectares devoted to vines in 1992, the canton is divided into three distinct areas. The first and largest of these areas is the right bank or Mandement region, which has over 850 hectares of grapes. The second is the area referred to as Entre Arve et Rhône, (Between the Arve and the Rhône), comprising the most westerly of Geneva's vineyards with 330 hectares producing grapes. The third and last major area is formed by the vineyards Entre Arve et Lac (Between the Arve and the Lake) which includes all the vines on the left bank of Lake Geneva, totaling just over 280 hectares.

Among the leafy suburbs of Geneva such as Cologny in this last area, one finds arguably some of the most valuable land planted in vines in the world. Although Geneva is one of the smallest cantons of Switzerland, the relative amount of land devoted to grapes, (six percent of the total arable surface), is the highest in the country. (In 1994 the calculation for Geneva was reduced by 150 hectares to exclude the vineyards which are Swiss-owned but located across the border in France. These vineyards have a long history in Swiss hands and previously were included in Geneva's total acreage.)

Compared with the spring and summer in the rest of Switzerland, Geneva's seasons come early. In addition, falls are long and mild, providing a more than acceptable growing season. Lake Geneva exerts a moderating influence on the climate, although the two mountain ranges which enclose the city cause temperature inversions in winter which block the sun for weeks on end with a layer of uninviting heavy, grey fog.

The soil of the scattered Geneva vineyards varies between sandy, clay and alluvial. The level of chalk changes from region to region. Although in general the Genevois vineyards have withstood the onslaught of suburban developers, in the last several decades some land previously devoted to grapes has been developed into more immediately lucrative suburbs or villas.

The vineyards of Geneva

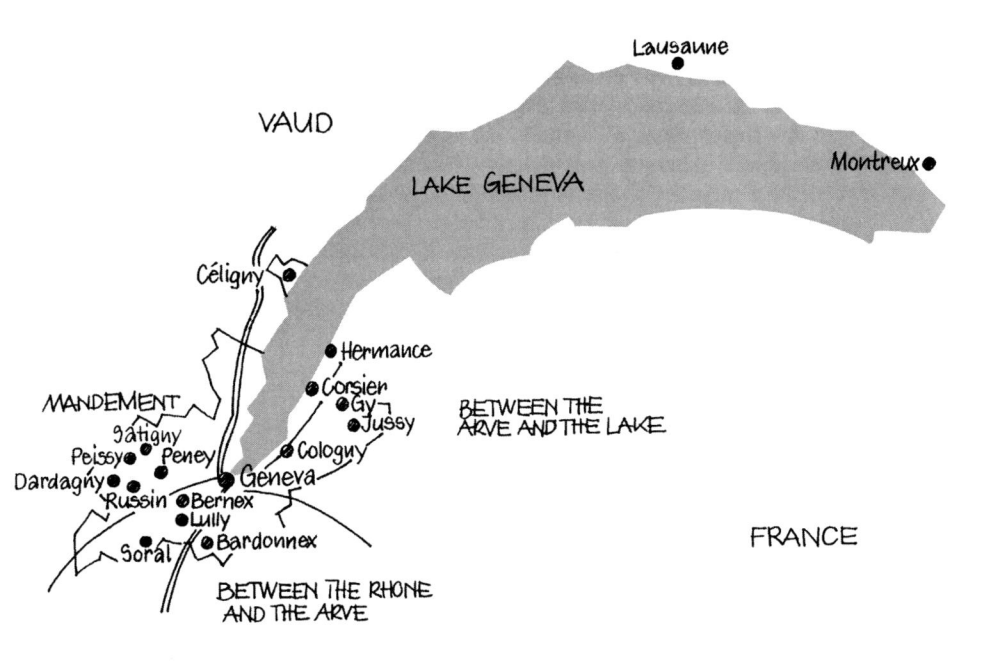

The vinous history of Geneva stretches back 2,000 years to the time when vines were first cultivated on the banks of the Rhône and Arve rivers outside the city's fortified walls. The site now occupied by Geneva has always been of strategic importance because of the transportation routes that pass through the area. From the 5th century, the Burgundians established one of their regional capitals at Geneva and encouraged grape cultivation with laws to protect the vines and the livelihood of the growers. The rather severe royal provisions of the Law of Gombette allowed vineyard workers to kill grape thieves without fear of legal sanction. In 912 the Countess Eldegarde bequeathed important vineyards to the Augustinian monks of the Monastery of St. Pierre in Satigny, still one of the most important vine-growing satellite villages of Geneva. Eventually the best parcels were taken over by the bishops of Geneva. The earliest mention of grapes on the left bank of the lake is in an obituary dated 1178 which mentions the donation to the church of St. Pierre by the Count of Geneva of a *tonneau* of wine from Bossey at the foot of the Salève cliffs.

In the later medieval period, the development of Geneva as a commercial center encouraged a flourishing bourgeoisie. Because of the economic success of the town, a commune was established in the latter part of the 13th century – the same time that the cantons of Uri, Schwyz and Unterwald united to create the core of present day Switzerland. Eventually the sale of wine became a privilege granted to the emancipated inhabitants of the city. Charters from 1387 specify that a wine seller must be a member of the bourgeoisie, a citizen or a monk. Such ordinances were also meant to encourage the sale of local wines by allowing the wine from the immediate vicinity to enter the city duty free. At the same time the charters set up a monopoly over the sale of wines from outside Geneva proper.

By the 16th century certain of the episcopal estates had established considerable reputations, including the Clos du Paradis, the Clos des Seigneurs and the Contamines. All of these still exist as identifiable vineyards in Jussy, Laconnex and Compesières respectively. Quite separately, from the 16th century onward, Geneva also became a significant international city, offering refuge to the politically persecuted, artists out of favour, visionaries and revolutionaries, as well as to Huguenot bankers, clock-makers and the occasional *vigneron*. The total area of the canton devoted to grapes in the 17th century was five times the current level, and the production of wine was critical for the health of the local economy.

By the time Geneva again entered the Swiss Confederation in 1815 it still had 2,500 hectares of grapes under cultivation, although they were generally grown at random, without alignment, or in *hutins,* where the lengthy vine stocks were attached to trees. Such viticultural habits were inherited from the neighbouring region of the Savoie, but they were discarded almost entirely by the end of the 19th century when the vineyards were replanted after invasion by the phylloxera louse and the damage from the other 19th century scourges. This replanting also reduced by half the land growing wine grapes in Geneva.

As mentioned above, the dominant force in the Geneva wine world from 1933 to the early 1990s has been the Genevois cooperatives. Until late 1992 this structure operated under the name Vin Union and, after its bankruptcy, subsequently as La Cave de Genève. The cooperative was born out of the social and economic turbulence of the 1920s and 1930s which afflicted agriculture, generally, and wine production specifically. Economic pressures forced individual grape growers and *vignerons* to unite to protect their basic interests. The first cooperative cellar, La Souche, was founded in 1929 at Pallanterie, a 15th century fortified site in the left-bank village of Collonge-Bellerive, just outside of Geneva. The considerably larger Cave du Mandement on the right bank followed in 1933. Growers from the area around Lully, in the region between the Arve and the Rhône, joined the cooperative after the Second World War.

Overproduction of inferior white wines in the late 1920s caused a severe drop in market prices. In response, production was limited to areas most suitable to grapes; yields were reduced; grape types were improved; vinification methods changed; and, more recently, the production of red wines, particularly the Gamay, was increased to complement the production of Chasselas. Similar efforts have continued ever since, a testimony to the ongoing challenges of achieving balanced and profitable wine production in Geneva.

Geneva's production of wine was 11.5 million liters in 1995. Chasselas still dominates white grape varieties and in 1995 still accounted for over 40% of the canton's vineyards. This figure is down from well over 50% only a few years earlier. Selected white grapes such as Aligoté, Pinot Gris, Pinot Blanc, Chardonnay and Muscat receive increasing attention with about 10% of total production. Almost one-half (47.5%) of total output is red, largely Gamay, (almost one-third of all wines) which is often used to produce the Genevois equivalent of Beaujolais nouveau. The Gamay grapes are complemented by red wine made from Pinot Noir, some 13% of vineyards, and plots of other classic grapes such as Cabernet Sauvignon and Merlot. These last three grape varieties will play an increasingly important role in Geneva's wine future as recent plantings of these new varieties, some of which are not yet fully producing, are greater than the regeneration of the more traditional grape varieties.

In general, there is a trend away from reliance upon traditional high-yield varieties and growing techniques towards greater discipline and high quality (albeit less bountiful) grapes. These changes have brought notable innovations and improvements to local wine production as the trend in the grapes grown in Geneva's vineyards reflects the evolution of experience and wine fashion. Overproduction is, however, still a problem. The average production (hectoliters per hectare) in 1994 was 102 for white wines and 81 for reds. These figures were only exceeded by the vineyards of Vaud.

As can be seen from the table on the next page, the Chasselas has steadily lost ground to the Gamay and Pinot Noir. Hybrids, once popular in the area, virtually disappeared between the 1960s and 1980s. The relatively high-yielding Riesling x Sylvaner was very popular for a time but by the 1990s its acreage had fallen back. More important for the long-term is the increase of the acreage of other quality vinifera grapes such as Aligoté, Chardonnay, Pinot Gris, Gewürztraminer, Pinot Blanc, Merlot and Cabernet Sauvignon.

The gentle, protected fields of Geneva distinguish its vineyards from those of Vaud and Valais. Terraces are generally not required. Mechanization, therefore, arrived earlier here than in most other parts of Switzerland The introduction of the medium-height *guyot* system of trellising allowed for greater utilization of machines. Geneva, and the next-door La Côte region of Vaud, are now two of the most mechanized grape growing areas of Switzerland.

Table VIII: Grape types planted in Geneva (%)

	1957	1986	1994
Chasselas	68	50	43
Gamay	6	36	29
Riesling-Sylvaner	1	8	4
Pinot Noir	-	4	13
Other Vinifera	4	2	11
Hybrids	25	-	-

The Genevois were in the forefront of the Swiss producers in adopting a system of *appellation contrôlée,* perhaps reflecting the influence of France which geographically surrounds the small canton. A conscious effort began in 1984 to limit production to meet market demand for improved quality. In 1988 the first formal system of control was introduced, although not without controversy. The new system was divided into two categories, *appellation d'origine* (AO) and *appellation d'origine contrôlée* (AOC). The former is a recognition of basic quality and authenticity. The latter, however, must meet stricter criteria, including limitations on age of vines, production and must weight, and vinification techniques. Yields for AOC wines must be below 1.2 kilograms per square meter while the pressing must be sufficiently light to give not more than 70 hectoliters per hectare. Sugar, however, can still be added to improve the musts, although its use is limited to a maximum of 40 grams per liter. The AOC group is further divided into two sub-categories – a simple AOC and an AOC "grand cru" or "premier cru".

The initial introduction of AOC wines was largely confined to production from the better vineyards that were connected to the cooperative. This occasioned rather heated debate, particularly from some of the independent producers, about how strict the parameters really were. The *Association des organisations viticoles genevoise,* (AOVG or Geneva Association of Wine Producers), created in 1990 and composed of both cooperative growers and the independent producers has sought to develop a consensus on the appropriate commercial and qualitative standards for a credible AOC system.

The future of the Genevois Cooperative

As of the 1994 harvest, the future of the Geneva cooperative was very uncertain. The cooperative marketing arm, Vin Union, controlled nearly four-fifths of the canton's grape harvest in the 1970s. By the late 1980s, this had fallen two thirds. According to one account, Vin Union produced wine under almost 150 different labels. Traditionally, the cooperative was known particularly for its high-yield varieties and, as a consequence, many of its wines had considerable difficulty in establishing recognized and commercially viable market niches. Attempting to establish a better reputation for their wines, Vin Union producers put a considerable effort into developing the canton's *appellation controllée* system. This work was beneficial but was not enough to save the cooperative.

The cooperative's financing was never fully secure and Vin Union was forced into bankruptcy in late 1992. A smaller, but more focused successor organization, La Cave de Genève, was established in October 1993. It too, however, lacked financial stability and had to seek protection early in 1994 and was declared bankrupt and liquidated in May 1994. A third entity, La Cave de Genève SA (a limited liability company rather than a cooperative) was established just before the harvest in September 1994. Efforts to secure its economic viability continue but, in the meantime several cooperative members, including some of the better estates that used to be marketed under the Vin Union/La Cave de Genève labels, have struck out on their own and are now operating independently. As a result, in 1994 for the first time, less than half of Geneva's harvest was gathered by members of the Genevois cooperative.

Given its importance for the canton, it seems unlikely that the cooperative will, or could, disappear entirely. The immediate future does promise to be unsettled while the financial fall-out from the initial Vin Union bankruptcy is worked out. The failure of Vin Union has already fundamentally shifted the balance of power towards the independent producers. Given their track record in terms of innovation and efforts at quality improvement, this is not a bad thing. A successful successor organization will have to be more focused and better at establishing a closer link between quality grape growing and wine making, as well as consumer acceptance of its range of wines. As such, the greater agility that comes from reduced size will probably work in its favour as the cooperative will be able to concentrate on a reduced range of higher quality wines. Only time will tell if this transition can be made successfully.

Given the uncertain state of the future of the Genevois cooperative, except where noted, the section on Geneva's vineyards includes reference to the cooperative's wines up to the early 1990s.

White Wine Grapes

Chasselas (Perlan)

In general the Genevois Chasselas, or Perlan, is dry, slightly bitter and sometimes *petillant*. These wines are best served on their own, as an aperitif, or with lake fish such as the *omble chevalier* or *filets de perche*. The alcohol level varies between ten and twelve degrees. Increasingly wines are marketed with higher alcohol levels although there has been concern that not all the additional strength comes from natural grape sugars!

The effort to create a separate and recognizable Genevois *appellation* through the promotion of the "Perlan" has so far met with mixed success. The challenge is to determine a minimum quality level which is economically viable while also supporting a higher-class product. The wine makers of Geneva are still working towards the creation of a particular niche for their wines. Unless they find it, one wonders whether the "Perlan" might suffer the fate of the now discontinued "Dorin" of the Vaud as a marketing tool.

The above is not, however, to say that Geneva does not produce good Chasselas. In fact, quite the opposite. Some excellent white wines are made from the Chasselas, but only by those producers who exert the additional discipline and understanding that produce a product a cut above the others.

Pinot Gris

Many of the better Pinot Gris are from the Mandement region, particularly around the village of Dardagny. Some of the better producers will reserve small sections of their vineyards for this quite successful wine which should balance a floral nose with an acidic crispness. This is certainly a grape type to look for, although Pinot Gris wines usually demand a premium compared to the price of a Chasselas from the same producer.

Pinot Blanc

The Genevois Pinot Blancs have also established a reasonable reputation, although they still remain slightly in the shadow of the more successful Pinot Gris. The Mandement region between Satigny and Dardagny, including the villages of Peney and Peissy, is an area where the Pinot Blanc grape grows particularly well.

Aligoté

The increased planting of Aligoté is clearly one of the success stories of the renovation of the Geneva vineyards over the past several years. The area devoted to this grape should continue to expand if one judges by the promising results to date. The number of growers producing the Chardonnay grape outnumbers those producing the Aligoté, undoubtedly for commercial reasons. But the future, certainly in terms of a happy marriage between production and quality, may definitely rest more with increased plantings of the Aligoté grape.

Chardonnay

Although considerable progress has been made in recent years, really successful Chardonnays from the Geneva area are still difficult to find. The local soils may be just too rich, or the pruning too relaxed to force the character and depth required to produce convincing Chardonnay. As a consequence, Genevois growers seem best placed to explore the potential of Burgundy's less exclusive grape, the Aligoté, and leave the Chardonnay to more suitable climates. This is not, however, to say that some pleasant wines produced from the Chardonnay grape cannot be found in and around Geneva. Consumers, however, must take care to purchase their Chardonnay from a serious producer.

Riesling x Sylvaner and other white varieties

The Riesling x Sylvaner (Müller-Thurgau) is fairly successful in preserving its fruit and "muscaty" nose in the Geneva environment. The final product can, however, be less than inspiring compared to the better producers of eastern Switzerland. Again, successful producers will prune vigorously. Other white wine grapes grown in Geneva include the Gewürztraminer which is grown mainly in the Mandement, as well as the Findling, a rare Müller-Thurgau clone grown mainly in the Mosel.

Red Wine Grapes
Gamay

Grown in the less chalky regions of Geneva, the local Gamay has achieved considerable success. There is now even an imitative "Gamay nouveau" which is marketed each fall, just before the equivalent wine from Beaujolais is released on the local markets. If properly vinified, the Genevois Gamay can capture the fruity, forward, violet bouquet responsible for this grape's international reputation. Some of the more creative independent producers have managed to extract wines from their better Gamay clones which compare favorably to Gamay-based wines anywhere.

In addition, certain Genevois wine makers go one step further and produce a specially selected Gamay, often from older vines, which is then aged in oak. The attention these wines receive adds a facet rarely found in other Gamays – a more intense, developed wine which somehow manages to preserve the fruit both on the nose and in the taste. Interestingly the Gamay/Pinot Noir *mélange,* common as the Salvagnin in Vaud and Dôle in Valais, is rarely made in Geneva. But perhaps this more intense Gamay fills the gap.

Pinot Noir

As is the case with the Gamay, two distinct types of Pinot Noir are produced in the Geneva region, standard and oak-aged. The latter commands a notable price premium, although it is not always the better wine since the oak, if not used skillfully, can overpower the delicate fruit of the grapes. In fact, with some exceptions, Pinot Noir generally is not as successful in Geneva as the more lowly Gamay. At its best the Genevois variety resembles a good, fruity but fairly light Alsacian Pinot Noir. Rarely do they acquire the finesse and depth that are associated with the best producers of Valais or the Neuchâtel region. The determinants of soil, slope and climate work against the Genevois producers. Because of the prestige and commercial return associated with growing Pinot Noir, however, almost as many independent growers produce a version of Pinot Noir, either standard or oak-aged, as produce Chasselas. In the Mandement region, the growers of Peissy and Dardagny again dominate production of quality Pinot Noirs.

Other red varieties

The recent plantings of Merlot and Cabernet Sauvignon in Geneva are only just coming into commercial production. The total acreage of these varieties will remain small but qualitatively they could become increasingly significant as Genevois producers continue to search for better wines with aging potential. Some examples of wine from these grapes have been exciting successes.

The Vineyards

The Mandement

Of the three distinct Genevois wine areas, the Mandement on the right bank is the largest and economically most important. With nearly 860 hectares recorded in 1992, it represents almost two-thirds of the canton's total production. The name *"mandement"* comes from the French term for summons or mandate. In the 16th century when the vineyards of Jussy and Satigny were attached to Geneva by a special "mandate", they were still physically separated from Geneva proper by lands belonging to the independent authorities of Savoie and Gex. Hence they inherited a separate designation which has stayed with time.

Today the Mandement area is considerably larger than the original mandate. It includes the villages of Peney; Bourdigny (upper and lower); Peissy (site of the largest single independently-owned vineyard in Switzerland, the 50-hectare Cave des Bossons); Russin; Essertines, and Dardagny. These are all lovely little villages that have remained close to their agricultural roots and architectural traditions. A mid 19th century landscape painting of the village of Dardagny by the French artist Camille Corot which hangs in the Metropolitan Museum in New York attests to the success of the preservation efforts. Today's buildings are clearly identifiable nearly 150 years after they were painted. A sister painting, *Dardagny, Morning,* is in the collection of the National Gallery in London.

The center of the region remains Satigny which, with its 450 hectares, is the largest viticultural commune in Switzerland. It is also the site of the Cave du Mandement, headquarters and largest winery of the La Cave de Genève group. A very large proportion of Geneva's light, fruity and often *petillant* Chasselas-based Perlan issues from the Cave du Mandement. The various versions of Perlan produced by the Mandement and the other cooperative cellars should generally all be drunk quite young, regardless of whether they are generic selections or single

---

Dardagny with its Château

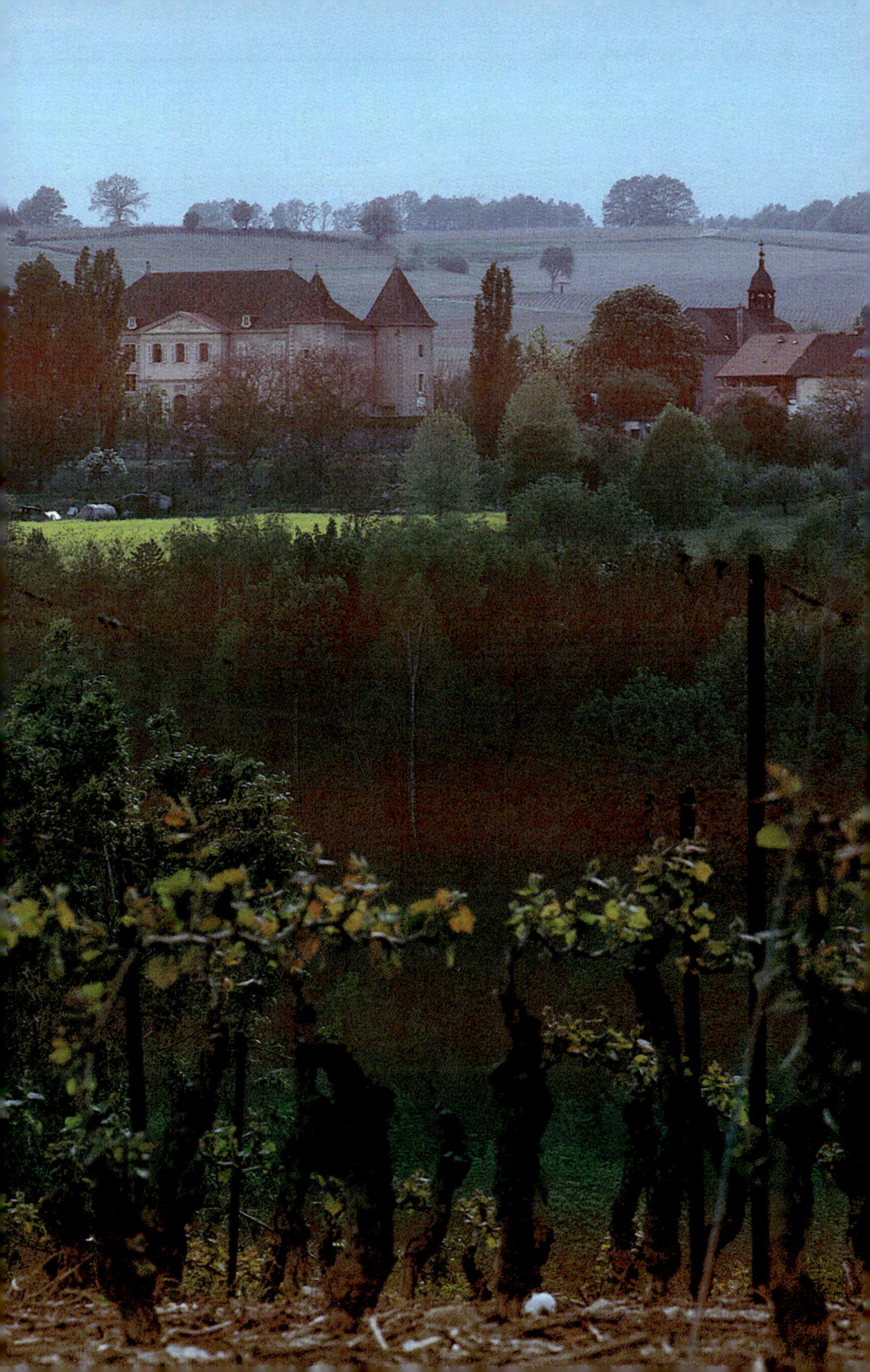

vineyards under the name "Vitis", the new mark for superior wines from La Cave de Genève. Other white wines available from the cellars in Satigny include a Chardonnay and a Riesling x Sylvaner.

La Cave de Genève also markets a selection of Gamays from various sites around Satigny. These are enjoyably acceptable wines and widely available, although they lack the intensity found in some of Geneva's independently-produced Gamay wines. On the other hand, the cooperative's Pinot Noir wines have not had great success.

Château Barillet, formerly part of the cooperative group, is the producer of one of Geneva's more accessible Chasselas. The Chateau is an old rambling 16th century estate just above Satigny, whose cellars are often used for educational tastings. The Château's Perlan has, on occasion, been mistaken for a more intense Valaisan Fendant. The output, however, can be inconsistent as some vintages do not always show a bouquet or taste with a consistent level of crisp authority. The Chateau's Gamay has been solid if not inspiring. Independence from the cooperative may encourage Chateau Barillet to concentrate its efforts more narrowly on quality wines.

Although the Cave de Mandement dominates the village center, the wines of La Cave de Genève certainly do not have an exclusivity in the area of Satigny. Among the notable wineries is Charles and Jean-Michel Novelle's Domaine Le Grand Clos. A greater contrast between the massive Cave de Mandement and the headquarters of Le Grand Clos across the street is hard to imagine. Charles Novelle and his oenologist son Jean-Michel are known as perfectionists. Their commitment to producing fine wine borders on the fanatical and recognition is beginning to arrive. In 1994, the influential Gault Millau magazine recognized Jean-Michel Novel's rising status by awarding him the accolade of the "Swiss wine maker of the year".

From three grape varieties grown some years ago, the winery now produces 20 wines from 17 different varieties on seven hectares. Yields are kept extremely low and Jean-Michel claims, with considerable authority, that his vines are the most expensive in Geneva to harvest. Healthy fruit, a sympathetic handling of the grapes, the highest technical standards and sensitive barrel-aging are hallmarks of this winery. Among the whites that spend some time in oak are the Novelles' Sauvignon, Chardonnay and Pinot Gris. A Grand Clos standard Chardonnay from the late 1980s exhibited an intense but slightly uncharacteristic nose. The limited quantity, up-scale oak-aged version of the Grand Clos Chardonnay is sold at a considerable premium. In the difficult year of 1993, Le Grand Clos chose not to release any single variety wines but rather produced white and red blends from Pinot Blanc/Chasselas and Syrah/Merlot/Pinot Noir/Gamay, both under the label Empreinte. For 11 Swiss francs, the white wine is an exceptional effort in the circumstances. As Jean-Michel notes, it's years like 1993 when oenologists justify their existence!

Merlot, Pinot Noir, Syrah, Cabernet Sauvignon are all part of the repertoire of fine red wines from Le Grand Clos. The Novelles are one of the canton's very best producers of Merlot. Their version is an attractive forward wine which also has sufficient fruit and soft acids to age well. In 1993, Le Grand Clos also released several innovative *vin liquoreux* (one based on a Chardonnay/Pinot Blanc/Pinot Gris *assemblage*) and a Cabernet Sauvignon/Merlot release is scheduled for 1995. Jean-Michel likens his approach to that of a fashion designer who "presents" a certain number of top-quality items each year. Only the best will make it through his exacting standards. One can only hope that this intense spark of creativity will continue to shine bright.

Slightly up the hill from Satigny is the village of Peissy, also home to some more of Geneva's better vineyards and wine makers. Even the cooperative seems to improve on Peissy's slopes. The La Cave de Genève's Coteau de Peissy Chasselas actually lives up to its "Perlan 1er Cru" status. The wine is slightly *petillant*, smoky but well-rounded. Despite its lack of a "Château" title, this is one of the better products from La Cave de Genève. In fact this 1er Cru is better than other "Grand Cru" wines from the cooperative.

Bernard and Brigitte Rochaix, who cultivate 35 hectares using integrated production techniques, produce as full a range of wines as anyone in Geneva. They are among the larger producers in Peissy. The Rochaix have built an enviable reputation for their wines over the years and their better selections can be found considerably farther afield than most Genevois wines. The selection of their Domaine Les Perrières whites include a solid Chasselas de Peissy Les Millerands, Riesling x Sylvaner, Chardonnay and Pinot Gris. The Riesling x Sylvaner is one of the best of the canton. But Rochaix's Aligoté from the early 1990s, although pleasant, could be better. It lacks some intensity and is not Rochaix's best wine. Their Chardonnay comes in a regular and barrel-aged versions. The reds include two styles of Gamay and a barrel-aged Pinot Noir.

Also located in Peissy is the relatively new cellar of Bernard Conne, Domaine des Charmes, whose wines are consistently well-made and comparatively inexpensive. His vineyard, which combines new plantings with some much older plots, produces a well-made Chasselas, Les Crécelles, which, in terms of value for money, is surely one of the better finds in Switzerland. The wines from Conne (not to be confused with the Connes of Chexbres in Vaud) are very pleasing, honest and fresh, if not particularly complex. Conne also produces some passable Riesling x Sylvaner and Findling at Peissy. The latter wine is bottled under the label Le Griset Blanc.

It is, however, Conne's Gamay Le Baron Rouge that is exceptional. This wine is a first-rate example of the concentrated, oak-aged style of Gamay occasionally found in Geneva. This "more serious" style of Gamay is surprisingly stylish and successful. In addition to Domaine des Charmes, this innovative approach to the Gamay is followed by other Genevois estates such as Domaine des Rothis in Dardagny and Domaine des Balisiers in Peney. These are wines well worth searching out, even if in some cases production is fairly limited.

Le Baron Rouge presents a strong and immediate impression of concentrated fruit, possibly drawing strength from the older vines that exclusively provide the grapes for this wine. The wine has good colour, depth and structure, and is a good example of what creative and slightly non-traditional wine-making can do. In addition to the specially handled Gamay, Conne also produces a regular bottling of Gamay de Peissy as well as a rather good pink Gamay Rosé which is marked by its fruity, refreshing taste.

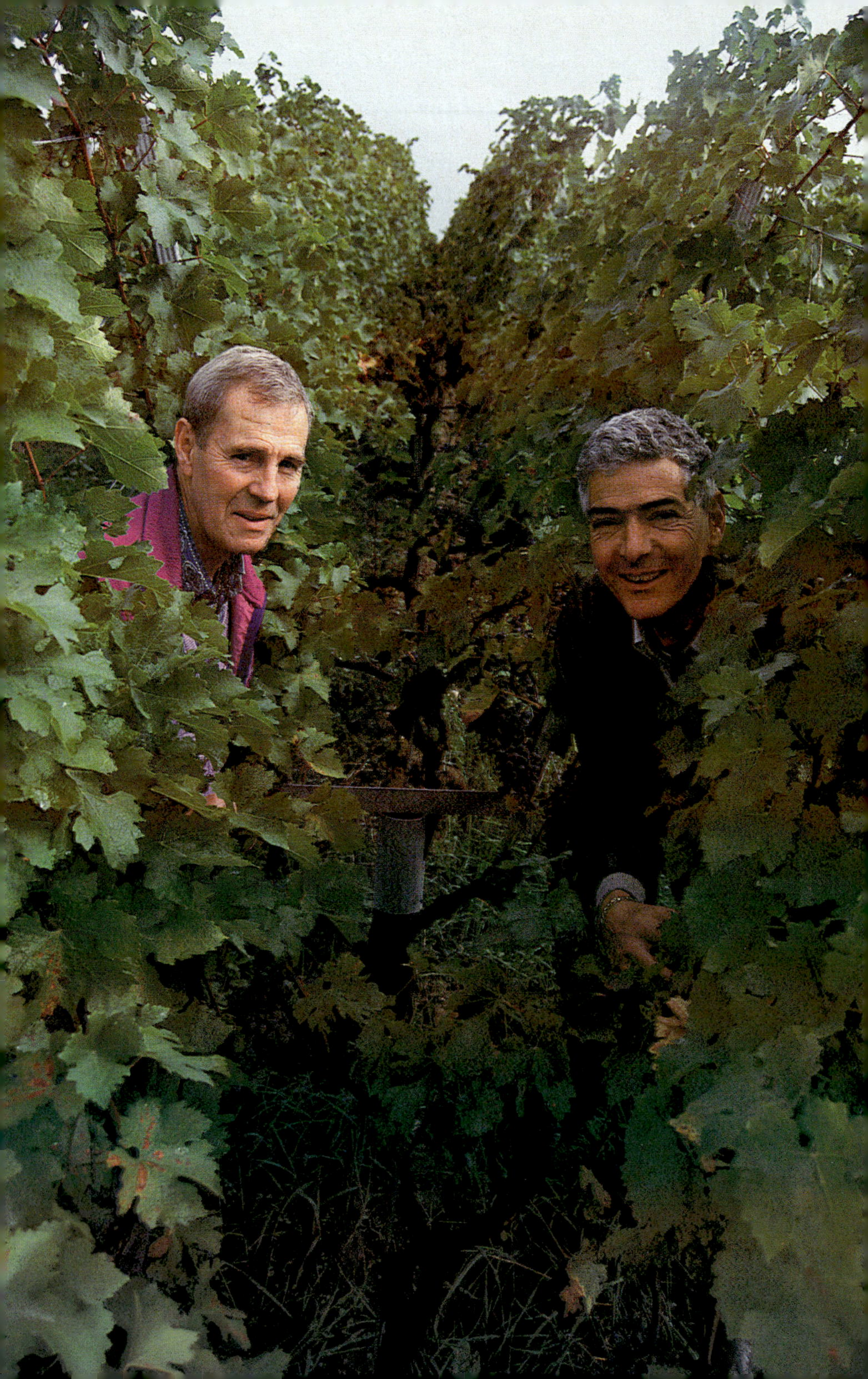

The very large, by Swiss standards, 50-hectare Cave des Bossons produces both standard and oak-aged versions of Pinot Noir which are well-regarded. The Cave des Bossons Pinot Gris is also a wine which has received its share of plaudits.

And finally in Peissy is the well-respected Domaine des Trois Etoiles of Jean-Charles Crousaz. This vineyard produces a range of straightforward, honest and occasionally innovative wines, including a Chasselas, Aligoté, and Chardonnay. The reds include a forward Pinot Noir/Gamay blend, named after the law-giving King Gondebaud, and a relatively rare Genevois Merlot. Although not overly concentrated, the Merlot bears a very credible resemblance to a *cru classé* from St. Emilion. The success of Trois Etoiles Merlot is a good sign for the future prospects of this grape in Geneva. The Domaine's production is approximately 8,000 cases from a total estate of 10 hectares.

Down the hill and closer to the Rhône from Satigny are the vineyards of Peney-Dessus, home to the vineyards of Les Balisiers, the property of Gérard Pillon and Jean-Daniel Schlaepfer. These two wine enthusiasts are also authors of the informative and opinionated book, *Les Vins de Genève*, which strongly defends the interests of the independent producers confronted by the economic and technical clout of cooperative. They also strongly argue that if Geneva is to establish a firm and credible reputation for its wines, it will not be through producing high-yield, thin "Perlans", but rather through experimentation and propagation of more demanding varieties, suitable for laying down such as Merlot, Syrah and Cabernet Sauvignon. Wherever possible these two *vignerons* practice biological viticulture which prohibits the use of chemical weedkillers and encourages only organic manure. Other chemical interventions are kept to the absolute minimum.

The Chasselas from Les Balisiers, which is not labeled Perlan, is well-made, refreshing and forward. The Pinot Blanc selection is also generally light, but has a pleasant, balanced taste. The Les Balisiers Pinot Noir, while not a particularly deep wine, will still benefit from some aging. The wine shows a respectable strawberry-leaf aroma on the nose and with its reasonable length is a worthy effort at a Genevois Pinot Noir. Also not to be overlooked is the Balisier oak-aged Gamay, Dame Noire. This estate in fact established the serious-style oak-aged Gamay in Geneva as far back as 1984 and now successfully produces 30,000 bottles of this wine annually.

This winery, however, has achieved real recognition for its rich and opaque Comte de Peney Cabernet Sauvignon. This wine is surprisingly well structured and fragrant after only several years in the bottle and is a wine for keeping. The 1990 Comte de Peney was judged one of the top five oak-aged Swiss red wines by the Swiss wine magazine *Vinum*. And in a competitive tasting of Cabernet Sauvignons in December 1993, the same wine not only placed third overall, and the top Swiss wine, but was also evaluated higher than more famous châteaux such as of 1989 Cos d'Estournel, 1988 Chateau Latour and 1988 Sassicaia. The value of competitive as versus comparative tastings may be open to question, but there is no doubting this is a very fine wine.

Gérard Pillon and Jean-Daniel Schlaepfer in their vineyards of the Domaine des Balisiers in Peney..

Just up the hill from the *chai* of Les Balisiers is the rustic but elegant hotel and restaurant, Domaine de Châteauvieux. The wine list is as good as the food, and the view over the vineyards of Peney, with the Rhône and the Salève cliffs in the distance, is exceptional. Châteauvieux's owner and chef, Philippe Chevrier, was awarded his second Michelin star in 1993.

Between Satigny and Dardagny is the village of Russin, which hosts one of Geneva's better-known fall wine festivals. From here La Cave de Genève bottles both a white and red Côtes de Russin. Despite a "Grand Cru" designation, the Côtes de Russin white has been generally only a passable wine. The Gamay-based Premier Cru red is slightly better with a fresh and fruity taste, but it is still not as good as some of the nearby vineyards.

Finally, in the Mandement are found the producers clustered around Dardagny. This village has more than its fair share of conscientious independent wine makers. It is also perhaps the most picturesque wine-village and a producer of some of the best wines of the canton. Located here are wine makers such as Edouard Ramu et Fils of Domaine des Esserts; Claude Ramu of Domaine du Centaure; Mistral-Monnier of Domaine des Faunes; Guy Ramu of Domaine de Chafalet; and Jean-Pierre Rothlisberger of Domaine des Rothis. Many of these *propriétaires-encaveurs* are best known for their wines from grapes other than the Chasselas, but virtually all of them still produce more than acceptable versions of the Chasselas. The wines of Dardagny are straightforward, floral and well-balanced. In good years the more disciplined producers can take advantage of the soils and well-exposed rolling slopes around the village to produce wines with a definite qualitative edge over those from more ordinary sites.

One of the largest firms is that of Domaine Les Hutins, belonging to Jean and Pierre Hutin. They have a relatively wide selection of wines from 18 hectares and produce approximately 100,000 bottles annually. There are at least two different Chasselas wines, a Pinot Gris, a Sauvignon and a respectable Chardonnay. Pale when young, their Chardonnay displays good varietal characteristics which would evolve still further if left for an additional year or two. Their oak-aged Gamay Domaine des Hutins is well worth searching out.

The Pinot Blanc from Edouard Ramu et Fils of Domaine des Esserts is one of the best from the village. The wine is well-made and tightly structured. Ramu's Pinot Gris has been also particularly impressive with a surprisingly attractive nose and good depth. The Domaine des Esserts Aligoté is also certainly a very acceptable wine.

Claude Ramu's Domaine du Centaure Aligoté confirms why the future of Geneva's white wine should tend more towards Aligoté. Clean and crisp, this wine is an example of the Aligoté's potential to provide an immediately attractive nose and good acid balance. Ramu is developing a real reputation for his white wines. His Domaine du Centaure Pinot Blanc is fresh, well-focused wine. A two year old Pinot Gris from tasted at the fine Geneva lakeside restaurant Perle du Lac, was a superior, well-structured wine showing good fruit and acid balance. It is a wine with sufficient character to complement a dish as strong as smoked duck. Although immediately smooth, it would still benefit from cellaring. Finally, Ramu's Saturnale is a Dardagny wine made from the Kerner grape. It is smooth, fragrant, well-rounded and sweet with a dry finish. This wine would make a lovely aperitif or could be drunk on its own.

Not to be outdone, Guy Ramu and his wife Sylvie of Domaine de Chafalet have concentrated on an intriguing range of wines, some of them from vines grown on slopes too steep for mechanization. His wines, under the label of Le Chafalet, include a Chasselas aged in oak, a Chasselas grown in Thoiry across the border in France, a Pinot Gris, a Pinot Blanc (as of the 1994 harvest), two Gamays and two Pinot Noirs, one of which is aged in oak. Guy Ramu left the Genevois cooperative in 1988 and although it hasn't been easy, he has not looked back. This is a serious winery where the *chai* is a metal shed and the entire operation very much has the air of a working farm. In 1994 Ramu also produced small casks of the cross Garmet and the Valaisan grape Cornalin. The former tasted exceptionally well from the barrel and is a sign of continuing positive experimentation.

It may seem surprising but the Ramus do not have Dardagny entirely to themselves. Other producers of Pinot Gris include the Domaine des Rothis of Jean-Pierre Rothlisberger. The wine demonstrates a straightforward nose but greater complexity on the palate. It consequently will improve for a year or so. Their best Gamay, La Rose Noir from Domaine des Rothis, is another excellent example of the more concentrated style of Gamay. This full but still fruity wine has good depth and is quite good value considering the care put into its production.

The Domaine des Faunes Chardonnay from Mistral-Monnier is a pleasant, if not deep wine, with a forward but reasonably characteristic Chardonnay nose. The taste confirmed a good balance between the fruit and acid. The Réserve des Faunes Gamay has developed a solid following while their Pinot Noir is rated among the best of the canton.

La Cave de Genève also markets a quite drinkable red Gamay-based "1er Cru" Coteaux de Dardagny from the cooperative's vineyards around the village.

Between the Arve and the Rhône

The second wine region of Geneva is the area between the river Arve and the Rhône. The banks of these two rivers form the northern extremes of the region, while the south and west are delimited by the border with France. In this region the vines extend to the west of the city of Geneva on the Aire plain. This area remains one of mixed farming with grapes enjoying the better exposed slopes. Total acreage for grapes is over 330 hectares. The area has been inhabited since Roman times, and a long history is shared by the small pastoral villages such as Soral, Avully, Lully, Sézenove, Bernex, Bardonnex and Troinex.

Lully, in particular, is a village whose better exposed slopes are well-regarded, and here La Cave de Genève cooperative uses the name La Cave de Lully for its wines from this region. Their wines are generally bottled under the label Coteau de Lully "1er Cru" although in fact after harvesting, the cooperative's grapes are transported to Satigny for processing. Some of these Lully wines can also be bottled separately. The wines are considered by some to be more "feminine" than those of the Mandement, although they certainly share a light, refreshing familial resemblance.

Separate from the cooperative, the well-drained Lully vineyard, Domaine des Curiades, produces some of the canton's more successful wines. This firm is known particularly for its Aligoté, Chardonnay and Pinot Noir. The Chardonnay receives some oak aging. Unfortunately not all the growers from this area produce well-structured wines, perhaps in part a consequence of not setting the AOC standards high enough. In such cases the wines will lack concentration and the result is little more than a pleasant but uninspiring drink.

On the other hand, Bernard Cruz is well known for his Beauvent Chasselas from the Cave de Beauvent in Bernex. His wines range from a simple Chasselas to Aligoté and Pinot Blanc. His rosé is Gamay-based, although he also grows some Pinot Noir which is bottled under the name La Croix. Cruz's Gamay de Bernex, Les Gries, is a fragrant, well-balanced wine. Bernex is also the site of the superior Côtes d'Enfer and the Clos de Murcie vineyards and, along with vineyards near Avully, is the site for much of the Riesling x Sylvaner grown in this area.

The Pinot Gris from the Cave de Sézenove, run by the Bocquet-Thonney family in the village of Sézenove is considered the equal of the same wines from Dardagny and Peissy in Mandement.

The village of Soral is right on the French border. Here Paul Dupraz of Domaine du Château de Rougement has won applause for his Gamays. In the Soral area La Cave de Genève has its "Grand Cru" Rougement, which is not to be confused with the Domaine du Château de Rougement. Although this wine was one of the first three Geneva AOC wines to be labeled "Grand Cru" in 1988 (along with Côtes de Russin red and white, and Chasselas La Feuillée, also from Soral), this wine has a mixed reputation. Examples from the late 1980s tended to the heavy side.

Between the Arve and the Lake

The third and final region of Geneva is the area between the river Arve and the Lake on the south shore of Lake Geneva, extending from the Geneva city limits to the French border at Hermance. The expansion of the city and the rise in land values for residential development are most pronounced in this area. As a consequence many of the smaller producers might have slowly disappeared without the support of the La Souche cooperative.

The vineyards alternate with built-up areas throughout the suburbs which lie between Geneva and the nearby French border. The wines here are generally not of the same caliber as their right bank counterparts, but pleasing wines can definitely be found. The future of some of these vineyards remains uncertain, particularly in light of the land pressures from the expansion of Geneva's suburbs.

Several of the villages, in particular those along the lake such as Anières, are little more than residential extensions of Geneva. They have managed, nonetheless, to keep at least some vines. Hermance maintains ten hectares, Anières fifteen, Cologny five and Corsier ten. Collonge-Bellerive, site of the La Souche winery, tends twenty-eight hectares. Further back from the lake, and somewhat distant from direct urban pressure, the village of Choulex has 27 hectares of grapes. Meinier is the largest with 45 hectares. Gy, on the border with France, maintains 14 hectares while nearby Jussy, site of the well-known Château du Crest, divides 30 hectares among a dozen *vignerons*. Finally the villages of Presinge and Puplinge have some 10 hectares. Even Vandoeuvres, virtually at the gates of Geneva, maintains a few small plots, largely planted with Gamay and a very little Pinot Noir.

Literally on the outskirts of Geneva in Cologny are the vineyards of Côteau de la Vigne Blanche of Roger Meylan. His basic white is a fresh, forward wine with good balance; a quite acceptable Chasselas. It is the "house" wine of the Michelin two-star restaurant Lion d'Or in Cologny. Meylan's Cologny vineyards could be turned into fabulously expensive villas without difficulty, although one hopes that the vines will survive.

Meylan, is also a recognized producer of one of the better Genevois rosés made from the Gamay grape. In general these wines are for light summer drinking on a patio or at the outdoor cafés that provide a civilized touch to Geneva's summers. They have few pretensions and are thoroughly enjoyable light, quaffable wines. Meylan's Gamay rosé has more structure than most, without losing its pleasing freshness. More substantive is the Pinot Noir Meylan vinifies for La Tour de Pressy owned by Roland Cramer in Vandoeuvres. This wine is surprisingly full, well-balanced and even complex.

From the vineyards which rise behind the lakeshore village of Anières, ever closer to the French border, comes the Chasselas of Pierre Villard et Fils. This simple, pleasing wine is one of the standard house offerings of the upscale Hotel Metropole. Villard's Chardonnay is also often among the canton's best. The Pinot Blancs and Gamays of the La Côte d'Or vineyard of J.J. and P. Gavillet also in Anières are well-regarded.

Some of the better wines on the plateau that spreads east from Cologny are found at Daniel Corthay's Domaine de la Tourelle at Carre d'Aval and at Edouard Béné's Domaine de la Tour in nearby Meinier. Corthay's Gamay is straightforward, although at times a touch acidic.

Farther back on the plateau, near the French border is the excellent Château du Crest from the commune of Jussy. The Château has been in the hands of the Micheli family since 1637 and the annual production is now around 34,000 bottles. For many years the Château du Crest was marketed through the Vin Union cooperative although in 1993 the Michelis established themselves as independent *vigneron-encaveurs*. In good years their Gamay wine is robust, fruity and easy to drink – just what a good Gamay should be. A late 1980s vintage was filled with fruit, well-balanced and forward, a refreshingly good reason why plantings of this grape have risen so dramatically in recent years.

Céligny

The last vineyards in the chapter on Geneva are those of Céligny, a small Genevois enclave on the right shore of Lake Geneva, totally surrounded by Vaudois territory. In fact Founex, mentioned at the end of the chapter on Vaud, is closer to Geneva than Céligny. The Clos de Céligny produces a relatively inexpensive, fairly full, well-balanced Chasselas which is widely available in Geneva. The wine, Le Clos de Céligny, "Sur la Côte", was chosen as the best-value wine at a blind tasting of Swiss Chasselas which included many wines with more distinguished pedigrees from both Vaud and Valais. Prices have, however, risen somewhat in the early 1990s.

The Clos de Céligny, not to be left behind, has also jumped on the Chardonnay bandwagon. The results are somewhat mixed. The wine is certainly acceptable, forward but without great Chardonnay distinction. As might be expected the wine is more expensive than the Chasselas, and offers less value for money. Their Gamay tends to a lighter style with good fruit. The Gamay is reasonable value but the Pinot Noir is the better and more complex of their two reds. It is still somewhat lacking in extract and concentration and needs slightly stricter selection and vinification. This wine is again relatively good value for money.

Académie du Cep

Geneva has its *Académie du Cep*, founded in 1953 to develop a greater awareness of Genevois wine nationally and beyond. Many of its events are held in the Château of Dardagny, one of the most lovely estates of the Mandement.

Useful Addresses in Geneva:

Recommended Wine makers

Edouard Béné, Domaine de la Tour, Carre d'Aval 1252 Meinier (022) 750 13 71: One of the better producers on the right-shore plateau.

Bernard Conne, Domaine des Charmes, 11 Route de Crédery, 1242 Peissy, Satigny (022) 753 22 16: Good value wines. Certainly one of the better new breed vignerons in Geneva.

Bernard Cruz, Cave de Beauvent, Rue de Bernex 265, 1233 Bernex (022) 757 11 96: These vineyards are very close to Geneva's western limit. An easy trip from the city for good wine.

Jean-Charles Crousaz, Domaine des Trois Etoiles, Route de Peissy 41, 1242 Peissy (022) 753 11 08: A dependable producer of carefully made wines. The Merlot shows considerable promise.

Paul Dupraz, Domaine du Château de Rougemont, Route Creux de Boisset 40, 1286 Soral (022) 756 14 08. Slightly isolated in Soral but one of the best regarded wine makers in the region between the Rhône and Arve.

Jean & Pierre Hutin, Domaine des Hutins, Chemin de Brive 8, 1282 Dardagny (022) 754 12 05: One of the largest producers of quality wines in Dardagny. The Hutins market a full range of wines.

Roger Meylan, Côteau de la Vigne Blanche, Route de Vandoeuvres 13, 1223 Cologny (022) 736 80 34: One of the best wine makers on the left-hand side of the lake. His cellars are almost in the city of Geneva.

G. & D. Mistral-Monnier, Domaine des Faunes, 1282 Dardagny (022) 754 14 46: Another Dardagny producer with a solid reputation. Look for their Chardonnay.

Charles & Jean-Michel Novelle, Domaine Le Grand Clos, 201 Route de Mandement, 1242 Satigny (022) 753 10 09: Increasingly recognized as one of the real up-and-coming Swiss vineyards. Fanatical on quality, these are wines well worth searching for.

Gérard Pillon & Jean-Daniel Schlaepfer, Domaine des Balisiers, Route de Peney-Dessus 12, 1242 Peney (022) 753 19 58: Two outspoken wine makers who practice what they preach. Balisiers produces some very interesting wines and their Comte de Peney Cabernet Sauvignon is exceptional.

Claude Ramu, Domaine du Centaure, Route de Mandement 480, 1282 Dardagny (022) 754 15 09: Good whites in particular. The Pinot Gris is excellent.

Edouard Ramu et Fils, Domaine des Esserts, Chemin de Chafalet 17, 1282 Essertines (022) 754 12 47: Good selection of well-made wines. Also available at the village *caveau* in Dardagny.

Guy Ramu, Domaine de Chafalet, Chemin de Chafalet 16, 1282 Essertines (022) 754 11 79: A serious producer of some of the better wines of Dardagny including good Gamay and Pinot Noir. Try the Gamaret if it is ever commercially released.

Bernard Rochaix, Les Perrières, Route de Peissy 54, 1242 Peissy (022) 753 15 98: Sometimes a bit uneven but generally a solid producer of attractive wines.

Jean-Pierre Rothlisberger, Domaine des Rothis, Chemin Côte 13, 1282 Dardagny (022) 754 13 61: La Rose Noire is one of the best Genevois Gamays. Rothlisberger's other wines, especially the Pinot Gris, can be very good.

Cooperative

La Cave de Genève, 140 Route de Mandement, 1242 Satigny (022) 753 11 33: Still an important producer in Geneva although the future remains uncertain. Look in particular for the single vineyard wines.

The vineyards of Neuchâtel

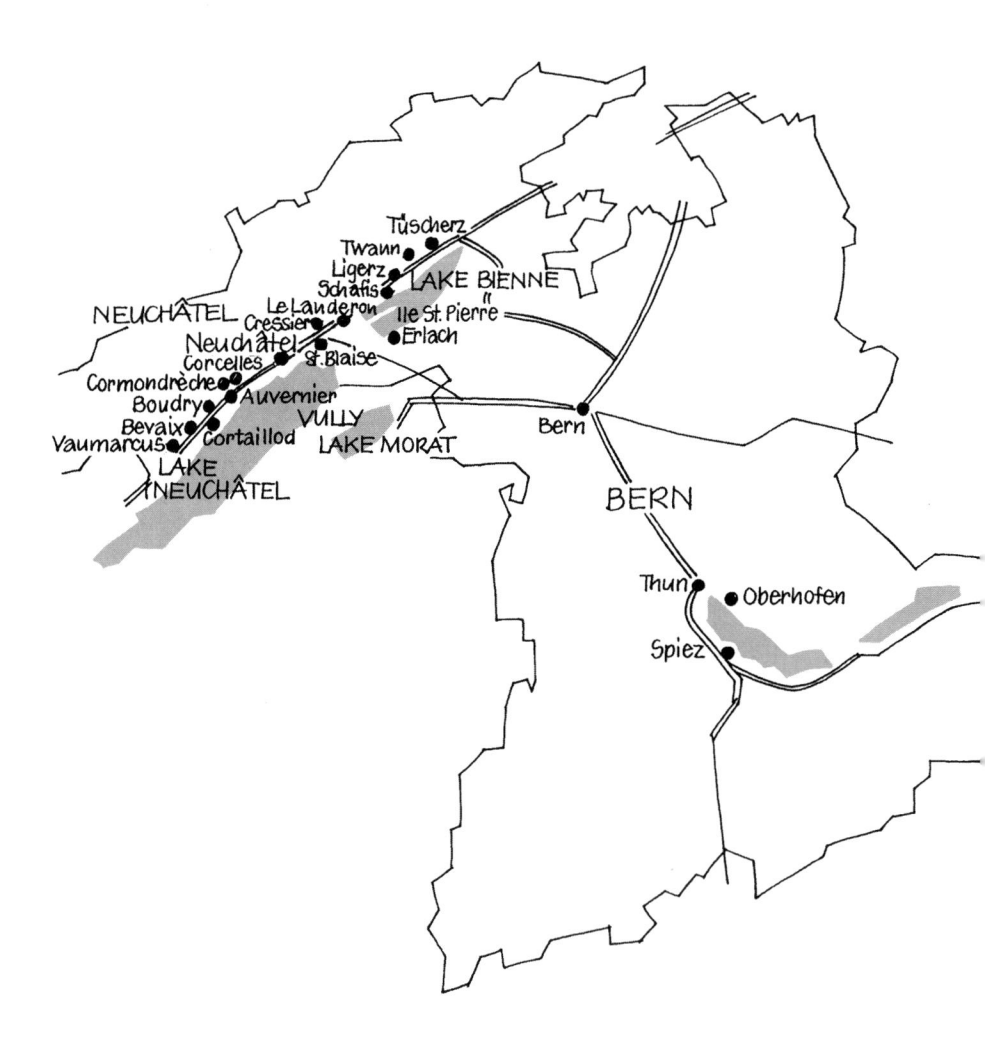

IX

Neuchâtel, including Berne (Lake Bienne) and Jura

"The wine of Neuchâtel is excellent for extinguishing thirst, encouraging the appetite, accelerating digestion, facilitating circulation, re-enforcing the heart and intestines, correcting moods (humeurs) and restoring the entire organism."

- François Prince, Doctoral thesis, University of Basel, 1743

The Region
Neuchâtel

Every wine region in the world has its unrecognized philosopher who, in times long past, sang the praises of the local wines. In this, Neuchâtel is therefore not alone. However, given the relatively small production, the wines are sometimes difficult to find outside the native area, although internationally Neuchâtel is known as well as any of the Swiss regions. Minor quantities are exported and they survive the rigors of international transportation. In the 1970s Neuchâtelois Oeil-de-Perdrix were even known to turn up in the markets of South America, one of the few European wines available and none the worse for its long voyage across the Atlantic. Other Swiss wine makers might begrudge the international success of the Neuchâtelois by claiming that the reputation of these wines was established by the local watch makers who used to smooth the sale of their precision time pieces with gifts of local wine to favoured customers. In today's market, however, the reputation of the Neuchâtel wines will sink or swim on its own merits.

Records mentioning wine-making in the area go back at least 1,000 years. As early as 998 A.D. Rodolphe, Seigneur of Lausanne, sent the first vines to the Abbey of Bevaix on the north shore of Lake Neuchâtel. As is the case in many regions in Switzerland, the origins of grape-growing extend back even further to Roman times or earlier. Grape seeds from Neolithic sites (3,000-1,800 B.C.) have been found in St. Blaise at the north-eastern end of Lake Neuchâtel. By the Middle Ages large monasteries were instrumental in the cultivation and expansion of grape-growing lands. A historical footnote that merits some thought suggests that were it not for the 1476 defeat of Charles the Bold of Burgundy by the Swiss Confederation forces at nearby Grandson and Morat, the region of Neuchâtel might have come under the sway of the dukes of Burgundy. Who knows what this would have meant for the canton's vinous development.

Traditional mixed farming methods in this area interspersed vines with other crops, even to the point of mixing fruit trees and vegetables with grapes. In time the expansion of vines occurred at the expense of basic cereals which, following the ravages of the Thirty Years War from 1618 to 1648, provoked a ban on new grape plantings and the uprooting of marginal vineyards. As early as 1687 the Compagnie des vignerons de Neuchâtel was founded to improve viticultural practices. And in the 18th century, the Société d'Emulation Patriotique attempted to match soils with particular grape varieties.

More recent history has also influenced viticultural development in the canton. A private property of the King of Prussia since 1707, Neuchâtel only became a part of Switzerland after the Napoleonic wars of the early 19th century. The Congress of Vienna in 1815 formally attached Neuchâtel along with an enlarged Geneva and the canton of Valais to the Swiss Confederation.

Neuchâtel is the smallest of the major wine cantons in Switzerland, just over half the size of Ticino. The area of grapes under cultivation is only 613 hectares or 4.3% of the national total. The vineyards of Valais, Vaud and Geneva are larger than those of Neuchâtel by ten, six, and two and one-half times, respectively.

The geography of the Neuchâtel region divides into two major grape growing areas which stretch along the north shore of Lake Neuchâtel to the west and east of Neuchâtel city. The lakeshore wines of the canton extend from the south-west to the north-east, through twenty villages strung out over forty kilometers along the northern shore of Lake Neuchâtel. They begin at the western border of the canton between the Vaudois towns of Concise and Vaumarcus, and continue until they are interrupted by the suburbs of Neuchâtel.

To the east of the city, the vineyards begin again at St. Blaise and end at Landeron on the north shore of Lake Bienne, the border with the canton of Berne to the east. The vines occupy the south-facing slopes and they enjoy the reflective heat rising from Lake Neuchâtel. Immediately behind the vineyards, the Jura mountains protect the vines from cold northern winds and excessive rains from the west.

The Neuchâtelois are so taken by the beauty of their vineyards which seem to flow effortlessly from flowered village to flowered village, that they have created a "Route Joyeuse du Joli Vin de Neuchâtel" (Joyous road of the Pleasing Wines of Neuchâtel) to entice the enthusiast to explore the canton's wine-producing areas. The route twists and turns its way through the villages which line the north shore of Lake Neuchâtel, often providing an unrivaled view of the lake and the Alps farther to the south against a backdrop of vines. The opportunity to stop and visit some of the many *caves* on the route, or to break for lunch in one of the many village restaurants is almost irresistible.

The canton's 18 wine-producing communes usually turn out between four and five million liters annually, although in 1992, total production fell just short of three million liters. In 1995, wine production rose to just under four million liters. The soils of the Neuchâtel region are generally rich in chalk and poor in humus and the elevation of the vineyards ranges between 430 and 600 meters above sea level. There are approximately 1,300 grape cultivators but most of the output is processed by 80 larger cellars grouped in five major associations. A number of larger independent Châteaux still exist.

The grape types allowed in Neuchâtel are defined by the decrees of the Conseil d'Etat. For reds only the Pinot Noir is authorized, although some experimental plots of Cabernet Sauvignon can be found. For the whites, the selection is limited to the Chasselas, Riesling x Sylvaner, Sylvaner, Pinot Blanc, Chardonnay and Pinot Gris. Throughout the 1980s Chasselas provided just over three-quarters of total production and Pinot Noir 22%. Pinot Gris, Chardonnay and Riesling x Sylvaner share the remaining three percent of the harvest.

The best of the Neuchâtel Chasselas is slightly acidic, refreshing and often *petillant* from being bottled *sur lie*, i.e. without separation from the sediment thrown off during fermentation. The light and spritzy character of the Neuchâtelois Chasselas make these wines particularly agreeable as aperitif drinks. Outside of Switzerland, Neuchâtel is best known for its Oeil-de-Perdrix rosé made from briefly macerated 100% Pinot Noir, which provides its distinctive "partridge-eye" colour. Over the years this rosé wine has found its own export niche. The Neuchâtelois can certainly lay claim to having "invented" the Oeil-de-Perdrix style of wine. While the style is now widely copied elsewhere, the local *vignerons* believe this wine can be "imitated but never equalled". Because of the growing demand for Neuchâtel reds, some Chasselas vineyards have been replanted with Pinot Noir which now provide over 12,000 hectoliters annually.

In recent decades there has been a reduction in the grape growing area of Neuchâtel from 870 hectares in 1940 to 740 hectares in 1960 and then to just over 600 hectares in 1995. The loss of almost one-third of the area under cultivation in the last 50 years has encouraged an increased emphasis on quality over quantity. The authorities of the canton have supported this transition with efforts to restrict overall production while protecting the livelihood of producers and improving the reputation of the canton's wines. One result is that the average output is the lowest of all the major *Suisse romande* cantons at 77 hectoliters per hectare for whites and 58 for reds in 1994.

In the canton there are nearly 50 bottlers, of which the five major associations of growers vinify and bottle the majority of the wine. The largest of these is Samuel Châtenay in Boudry which controls some 85 hectares of vineyards. The rest is divided among various independent producers, including some rather large individual vineyards such as the Domaine of Champréveyres (André Gerber of Hauterive bottles the Cru de Champréveyres), and the almost twelve hectares controlled by Caves de Troub/Hôpital Pourtalès of Jean-Paul Ruedin in Cressier.

The canton has introduced a three category classification system for Chasselas and Riesling x Sylvaner whites and a two-category system for reds. Category I corresponds to *"appellation d'origine"* and, as of 1990, the harvest from Category I vineyards is limited to one kilogram per square meter. The average production for the Pinot Noir was only 680 grams per square meter from 1979 to 1989 and, therefore, the authorities have not instituted a similar limit on the red grapes yields. There is also a quality label "La Gerle", awarded by the Federation of Neuchâtel vignerons for Chasselas that pass a tasting test.

James Joyce and Swiss Wines

This is an appropriate point to note that there are several different stories that link the great Irish writer, James Joyce, with Swiss wines. Joyce lived off-and-on in Switzerland from 1915 and died in Zurich in 1941. One story has circulated that Joyce was particularly fond of Valaisan Fendant. Unfortunately for the producers of the Valais, it would appear that Joyce enjoyed his wine but, according to the family, (as related to the author by Joe Wheeler, formerly of the OECD Secretariat in Paris), his preference was more often for the wines of Neuchâtel rather than those from the Valais, most likely a rosé d'Auvernier. Joyce was also known to be partial to the Château d'Auvernier. Other stories circulate about Joyce's love of Fendant de Sion in the eating houses of Zurich where he is still well-remembered.

The Vineyards

Vaumarcus and Fresens

Moving along the shores of Lake Neuchâtel from the western frontier with the Vaud towards the city of Neuchâtel in the east is a series of wine villages, including Vaumarcus, St. Aubin, Cortaillod, Boudry and Colombier. Here the Chasselas and Pinot Noir dominate, although occasional pockets of Pinot Gris and Chardonnay can be found.

Beginning near the small village of Vaumarcus, the first vines of the canton are dominated by the 18th century Château of Vaumarcus, built on an imposing 15th century sloping buttress, and itself the site of an earlier 13th century château. The wines of Domaine Château Vaumarcus are now marketed by the firm of Samuel Châtenay in Boudry. Established on chalky soil, the vineyards include almost nine hectares of Pinot Noir, seven hectares of Chasselas and almost one hectare of Pinot Gris. The Chasselas from this estate is reminiscent of a Vaudois white – slightly *petillant* and a touch acidic but with a pleasant hint of apricots on the nose. The Pinot Gris is a floral, but well-structured and surprisingly powerful wine. Reflecting the marketing reach of Samuel Châtenay, the wines of Domaine Château Vaumarcus have made their way into at least some North American export markets.

Rising behind Vaumarcus are the small vineyards of Fresens. Here a small holding totaling 315 ares (3.15 hectares) is split among twenty producers making Chasselas, Pinot Noir and Riesling. Despite the relatively high elevation, this acreage has a micro-climate which produces sufficiently high sugar levels to produce reasonable wines.

Along the north shore of Lake Neuchâtel, Samuel Châtenay is the dominant producer. The firm markets a selection of basic wines from various villages between Vaumarcus and Boudry. There is not a great variation between these Châtenay wines from Auvernier, Colombier, Cortaillod and Boudry as they are all straightforward, well-made, refreshing and slightly acidic, if not terribly complex.

Continuing along the lake, the picturesque villages of Gorgier and St. Aubin, known as the Neuchâtel Riviera because of the mild micro-climate, both have small plots of vines. In St. Aubin, the wine route provides a post card-view of a well-ordered little port jutting into the lake. The popular Oeil-de-Perdrix La Béroche comes from this area. The 55 hectares of vines at Bevaix, among the oldest vineyards of the region, are guarded by the ancient Abbaye of Bevaix and the state vineyards that surround it. Below the isolated but imposing buildings of Bevaix, the wedge-shaped Point du Grain thrusts out into Lake Neuchâtel. The well-exposed vines of this point lead on to the vineyards of Cortaillod.

Cortaillod

Cortaillod is an important Neolithic site perched on a small hill above the lake. It is particularly well-suited for Pinot Noir and can produce full wines that benefit from laying down. For much of the 19th century, the Pinot Noir in Switzerland was known by the name "Cortaillod" in recognition of the development in this area of Pinot Noir grape stocks adapted to Swiss conditions. Here the *vin du diable* (devil's wine) gained a reputation for quality. Thirty percent of the commune's production, drawn from a total of 54 hectares of vines, is devoted to Pinot Noir for the *vin du diable*.

Vin du Diable is today produced by the Caves des Côteaux in Cortaillod. Unfortunately the contemporary wine does not fully live up to its reputation which claims a history that extends back to 1620 when a *vigneron* from Cortaillod was burned at the stake for having been seen dancing with the devil. The reputation of the wine was appropriately enhanced in 1806 by the French General Oudinot, Napoleon's victor at Austerlitz. Trying to ride after a day of imbibing red wine during a visit to a fellow officer at Cortaillod, the general fell from his horse, exclaiming as he went down, *"Il est du Diable, votre vin, Colonel"*, (Colonel, your wine is from the devil!). The Caves des Côteaux cooperative also produces a Cortaillod Chasselas. This wine is usually slightly *petillant* with a restrained nose, although it can be somewhat flat despite the spritz. Their Pinot Noir also has a slight spritz which, for a red, is somewhat rare but not unknown. However it has very little stuffing.

Another producer in Cortaillod who has developed a special reputation for his Pinot Noir is Albert Porret. These wines are from 6.2 hectares of steep red-soiled vineyards near the lakeshore. Porret uses a locally-propagated small berry Pinot Noir clone at his vineyard, Les Cèdres, which produces only 300-400 grams per square meter. Along with the wines of Château d'Auvernier (see below), Porret's wines are probably the most respected of this area of Neuchâtel. In addition to Pinot Noir he also produces wines from Chasselas, Pinot Gris and Chardonnay. To the north of Cortaillod is the village of Bôle with 10 hectares of vines where Michel Egli has also developed a loyal following for his full range wines.

Boudry and Colombier

Boudry is perhaps best known for its restored 13th century Château which perches over this small wine town. The Château is the site for many of the activities of the *Compagnie des vignerons de Neuchâtel*, a wine fraternity established in 1951 to promote the wines of Neuchâtel. The thick Château walls also house the canton's small but informative *Musée de la vigne et du vin* (Museum of the Vine and Wine). Surrounding the town are 57 hectares of vines and, traditionally, almost every house had its wine press and cellar. 1000 years ago, wine production was already the major industry of the area. It reached its peak in the 17th century, but today only a very few of the village's cellars are still used for their original purpose.

Boudry is also the headquarters for the important Neuchâtelois producer, Samuel Châtenay. The firm, the largest in the canton, markets a full range of wines from selected sites throughout the commune. Châtenay is also one of the more export-oriented firms in Switzerland. Their generic Oeil-de-Perdrix has played no small part in establishing the international reputation of this Neuchâtel product. Other Châtenay wines from Boudry include a clean and sharp Pinot Gris with good weight. Some of the vineyards climb the hills immediately behind the firm's tasting and reception center just off the main road. Another recognized producer in Boudry is the Domaines des Repaires.

The nearby town of Colombier maintains 62 hectares of grapes on the Côteaux de Planey, surrounding the village's 15th century Château. The Château houses both a military and printed fabric museum The most-easily found of Colombier's wines are the local Chasselas marketed by Châtenay.

Auvernier

The cobble-stoned village of Auvernier lies between Boudry and Neuchâtel city. Its vineyards stretch out on three sides of its celebrated 16th century Château. Like Cortaillod, Auvernier is also an important Neolithic and Bronze Age site, famous for its lake dwellings. Today it is very much a village of *vignerons* as well as being the site of Neuchâtel's cantonal viticultural school, established in 1891. It has become an experimental viticological station and has influenced the development of vines and wine-making throughout the canton over the last century.

The graceful and well-preserved facades lining the village streets are particularly appealing. Although Auvernier is the smallest commune in the canton, it also has more land growing grapes than any other. One-third of Auvernier's 70 hectares of grapes is planted in Pinot Noir, while most of the remaining vines are Chasselas.

Auvernier is in fact home to some of the best wines of the canton. In particular Thierry Grosjean at the Château d'Auvernier has an excellent reputation for his standard Chasselas and Pinot Noir, and for some experimental efforts from small plots of Cabernet Sauvignon and Chardonnay which are just beginning to come into production.

The walled vineyards which surround the turreted Château on the outskirts of the village produce between 400,000 to 450,000 bottles from 35 hectares. At the Château, Chasselas yields average 1.1 kilograms per square meter. Sixty percent of the Chasselas production is sold in the canton; 38% in the rest of Switzerland; and just two percent outside the national borders. This wine is, however, available in London and in North America. Seventy percent of the Pinot Noir is transformed into Oeil-de-Perdrix rosé, half of which is sold in the canton, and half in German Switzerland. The remaining 30% is bottled as straight Pinot Noir. The older vines are used exclusively for the Château's Pinot Noir, while vines less than 12 years old are used to create the Oeil-de-Perdrix.

The Chasselas from Château d'Auvernier has a somewhat misleading light pale colour. The wine is textured and complex with a smoky nose and flinty taste. It is a very good wine with considerable finesse and length. The Oeil-de-Perdrix has sufficient Pinot Noir extract to produce a substantial rosé, while the Château's Pinot Noir is certainly one of the better wines of the canton. The Château also has small quantities of Pinot Gris (6,000 liters) and Chardonnay (2,000 liters). The Chardonnay is aged for two years in Burgundy oak casks for extra texture. These two wines are unlikely, however, to be commercially important.

Auvernier also has other producers who have established good reputations. At the local restaurants one can sample an unusual "non filtré" (unfiltered) Chasselas from H.A. Godet. The 1990 vintage (tasted in 1992) was full but slightly acidic, with a faintly yeasty nose and taste as if it were still slightly fermenting. This wine needs time to settle down. Another local producer is Domaine de Montmollin. Their Chasselas unfortunately suffered from an initial excess of sulfur on the nose which masked its qualities. The wine is light and without much of an acidic balance to provide equilibrium. On the other hand, the firm's Pinot Noir, Domaine de la Brosse, is a well-balanced, forward, cherry-nosed wine. One of the local reds is a Cru d'Auvernier from Les fils de Arthur Perret, a bright wine with good fruit and balance.

Farther back from the lake are the villages of Cormondrèche and Corcelles which lie to the north-west of Neuchâtel. It was in the cellars of the Château in Cormondrèche, the Prieuré, that the monks of Val-de-Travers vinified their harvest. The Caves du Prieuré in Cormondrèche is still a major operation, although the grapes for their extensive range of wines come from an area wider than the immediate vicinity. Increasingly, however, the expansion of the suburbs of Neuchâtel has taken its toll of land which used to be devoted to grapes. The village of Peseux now has only 13 hectares of vines, the same amount found within the city of Neuchâtel itself.

Hauterive and St. Blaise

To the east of Neuchâtel is the second major vineyard region of the canton. The first vines are found around Hauterive, a region which unfortunately has also lost much of its former vineyards to modern construction. Here, some well-restored *vigneron* houses from the 15th and 16th centuries preserve the memory of the past importance of wine. In addition, the vines of some of the best-known Hauterive vineyards actually continue to line the main Neuchâtel road as a reminder of past glories.

St. Blaise, a village with a tradition for quality wines that goes back at least to the 16th century, has also had its vineyards reduced over the last century to a mere 28 hectares by a combination of railroad construction, phylloxera and urban sprawl. Situated at the extreme eastern end of Lake Neuchâtel, the remaining vineyards are well protected by unusually high and thick walls, some of which date to the 16th century. These stone walls were constructed to shelter the vines from destructive winds, called locally the *"joran"*, which occasionally sweep down the valley.

One of the producers in St. Blaise is the firm of Jean-Claude Kuntzer and Fils whose overall quality is very good. Particularly well-regarded are this producer's Pinot Gris and Pinot Noir. The former is slightly *petillant* but has a rounded, full nose and pleasing lingering aftertaste. Kuntzer's well-structured Pinot Noir is not an overpowering wine but rather tends to freshness and elegance. Another producer located in St. Blaise is François Haussener whose wines are marketed under the name Vieux Pressoir. Haussener's Oeil-de Perdrix has good colour, a faintly floral nose and a well-balanced smooth taste with an agreeable touch of sweetness. It is a well-made wine.

Cornaux and Cressier

Between the Lakes of Neuchâtel and Bienne are the towns of Cornaux, with 12 hectares of vines and Cressier with 47 hectares. Near Cressier is one of the most famous vineyards in the canton, Domaine de l'Hôpital Pourtalès from Caves de Troub. This vineyard produces a barrel-aged Pinot Noir particularly known for its richness and concentration as well as Chardonnay, Chasselas and normal Pinot Noir. Unusual public auctions are held at the property the last Monday in February. Other wines from Cressier include an Oeil-de-Perdrix from Vins La Rochette of François Ruedin, which has a good structure and fruit, and even some length on the palate which is relatively rare for rosés. A Cressier Blanc, also from La Rochette, lacks the distinctiveness of the Oeil-de Perdrix. It is a pleasant wine but without noteworthy attributes. Finally, one of the more respected wine makers of Cressier is Jacques Grisoni whose wines are highly regarded by other producers in the canton.

The Plaine of Thièle which joins Lake Neuchâtel and Lake Bienne is the site of Le Landeron, an ancient fortified town. More than 60 hectares of vines produce mostly white wines, although some good Oeil-de-Perdrix is produced. Close by is the dividing point between the cantons of Neuchâtel to the west and Berne, to the east and south. It is also another of the linguistic dividing lines between German- and French-speaking Switzerland.

The Berne (Lake Bienne) Region

The canton surrounding the Swiss capital of Berne today maintains only 260 hectares of vines, the vast majority situated on the north shore of Lake Bienne – a natural continuation of the wines of Neuchâtel. In terms of the linguistic divisions of Switzerland, the wines from the canton of Berne would normally be included in the chapter on the German-speaking regions. As both the climate and the ownership of many vineyards are shared with the Neuchâtel region, these wines are dealt with as a natural extension of the production from Neuchâtel.

Two hundred and forty of the Bernois hectares of grapes are on the slopes of Lake Bienne. The next largest holding of only 14 hectares is located along the shores of Lake Thun, well to the south-east of the city of Berne. The remainder is scattered throughout the canton. Moving along the northern shore of Lake Bienne one crosses from the French-speaking *Suisse romande* into Germanic Switzerland. The transition from one region to another is most evident in the language, but this is not the only change. A *vigneron* in Vaud, Valais or Neuchâtel, for example, would look towards the agricultural station at Changins in Vaud for viticultural expertise and technical support, whereas in the German-speaking areas, the influence of the eastern Swiss agricultural station at Wädenswil on Lake Zurich predominates.

The current modest holdings of vineyards by Berne is certainly not a reflection of the canton's history. In its heyday, "The Republic of Their Excellencies of Berne" had extensive vine holdings in Vaud and used their near-absolute control over the flow of "foreign" wine into their Republic to promote their own vineyards, much to the chagrin of neighbouring cantons such as Neuchâtel. Unfortunately for the Bernois *vignerons*, even today the Bernois remain great consumers of Vaudois wines, while the reverse flow is considerably more restrained. In general, however, wine production came fairly late to this region. Historically, the main promoters of vineyard expansion were, perhaps not surprisingly, the Bishops of Basel, the Benedictines from the Cloister of Engelberg and the City of Bienne.

Ligerz and the Isle St. Pierre

The vineyards located in the western section of Berne enjoy conditions similar to those of Neuchâtel. Protected by the Jura mountains behind Lake Bienne, vines stretch along the north side of the lake from La Neuveville in the west through Schafis, Ligerz, Twann, and Tüscherz finally arriving at Vingelz near Bienne.

Total annual production of the Bernois region of Lake Bienne is approximately one million liters of white and two hundred thousand liters of red. Although there are nearly 400 grape growers in the area, only 60 actually vinify, age and sell their own wines. In addition to the independent *vignerons,* there is also a cooperative at Neuveville.

Lake Bienne

The white wines of Lake Bienne are similar to their Neuchâtel cousins, although they can be more dry and fruity because of a slightly more chalky soil. Although the climate of the two regions is virtually the same, the slopes leading down to Lake Bienne are generally steeper than those above Lake Neuchâtel. This is important when growers are trying to coax the last degree of ripeness out of their Pinot Noirs.

Between 75% and 80% of the harvest is Chasselas. The remainder is virtually all Pinot Noir except for very small amounts of other specialty white wine grapes such as Muscat, Sylvaner and Pinot Gris. The whites, in particular, are meant to be drunk young to take advantage of their light, fragrant and fresh character. Similar to the Neuchâtel wines, they are generally considered to be good aperitif wines. The reds are ordinarily lighter than the Pinot Noir of Neuchâtel's Cortaillod region. But when the reds are grown and vinified by an exceptional *vigneron*, they can be wines of exciting depth and complexity, rivaling much more famous vineyards in Switzerland and elsewhere. If vinified to a rosé, the Pinot Noir of the region can also be styled Oeil-de-Perdrix.

The greater part of the production on Lake Bienne is located in the west. Moving from Landeron on the Neuchâtel side of the border, the first vineyards in the canton are found in La Neuveville. The town maintains its late medieval character, and trophy cannons captured in the 15th century by the Swiss forces from the Burgundians after the defeat of Charles the Bold are still on display at the Hôtel-de-Ville. La Neuveville is the site of the cellars of the Domaine de la Ville de Berne which has a total of 21 hectares, mainly from Schafis. The famous bears of Berne figure prominently on the red and yellow label. Although best known for their Pinot Noir, the estate also produces Chardonnay, Chasselas, Pinot Gris and Sauvignon Blanc. The Pinot Noir is fresh and straightforward, with a hint of cherries on the nose but perhaps lacking the authentic fruit that one would expect.

In addition, on the south-west side of Lake Bienne, vines are planted eastwards towards the villages of Erlach and Tschugg. A small vineyard belonging to the *Hôpital des Bourgeois* of Berne is still cultivated in the northern portion of the Isle St. Pierre, a peninsula which extends into the middle of the lake. This wine is sold under the name Inselwein. Jean-Jacques Rousseau fled to this idyllic spot for six weeks in 1765, before being summarily expelled by the nervous Bernois authorities. About this short but happy period Rousseau penned views, quoted in

Matthew Josephson's biography, that could be as valid today as they were in the 18th century:

"Why can I not go to finish my days in this beloved island, never to quit it, never again to see in it one dweller from the mainland to bring back to me the memory of all the calamities of every sort that they have delighted in heaping on my head for all these long years?"

Schafis and Ligerz

Wines labeled Schafiser, Ligerzer (which includes Schernelz, a small village belonging to the same municipality), and Twanner are the best known among the light, fruity white wines produced along the north shore of Lake Bienne. They are usually drunk young as aperitifs, or to complement the local fish, especially the delightful *omble chevalier.*

In this intermediate zone between the purely French- and German-speaking parts of Switzerland, "Schafis" is German for Chavannes (the French name of the village), while "Twann" is the German name for Douane. The same appellations apply for the other villages that stretch out along the shores of Lake Bienne – Tüscherz (Taucher in French), Ligerz (Gléresse), La Neuveville, and Vingelz.

Schafis is the first town on the north shore of Lake Bienne. Heinz Teutsch's Schlössli in Schafis is one of the best regarded producers in this area. His deep, red Pinot Noir, Schafiser Réserve du Petit Château Barrique is both strong and elegant, exhibiting a slight taste of vanilla and oak alongside agreeable tannins. Teutsch's inspiration certainly comes from Burgundy. Tastings take place in one of the region's most fabled oak-barreled wine cellars. Other wines from his three hectare estate are the classics of the region – Chasselas, Pinot Noir and Oeil-de-Perdrix.

This part of Lake Bienne is also home to one of the most successful small wine makers in Switzerland. The vineyards of Charles Steiner are stunningly located above the lake, directly uphill from the lakeshore town of Ligerz. Steiner is an impressive representative of the new generation of wine maker in Switzerland which is totally committed to the integrated approach to grape-growing promoted by the Federal Agricultural Station at Wädenswil. He produces wines varying from a smoky, complex Chasselas to a perfumed, forward Gewürztraminer from the village of Schernelz. Steiner also producers a very acceptable Oeil-de-Perdrix, Le Landeron, which fully reflects its Pinot Noir origins.

The real show-wine of this conscientious producer, however, is his reserve Pinot Noir, Schernelzer Pinot Noir Cuvée spéciale, a remarkable wine by any standard. Steiner feels strongly that the Neuchâtel/Bienne region produces the best red wines in all Switzerland, and his oak-aged Pinot Noir, which regrettably is produced in very limited quantities, must rank as one of the contenders for top honours. The 1989 vintage, which spent 18 months in new oak casks, offers a complex nose with hints of strawberries, vanilla and chocolate. The taste is full and round with fantastic length, and despite lots of tannin, the wine was very drinkable even just two and a half years after harvest. The same wine from 1985, which also spent 18 months in oak, was equally complex but with a sweet, refined nose which developed during additional aging. The older of the two wines also displayed an excellent length. This is wine-making at its best in a location that can hardly be described as a traditional center for top quality Swiss wines. According to Steiner, one of his simple secrets may be the relatively long time the must remains in contact with the pressed grapes. This produces the concentrated fruit, ruby-red colour and complexity for which his wines are known. The other simple secret is healthy, concentrated grapes. Steiner's grapes enjoy a marvellous south-east exposure; a favourable micro-climate enhanced by the important reflective capacity of Lake Bienne; a strict limitation on the harvested yield (only 450 to 700 grams per square meter) to concentrate the juice of the plant; and a sympathetic but educated vinification. The winding road to Steiner's cellar and the nearby family restaurant, Aux Trois Amis, may be difficult to find but is worth the trouble not only for the Pinot Noir, but equally for the marvelous view over Lake Bienne and the entire range of Bernese Alps, including the peaks of the Eiger, Mönch and Jungfrau.

In the lakeshore village of Ligerz is the Musée de la vigne au lac de Bienne (Lake Bienne Museum of the Vine), another of Switzerland's small wine museums.

Twann

One of the best known areas bordering Lake Bienne is the village of Twann. Of particular note here are the *"non filtré"* wines from Fritz Peter Hubacher. Filtering remains standard practice at most Swiss wineries so Hubacher's more adventurous approach stands out. His white wine is naturally made from Chasselas grapes but, unusually, is matured in oak barrels and then bottled without filtration – two interesting innovations. The Chasselas from Werner K. Engel is sold as Twanner Frauen-Kopf. This is a full wine, perhaps lacking some elegance but it enjoys correct balance and acidity. The Engel firm also produces Pinot Gris and a Twanner Brut sparkling wine.

Hans-Peter Rüfenacht, in Tüscherz at the eastern end of Lake Bienne, has 2.5 hectares scattered topographically in very difficult small parcels, from which he produces about 15,000 bottles of Chasselas, Chardonnay and Pinot Noir. Rüfenacht's carefully-made wines have already won a number of gold medals in various tasting competitions. His Chardonnay, grown on a steep, well-exposed chalky soil, is a particular specialty. Rüfenacht's winery is well worth visiting, particularly for the cellar tastings which take place in the shadow of a massive 12,000 liter oak barrel built in 1630. A local red wine is the Twanner Roter from Peter Posch-Jutz at Tüscherz. This is a pleasantly light and fruity wine but without much concentration.

The Jura Region

The canton of Jura is Switzerland's 23rd and most recent canton, created on September 24, 1978. At that time it was also the only one of the six French-speaking

The picturesque wine-growing village of Ligerz on Lake Bienne.

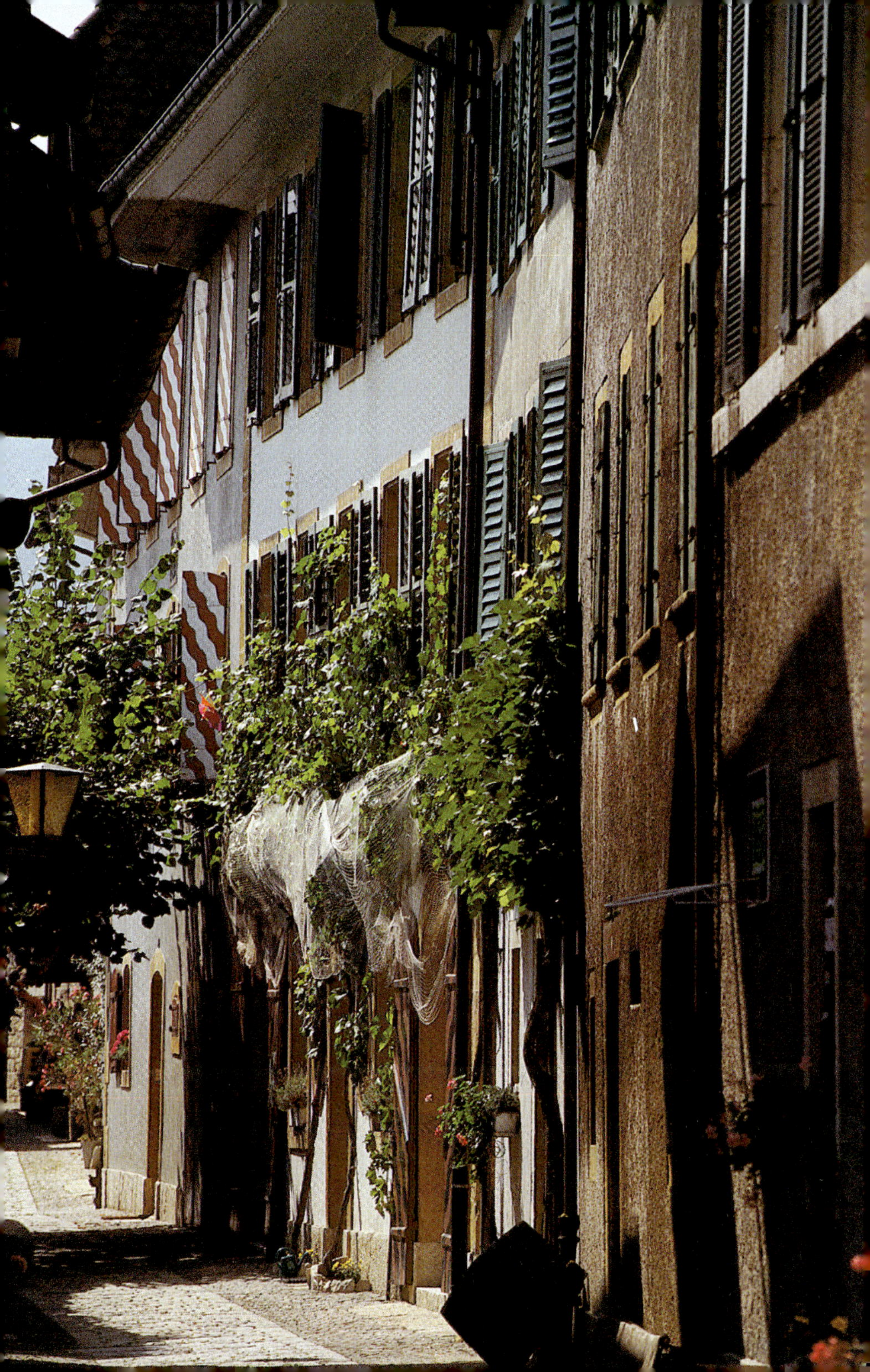

cantons of the *Suisse romande* to be vineless. This unfortunate situation was rectified in 1986 when two hectares of grapes were planted on favourable ground. The vineyards of the canton have now grown to five hectares producing some 15,000 bottles annually, almost all of which is consumed locally. Two-thirds of the production is red from Pinot Noir and the Granoir (Gamay x Reichensteiner) grapes, while the whites are made from the Riesling x Sylvaner and the Pinot Gris. The main vineyard, "Les Cantons", is located near Porrentruy, and there is an additional small planting at Soyhières outside the town of Delémont. To regulate its new industry, the canton of Jura introduced a wine law in 1988, which included minimum sugar levels for the wine musts.

Useful Addresses in Neuchâtel, Berne and Jura:

Neuchâtel

Office des vins de Neuchâtel, rue du Trésor 9, C.P. 1417, 2001 Neuchâtel (038) 725 71 55

Recommended Wine Producers:

Caves Châtenay SA, Route du vignoble 27, 2017 Areuse (Boudry) (038) 842 23 33: Wide distribution makes these sound wines the easiest to find of the canton.

Thierry Grosjean, Château d'Auvernier 2012 Auvernier (038) 731 21 15: The reputation of the Château is well-deserved. Look for both the Chasselas and Pinot Noir.

François Haussener et Fils, Encavage du Vieux Pressoir, Petite-France 6, 2072 St. Blaise (038) 753 21 42: Good, typical wines from the region east of Neuchâtel.

J-C Kuntzer et Fils, Rue Daniel Darnel 11, 2072 St. Blaise (038) 753 14 23: One of the larger producers east of Neuchâtel with a wide selection including Chardonnay, Pinot Gris and Gewürztraminer.

Albert Porret, Domaine des Cèdres, Goutte d'Or 20, 2016 Cortaillod (038) 842 10 52: Considered by many to be the most conscientious producer in Cortaillod, if not the canton, known especially for his Pinot Noir.

Jean-Paul Ruedin, Hôpital Pourtalès, Caves de Troub, Route de Troub 4, 2088 Cressier (038) 757 11 51: Hôpital Pourtalès is one of the stars of Neuchâtel.

Berne

Fritz Peter Hubacher, Johanniterkeller, Dorfgasse 170, 2513 Twann (032) 315 11 06: A creative wine-maker with some interesting innovations.

Hans-Peter Rüfenacht, Wybuur Rüfenacht, Hauptstrasse 33, 2512 Tüscherz (032) 322 39 88: Look for this producer's Chardonnay, although all his wines are good.

Charles Steiner, 2514 Schernelz (032) 315 23 24: A producer of exceptional wines, especially his oak-aged Pinot Noirs, ranking with the best Switzerland offers.

Heinz Teutsch, Ligerz, 2514 Schafis (032) 315 21 70: Another producer of excellent Pinot Noirs.

Jura

Coopérative Center Ajoie, 2942 Alle (066) 471 24 24.

X

Ticino

The Region

Perhaps more than any other part of Switzerland, Ticino is a wine region in search of an identity. While progress in this regard since the end of World War II has been nothing short of remarkable, Ticino began well behind the pack and consequently has had to focus and define its efforts to bring its wines into line with the competition. The canton's better wine makers are actively distancing themselves from a reputation for producing "flabby" Merlots. They have taken good advantage of recent technical innovations to solidify their hard-won reputation as producers of premier wines. The quest for quality has been made slightly easier because of early steps taken by the canton's wine authorities to reward superior quality with a recognizable seal of approval. Growers have concentrated their energies almost exclusively on the Merlot grape, a variety not often found elsewhere in Switzerland but one well-adapted to Ticino's particular situation.

The most southerly of the Swiss cantons, Ticino is the bastion of Italian Switzerland. The country's fourth largest wine canton is blessed with a mild, inviting Mediterranean climate which accounts for the wonderful anomaly of palm trees in the Alps. The average temperature is 11.7°C, a full 3°C higher than experienced by the more northern cantons. The canton receives an average of 2,100 hours of sunshine annually, somewhat less than Bordeaux, and 1,800 mm of rain. Heavy spring storms can be particularly destructive. These violent downpours explain why many traditional Ticino villages cling to the sides of mountains, well away from the plains which are prone to flood damage.

In parts of Ticino the welcoming climate is counterbalanced by a steep and rugged terrain, with limited pockets of southern exposure. Plots are often small and the costs of production are exceedingly high. Machine cultivation and automated harvesting are virtually impossible for many of the best vineyards, so manual labour remains an important, and expensive, factor in production. A large number of the over 6,000 grape producers are small-scale "weekend" cultivators who sell their grapes to a cooperative or larger firm, or produce an amount of wine that is not commercially viable.

Physical limitations on expansion will prevent the region from becoming competitive in terms of quantity. As Ticino contains less than eight percent of

The vineyards of Ticino

Switzerland's grape growing lands, its appeal will be for a recognizably unique product. Concentrating to such a degree on Merlot has already provided a certain recognition factor. Continuing efforts towards raising the overall quality level, in addition to the special efforts of the smaller, high-quality "boutique" wineries are other elements in the canton's longer-term marketing strategy. Certainly the region has proven that it can produce a premium product despite the relatively recent development of commercially-viable vineyards. For some of the more traditional producers in the canton these ongoing improvements will mean changes in how grapes are grown and vinified. Limiting output even further, or contracting vineyards to only the best sites, imposes a potential economic dislocation that will be difficult to accept.

The "Merlot del Ticino" is without question the wine for which the canton is known. A parallel can undoubtedly be made with the equally successful plantings of Merlot found across the border in the Friuli and Veneto region of northern Italy. The range of wines produced from the Merlot grape would surprise, if not shock, some traditional Bordeaux producers. In the hands of the inventive and practical Swiss, this distinctive, thin-skinned grape is used to produce not only flavourful, rich and forward reds but also near-whites, rosés and even sparkling Spumante. Some Pinot Noir is grown at higher elevations, and vestiges of earlier varieties such as the Bondola as well as most of the few "American" *(vitis labrusca)* grapes found in Switzerland, are still found in the northern part of the canton. Only two percent of Ticino's total production is from other white wine varieties, such as Chasselas, Semillon, Sauvignon Blanc and Pinot Gris.

The Merlot is a late immigrant to Ticino. The variety was first introduced into the canton in 1907 as part of the continuing response to the attacks of phylloxera and mildew. Seven thousand hectares of grapes had been reduced to a mere 800 hectares by the turn of the century and, in response, twelve thousand cuttings of Merlot were initially imported from Bordeaux for distribution among growers. The expansion of the plantings of the Merlot grape has been steady ever since. Today nearly 90% of the Ticino vineyard area is devoted to Merlot and it continues to increase its acreage in all the most favoured sites at the expense of the indigenous Bondola, now limited to just 2.5% of production, and other grapes. Total production in 1995 was just over 29,000 hectoliters of red wine and only 1,513 hectoliters of white wine. Average production is generally among the lowest of all the major Swiss wine-producing cantons: 47 hectoliters per hectare for reds and 37 hectoliters per hectare for whites in 1994.

The successful introduction of the "foreign" Merlot grape reflects something of the nature of the canton and its people. Until very recently Ticino has been one of the most backward, rural and economically deprived parts of Switzerland. At times, Ticino's most notable success was the emigration of its inhabitants who, discouraged by their prospects at home, fled as far as Australia and California to start anew. The Italian Swiss Colony vineyard near Santa Rosa California is one result. Although many urban dwellers idealized the pastoral life led by Ticinese peasants, the reality was a grinding, if dignified poverty. Switzerland's industrialization of the early 19th century largely bypassed the valleys of Ticino and it was only later, with the introduction of silkworm farming and tobacco processing to take advantage of cheap labour, that a non-agricultural base was established. Between 1881 and 1930 over 25,000 inhabitants of the canton emigrated abroad, a remarkable number for the time.

Developments since the end of World War II have changed the situation dramatically. Depopulation of the truly rural and mountainous areas continues, but rather than moving abroad these migrants quickly establish themselves in the canton's major urban centers such as Bellinzona, Lugano and Chiasso. Industry has thrived and, in particular, a flourishing financial services sector has matured, responding to the needs of Italians and others wishing to protect personal funds from the prying eye of the invidious tax collector. Ticino has traditionally produced more than its fair share of Switzerland's lawyers.

Today, rather than emigration, the major concern of the canton is the invasion of German-speaking Swiss and German weekenders searching for a place in the sun. The influx of these prosperous outsiders is such that one in four houses built in recent years is a holiday home, used only occasionally throughout the year. Many have headed up the alpine valleys to renovate deserted properties. Others, however, have established more permanent roots. The list of leading wine makers in Ticino now includes many names of German rather than Italian origin, several of whom established their wineries in the early 1980s.

In 1980 only just over 870 hectares were planted with grapes. This figure rose to over 1,200 by 1990 but since then has fallen dramatically. In 1995, the canton's 900 hectares of vines are divided among 6,000 (some estimates range as high as 10,000) small *vignerons*. This means an average of one-fifth of a hectare per grower. Most plots are too small to be economically viable on their own and, hence, the role of the cooperatives is comparatively important. Most notable are the Cantina Giubiasco in the northern region of Sopraceneri, founded in 1929 and comprising 600 growers producing 2.5 million liters annually. Its equivalent in the southern region of Sottoceneri is the Cantina Sociale Mendrisio, founded in 1950, with 950 growers whose annual production is in excess of 3 million liters. Twenty independent *vignerons-encaveurs* bottle and sell about 20% of the harvest, while the remaining amount falls under the control of the major *négociants*, who are often themselves owners of large estates in the canton.

Sopraceneri

Ticino is divided into two large wine regions, the Sopraceneri in the north and the Sottoceneri in the south. The names mean, respectively, "north" and "south" of Mount Ceneri, a major dividing point in the canton near the capital city of Bellinzona. Although the Sopraceneri has slightly more land devoted to grapes than the Sottoceneri, virtually all the better vineyards are located in the south of the canton.

Most of the vineyards of the Sopraceneri are found along the course of the Ticino River, which flows into Lake Maggiore, and its tributaries. This valley, along with the former tobacco-growing plain of Mendrisio in the far south of the canton, is one of the very few parts of Ticino suitable for agricultural production. Given the proximity of the northern vineyards to the Alps, it is not surprising that the soil is largely granite with very little limestone. In general the vineyard sites are well-drained, and recent stepped reconstruction using *banquettes* or *gradins*, has now made mechanization possible. This is the area of high production, but generally lesser quality wines.

The Sopraceneri is composed of the districts of Bellinzona, Blenio, Leventine, Locarno, Rivera and Valle Maggia within the communes of Gordola, Bellinzona, Camorino and Malvaglia. In Blenio and the Valle Maggia are still found vineyards where grapes are grown using traditional trellises or "pergola" with the high vines supported by granite pillars.

The Merlot dominates, as is not surprising, but the Sopraceneri is also home to many of Switzerland's remaining *labrusca* varieties, such as the Isabella and Clinton, which were first imported during the post-phylloxera reconstruction of the vineyards. Most of the output from these grapes is now allocated for grape juice, although some is fermented for local consumption and is known as "Americano" in recognition of the origins of the vines. Part of this production is also made into Grappa. The other traditional wine, "Nostrano", contains only *vinifera* grapes and is usually composed of four-fifths Bondola combined with other *vinifera* varieties, including Merlot, Malbec, Freisa and Bonarda. These distinctive blended wines reflect the "imported" origins of many of the grapes now grown in a region where, at one time, most wine was from vines brought back by migrating labourers, with little regard for the provenance or vinous purity of the blend.

Sottoceneri

The southern Sottoceneri is divided into two areas: the Luganese to the north, and the Mendrisotto to the south with most of the production coming from the communes of Chiasso, Morbio, Castel San Pietro, Coldrerio, Novazzano and Stabio. It is here that the Merlot achieves its greatest success in Switzerland. The vines are often grown on steeply terraced slopes such as those overlooking Lugano's Agno airport. These vines, although requiring prodigious care, have adapted well to the poor chalky, alkaline soil found throughout the region. The Mendrisio plain in the far south of the Sottoceneri provides the only appreciable piece of flatter land suitable for normal farming techniques.

Ideally the wines of the Sottoceneri have the Merlot's typical fragrant nose and rich, black cherry taste, without losing a certain elegance. To achieve its best, and to avoid the slight herbaceousness found in younger Merlot wines, several years' aging may be necessary. This is also the region where the canton's small plantings of Cabernet Sauvignon and Pinot Noir are found.

VITI

Since 1948 the better Merlot wines of Ticino have been distinguished by a conspicuous red and blue bottle label, featuring the word "VITI". Initially established to recognize the superior 1947 vintage, the VITI mark was one of the first marketing efforts to identify the better wines of a particular canton. Only 100% Merlot wines are eligible for the label and the wines must pass both chemical

Colli degli Ulivi, Lamone, from where the Collivo wine of Eredi Carlo Tamborini originates.

analysis and a taste test conducted by a seven-person government-appointed commission. Minimum sugar levels are established but there are still no defined limits on production of grapes per square meter or hectare, a gap that may be filled with more experience. In an average year only about one third of the total production of Merlot is awarded the VITI accolade and must be bottled in classic bordeaux-shaped bottles. A minimum production of 2,000 liters is required to receive the VITI label and only a specific number of labels, corresponding to the amount of wine submitted for the test, is distributed to ensure that non-eligible wines are excluded.

The VITI symbol is regarded by the best producers as an important but by no means final step on the long road to real quality. Some believe the VITI recognition could become the sign of a good, well-made, medium-quality wine from the Ticino, eventually comprising between 60%-70% of total production. A separate category for the best 15%-20% of production has been proposed which would include higher-quality wines with production per hectare limited to well-defined maximums. A third category would identify declassified wine known simply as Ticino red, i.e., a table wine with few if any production limits. Whether a system such as this is ever implemented remains to be seen, but the proposal is symptomatic of the search by the better producers for recognition and a long-term, commercially viable, niche for their wines.

The Wines

Among the leading *vignerons* of Ticino, there are five producers who regularly appear on lists of the canton's best wine makers. They are all headquartered in the Sottoceneri and their reputations are founded on a solid base of superior Merlots. In most cases, however, they have also branched out to produce variations on the Merlot theme, or other wines from soils and micro-climates better suited to different varieties. Some even produce their own Americano for amusement, although we are unlikely to see any of it in the stores.

These leading wine makers are Cesare Valsangiacomo of Fratelli Valsangiacomo in Chiasso, a family producing wines since 1831; Sergio and Ivo Monti of the Cantina Sperimentale di Sergio Monti & Figli in Cademario; Hans Imhof of Tenuta Bally (Crespero) in Breganzona; Adriano Kaufmann in Beride; and Daniel Huber in Monteggio. Each has developed an individual approach to wine making.

Valsangiacomo is among the largest of the fine wine producers in the canton and has played a leading role in developing the reputation for fine Ticino wines through barrel aging and selection of premium *cuvées* for special attention. Sergio Monti, Adriano Kaufmann and Daniel Huber, by contrast, are fairly recent entrants into the wine business. Monti is a former banker, while the other two are engineers who established their small vineyards only in the 1980s, but who quickly have become known for their high standards. Valsangiacomo and Monti both largely concentrate on the Merlot. The former even includes a sparkling Spumante Extra Brut in his range of wines. The other three have also produced Cabernet Sauvignon in minute quantities to complement their other varieties.

This small coterie of superior wine makers is by no means unchallenged as there is an important group, often equally successful, very close behind. Some of their names can be found in the list of recommended wine makers below.

White Wines

White grape production is so limited in the Ticino that it merits only a brief mention. The majority of white wine vines are made from the classic Chasselas grape. If properly tended and vinified, Ticino Chasselas can produce a relatively intense, tart and satisfying wine. These are honest and useful white wines, lost in a red sea. In addition to the Chasselas, the most common grapes are, perhaps not surprisingly given Ticino's viticultural connections with Bordeaux, the Semillon and Sauvignon Blanc. More often these three grapes are blended together to produce Bianco del ticino, rather than bottled separately. Riesling x Sylvaner, Chardonnay and Pinot Gris more or less complete the list, although they are mainly grown in experimental plots. It is unlikely that these wines can be easily found outside their region of production. Few other producers have specialized in white varieties, although some of the better producers do include a white *tincinese* blend in their product range. A good producer's blend should display a focused, concentrated nose and even some backbone.

A Bianco di Merlot is also marketed in limited quantities by certain producers, including the Sopraceneri cooperative Cantina Giubiasco which is sold under the name Bucaneve, Bianco di Merlot. Traditional Merlot producers from Pomerol or St. Emilion might argue that a white Merlot is a contradiction in terms, if not complete sacrilege. A comparison, however, might be made with the white Zinfandels of California — a fragrant, if trendy wine that, if little else, adds one more variation to the complex incarnations of the grape.

These wines can show a good floral nose, a touch of peach on the palate and some depth. If the wines are well-balanced, they should give pause to those who believe that it is a pity to produce a white wine from the Merlot grape. Only time will tell, however, if white Merlot is more than a passing fancy.

Red Wines
Merlot

The Merlot is not a particularly easy grape to grow and is very sensitive to overproduction. Yields of over one kilogram per square meter provoke a rapid reduction in the quality of the final product. In addition, it can rarely be grown successfully over an altitude of 550 meters in the Ticino, and even at this level it is pushing its limits.

The most straightforward Merlots are generally those grown in the larger, mechanized vineyards of the Sopraceneri. Although commercially successful and widely marketed in Switzerland, these wines have contributed to the less-than-stellar reputation of Ticino reds. Generally these are light wines with some, but not very noticeable, tannin. Technically correct, these wines are one-dimensional and unexciting Merlot and do not repay long cellaring. They can be quite inexpensive if purchased for current drinking, although young, green Merlot is not always the most approachable of wines. The firm of Matasci Fratelli with their Selezione d'Ottobre wines have perhaps been the most adroit Swiss producer in satisfying the demand for inexpensive, immediately drinkable Ticino Merlot.

Good, complex wines can, however, be produced in the Sopraceneri region. Names to look for among the Sopraceneri producers include Angelo Delea of Losone and Werner Stucky of Rivera, who cultivate ten and three hectares respectively. All specialize in serious Merlots although other wines such as Americano, Bondola, Pinot Blanc and Muscat are found on their lists. In addition, some of the more successful southern wine makers also own or purchase small quantities of grapes from northern growers for separate vinification. The wine maker's reputation is the best quality guide in such cases.

Fine wine production in the southern Sottoceneri region is the best proof that good Swiss Merlot needs time to show its qualities. In 1992, a 1985 Dionisio, Merlot di Morbio, from Fratelli Valsangiacomo in Chiasso, was still thick and dark, with a nose only just beginning to open up. After some time in the glass, the wine combines the taste of soft berries with excellent length. This wine is only made in the finest years such as 1961, 1985 and 1990, and quantity is strictly limited at around 4,000 liters.

The other top-quality, limited production Merlot wines from Valsangiacomo are bottled under labels such as Rubro, for their smooth but full oak-aged Merlot from the Lake Lugano region, Roncobello and Reserva di Bacco. The

Valsangiacomo family produce wines from a large holding of 22 hectares. The firm concentrates almost exclusively on Merlot although a small amount of white from blended Chasselas, Sauvignon and Semillon is made.

Representative of the approach to wine-making by the smaller boutique wineries in the Sottoceneri is that of Sergio and Ivo Monti. Their minuscule production, about 7,000 bottles a year, is bottled under the label of Cantina Sperimentale di Sergio Monti & Figli. The word "cellar" is a bit of a misnomer in describing the Monti establishment. This small, modern and spotless operation is perched precariously on a hillside overlooking the slopes of the Malcantone region and Lugano. Their small output makes their wines difficult to find, but the quality rewards the effort.

The firm produces two quite different Merlots, under the labels Rovere and Malcantone. The Rovere is vinified from grapes purchased in more-or-less equal portions from selected growers in the north and south of the canton whose vines have an average age of over 35 years. These wines are rich and almost alcoholic, with a hint of violets on the nose. They will only begin to show their complex best after five or six years. When still in the barrel, the Rovere wines display a sweet and attractive but powerful nose.

The majority of the Monti's production is their Malcantone from their own vines planted in the 1970s on the steep slopes of the Malcantone region, just outside Lugano. They are slightly more forward than the Rovere, displaying a fragrant Merlot nose and a soft, lingering finish. As of 1990, the Monti's Malcantone included 10% Diolly (the Pinot Noir clone developed in Valais) and four percent Cabernet Sauvignon.

Claudio Tamborini of Eredi Carlo Tamborini in Lamone produces an extensive range of Merlot beginning with a straight-forward non-oaked Collivo (Hill of Olives) to a new and rather remarkable peppery Castel di Morcote, a wine produced from strictly limited yields (20-25 hectoliters per hectare) and aged in oak (20% new) for 12 months. The grapes for this wine come from the Mendrisio region of Ticino. In between, Tamborini has a selection of other Merlots showing different styles and intensity including his Vigna Vecchia and a strikingly bottled Ronco dell'Angelo.

Various premium producers have taken to either oak-aging their Merlot or adding a touch of Cabernet Sauvignon to the blend for structure. Barrel-aging has been increasing in popularity and most top firms such as Valsangiacomo will have at least one or more top selections spend at least some time under oak. Another small Merlot producer well worth searching out is Joe Pfister of Castelrotto who produces consistently good wines on his 2.5 hectare plot. The list of different Merlots produced by individual producers can be almost bewildering at times and the only way to understand the differences is to visit the cellars.

Experimental blending has also been gaining adherents of late. For example, those adding some Cabernet Sauvignon in a blend include Crespera of Tenuta Bally and Werner Stucky in Rivera. Daniel Huber not only combines Merlot with Pinot Noir but also throws in some Syrah for good measure. The results from these efforts have been quite positive and experimentation is set to continue on cépages and aging styles.

Bondola

The Bondola is to Ticino what the Humagne Rouge and Cornalin are to Valais — an indigenous red *vinifera* grape unique to the region. It produces an unabashedly ruby and "rustic" wine. The Bondola is the main constituent in the Nostrano blend unique to Ticino. It should not be confused with the wine produced from the increasingly rare *vitis labrusca* vines used in the other Ticino specialty, Americano. This authentic, native grape has survived the arrival of imported varieties which have invaded its native soil although production of Bondola is now limited to the Sopraceneri.

Annual yields are just over 1,000 hectoliters of wine. The Bondola of Ticino has shared with its indigenous counterparts in Valais a modest renaissance as *vignerons* find new ways to coax out the grape's inherent qualities. Ultimately, however, the Bondola rarely develops the complexity and aging potential which underlies the recent interest in the Humagne Rouge. It remains a pleasant, hearty, but often short and one-dimensional wine. The northern cooperative, Cantina Giubiasco, does market a typically forward, slightly rough but tasty Bondola.

Pinot Noir

The introduction of the Pinot Noir into Ticino has met with mixed success. The advantage of this grape is that it can be grown above 550 meters, the upper limit for the Merlot to thrive. Unfortunately, the wines have lacked sufficient extract and concentration, even when fermented for lengthy periods, sometimes as long as three weeks. Consequently there may be a move away from red Pinot Noirs towards a rosé made from 100% Pinot Noirs, similar to the "Oeil-de-Perdrix" of Neuchâtel.

Cantina Sperimentale has experimented with Pinot Noir for some years and the results, although not without promise, have failed to produce the type of wines which were initially expected. Very few single Pinot Noirs appear on the market. Occasionally, as in the case of Daniel Huber noted above, Pinot Noir is blended in an unusual combination with Merlot.

Ordine dei Grancoppieri

The Ordine dei Grancoppieri is the equivalent in the Ticino of wine fraternities found in all other parts of the country. Founded in 1961, it has been consciously modeled on similar organizations in Italy and France and seeks to promote both a better understanding of the wines of Ticino, while working conscientiously to increase the quality of the canton's wines.

Useful Addresses in Ticino:

PROVITI: Piazza Cioccaro 2, 6900 Lugano (091) 923 82 18.

Recommended Wine Makers:

Angelo Delea SA, 6616 Losone (091) 791 08 17: A good producer from the Sopraceneri. An unusual Americano complements his range of Merlots.

Stefano Haldemann, Via dei Colli, 6648 Minusio (093) 743 13 96: Produces 8,000-9,000 bottles annually. Look for his elegant barrel aged Piccola Riserva.

Daniel Huber, 6998 Monteggio (091) 608 17 54: 15,000-20,000 bottles are produced by this conscientious wine maker who concentrates on Merlot or Merlot/Cabernet and Merlot/Pinot Noir blends.

Adriano Kaufmann, 6981 Beride; (091) 608 13 71: Look for his Pio del Sabato and Pio del Sabato Barrique Merlot/Cabernet Sauvignon wines. Also produces a Malcantone white.

Erich and Fabienne Klausener, 6989 Purasca (091) 606 35 22: Merlot specialists producing 15,000 bottles a year, including an oak-aged Gran Reserva.

Sergio Monti & Figli, 6936 Cademario Ronchi (091) 605 34 75: Their Rovere and Malcantone wines are both excellent. Some white is also produced.

Mauro Ortelli, 6851 Corteglia (091) 646 05 04: Produces 9,500 bottles of a good white blend and an intense Merlot del Ticino.

Joe Pfister, Ronco, 6981 Castelrotto (091) 608 22 91: Very small production but high marks as one of the best producers in the northern Sopraceneri region.

Werner Stucky, Casa del Portico 6802 Rivera (091) 946 12 82: One of the top northern producers. The Conte di Luna wine is 50% Merlot, 50% Cabernet Sauvignon.

Eredi Carlo Tamborini Vini SA, Strada Cantonale, 6814 Lamone (091) 945 34 34: Claudio Tamborini produces 35,000 bottles annually and over a half dozen Merlot bottlings. The new Castel di Morcote is excellent.

Tenuta Bally, Via Crespera 55, 6932 Breganzona (091) 966 28 08: A limited range of very fine wines, particularly the Crespera Riserva.

Vinattieri Ticinesi, 6853 Ligornetto (091) 647 33 33: Producers of a good firm "Bianco Ticinese Vinattieri".

Fratelli Valsangiacomo SA, Corso San Gottardo 107, 6830 Chiasso (091) 683 60 53: Any Valsangiacomo wine should be good. The range of Merlots under the names Rubro Barrique, Roncobello and Cuvée Spéciale are particularly fine.

Christian Zündel, 6981 Beride (091) 608 24 40: Concentrates on Merlot. Orizzonte is the firms Merlot/Cabernet blend. The total vineyard is only 3.5 hectares.

Cooperatives

Cantina Giubiasco: 6512 Giubiasco (091) 857 25 31: The Sopraceneri cooperative which produces a full range of Merlot wines, some reasonably interesting.

Cantina Sociale Mendrisio: Via Bernasconi 22, 6850 Mendrisio (091) 646 46 21: The Sottoceneri equivalent of Cantina Giubiasco. Produces both a Merlot VITI and a Merlot Reserve.

The vineyards of eastern Switzerland

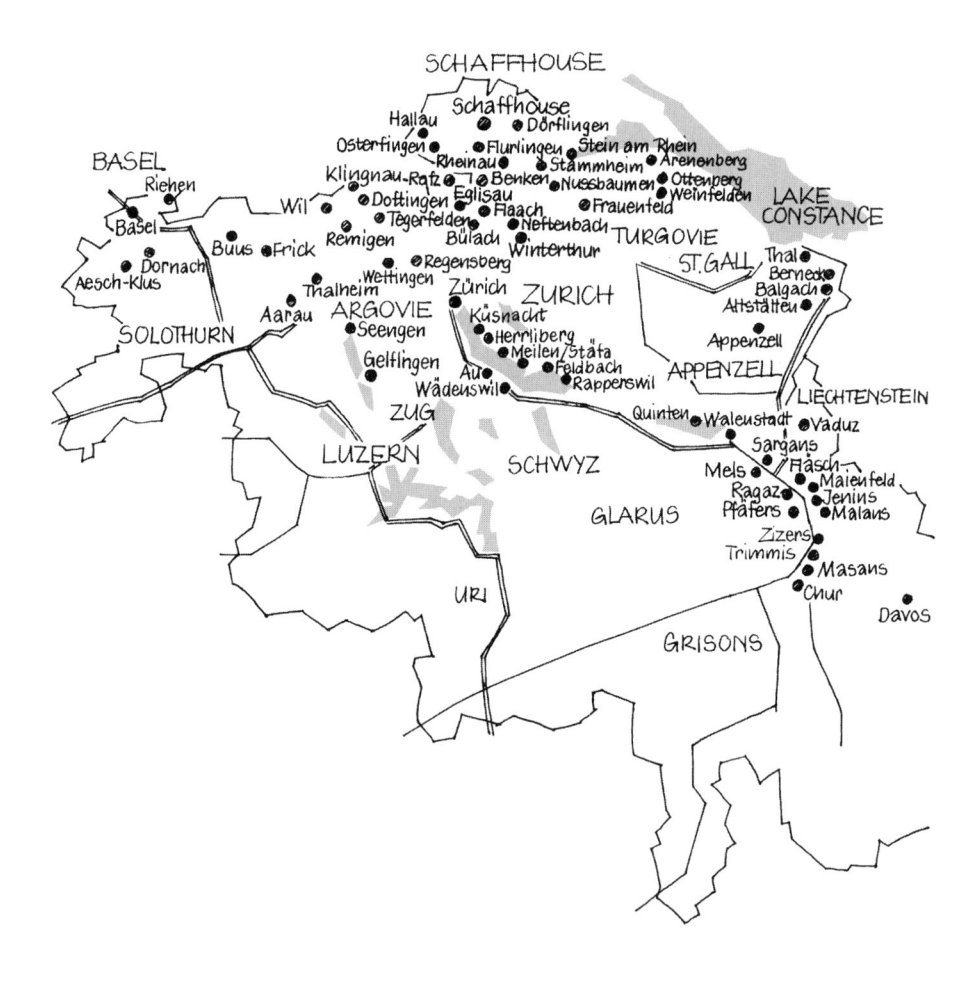

XI

Eastern Switzerland

The Region

The vineyards and wines of the eastern German-speaking part of Switzerland tend to be grouped together. The region is called *Ostschweiz* in German or *Suisse orientale* in French and includes all the vineyards located in the German-speaking cantons except for the Lake Bienne vineyards of the canton of Berne which were dealt with in the section on the canton of Neuchâtel. Almost all the vineyards are found in or around the Rhine river and its tributaries. Prevailing climatic conditions just barely permit the production of fine wines. In regions such as the Bündner Herrschaft in the canton of Grisons, only the influence of the warm fall *foehn* winds, *Traubenkocher* in German, provides sufficient warmth to ripen the grapes. As a result, Swiss-German producers generally concentrate on a limited range of grape varieties with the Pinot Noir and Riesling x Sylvaner providing 96% of the area's harvest. Differences in micro-climate, soils and vinification techniques do, however, ensure considerable variety among the wines, a diversity reflected by the almost 22,000 different labels which grace the wine bottles of the region.

Grapes account for about 2,550 hectares in eastern Switzerland, one-sixth of the whole Swiss vineyard area, and produce an average of 150,000 hectoliters a year. There are very few large unified estates and, therefore, vineyards are generally widely scattered across the 17 wine-producing cantons of the region. It is useful to view the vineyards of the German-speaking cantons as a collection of separate micro-climates that have in common a combination of temperature, southern exposure and slope which make successful grape growing possible. Many of these vineyards are sandwiched between forests, orchards, fields and villages or cramped on well-exposed slopes at the base of jagged mountains. At other sites, such as the area around Zurich or along the shores of Lake Zurich, urban expansion remains a constant threat. Responding to a large and steady local demand, this small production enjoys a rather strong self-sufficient market and most of these wines are consumed not far from the point of production.

Eastern Switzerland is one of the regions where land devoted to grapes has continued to grow throughout the latter decades of the 20th century. From 1,583 hectares in 1970, the total vineyard area rose to 1,940 hectares in 1980, 2,311 hectares in 1990 and 2,551 in 1995. Although almost all cantons in eastern Switzerland grow some grapes, the seven most important regions of production are located in the cantons of Zurich, Schaffhouse, Grisons, Argovie, Thurgovie, St. Gall and the countryside around Basel. These seven leading cantons provide well over 95% of the area's production.

Table IX: Eastern Switzerland: Production (1981-91 Avg.)

Canton	Acreage (ha.)	Harvest (hl.)
Zurich	610.0	34,698
Schaffhouse	482.0	33,142
Argovie	354.0	18,646
Grisons (ex. Misox)	314.0	21,208
Thurgovie	253.0	15,890
St. Gall	176.0	8,941
Basel – Country	78.0	4,243
Basel – City	2.0	176
Schwyz	23.0	1,289
Berne (Thun)	14.0	941
Lucerne	15.0	739
Appenzell (AR)	2.5	144
Appenzell (AI)	0.6	33
Soleure	0.8	86
Glaris	1.0	40
Zug	0.4	24
Nidwalden	0.2	9
Total	**2,327.5**	**140,249**

The climatic conditions are generally less favourable for grapes than those in Valais or in Vaud. The widely accepted minimum conditions for mature grapes include an average annual temperature of 9°C, more than 1,500 hours of sunshine a year and between 700 mm and 800 mm of rain. Table X on the next page, from the book *Vignes et Vins de Notre Pays*, shows just how close eastern Switzerland is to the extreme.

The low average temperature for the Grisons town of Landquart confirms the importance of the fall *foehn*. These difficult conditions do not, however, impede the production of interesting wines by well-managed vineyards. On the contrary, the defining realities represent a challenge which disciplined but creative wine makers take up successfully.

Table X: Climatic Conditions in Eastern Switzerland

Region	Altitude	Avg. Temp.	Sunshine	Rainfall
Zurich	493 m.	8.7°C	1680 hours	1044 mm
Hallau	450 m.	9.3°C	1618 hours	845 mm
Basel	317 m.	8.9°C	1683 hours	813 mm
Landquart	579 m.	7.6°C	1709 hours	1033 mm

The altitude of the vineyards ranges between 350 and 650 meters with the Pfäffers vineyards at Ragaz in the canton of St. Gall rising to 720 meters. The cultivation methods used in the vineyards of German Switzerland also generally differ from those used in Vaud and Valais. Cultivation using trellises often replaces the *gobelet* and the *gobelet sur échalas* (pole support) systems, although the latter is still useful when frosts are a particular threat. Slopes range from 25° to 80° and where the ground is less steep, intensive mechanization is often used.

In contrast to the output in the French-speaking part of the country, 70% of the wine produced in eastern Switzerland is red. The Pinot Noir (Blauburgunder, sometimes called Klevner or Clevner — the latter name traditionally used for Pinot Noir in the canton of Zurich) is virtually the only grape used. It has progressively displaced the formerly popular white grape types Räuschling, Completer and Elbling. These once widely-planted vines have not totally disappeared, although for a time the rapid spread of Riesling x Sylvaner made this a distinct possibility. Reduced areas of Räuschling still exist along the shores of Lake Zurich, and small areas of Completer and Elbling can be found near Malans in Grisons, remnants of earlier vineyards which are of historical and sentimental interest, even if their economic importance is limited.

Grapes and Wines

Red Wine Grapes

Pinot Noir (Blauburgunder, Klevner, Clevner)

The Pinot Noir was first introduced into the region of Maienfeld between 1630 and 1635 by the Breton Duc de Rohan who commanded a local garrison of French troops on behalf of Louis XIII. Legend suggests that the Duke was not impressed by the local thin white wines and therefore introduced his favorite vine from France.

Over time, varietal selection for the Pinot Noir has focused on developing strains which are both productive and *pourriture* (rot) resistant. Specific clones such as the Mariafeld have been developed to respond to local climatic conditions, although there have been problems with strains which are too fecund and trade high yields for inferior quality. In the region between the Rhine river and the Alps, the Pinot Noir does not always reach the optimum must weight. However, if planted on well-exposed slopes with soil of sufficient depth and drainage, the grapes can produce reasonably rich and complex wines without the heady alcoholic fullness found at times in the more southern cantons. *Vignerons* here aim for greater subtlety along with an attractive, fruity bouquet. These Pinot Noir wines can be surprisingly elegant and classy. They have a recognizable fruity character and a natural vivacity. These wines are often drunk slightly cool but few are kept much beyond two or three years after the vintage. The very best producers are creating Pinot Noirs with sufficient fruit and structure to withstand and benefit from aging in oak.

The Pinot Noir is also used in the production of the three different types of rosé found in eastern Switzerland. Federweiss is a white or off-white wine produced from the red-skinned Pinot Noir. Its style resembles that of the Oeil-de-Perdrix of Neuchâtel and Valais. Schiller is a combination of both red and white musts; Pinot Noir which predominates for the red and, traditionally, Elbling for the white, although this grape has generally been replaced by Riesling x Sylvaner. Süssdruck is a *petillant* rosé. Much of the production of these wines comes from the Churer Rheintal region of the canton of Grisons although similar rosés are produced throughout eastern Switzerland.

Although the Pinot Noir grape is the only economically significant red grape cultivated in this part of the country, mention should also be made for the record of small plots of Cabernet Sauvignon and the fact that the Merlot and Bondola, discussed in the chapter on Ticino, are both cultivated in the far south of the Grisons region in the Italian-speaking region of Misox. These vineyards reflect the climatic and historical affinity between Misox and the neighbouring Italian-speaking section of Switzerland. In addition, one can find pockets of Gamaret and Granoir, the two Gamay x Reichensteiner crosses popular for their colour and ripening abilities, but both rarely cultivated today. Finally, several recently introduced red hybrids, selected to accommodate the unique growing conditions found in the area, are grown in the cantons of Argovie and Basel.

White Wine Grapes

Riesling x Sylvaner (Müller-Thurgau)

From the growers point of view, the Riesling x Sylvaner is one of the most suitable white grape types for cultivation near the northern climatic limit as it combines early maturation with a highly fruity taste. The dominance in eastern Switzerland of the Riesling x Sylvaner, a low-acid, bountiful, easily-grown grape, approaches the pre-eminence of the Chasselas in the French-speaking part of the country. The Riesling x Sylvaner is, however, sensitive to mold and the vines must be severely pruned to produce sufficiently concentrated wines. Overproduction of this grape rapidly leads to an insipid wine. In addition, some wine makers have recently been experimenting with only partial or no malo-lactic fermentation to preserve a necessary level of acid in the wine.

After the refinement of the cross-breed at Wädenswil on Lake Zurich late in the 19th century, the Riesling x Sylvaner was first formally cultivated in 1925 in vineyards around Malans in the canton of Grisons. Its subsequent success in this part of Switzerland and much of Germany has been remarkable, although in recent years some of the varieties displaced by the advance of the Riesling x Sylvaner have been making a comeback.

As the Riesling x Sylvaner grapes mature rapidly, it can be grown where other varieties would not fully ripen. The grapes should be quite fruity, and produce a smooth, at times velvet, taste. The slight musky perfume can enhance the fragrant bouquet. The wines are usually consumed after one or two years.

Räuschling

Traditionally, the Räuschling grape produced the characteristic white wine of German-speaking Switzerland until it was largely replaced in the 20th century by the Riesling x Sylvaner. Its origins are unknown, although the Räuschling could be a derivative of the Kipperling, a grape formerly cultivated in the Pfalz region of Germany and in Alsace. The Räuschling is now grown sparingly on the shores of Lake Zurich and in the Limmat river valley. The grape has a fragile flowering and matures late, which limits its utility compared to the Riesling x Sylvaner.

Wines made from fully-ripened Räuschling grapes exert a particular appeal for Swiss palates. In addition, Räuschling wines do not necessarily have to be consumed as rapidly as some of the other regional "specialty" white wines. They combine a delicate but fruity flavour with well-balanced acids. As a result of the attractive qualities of this grape type, it has enjoyed a minor revival in recent years. The Räuschling has even been blended with Riesling x Sylvaner to use Räuschling's natural acid level to balance the floral characteristics of the Müller-Thurgau.

Completer

The Completer grape is also named "Malanserrebe" and may be related to the Lafnetscha, one of the minor grapes of the Haut Valais. It is grown almost exclusively around the Bündner Herrschaft village of Malans where it is still cultivated on the perfectly exposed slopes of the "Completerhalde" to produce much sought after wines. Small plots of Completer are also found around Lake Zurich. The use of this grape is limited by the sensitivity of the flowering and by its susceptibility to adverse climatic conditions. It is also a late maturing variety which in less-good years produces a very thin wine. In good years the Completer can produce musts with an Oechsle reading of over 100°. The wines still have a high acid content but are long-lasting. Folk traditions suggest this wine was drunk by monks after their evening prayers, or *complines* — whence came the name.

Pinot Gris and Pinot Blanc

The Pinot Gris grape needs the best and warmest growing conditions to allow the must to reach at least 90°Oe. It is not extensively planted in eastern Switzerland, but occasionally very successful examples can be found. Sometimes the grapes are

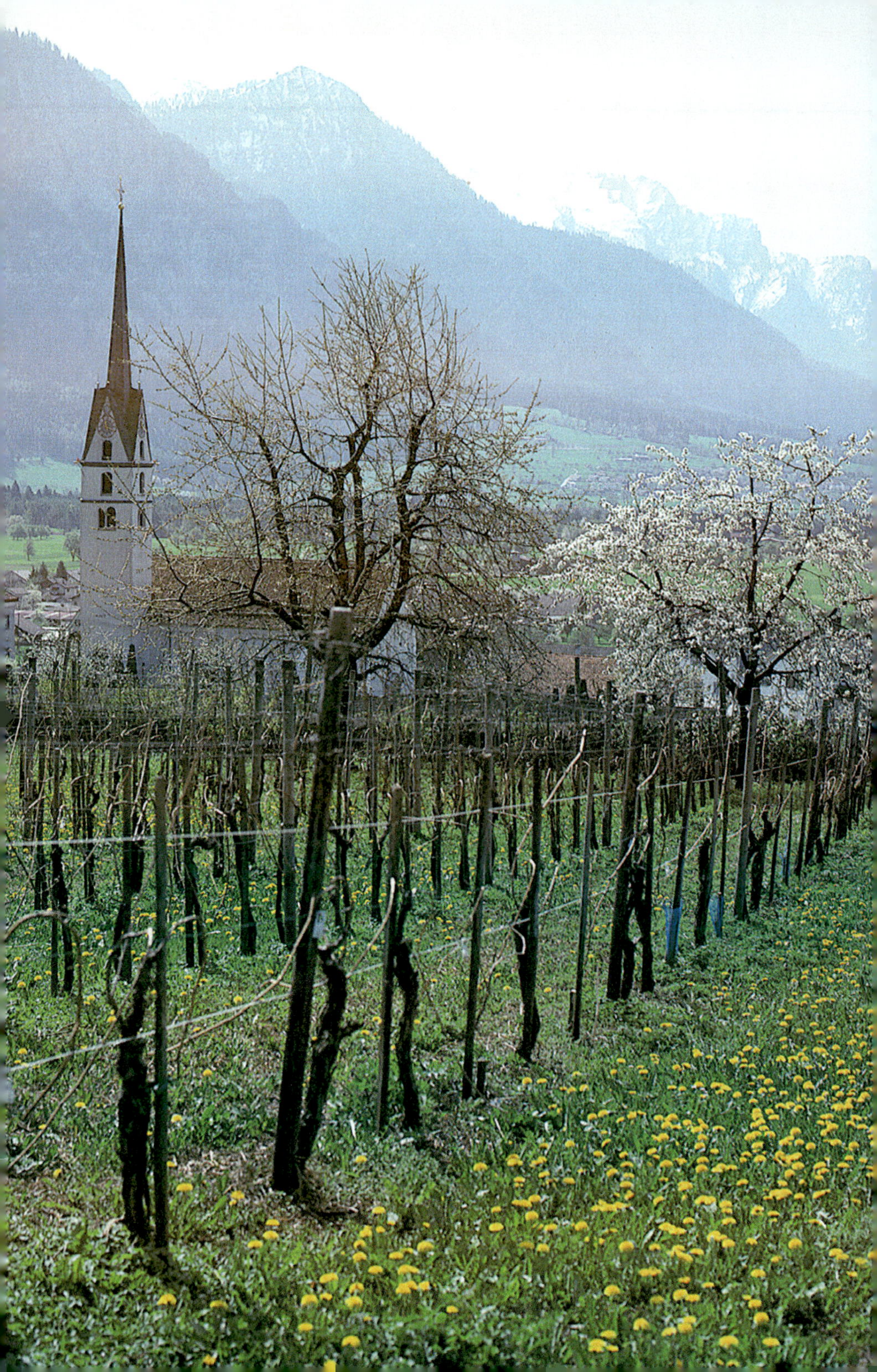

left on the vines to achieve an extra degree of sweetness. In such cases the wine from the overmature grapes resembles the *flétrie* Malvoisie wines of Valais. Pinot Blanc is even less often cultivated in eastern Switzerland as it is a more difficult grape to ripen under most conditions. Some *guyot* and high-trellised vines are now being grown in Malans with considerable success.

Elbling

The ancient Elbling grape produces an overly acidic wine and consequently has almost disappeared. The high acid content of the grapes remains a particular problem for wine growers when the grapes cannot ripen sufficiently in rainy summers. Most Elbling is cultivated in the canton of Argovie, although in Grisons it is still occasionally grown together with Pinot Noir to produce a traditional rosé Schiller wine.

Gewürztraminer

The Gewürztraminer, unlike the Riesling x Sylvaner, needs privileged climatic conditions and is therefore cultivated on the best exposed slopes along the banks of Lakes Zurich and Constance. As is the case when this grape is grown elsewhere, in eastern Switzerland the grape produces an original wine with a unique fruity and aromatic bouquet.

Freisamer

The Freisamer is a cross between Sylvaner and Pinot Gris, developed in the German city of Freiburg in the early part of this century. As with the Sylvaner, the Freisamer grapes remain green when mature. It needs a forgiving climate as well as good soil conditions. Given the infrequency of this combination, the distribution of this grape is very limited although some of the better wine makers around Lake Zurich and in the Bündner Herrschaft have experimented quite successfully with this variety to produce well-rounded, fresh wines.

The Wine Cantons of Eastern Switzerland

The German-speaking cantons of eastern Switzerland are divided into three broad regions: i) Central (Zurich, Schaffhouse, Thurgovie, Schwyz and Glaris); ii) Western (Argovie, Basel, Berne (Thun), Lucerne, Soleure, Zug, Nidwalden and Uri); and iii) Eastern (St. Gall, Appenzell and Grisons).

Spring in Malans, Bündner Herrschaft

The Central Region

Zurich

The first evidence of grape-growing and wine-making in Zurich is found in the Roman period when the Lindenhof, on the left bank of the Limmat river, was fortified from the 2nd century A.D. A many-towered citadel was added 200 years later, but after the invasion of the beer-drinking Alemanni tribes from the north in the 5th century, grape-growing disappeared from the region. Viticulture was again introduced by Charlemagne at the beginning of the 9th century. The first documented reference to grape-growing is dated 834, when a small vineyard in Stammhein was donated to the Benedictine Monastery of St. Gall. During the Middle Ages, grape-growing and wine production were further promoted by the monasteries, particularly by those of St. Gall and Einsiedeln.

Zurich is the leading wine canton in eastern Switzerland with 632 hectares of grapes which produced 37,000 hectoliters in 1994, down from 44,000 hectoliters in 1991. These vineyards provide one-quarter of the production of eastern Switzerland and the canton is ranked sixth among all the wine-growing cantons of Switzerland. Formerly Zurich's vineyards were of even greater importance with 5,000 hectares under cultivation at the beginning of this century. Since then, however, strong pressures from urban expansion, economic dislocation, diseases, imported wines and the concentration of production in the better vineyards have taken their toll. Over 80% of the former vineyards have disappeared.

The vineyards are now scattered throughout the canton and are usually found only in small parcels. Individual areas are sometimes subject to quite different climatic and geological conditions. The shores of Lake Zurich and the slopes of the Limmat and Rhine valleys are the most favoured for grape growing. The warm *foehn* wind from the south helps mature the grapes and gives some protection against the winter and spring frosts which are serious problems. The heat reflected from Lake Zurich also contributes to achieving acceptable median temperatures.

The Pinot Noir grape dominates over 60% of the total vineyard area. The Riesling x Sylvaner comes second, with just under half as much land planted. The other white grapes such as Räuschling, concentrated on the shores of Lake Zurich, Gewürztraminer, Chardonnay, Kerner and Pinot Gris make up most of the remainder. Total white wine production, 37% of the harvest, was 13,400 hectoliters in 1994. The topography allows cultivation using trellises, except on the northern flank of the lake where terraces have been built up.

Under the pressure for higher quality wines, the harvest increasingly has been strictly limited. Currently, 800 to 1,000 grams per square meter for Pinot Noir and 800 to 1,100 grams per square meter for Riesling x Sylvaner are normal. The Oechsle sugar readings can vary substantially from year to year. Between 1982 and 1991 the range for Pinot Noir averaged between 77°Oe to 94°Oe, while for Riesling x Sylvaner the average variation ranged between almost 70°Oe to 85°Oe. In some very good years, such as 1985 and 1990, the Oechsle readings in particularly well-exposed vineyards have reached extremely high levels such as 134°Oe for Pinot Noir and between 103°Oe and 115°Oe for Riesling x Sylvaner.

The white wines of Zurich are generally less fragrant than similar wines from other parts of eastern Switzerland. The reds should be well-structured and can benefit from short aging. However, apart from exceptional years, or the production of local "specialities", the wines of Zurich tend to be slightly acidic. If the wines are not produced with care, the results can be rather thin and lacking the charm of other Swiss wines. The exceptions are, however, worthy of note.

There are four distinct wine-growing regions within the canton of Zurich. The first is made up of the vineyards along the shores of Lake Zurich. The second lies along the banks of the Limmat river which exits the north end of Lake Zurich on its way to join the Aar and the Rhine rivers. The third, *Weinland* (Wineland), between Winterthur and Schaffhouse, is partially an extension of the vineyards of the neighbouring canton of Thurgovie and is the largest wine-growing area of the canton. The fourth, *Unterland,* is the area directly north of Zurich between the city and the Rhine river.

The city of Zurich has also managed to maintain a few vines within the municipality, and their production is sold under the labels of Bürgli, Sonnenberg and Höngg. These are, however, of limited commercial importance.

Lake Zurich

The vineyards bordering Lake Zurich produce some of the best wines of the canton. The north shore of the lake from the city of Zurich to the border with the canton of St. Gall has a string of well-known wine communes. The first vineyards can be found in Zollikon. They continue along the line of south-west facing hills that rise behind the lakeshore villages of Küsnacht, site of the highly-regarded Kunststuben restaurant, Erlenbach, Herrliberg, Meilen, Stäfa, and Feldbach. Stäfa is the largest wine-producing commune in the canton and is known for its Hasenhalde, Appenhalde, Chorherren and Sternenhalde vineyards.

Moving down the north shore of the lake along the well-travelled "gold coast" road from Zurich, among the recognized growers is Jürg Schneider in Feldmeilen who produces one of the best Riesling x Sylvaner along the northern shore from his Chorherren vineyards in Meilen. These wines can be elegant and slightly acidic with a light Muscat perfume. Schneider concentrates on a limited range of Riesling x Sylvaner, Räuschling and Pinot Noir. His five hectares produce 50,000 bottles a year.

Also in the vicinity is the outgoing and creative *vigneron* Hermann Schwarzenbach who has six hectares concentrated around the village of Meilen. Schwarzenbach worked for a time in Australia, which perhaps explains his bubbling enthusiasm for experimentation. He offers well-constructed quality Riesling x Sylvaner, Räuschling, Pinot Gris, Freisamer, Chardonnay and Pinot Noir and even a touch of the rare Completer. In order to preserve an adequate level of acidic freshness, Schwarzenbach often stops the secondary malo-lactic fermentation of his Riesling x Sylvaner before it is completed. Especially noteworthy are his Räuschling, a very concentrated Riesling x Sylvaner Beerenauslese, and his barrel-aged specialities, Chardonnay and Pinot Noir. The labels distinguish his two Pinot Noir selections: the Meilener Clevner is the regular selection while Meilener Pinot

Hermann Schwarzenbach from Meilen on Lake Zurich.

Noir is reserved for his aromatic barrel-aged wines. Schwarzenbach is also experimenting with blending, still a rare art in eastern Switzerland. A judicious combination of Riesling x Sylvaner and Räuschling, labelled Meilener Grande Cuvée and released for the first time in 1994, promises to be a very attractive and successful wine.

Farther down the lake, wines from the commune of Stäfa are particularly prized in the restaurants of Zurich. In 1991, in a competition celebrating the 700th anniversary of the foundation of the Swiss Confederation, the commune of Stäfa won a gold medal for a wine from the Sternenhalde vineyard made from the local Räuschling, a grape that has survived particularly well in this area. Hansueli Hasler in Uerikon, a suburb of Stäfa, is one of the leading producers of Räuschling. He is particularly known for his Stäfner Rütihof Räuschling. Hasler emphasizes quality over quantity. From his 5.3 hectares, he only produces between 30,000 and 50,000 bottles per year of Riesling x Sylvaner, Räuschling and Pinot Noir.

Across the lake on the southern shore, is the well-travelled autoroute from Zurich to the Grisons mountains and the popular ski areas of Arosa, Davos and St. Moritz. Here grape-growing plots are located on the Au peninsula which extends into Lake Zurich. These belong to the influential Federal Agricultural Research Institute of Wädenswil, which remains the source of much inspiration throughout the German-speaking cantons of Switzerland. The research station has also built a wine museum, the Weinbaumuseum zum Zürichsee (the Lake Zurich Wine Museum), which is worth a visit.

Still on the south shore, the firm of Gebrüder Kümin is located in the town of Freienbach, actually just across the border between the cantons of Zurich and Schwyz. Kümin's holdings of 14 hectares are quite spread out and include vineyards on the small islands in Lake Zurich, on the north shore of Lake Zurich in Rapperswil and in the isolated vineyards of Quinten on Lake Walensee.

The Limmat Valley

Departing north from the suburbs of Zurich along the Limmat river, one encounters scattered grape-growing areas between the city of Zurich and the Unterland wine region farther to the north. The two major wine-producing centers in this area are the communes of Weiningen, the second most important vine-growing commune in the canton, and Regensberg. In both areas, geological fate has given the local hills a particular southern exposure conducive to grape-growing. The Limmat valley is again blessed by the beneficial effect of the warm fall *foehn*.

Weiningen is a quaint village, tucked off in a small valley to the east of the Limmat, almost in the suburbs of Zurich. Two producers of note in Weiningen are Heinrich Haug and Peter Vogler who both produce Riesling x Sylvaner and Pinot Noir. Haug also bottles a Räuschling while Vogler produces a rather rare Weininger Gewürztraminer. To the northeast of Weiningen is the carefully preserved hilltop town of Regensberg. Here Thomas Weidmann sells 30,000 bottles a year which include Pinot Gris, in addition to Riesling x Sylvaner, and even an uncommon sparkling wine, Regensberger Schampus. The vineyards of Regensberg spread out in a natural south-facing amphitheater which unfolds directly below the schloss. Without in any way downgrading the local wines, Regensberg is known equally, if not more so, for its flowering roses, including a red variety named after the town.

Weinland

The third major area in the canton of Zurich is Weinland. It includes the vineyards beginning at Winterthur, an important industrial center north-east of Zurich, and extends north to the border with Schaffhouse, and east to the border of Thurgovie. Around Winterthur the vineyards in the communes of Neftenbach and Wiesendangen have good local reputations. Neftenbach is north-west of Winterthur and here Hans Herzog's five-hectare Domain Zum Taggenberg produces a wide variety of grapes including Riesling x Sylvaner, Pinot Gris, Chardonnay, Räuschling, Pinot Noir, and even Sauvignon Blanc, Cabernet Sauvignon and Merlot — three varieties rarely found in eastern Switzerland! Herzog also devotes considerable attention to the presentation and marketing of his wines, and produces some striking bottle labels. His Taggenberg Pinot Noir, which is labeled Auslese, or Spätlese for the barrel-aged selection, is his most highly valued wine. Annual production is 30,000 bottles.

Farther north along the Kohlfirst hills in Truttikon, Waldemar Zahner's Domain Bächi produces a total of 55,000 bottles per year of Riesling x Sylvaner, Gewürztraminer and Pinot Noir from six hectares of vines. Of particular interest are his unusual Truttiker Spätlese, a late-harvested Pinot Noir which is a deep red, aromatic wine after maturing two years in barrels. This wine will keep for several years. Zahner's red contrasts well with his rosé Truttiker Federweiss, a light, pale yellow wine which still retains an intense Pinot Noir nose and a good length.

Heiner Hertli in Flurlingen, along the Rhine, is one of the few producers known for his Pinot Gris, which is labeled Flurlinger Tokayer. A favourable topography and climate, as well as the chalky soil on his 3.4-hectare vineyard, combine to produce a range of unique wines. Hertli's several different variations of Tokayer include a late harvest Spätlese dessert wine, and two Auslese versions which are made from musts with Oechsle readings of 100° and 104° respectively.

Other important wine-producing areas in the Weinland are Andelfingen, Oberstammhein and Rheinau, the latter perched precipitously in a sharp bend in the Rhine river. Rheinau is the site an ancient convent where the ice-wines of Volken are vinified. These grapes are picked in the cold of January, often in freezing weather after midnight, when the grape sugars have reached 140° Oe. The wines have around 16% alcohol. Rheinau also is a convenient crossing point on the wine trail for entry into Germany. Depending on where one is starting from, passing through Rheinau can be the most direct route to the vineyards of Hallau in the canton of Schaffhouse.

Unterland

The last important production area is the *Unterland* with about 110 hectares, mainly in areas around the villages Teufen, Eglisau, Wil and Rafz, all in the northwest of the canton of Zurich and quite near the border with Germany. The vineyards of Wil and Rafz rise directly from the Rhine. These vineyards are part of the Jura region and are protected by the Jura mountain range.

In Teufen, Geri Lienhard produces 20,000-30,000 bottles a year of Riesling x Sylvaner, Räuschling and Pinot Noir. His Pinot Noir comes in four different versions from a Federweiss rosé to a barrel-aged Gramat Auslese. Mattias Angst in Wil produces 40,000 bottles of respected Riesling x Sylvaner, Gewürztraminer, Chardonnay and Pinot Noir; in Rafz, Kurt Neukom cultivates three hectares of Riesling x Sylvaner, Pinot Gris and Pinot Noir. The skill with which he grows and vinifies his grapes was recognized in 1990 with a gold medal at the annual Swiss Wine Competition. Also of note are his two types of Pinot Gris: one a fruity wine with a good structure; the other a well-rounded dessert wine, meant to be served appropriately cool.

Schaffhouse

The city of Schaffhouse is located just above a series of impassable rapids on the Rhine river. This strategic location made the town a natural transportation center as all goods had to be transshipped to cross the river. As early as the 11th century, the abbots of the Benedictine monastery of Allerheiligen (All Saints) contributed significantly to the promotion of grapes and wine growing. When the monastery was closed in 1524, the town of Schaffhouse took over the properties of the monks, including its vineyards. After the Reformation, the area of vines under cultivation continued to grow, reaching as much as 1,170 hectares in 1800 compared to under 500 hectares today. This strong increase in vineyard size was due to the role played by Schaffhouse as a source of cereals and wine for the independent German Duchy of Baden. However, when Baden joined the German Custom Union in 1835, the economic prosperity of the local vineyards ended.

The vineyards of the canton of Schaffhouse straddle both banks of the Rhine and are protected to the north by the tail of the Jura mountain range. Traditionally Schaffhouse was a white wine region. Today, however, 80% of the production is red.

Although this is a northern vineyard, the prevailing climatic conditions, including 800 mm to 850 mm of rainfall per year and very little fog during the vegetation period, and a favourable warm autumn, all contribute to ripening the grapes. Nevertheless, the risks of frost and hail cannot be ignored. The vineyard terrain varies considerably. There are chalky soils in some areas, molasse or sandy soils in others and clay elsewhere. These differences contribute to the surprising diversity of wines — fresh and lively whites from pebbly and chalky soils, complemented by strong red wines on heavier soils.

Just over 480 hectares are devoted to grapes, of which 380 hectares produce Pinot Noir, 90 hectares are given to Riesling x Sylvaner, and the remaining 10 hectares to Pinot Gris, Chardonnay, Räuschling, Gewürztraminer, Kerner and Pinot Blanc. Variations in harvest conditions have an impact on the output. In the less-than-perfect 1987 vintage, for example, the median production was 43 hectoliters per hectare; two years later, in the exceptional vintage of 1989, it reached 103 hectoliters per hectare. In 1994 the yield was a generous but not overly excessive 73 hectoliters for red and 64 for white. The sugar content at harvest can also vary substantially: the average for Pinot Noir musts fluctuated between 79°Oe in 1987 and 90°Oe in 1990; for the Riesling x Sylvaner grapes, the sugar content varied between 71.5°Oe in 1986 and 78°Oe in 1990.

Over the last several decades, local wine makers have substantially enlarged their production. From 380 hectares in 1970, the average is up almost one third to 501 hectares in 1994. During the better vintages, vingerons have begun to mature some of their red wine production in oak. This operation remains delicate because strong oak tannins can overwhelm the relatively light bouquet and taste of the these Pinot Noirs. In addition, an important part of the Pinot Noir harvest has been used to produce off-white or rosé wines labeled as Rosé, Federweiss or Weissherbst, the latter name more commonly found in Germany. Wine makers here have also started to diversify their production by introducing limited plantings of new grape types, including Chardonnay, Pinot Blanc, Kerner and Bacchus among the whites, and the Gamaret or Granoir crosses among the reds. Even if it is too early to assess the ultimate success of these developments, the determination of these wine makers not to be left behind by experiments in other parts of Switzerland is striking.

In spite of pressures from urban sprawl, the city of Schaffhouse has managed to maintain four hectares of Pinot Noir and Pinot Gris within its boundaries. The vineyards on the slopes of the Munot hill, crowned by an imposing round dungeon which dominates both the city and the Rhine Valley, are impossible to miss. Protected by the walls of the ancient fortress and benefiting from long periods of sunshine, these pie-shaped vineyards produce a solid Pinot Noir, labeled Munotler in honour of the hill. Traveling westwards from Schaffhouse, the Rhine waterfall near Neuhausen is one of the most impressive in Europe.

The most important vineyards of the canton are concentrated in the Klettgau plateau to the west of Schaffhouse city. This 200 hectare plateau forms the largest continuous vineyard area in eastern Switzerland. For the communes of Hallau (153 hectares), Oberhallau (63 hectares), Wilchingen (61 hectares), Trasadingen (41 hectares) and Osterfingen (31 hectares), wine-making is the major economic activity. Pinot Noir dominates, with over 80% of production in Hallau and Oberhallau. In autumn, colourful processions with horse drawn *barouches* (carriages) are organized throughout the villages and the vineyards of the region. Hallau is also home to the Schaffausen Weinbaumuseum (Schaffhouse Wine Museum) founded in 1983.

Notable among Klettgau wine growers are Max and Ruedi Baumann of Baumann Weingut in Oberhallau. Max Baumann started producing wine many years ago and, after years of effort, he now turns out well-structured and personalized wines. His son Ruedi is increasingly important in the business. The Baumanns are keen on producing as natural a product as possible. They follow the regime of integrated pest management and have consequently reduced the use of insecticides and fertilizers to the absolute minimum. The domain of seven hectares produces between 40,000 and 50,000 bottles a year of Riesling, Chardonnay and Pinot Noir. Pinot Noir is, however, their passion. Oberhallau Beerli and Auslese are their two standard wines with 12.5% and 13% of alcohol respectively. These are both well-balanced wines with good length. The Auslese Pinot Noir is enhanced by rather fine soft tannins. The Baumanns have also started to produce a superior wine aged in French oak and labeled Classique. Only 700 liters were made in 1993. The latest innovation is a Pinot Noir Trockenbeere, a haunting wine from grapes picked in late October at 135° Oe. and then left to dry until mid-December to concentrate the juice and sugars before fermentation. A fabulously perfumed wine, the 1992 harvest has been released in half bottles.

The headquarters of the large but good Hallau producers Hans Schlatter are in the attractive town of Hallau. Schlatter's wines have achieved some international distribution and can be found in London. In addition to his Sanct Moritz Pinot Noir, Schlatter also produces a rather special Spätlese Pinot Noir under the label 16-Fahne Wy.

South of Hallau, almost on the border of a small slice of Germany that extends like an arrow into Switzerland, is the quiet village of Osterfingen, located up a dead-end valley off the main road. Here again geographic evolution has provided some excellent south-facing slopes. Jacob Richli is among the better producers in the village. Back on the main road are the cellars of a wine maker highly esteemed by his colleagues, Michael Meyer of the Familie Meyer winery in Bad Osterfingen. Meyer's own vineyards at less than two hectares are quite tiny, but he buys-in local grapes to supplement his production. As might be expected the winery concentrates on Pinot Noir. The Meyer winery's basic Pinot Noir red, served cool in the wood-panelled guesthouse restaurant above the cellars, is an extremely agreeable, soft and round wine with almost no tannin. The striking label features a map dated 1800 of the Meyer house. More substantive are Meyer's Badwy and Badreben wines, both from Osterfingen vines. The Badreben Pinot Noir is oak-aged and has done very well in competition, both domestically and internationally, against German and Alsacian Pinot Noirs. Meyer complements his Pinot Noir production with white wines made from Pinot Blanc and Riesling x Sylvaner grapes.

Continuing down the road from Osterfingen to Germany, after crossing a forested landscape one reaches the German town of Jestetten. From here you re-enter Switzerland by crossing the covered bridge at Rheinau. Not far away, but back in the canton of Schaffhouse, Pinot Noir and, to a lesser extent Riesling x Sylvaner, are cultivated in a bend in the Rhine at Buchberg and Rüdlingen.

Away from the Klettgau plateau, to the north of the city of Schaffhouse in the village of Thayngen, Thomas Stamm is gaining a solid reputation for interesting wines from his 3.5 hectare estate. Production includes oak-aged Pinot Noir in addition to the full range of wines commonly found in eastern Switzerland.

Pinot Noir and Riesling x Sylvaner are also grown farther up the Rhine valley towards Lake Constance at Stein-am-Rhein, a small walled town straight out of the Middle Ages with its stone bridges and ancient monasteries, including the famous Monastery of St. George built in 984. The local vineyards, in particular Blaurock and Chäfersteiner, produce quite interesting wines from 17 hectares of Pinot Noir and 3 hectares Riesling x Sylvaner. These wines can best be enjoyed in the authentic atmosphere of the restaurant Roter Ochsen (Red Beef), an old mansion with a gothic facade dating from 1615, and a fine renaissance period room with paintings by the noted Swiss artist, Andreas Schmucker.

Thurgovie

The vineyards of the canton of Thurgovie cover over 250 hectares, most of them between Lake Constance and the Rhine on the north and, to the south, the banks of the Thur river. The production is divided between Pinot Noir (67%) and Riesling x Sylvaner (32%), with some traces of Pinot Gris and Gewürztraminer. The wines of Thurgovie generally are similar to those of Schaffhouse and Zurich. They are floral and can be either mild or quite strong, depending on variations of location, vinification and climate, even within relatively short distances. The five major wine-producing areas in Thurgovie are the upper Thur valley, the lower Thur valley, Seebach, the banks of the Rhine and Untersee.

Upper Thur Valley

The vineyards of the upper Thur valley are located within the communes of Weinfelden (Winefields) and Märstetten, along the slopes of the Ottenberg range. The highly regarded Ottenberger wines are concentrated around the Bachtobel region between Märstetten and Weinfelden.

Here Hans-Ulrich Kesselring has a 5.5-hectare domain, Schlossgut Bachtobel, probably the leading estate in the canton. The vineyards are planted with Pinot Noir (80%) and Riesling x Sylvaner (15%), while the remaining five percent is devoted to Pinot Gris, Chardonnay and rare plot of Riesling. The vineyards are gathered around an old mansion, locally known as "the castle" which is featured on some of the domain's labels. Part of the Schloss dates from the 15th century, although the house was extensively done over in the French style some 200 years ago. The above-ground *chai* is protected by towering plane trees planted in the first years of the 19th century and features two massive grape presses, the oldest dating from 1584, four years before the Spanish Armada! It was last used in 1984. Kesselring is in fact an agronomist-engineer who specializes in oenology. He performs his own chemical analysis and uses his research to improve his vinification techniques. In recent years he has begun serious experimentation with barrel maturation for his reds with very encouraging results. "We have come back to wood, but not to the wood of our fathers" Kesselring perceptively commented.

Among his Schlossgut Bachtobel wines is a very good Riesling x Sylvaner where the necessary acidity is preserved by allowing only part of the final wine to complete the secondary malo-lactic fermentation. Production for the Riesling is restricted to 700-800 grams of grapes per square meter and the wine exhibits a hint of pineapples. Plantings of Riesling x Sylvaner are being reduced in favour of Pinot Noir and it is here that Kesselring excels.

His basic red wine, referred to as #1, is full of fruit and soft tannins. Fermentation lasts for five days. The working material for wine #2 is virtually the same grapes, but fermented at high temperature for two weeks. This wine is aged for 3-4 months in 800 liter French oak barrels to provide just enough oak to balance the fruit. The result is rounded but quite powerful. Finally, wine #3 is Kesselring's excellent Der Andere Pinot Noir, a ruby-hued wine produced from specially selected sites on the Ottenberg slopes. It is matured for one year in 225-liter French barrels, racked every two months, blended back together and again redistributed to the barrels. The harvest yield varies between 800 and 900 grams of grapes per square meter, but the 1992 yields were under 620 grams per square meter, reflecting both a serious effort to limit the harvest and the dryness of the vintage. This was a fine year for Pinot Noir in this area. When young, the Der Andere exhibits a "toasty" nose; after a year or two the scent recalls cinnamon while after three years the fragrance changes to cloves. This is a wine that sells out very quickly.

Lower Thur Valley

In the lower Thur valley, which produces the most wine of all the regions in the canton, vineyards are located in the communes of Niederneunforn, Oberneunforn, Uesslingen-Iselisberg and Warth-Weiningen on the north bank of the Thur river. Among the different local producers, the domain of the illustrious Charterhouse at Ittingen in Warth, and the property of Ulrich Haussmann in Iselisberg merit mention as conscientious producers.

Seebach

Pinot Noir is grown almost exclusively in the Seebachtal, the area to the north of Thurgovie's capital, Frauenfeld, and slightly to the north-east of the lower Thur valley. The villages of Hüttwilen, Herdern, Dettighofen and Nussbaumen are all recognized as producing among the better wines of the canton. Herdern is the site of Kalchrainer, the estate owned by the canton of Thurgovie. It produces a respectable Pinot Noir.

The Banks of the Rhine

Between the region of Seebach and the Rhine, vineyards are cultivated around the small town of Dissenhofen and in the village of Schlattingen. The Municipality of Dissenhofen grows a noted Pinot Noir, and even produces a Riesling x Sylvaner from properties on the other side of the Rhine, in German territory. The state-owned domain of St. Katharinethal is also located in this area.

Untersee

The vineyards of Untersee face the Untersee peninsula which juts out from Germany into the waters of Lake Constance. The main wine-producing communes are Salenstein, Stechborn and Ermatingen. This area produces the best Riesling x Sylvaner in the canton.

The wines of the Arenenberg domain in the commune of Salenstein are often singled out for attention, although like so many wines of eastern Switzerland, they are mainly consumed *"sur place"*. The historical reputation of Arenenberg is not due solely to the Riesling x Sylvaner of the agricultural school of Arenenberg, but rather to an illustrious guest of the castle, Napoleon's nephew, Louis Napoleon Bonaparte, who himself ruled as Emperor of France from 1848 to 1870. After his uncle was deposed in 1815, Louis Napoleon took refuge in Arenenberg. He was educated there and was even granted citizenship from the canton of Thurgovie in 1832, prior to returning to France as Emperor Napoleon III in 1848.

A short driving distance from Arenenberg, on the way to the towns of Kreuzlingen and Constance, is Scherzingen, home to Walter Rutishauser's wine cellars, Rutishauser Weinkellereien. Rutishauser, who is also a wine trader, grows and vinifies his own grapes from 16 hectares. His winery also processes grapes grown at sites found across six cantons in eastern Switzerland which collectively are far larger than his core 16 hectares. Rutishauser's production consists largely of Pinot Noir and Riesling x Sylvaner, with traces of Pinot Gris, Gewürztraminer and Chardonnay. By limiting the harvest to 700-800 grams per square meter for his reds, and to 900-1000 grams per square meter for the whites, Rutishauser releases wines with good concentration which have scored well in national wine competitions.

Schwyz

The 23 hectares of vineyards in the canton of Schwyz are along the south-east side of Lake Zurich, near Wollerau and Lachen. Riesling x Sylvaner (56%) and Pinot Noir (39%) dominate, while the remaining area is planted with Chasselas, Pinot Gris, Gewürztraminer, Räuschling and Freisamer. Mention was made in the section on Lake Zurich of the good Schwyz producer Gerbrüder Kümin whose grapes are spread across at least three cantons, Zurich, Schwyz and St. Gall. Overall, these wines are similar to the others produced in the region.

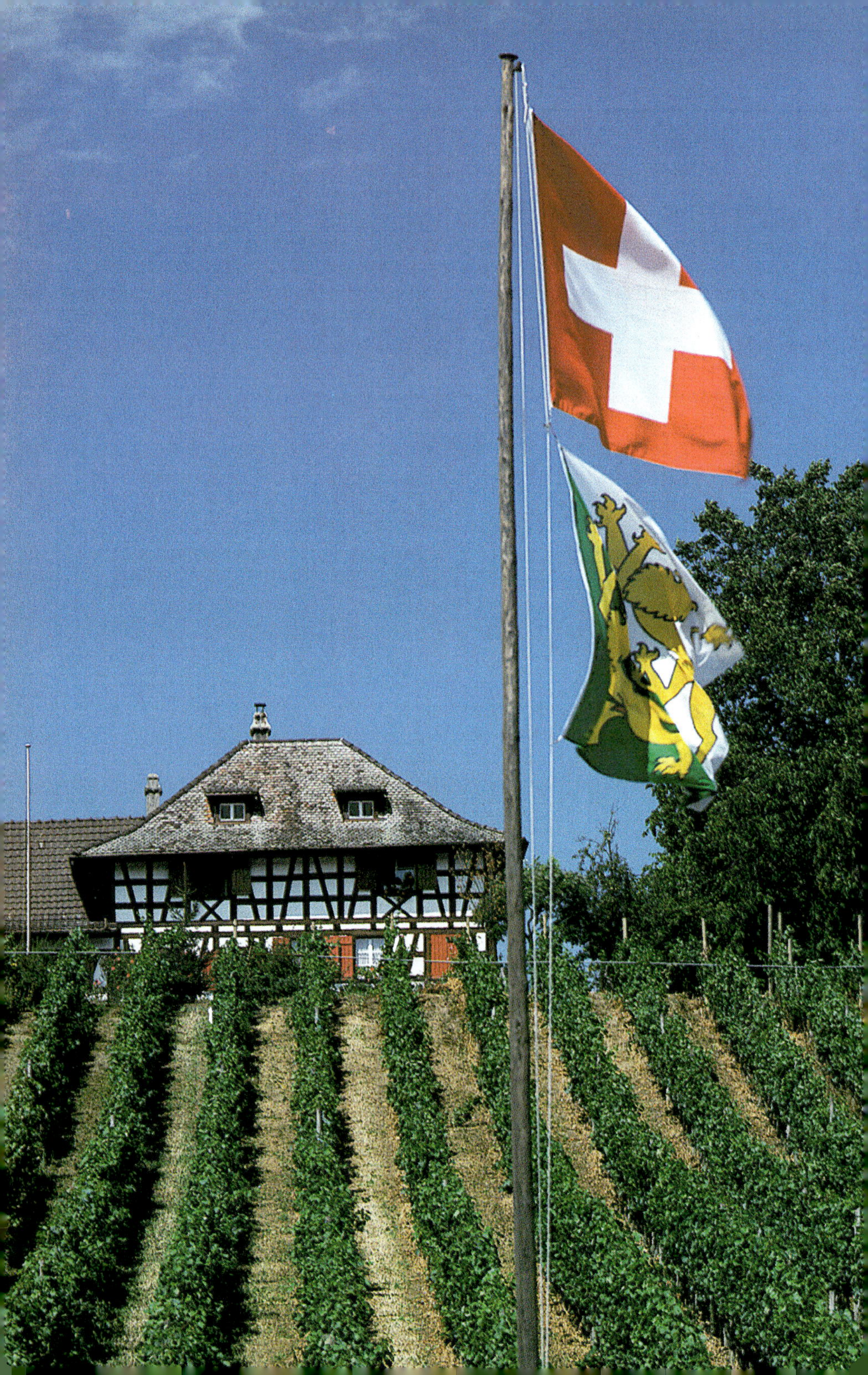

The Western Region

Argovie

The heavily urbanized canton of Argovie is in the heart of the industrialized triangle of Switzerland, to the west of Zurich in the direction of Basel and Berne. The canton's vineyards cover a total of 350 hectares.

The grapes most frequently cultivated are Pinot Noir (54%); Riesling x Sylvaner (43%); and traces of Elbling, Pinot Gris and Gewürztraminer. Trellises are the most common form of training the vines. The varied landscape and the climatic conditions have an important effect on the grape production. The sugar content of the Pinot Noir musts, and consequently the wines, vary considerably. They can be fruity or strong with the fuller versions sometimes exhibiting notable tannins. On the other hand, the Riesling x Sylvaner, when grown on chalky soils in the western part of the region, can distinguish itself by a muscaty perfume and a characteristic velvet texture. The output can vary greatly from year to year. In 1985 there was a minuscule yield of 10.6 hectoliters per hectare. In the more normal harvest of 1994, the average yields were 61 hectoliters per hectare for red wines and 59 hectoliters per hectare for whites.

Riesling x Sylvaner is the chief grape in the communes of Schinznach, Oberflachs and Thalheim, as well as in the vineyards of the leading local producer, the Cooperative of Schinznach. Over 80% of the grapes grown here are Riesling x Sylvaner while the rest are Pinot Noir. The Riesling x Sylvaner thrives on the chalky soils of this area producing fresh and elegant wines. In Schinznach, Emil Hartmann produces interesting wines of which the Thalheimer Chalöfner, a typical regional Pinot Noir, and a solid Chardonnay, have received particular recognition. He produces 60,000 bottles of Riesling x Sylvaner, Chardonnay and Pinot Noir from six hectares of vines.

The Pinot Noir is mainly cultivated on the slopes along the three rivers, the Aar, Reuss and Limmat which join in Argovie before flowing towards the Rhine. Pinot Noir also grows near Hapsburg, originally home to the Austrian imperial dynasty and Lenzbourg, a provincial town dominated by an imposing castle, founded around 1240 by one of the great warrior families in Swiss medieval history, the Kybourgs.

Anton Meier in Würenlingen is another Argovie *vigneron* worth special mention. Meier, who also runs a major tree nursery, continues to propagate Pinot Noir clones developed by his father. Although he holds some vines in Würenlingen, his best production is from the Kloster Sion vineyard in Klingnau to the north. He is one of the few producers who can claim total vertical integration — controlling his entire production from the root stock to the bottle of wine on the table. Meier is without doubt one of the leading wine promoters in the canton. On his six-hectares of property he produces 40,000 to 50,000 bottles per year of Riesling x Sylvaner, Pinot Gris, Gewürztraminer and Pinot Noir and his production includes selections from Würenlingen, Dottingen and Klingnau. Among his wines, the Kloster Sion Pinot

At Warth in the upper Thur valley.

Gris is a well focused, almost spicy white while the intense purple Kloster Sion Barrique Pinot Noir is his finest wine. Meier's wines hold pride of place at his countryside restaurant, the Zum Sternen in Würenlingen, and with luck, visitors might be able to purchase some of the oak-aged Pinot Noirs to take home.

To the north of Würenlingen, the quaint town of Tergerfelden is the site of the Argau cantonal wine museum. From Tergerfelden to Dottingen a south-facing line of hills boast an almost unbroken line of grapes on the upper slopes with the lower areas dedicated to fruit trees.

Across the River Aar, grapes are grown up the slopes which rise behind the villages from Villigen to Remingen. In the town of Remingen, Bruno Hartmann is another of Switzerland's "natural" producers who is making impressive wines at the Hartmann-Saladin winery. His 5.2-hectare winery concentrates on grapes from the Remigen and Villnachern regions and includes various specialties in addition to the normal range of wines.

Moving towards the west of the canton, the vineyards in the commune of Fricktal produce both red and white grapes. The team of Fehr + Engeli in Uekon obtain much of their production from Fricktal vines, although they also have holdings on the hills immediately above Uekon. Riesling x Sylvaner and Pinot Noir are the dominant grapes although some Riesling and Cabernet Sauvignon are also grown. Pinot Noir is used to produce their rosé and also for their light, pleasing Fricktal Schiller, a Pinot Noir/Riesling x Sylvaner blend. Among their other wines a Kaister Riesling x Sylvaner Special Cuvée which has not gone through its malolactic fermentation stands out, although in less-full years such as 1992 the wine can be quite sharp. Fehr + Engeli's premium wine is their Uekon Blauburgunder Barrique, a full bodied wine which not surprisingly sells out quite quickly.

Basel

According to Basel municipal records over 20,000 hectoliters of wine were produced in the canton in 1593, more than twice today's output. Of the 97 hectares of vines in the two Basel cantons, Pinot Noir (60%), Riesling x Sylvaner (20%) and Chasselas (10%) have the largest shares. There are also small plots of Pinot Gris and Gewürztraminer. The Pinot Noir dominates in the higher elevations of Buus, Maisprach and Sissach, while the Chasselas, which needs more warmth, only grows in lower sites such as Muttenz, Arlesheim and Biel-Benken and at Aesch in the Klus valley south of Basel. Even the northern Basel suburb of Riehen, hard by the German border, has its local Schlipfer wine and a small museum devoted to the history of the area and the role of the *vigneron*.

In Aesch, Kurt Nussbaumer produces Chasselas, Riesling x Sylvaner, Gewürztraminer, Räuschling, Pinot Gris, Pinot Noir and Granoir at his ten-hectare domain, Vordere Klus. Production is between 50,000 and 60,000 bottles per year. Nussbaumer and his wife also run a fine wood-paneled countryside restaurant situated among their vines outside of Aesch. Here the appropriate aperitif is Nussbaumer's sparkling Chrachmost, an elegant *méthode champenoise* wine composed of 60% Chasselas along with Riesling and Riesling x Sylvaner. Nussbaumer's Kluser Räuschling is a fresh, slightly acidic wine that is most agreeably drunk with a fine fish dinner. His Granoir, which has scored well in wine competitions, has a good fruity nose and some tannin. Nussbaumer also produces a rare oak-aged Riesling x Sylvaner along with his highly regarded Pinot Gris and Pinot Noir.

Berne (Lake Thun)

South-east of the city of Berne, towards the head-waters of the Aar and at the foot of the Alps, are the wines from the cooperatives of Spiez and Oberhofen on the shores of Lake Thun (Thoune). The area under cultivation is just 15 hectares and wine production is limited to Riesling x Sylvaner (65%) and Pinot Noir (35%) grapes. The small output has to meet a fairly large local demand and these wines are rarely found outside their native region.

Lucerne

In the canton of Lucerne, 15 hectares of vineyards are located on the shores of the Lake Lucerne and Lake Baldegg, as well as in the Seetal region. Riesling x Sylvaner is the grape most frequently cultivated (67%), while most of the rest is Pinot Noir. There is also some Pinot Gris.

Soleure

The canton of Soleure, located farther up the banks of the Aar river, produces low-alcohol wines from Chasselas and Pinot Noir, almost exclusively for local consumption. Over the last century the area of vines in Soleure has been reduced considerably due to the familiar pressures of urbanization and industrial expansion. Today only four hectares of vines remain, just one one-hundredth of the canton's former vineyards. However, Josef Müller in Niedererlinsbach is bravely carrying on the tradition of grape growing on a tiny 1.5 hectares of vines. His wines includes Riesling x Sylvaner and Pinot Noir.

Uri

Uri is not known as a wine producing canton and, if the truth be known, much of its better wines are vinified along the shores of Lake Zurich in Hermann Schwarzenbach's cellars at Obermeilen. The grapes come from the Planzer estate in Bürglen. There is usually just enough Pinot Noir grown to fill a large wooden barrel. The wine is surprisingly good. Fresh and well-rounded, it contains a good dose of tannin.

The Eastern Region

St. Gall

The famed monastery of St. Gall was founded by the saint of the same name in the early 7th century. The vineyards of the canton of St. Gall now cover 176 hectares, where mainly Pinot Noir (82%) and Riesling x Sylvaner (14%) grape are produced. The remainder is composed of Pinot Gris, Gewürztraminer and

Chardonnay. The two important grape growing regions of the canton are Rheintal in the north and Oberland in the south.

Rheintal

Rheintal, the first wine region of the canton of St. Gall, is in the north of the canton between Thal where the Rhine opens towards Lake Constance, and the small town of Altstätten across the Rhine valley from the Austrian border. The most important vineyards are those in Berneck, Balgach and Marbach. Produced from Pinot Noir grapes, these wines are marketed under the names of Bernecker, Balgacher, Sonnenberger, Rebsteiner, Marbacher, Pfauenhalde, Rosenberger, Eichholtz, and Monsteiner. To this list must be added the Buchenberger, known popularly as the "pearl of the Rhine valley".

The growing conditions here are similar to those of the better regions of Grisons to the south because they benefit from the southern, warming influence of spring and autumn *foehn* winds. The grape-growing conditions are anything but easy, as most of these vineyards are on the steep slopes at the base of the mountains which rise immediately to the west of the Rhine. Often the vineyards have a south-eastern rather than directly south exposure. The width of the Rhine valley does, however, ensure that sunlight reaches the slopes for much of the day. This difficult working environment helps explain why the vineyards have decreased by almost three-quarters since the end of the 19th century.

In Berneck, Jakob and Tobias Schmid are particularly respected. Jacob produces very fine wines from grapes grown on the steep slopes of the Rosenberg and the Pfauenhalde, two vineyards on the molasse outcrop reaching down to the Rhine valley and surrounding Berneck village. He owns a total of 6.5 hectares but vinifies more than this. His wines are immediately recognizable by their striking, almost medieval labels. Among other producers, mention should be made of Christian Herzog in Thal and the cooperative wine cellar of Berneck (Weinbaugenossenschaft). This is also the area which produces the rare and therefore fabulously expensive Forstwein of Altstätten. The demand for this local Pinot Noir "specialty" produced by Heini Haubensak is so great that its price has reached astronomical levels — even by Swiss standards. Another Altstätten wine is the Bergwein of Josef Besitzer, grown on the slopes below an imposing bright yellow and black shuttered tower overlooking the town.

Driving south from Altstätten towards Buchs, avoiding the autoroute leading to Chur one should not miss the small medieval village of Werdenberg with its *de rigeur* castle and vineyards. The reds of the castle of Werdenberg, together with those of the more southerly town of Pfäffers, (see below) are considered to be among the better wines of the canton. Indeed, the many archeological remains from the Roman and medieval periods — towers, castles, fortified villages and fortresses — all remind the tourist that this region was a significant crossroads between east and west, north and south.

Oberland

The second important wine-growing region of St. Gall, Oberland, is in the south of the canton. Its vineyards are scattered eastwards from Walenstadt to Mels and

Sargans and then on to Bad Ragaz, and Pfäffers. Sargans is famous for its brooding 12th century castle and square dungeon which dominates the Rhine valley at a critical three-way crossing point. The Schloss has its own grapes growing behind the battlements and part of the cellars, complete with an old wooden press, has been made into a display room for the wines of St. Gall. The chalky soil in this part of the canton, especially in Pfäffers where the domain of Porta Romana (Portaser) is located, gives the wines quite a different taste than that imparted by the molasse soil of the sites lower down the Rhine river. The Portaser vines at Pfäffers, almost directly across the Rhine valley from the Bündner Herrschaft village of Maienfeld, grow to an altitude of 720 meters above sea level, the highest vineyards in eastern Switzerland.

West of Walenstadt on the northern shore of Lake Walensee is the isolated village of Quinten producing grapes, chestnuts, and, curiously, figs. The village, well worth a visit, can only be reached by boat as there is no road. Quinten is wedged between the lake and the mountains of the Churfirsten chain, but its vineyards have an almost direct southern exposure and clearly benefit from the reflected heat of the lake. In addition to the Pinot Noir and Riesling x Sylvaner commonly produced in St. Gall, the growers of this corner of the canton produce a version of Federweiss, the white wine made from red-skinned grapes. The Schwyz producer, Gerbrüder Kümin, also produces a small amount of Chardonnay in Quinten. Among the local grape growers and wine makers, Bruno Bosshart of Walenstadt and Franz Müller in Heiligkreuz near Mels, are well-regarded.

Grapes are cultivated and wines produced in two more regions of St. Gall: the first near Rapperswil and Jona, on the north shore of Lake Zurich; and the second near Wil and Bronschofen, in the north-west part of the canton. Production is generally consumed locally.

Appenzell

For the record, there are two wine-producing communes of Wolfhalden and Lutzenberg in the neighbouring canton of Appenzell. These vineyards totaling 3.1 hectares are, in effect, an extension of the region of St. Gall. Production in Appenzell is divided about equally between reds and whites, with almost all production consumed in the canton.

Grisons

Today wine grape growing in the canton of Grisons covers approximately 310 hectares, 90% of which is planted in Pinot Noir and seven percent in Riesling x Sylvaner. The remaining three percent includes Pinot Gris, Pinot Blanc, Completer, Gewürztraminer, Chardonnay, Kerner, Elbling and Freisamer. The Grisons vineyards divide neatly into two major areas: the east bank of the Rhine valley below Chur (Coire), where are located the more important vineyards including the Bündner Herrschaft; and the small Italian-speaking enclave in the south of Mesolcina (Misox). In addition, a tiny harvest is recorded in Poschiavo, in the far south-east of the canton, although almost the entire production is consumed locally.

Until the 17th century very few red grapes were grown in the Bündner Herrschaft region of the Rhine valley. Traditionally the dominant grape types were the Completer and the Elbling, also known here as the white Veltliner. This variety should not be confused with the green Veltliner, Grüner Veltliner in German, which is well-known in Austria. Over time the Completer and the Elbling were progressively replaced by the Pinot Noir. A hero's monument, the Rohanschanze, is located in the middle of the vineyards between the towns of Maienfeld and Landquart to honour the Duc de Rohan, credited with introducing the Pinot Noir grape into the region during the 17th century. Interestingly, the phylloxera louse has never struck the canton, although in most cases the non-American root-stocks have gradually been replaced by phylloxera-resistant strains.

The Pinot Noir has adapted well to the growing conditions on the chalky floor of the Rhine valley. The musts can reach 88°Oe to 90°Oe in good years, and rise to more than 90°Oe during exceptional years. The wines are generally light, but refreshing, although Pinot Noirs of considerable depth and finesse are possible in very good years. Local wine makers use different methods of vinification to produce four different types of wine from the Pinot Noir: Beerliwein, Federweiss, Schiller and Süssdruck. The latter three wines are regional "specialities" and are only found in limited amounts.

Here Beerliwein is the common name for the "standard" wine made from Pinot Noir grapes picked at usual maturity. If justified by elevated sugar levels, wines from late-harvested Pinot Noir grapes will sometimes have an additional designation such as "Auslese" on the label. Similar to elsewhere in eastern Switzerland, Federweiss is a white or off-white wine produced from Pinot Noir grapes. Ideally Federweiss should be made from free-run juice and from grapes as healthy as those used for the regular cuvée. This is not always the case. Schiller is made from a combination of both red and white grapes. The blend is usually 90% to 95% Pinot Noir, together with five to ten percent of a white grape type, traditionally Elbling or increasingly Riesling x Sylvaner. The grapes for this wine are grown together in the same plots and then vinified together. The fourth wine, Süssdruck, is the fruity *petillant* rosé.

The must sugar levels of the Riesling x Sylvaner grown in Grisons commonly reach only 75°Oe to 80°Oe, which gives a somewhat acid juice with a pronounced bouquet. In years with higher Oechsle readings, the musky perfume diminishes and the wine becomes fuller and better balanced. The best vintages may be conserved for several years. Riesling x Sylvaner producers in Grisons are also experimenting with various levels of completeness for the malo-lactic fermentation, seeking a better balance for their wines.

The Pinot Gris, distinguishable from the Pinot Noir only from the onset of the maturity when the berries take on a copper hue, was introduced into Grisons during the 1950s. It is found on the best exposed slopes and often was planted to replace the Completer. Pinot Blanc is preferred to the Pinot Gris by some producers and experiments such as high trellising are ongoing to determine the best means of cultivation. Small plots of Chardonnay have been planted in recent years and some of the results are surprisingly good.

Bündner Herrschaft

One way of entering the Grisons is via Vaduz, the capital of the Grand Duchy of Liechtenstein. Although Liechtenstein is not part of Switzerland, its geography and climate are of course very similar to neighbouring Swiss wine regions. It is worth briefly noting that vineyards have long existed in this tiny Principality. Almost directly below the castle rock, where the Château houses the Grand Duke's renowned art collection, the Hofkellerei des Fürsten von Liechtenstein produces a full range of well-made, domain-bottled wines. The carefully-tended vineyards are impossible to miss as one enters the town.

A small road departs Liechtenstein, southward from Vaduz to Maienfeld back into Switzerland. It travels up the saddle of a gentle hill and past some rather impressive concrete military reminders of Europe's less-than-pacific past. Over the crest of the hill one first encounters the famous Bündner Herrschaft which descend down the south-facing slopes towards the village of Maienfeld. The Bündner Herrschaft vineyards are the center of Grisons' wine universe and rank among the best in eastern Switzerland. These vines are located in the communes of Fläsch, Maienfeld, Jenins and Malans, on the last, smooth slopes of the Rätikon mountain range before it descends directly to the valley floor where the Landquart river joins the Rhine. The villages of Fläsch, Maienfeld, Jenins and Malans are connected by a series of attractive walking and bike paths. On a warm spring day there is nothing more enjoyable than poking around from village to village, stopping in at cellars or cafés to enjoy a glass or two of very fine wine.

The area enjoys a particularly good southern exposure, long autumns, little frost and perhaps the most beneficial warm *foehn* winds in the entire country. If the *foehn* is blowing, daytime temperatures can rise to 25° and the night stay at a steady 20°. In exceptional years such as 1983, 1990 and 1994 the *foehn* makes an important contribution to the quality of the harvest. Trellises are the most common form of cultivation. Small-holding owner-cultivators predominate although a few larger estates exist. In a good year, grapes with an Oechsle reading of above 85° produce wines with 11° to 13° alcohol. The Pinot Noir is by far the most important grape type grown.

The vineyards of Fläsch hug the base of the cliffs that protect the village to the north. The excellent exposure is almost due south. Two good producers in Fläsch are Daniel Gantenbein and Daniel Marugg. As might be expected, Pinot Noir dominates their production, although both also produce Riesling x Sylvaner and Pinot Gris, while Gantenbein also adds a touch of Pinot Blanc, Chardonnay and some rare Riesling. Gantenbein's production is around 20,000 bottles a year from four hectares while Marugg's is about double that number. Gantenbein has experimented extensively with various combinations of oak-aging to find the best balance for his wines and his Pinot Blanc was praised by the UK wine writer Jancis Robinson as "probably the best Pinot Blanc I have ever tasted." He also produces a super-concentrated wine from Pinot Noir grapes that have been left to dry after harvest and which reportedly sells for a virtual king's ransom!

On the road from Fläsch, just before entering the town of Maienfeld, one encounters the impressive Schloss Salgenegg of Andreas von Gugelberg. The château's vineyards produce 60,000 bottles per year of Pinot Noir from 8.5 hectares. Framed by the mountains behind, the brownish buildings with their rust shutters make a magnificent site. The domain Schloss Salgenegg enjoys a privileged situation and is somewhat unusual in concentrating exclusively on one grape variety. Under the protection of the warm *foehn* winds in the autumn, the grapes can ripen to full maturity. Indeed, vine-growing has a long tradition at this site, as the monks of the Pfäffers monastery on the other side of the Rhine used to take advantage of Salgenegg's mild climate to grow their grapes.

The pride of the Schloss is its carefully-harvested, destemmed, centrifugally-pressed Pinot Noir which produces a wine with an aroma of lemon, almond, kiwi and fig. The result very much resembles a good Pinot Noir from Alsace with an appealing, almost cherry-like nose. The vineyard also boasts an admirable old chestnut grape press built in 1658. This ancient press was so large that after its construction thirteen pairs of oxen were required to move it to its resting site.

Slightly uphill in Jenins the vineyards spread out below the village in a gentle south-facing natural amphitheater that perfectly captures the late-afternoon rays of the sun. Here Christian Obrecht cultivates his domain, Weingut zur Sonne. His vineyard includes five hectares of Riesling x Sylvaner, Pinot Gris, Pinot Blanc, Chardonnay and Pinot Noir producing 30,000 to 40,000 bottles per year. Obrecht's output includes a wide range of wines, including a standard Riesling x Sylvaner; a Jeninser Beerliwein Barrique (a barrel-aged Pinot Noir); and a rare specialty, a Jeninser Schiller, made from the rather surprising combination of Pinot Noir, Pinot Blanc and Chardonnay, all grown and vinified together.

The next Bündner Herrschaft town on this wine route is Malans which is particularly known for its small production of the traditional indigenous grape, the Completer, although some of the commune's Pinot Noir are among the best in the area. Pinot Gris and Pinot Blanc, while only grown in a few scattered patches, produce full and well-balanced wines when permitted to age. They are vigorously sought out by Swiss connoisseurs although the Completer is the local specialty.

Peter Wegelin and his wife Elisabeth have established one of the best reputations in Malans for their wines which are vinified in the cellars of Château Bothmar. The château, owned by the von Salis family, boasts a fine 17th century wine press which still functions today. The plans are to use the press once a year so that the knowledge of how these magnificent machines function is not completely lost. The château also has an unusual formal French garden which was laid out in the eighteenth century in expectation of a visit by France's Louis XV. The visit, unfortunately, never took place but the garden still graces the Château property.

The large Winterthur firm of Volg Weinkellereien leases a parcel of the château's vines from which they produce their Château Bothmar wines. Some of Peter Wegelin's 4.5 hectares of vines adjoin the château, although the majority of his vines are to be found to the north-west of the village. He concentrates on a selection that includes Pinot Noir, Pinot Blanc, Pinot Gris, Riesling x Sylvaner Kerner, Completer and Aligoté, the latter from very old vines planted by his father. Wegelin was among the first to introduce the Pinot Blanc in to the area.

His wines are elegant and harmonious and he is not afraid to experiment, as is shown by his non-malo-lactic Riesling x Sylvaner; his rich alcoholic Pinot Gris with considerable residual sugar; and his *vendange tardive* Pinot Noir. The grapes for the *vendange tardive* wines are not picked until late October and then cool-fermented for almost two weeks. The result is a deep, complex but well-balanced wine which has done extremely well in international wine competitions. The attractive labels for each of the recent vintages of *vendange tardive* Pinot Noir complement the wines.

Other leading producers of Malans include Thomas Donatsch, who cultivates Riesling x Sylvaner, Pinot Blanc, Pinot Gris, Chardonnay, Pinot Noir and even Cabernet Sauvignon on his 3.5-hectare domain. He also runs a very sophisticated wine import operation while selling a good part of his production of 30,000 bottles per year in his Restaurant Ochsen in the middle of Malans. The verandah of the Oschen on a sunny day is a perfect spot to sip a glass of fine wine while nibbling on some local specialty.

Years ago, Donatsch began to mature his Pinot Noir and, later, the Chardonnay, in 225-liter oak barrels. The Chardonnay Selvenen is quite an elegant wine, showing a touch of oak but without allowing it to overpower the fruit. According to Donatsch, the soils of Malans are very similar to those of Clos de la Roche in Burgundy. Clearly his inspiration is solidly Burgundian and the wines reflect this attitude. His two Pinot Noirs are well worth tasting: the Malanser Selvenen, from 1991 had a strong youthful ruby colour, a more raspberry aroma, some tannin and good acidity; the Malanser Spiger also from 1991 had a deep ruby colour complemented by concentrated raspberry-blackberry perfume, a touch of vanilla, some cinnamon and a light bitter almond finish. The excellent 1990 version from the Spiger vineyard had all the above attributes enhanced by even greater depth and tannic reserve. Donatsch also produces very limited quantities of Cabernet Sauvignon from vines propagated from seeds brought in from Château Mouton Rothschild. The wine is rich, well balanced and round and seems to be developing a classic cassis/cedar nose.

Adolf Boner, also in Malans, is known mainly for his Completer, which, according to tradition, should be left to age for at least eight years. This wine is most appropriately drunk as an aperitif with the famous dried beef from the Grisons. Boner grows his Completer at several sites around Malans but leases one of the best exposed slopes in the Completerhalde area from the von Salis family of Château Bothmar. The Completerhalde, south of the village of Malans, combines direct southern exposure with a good steep slope to provide the perfect conditions needed to grow this difficult grape. In addition to his Completer, Boner also produces Riesling x Sylvaner, Pinot Gris, Gewürztraminer and Pinot Noir on his 5-hectare property, reaching an annual output of 25,000 to 30,000 bottles. As might be expected, Boner is a traditionalist who feels that Swiss growers should concentrate on grape types that have evolved successfully in a Swiss environment. He is not attracted by the latest fad. The quality of his production and his efforts to produce fine Completer stand as testimony to a wine grower of principle. Continuing up the Rhine valley from Malans, vines are grown in the areas of Zizers, Trimmis, the important transportation junction of Chur, Felsberg, Igis, Domat/Ems and Bonaduz. Occasionally the fruity and forward wines from Zizers and Chur can be found outside the region, but most are consumed near their place of production.

Separated from his main vineyards in the Bündner Herrschaft, Gian-Battista von Tscharner is the owner of the Schloss Reichenau in Reichenau, farther up the Rhine valley south-west of Chur. A picture of the Schloss graces some of the labels for his wines. On his four hectares of property, spread between the towns of Jenins,

Maienfeld and Chur, von Tscharner cultivates Pinot Blanc, Chardonnay, Pinot Gris, Completer, Gewürztraminer, Räuschling and, needless to say, Pinot Noir. Total production is not more than 25,000 bottles per year. Of particular note among the different wines of the Schloss Reichenau are the Jeninser Completer, a strong, gold or honey-yellow white wine, with a full taste; the Churer Schiller Süssdruck, an elegant, fruity and fresh, lightly sparkling rosé made from a combination of Pinot Noir, Pinot Blanc and Completer; and two Pinot Noirs — Jeninser Tscharnergut and Churer Beerli Barrique — the latter matured in oak barrels. Von Tscharner's Jeninser Tscharnergut 1988 was ranked among the very best Pinot Noirs in an international competition in 1990 in Burgundy and other wines have scored equally well in international competitions. His success is certainly not an accident, but rather due to the hard work and discipline that comes with being "the Lord of the castle".

Misox

In the south of the canton towards the St. Bernardino Pass and physically quite distinct from the other vineyards of Grisons, grape-growing remains important in the traditionally isolated Mesolcina or Misox valley. The vines here are subject to quite different climatic and soil conditions than are those in the rest of the canton. The viticultural influence comes from Italian-speaking Ticino to the west, rather than from the German-speaking north. The 45 hectares of vineyards in the communes of San Vittore and Roveredo exclusively produce red wine from the Merlot grape and a few hybrids. Much of the production is actually transported to cellars in Ticino for aging. Cultivated on mezzana-type trellises, the grapes produce a wine which has characteristics very similar to the Ticinese Merlot. Small quantities of grapes are also cultivated in the extreme south of the Bernina Pass, in the other Italian-speaking part of Grisons. Production is concentrated in Campocolombo and Campascio, in the Poschiavo river valley, near the border with Italy. Little, if any, of this wine is seen outside the region.

Swiss Wines in Italy?

The 150 hectares of vineyards in the Valteline, this time on the southern, Italian side of the Grisons slopes, deserve note. The reason for mentioning grape-growing in this Italian valley is twofold. First, this region was traditionally part of Grisons until the 1815 Congress of Vienna "reshaped" Europe and awarded this part of the Alps to Italy. Grisons growers, however, still play an important role in the local wine production. And second, a large part of the production (30%-35% out of a production of 150,000 to 180,000 hectoliters) is exported and consumed in Grisons. The topographic conditions are as steep and as difficult as in the Lavaux, the costs of production very high, and the output quite low. The grape types are the Nebbiolo, the *Pignola della Valtelina* (Pinot of the Valteline), Brugnola and Rossola which produce strong red wines, characterized by their deep ruby colour, relatively high acidity, and pronounced tannic taste when young.

* * * * *

The canton of Grisons completes our wine tour around Switzerland. The Glacial Express, a remarkable Swiss train that travels from St. Moritz to Chur and then over the glaciers which feed both the Rhine and the Rhône, provides a symbolic last link to complete the circle. From Chur, the train moves up the Rhine valley before entering the high alpine valleys. It's route passes the sources of both the Rhine and the Rhône, the two great rivers of western Europe upon whose banks or tributaries are located virtually all the vineyards discussed in this book. The Glacial Express ends its journey in the canton of Valais at the city of Brig, very close to where we opened this examination of the wines of Switzerland.

Useful Addresses in Eastern Switzerland:

Promotion

Schweizerischer Weinbauverein, Seestrasse 251, 8804 Au-Wädenswil (01) 781 42 88.

Wine Museums

Musée de la vigne et du vin du lac de Zurich, Vordere Au, 8804, (01) 781 35 65.
Musée de la vigne et du vin de Schaffhouse, "Zur Krone", 8215, Hallau (052) 681 20 20.
Musée cantonal argovien de la vigne, Alterberg, 5306 Tegerfelden (056) 245 27 00.

Recommended Wine makers

Zurich

Hansueli Hasler, Rütihof, 8713 Uerikon (01) 926 37 54: A reasonably large, good producer on the north shore of Lake Zurich.
Heiner Hertli, Dorfstrasse 30, 8247 Flulingen (052) 659 30 47: Hertli produces a unique range of very interesting Pinot Gris.
Hans Herzog, Zum Taggenberg, 8406 Winterthur (052) 315 15 51: In Neftenbach, outside Winterthur, Herzog is recognized as one of the best Weinland producers.
Kurt Neukom, Hegi 13, 8197 Rafz (01) 869 05 25: In the far north-west of the canton of Zurich, Neukom's Pinot Gris is especially well-regarded.
Jürg Schneider, Haldengässli 72, 8706 Feldmeilen (01) 923 04 40: Schneider produces of limited range of fine wines. He has plots in some of the best Meilen vineyards.
Hermann Schwarzenbach, Reblaube Obermeilen, Seestrasse 867, 8706 Meilen (01) 923 01 25: Very good holdings in Meilen. He produces both a Clevner and a concentrated Pinot Noir. Look for his new Räuschling-Riesling x Sylvaner blend.

Thomas Weidmann, Uterburg 67, 8158 Regensberg (01) 853 04 55: One of the best wine-makers in the Limmat Valley, the Regensberg Chlevinger Pinot Noir is his top wine. He also produces sparkling wine.

Waldemar Zahner, Rebgut Bächi, 8467 Truittikon (052) 317 19 49: Zahner is the recognized producer in Truittikon with a good range of Pinot Noir wines.

Schaffhouse

Max Baumann, Unterdorf 117, 8216 Oberhallau, Schaffhouse (052) 681 33 46: Max and Ruedi Baumann represent the best of the Hallau region. Their wines can be quite complex.

Familie Meyer, Gasthaus und Weingut, Bad Osterfingen, 8218 Osterfingen (052) 681 21 21: Always listed among the top producers by other wine makers. Excellent Pinot Noirs that deserve their high ranking. Thurgovie

Hans-Ulrich Kesselring, Schlossgut Bachtobel, 8561 Ottoberg, Thurgovie (071) 622 54 07: Kesselring concentrates on Pinot Noir. His vineyards are among the best situated in the canton.

Argovie

Anton Meier, Restaurant Zum Sternen, Endinger Strasse 7, 5303 Würenlingen (056) 281 14 12: Meier has a very wide range of well structured wines. His Kloster Sion wines from Klingnau are especially well-respected.

Fehr + Engeli, Hauptstrasse 33, 5028 Uekon (062) 871 33 73: The best producer in the western portion of Argovie. Good basic wines with a special barrique-aged Pinot Noir that is quickly snapped up.

Basel

Kurt Nussbaumer, Klusstrasse 177, 4147 Aesch (061) 751 16 85: Another wine producer that combines vineyards with running a restaurant. His sparkling "Chrachmost" is an original aperitif.

St. Gall

Jakob Schmid, Tramstrasse 23, 9442 Berneck (071) 744 12 77: A relatively large producer with a wide selection of Pinot Noirs from some of the best sites in Berneck.

Grisons

Adolf Boner, Completer-Kellerei, Untere Kirchgasse, 7208 Malans (081) 322 14 80: One of the worthy wine producers who keeps the Completer alive.

Thomas Donatsch, Restaurant "Ochsen", 7208 Malans (081) 322 11 17: A leading producers in Malans — look for his single vineyard Pinot Noirs.

Daniel and Martha Gantenbein, 7306 Fläsch (081) 302 47 88: Very fine wines from only four hectares. Jancis Robinson raved about the Pinot Blanc and the "serious" Pinot Noir.

Christian Obrecht, Weingut zur Sonne, 7307 Jenins (081) 302 14 64: Produces a full range of Grisons wines, including Schiller and Federweiss, in addition to several variations of Pinot Noir.

Andreas von Gugelberg, Schloss Salgenegg, 7304 Maienfeld (081) 302 11 51: Von Gugelberg concentrates on producing a harmonious, elegant Pinot Noir which is among the best of Grisons.

Gian-Battista von Tscharner, Schloss Reichenau, 7015 Reichenau (081) 641 11 95: Although the Schloss is beyond Chur, von Tscharner's vineyards are well-located in the Bündner Herrschaft.

Peter Wegelin, Weinbau Scadena, 7208 Malans (081) 322 11 64: A top producer in Malans, Wegelin's full range of wines is extremely good. His *vendage tardif* Pinot Noirs are superb.

Vigneron Waldemar Zahner, Truttikon, in the canton of Zurich.

XII

The Legal Framework and Agricultural Support Systems

The protection of agricultural production and, particularly, wine, has a long and detailed history in Switzerland. As far back as the Middle Ages when the production and sale of wine were usually under the control of church institutions, taxes on its consumption were important sources of revenue for the local bishop. Naturally the local product was taxed at a preferential rate compared to wines from further afield. In 1368 new local wine entering Geneva was taxed at six *livres*, while the similar product from Soumont (i.e., La Côte section of Vaud) was taxed at seven *livres*.

Over the next century the difference grew even more marked: consumption taxes were 20 *sous* for a *bossette* (324 litres) of wine from Chautagne; 14 sous for a similar amount from Soumont; and only 6 sous for the Genevois *vin du pays*.

The dual objectives of generating revenue from consumption, while also protecting and encouraging local production, are still evident today in the national and cantonal regulations which govern the production and sale of wine in Switzerland. National and cantonal legal measures also seek to protect consumers from dangerous or fraudulent substances and, to the extent possible, to encourage the orderly and efficient marketing of the annual grape harvests.

At the same time, the movement towards the harmonization of trade restrictions throughout Europe will have an important effect on competition in the Swiss market. Although Switzerland has chosen to remain outside the European Union, the dismantling of non-tariff trade restrictions will continue and eventually there should be unrestricted entry for quality bottled wines, both red and white, from foreign producers.

The former quota system, which physically prevented importation of certain wines, is being replaced by a more transparent system of tariffs. The increased competition, especially for white wines in the CHF six or less per bottle range, will have an immediate effect on the Swiss domestic market. To the extent possible change has been introduced in stages.

In 1992 the quota system for bulk reds was transformed into a global quota. In 1993, the global quota for reds became a tariff-based system. Finally, and most importantly, the quota system for whites has been replaced by tariffs in the course of 1995.

The Contemporary Legal Framework

Federal Regulations

The contemporary Swiss legal structure is quite complex, particularly regarding the division of powers between the national federal government and the individual cantons. In the Swiss Confederation, the federal authorities establish the general policy guidelines regarding vinicultural and viticultural matters, but the responsibility for developing the specific regulations and criteria for implementation rests with the individual cantons which apply the federal laws to local conditions. Canton authorities are therefore responsible for the quality standards, certain financial measures to encourage or improve cantonal wine-making, and the criteria required for a wine to meet the standard for a cantonal *appellation contrôlée* system.

The significant federal regulations dealing directly with grapes and wine are the Law on Agriculture *(Loi sur l'agriculture)*; the Federal Legislation on Viticulture *(Arrêté fédéral sur la viticulture)*, in principle revised every 10 years; and the Wine Statute *(Statut du vin)*. In addition, the Regulations Concerning the Wine Trade *(Ordonnance sur le commerce des vins* (OCV)) are applied as appropriate.

The Law on Agriculture, or more precisely, the "Federal Law Concerning the Promotion of Agriculture and the Preservation of a Sound Agricultural Community" remains the primary piece of federal legislation. This regulation guarantees a base price for quality grapes sufficient to meet the producers operational costs, while at the same time establishing limits on total production. It includes provisions for a national vineyard survey *(cadastre)*, a list of authorized grape varieties and root stocks, and regulations governing the propagation and commercialization of vines. Only within specifically determined areas are vineyards allowed, and the planting of new vines in other areas is prohibited. Even within designated wine regions, permission from the authorities must be obtained before new vineyards are planted. Article 42 of the law is quite clear that, within the limitations imposed by the natural environment, regulations must be sensitive to the needs of the local market and the ability of the national market to absorb more wine.

The Law on Agriculture is, in turn, implemented along lines set out in the Federal Decree *(Arrêté)* which was revised in 1979 in 1992. Its provisions reflect the evolution of Swiss wines towards higher overall quality levels and the use of specific *appellations* to establish marketable wine types. One of the innovations is the establishment of three categories of wines based on a minimum natural sugar level of the grape musts at harvest. Only Category 1, with minimum sugar levels of 60°Oe for whites and 65°Oe for reds, will be eligible for an *appellation* status. The Federal Decree also insists upon increased respect for the environment, and it provides a precise definition of what is meant by the "provenance" and *appellation* of a wine – which are not the same – and the criteria to be considered when cantons establish *appellation* systems.

The other federal legislation directly affecting the wine industry are laws regarding the commerce of food products applied under the Ordinance on Food Products *(Ordonnance sur les denrées alimentaires* (ODA)), referred to in the chapter on vinification. The overriding objective of this legislation is consumer protection: it defines types of wine; prescribes limits on the addition of sugar to the must and blending of wines; sets out labeling regulations; and establishes what substances can be safely used in treating wines during the vinification and aging processes. Revised ODA legislation will enter into effect in mid-1995, although the full application of the new laws will not be until 1997.

Also worth noting is that Switzerland has a national "wine fund" *(fond vinicole)* collected from a tax levied on imported wines. This fund finances the quality control measures undertaken at harvest time; the federal viticultural stations at Changins and Wädenswil; viticultural and oenological research; and the underwriting of more general measures to improve wine quality. Other financial support has been made available to encourage the non-alcoholic use of wine, industrial use, other measures to encourage placement of the harvest, vineyard restriction and harvest control.

A federal commission on the wine trade *(La Commission fédérale du commerce des vins)* shares with the cantons the responsibility for the effective implementation of the federal and cantonal regulations governing the wine industry.

Cantonal Regulations

Of late, much attention has focused on how the cantons are establishing their *appellation contrôlée* regimes under the general framework provided by the federal legislation. An important distinction must, however, be made between the *appellation d'origine* (AO) measures which have been in place for some years in most cantons, and the more stringent *appellation d'origine contrôlée* (AOC) regimes which are gradually taking hold throughout the country, but which are determined and administered by the cantonal authorities. AOC regimes will not, in one sweep of the bureaucratic brush, eliminate all the problems that confront the Swiss wine industry. The establishment of appropriate and recognizable minimum standards will undoubtedly help raise overall quality. As the Swiss system evolves, one might usefully remember the controversy which surrounded the introduction of the Italian DOC and DOCG regimes several decades ago, and the benefits which, in time, accrued to Italian wines on international markets from having established recognizable bench marks.

The June 1992 federal decree on viticulture sets out the areas which are appropriate for *appellation* standards:

- delimited zones of production;
- grape types;
- growing methods;
- minimum natural sugar levels;
- harvest per unit of terrain;
- vinification procedures;
- analysis and testing.

Based on criteria established in these areas, the cantonal authorities are introducing and administering the revised systems of *appellations d'origine contrôlées* (AOC). The cantons which have lagged behind can do nothing but follow because of the marketing advantage that comes from establishing a recognized *appellation* standard..

Trial and error, and improvement based on experience, is still the *modus operandi* as the grape growers, wine makers, merchants and cantonal authorities continue to learn from experience. Somewhat surprisingly, Geneva anticipated the introduction of federal criteria for AOC with its own regulations in 1988. The cantonal standards recognize a basic *appellation*, and a separate category for "grand cru" and "premier cru". As mentioned in the chapter on Geneva wines, the introduction of the higher category was accompanied by some controversy because the regulations recognized certain larger Châteaux managed by the local cooperative at the expense of some of the better independent producers. The "cutting" of the wine is prohibited for AOC categories and both the harvest (a maximum of 1.2 kilograms per square meter for whites) and the pressing output (70 hectoliters per hectare) are controlled. The addition of sugar is limited to a still very generous four kilograms per hectoliter.

In Valais, a 1981 decree which promoted more controlled yields has been complemented by another decree in 1990 (subsequently modified) which establishes three categories of wine – along the same lines as the federal legislation. Only wines which meet the standards for Category 1 (whites) and Category 1a (reds) have the right to an AOC designation. Wines with labels such as Fendant, Johannisberg, Dôle and Oeil-de-Perdrix, by definition, are judged to have met the AOC standards and are subject to additional analytical and occasional tasting controls.

In Vaud the cantonal *appellation d'origine* regulations date back to 1985. In total the canton has 26 *appellations* which are recognized, although the canton has yet to introduce AOC standards. The use of the word "cru" can also be attached to vineyards which are officially recognized by the canton, although, as was evident in the chapter on Vaudois wines, the usage of "cru" and "grand cru" probably requires additional clarification to assist consumers.

Neuchâtel is proud of its wine regulations which remain among the severest in the country. The standard three classes for grapes were established in 1984 and again only Category 1 is eligible for *appellation d'origine* status. As of the 1990 harvest, Chasselas in Category 1 is limited to 1 kilogram of grapes harvested per square meter – one of the strictest cantonal restrictions in the country. All the wines are, however, grouped under a single broad *appellation*, "Neuchâtel". Only if a wine meets the additional criteria, and exhibits the accepted characteristics for one of the sub-*appellations d'origine*, can the label designate the wine as Oeil-de-Perdrix, Pinot Gris, Auvernier, etc.

As might be expected, Ticino has its own unique *appellation* criteria. The VITI label for Merlot del Ticino is a successful example of using agreed cantonal regulations to produce valuable marketing recognition. A cantonal commission will award a VITI seal only after a taste test, a chemical analysis and proof that minimum natural sugar levels have been reached. Annually only 30% of the Merlot grapes grown in Ticino receive the VITI designation and, although the process isn't perfect, it has contributed to an improvement of overall quality.

In the German-speaking cantons, the situation is more complex. Each wine-producing canton has some form of viticultural commissioner and there exists an

Association of wine makers of eastern Switzerland (Schweizerischer Weinbauverein). As wines are sold under the name of the grape type in addition to marketing under *appellations d'origine*, there are widespread differences between the cantonal-level regulations in the German-speaking cantons and the rest of the country. The success of the new *appellation d'origine contrôlée* systems in the French-speaking cantons will influence the evolution of regulations governing wine throughout the country. Some of the larger cantons such as Zurich, Schaffhouse and Thurgovie began in 1990 to limit their harvest in order to establish a better balance between markets, demand and quality.

Import Controls

Import controls also have a long history in Switzerland. For example, before 1685 the sale of "foreign" wine in Geneva was prohibited seven months of the year. By 1685 the prohibition covered nine months of the year. Eventually a total ban on the sale of all imported wines was imposed in 1704.

Until the early 1990s, a series of trade measures supported internal price levels in Switzerland, especially for white wine. A quota was set by region and by quality to control imports from 23 countries, including individual member states of the European Union. In particular, separate regulations affected both wine imported in casks and higher-quality bottled imports. Restrictions on wines imported by cask were first introduced in 1933 and, until the quota system was revised in 1992 for reds and 1995 for whites, imports of white wine for current consumption in cask or bottle were effectively banned. Bulk imports of white wine were allowed only to ameliorate domestic production shortfalls or for industrial purposes. Restrictions on bottle imports were first introduced in the 1970s. Some quota was possible for quality imported white wines in cask while quality imported white wines in bottles could normally not exceed 35,000 hectoliters.

These restrictions are being replaced during 1995 as Switzerland brings its regulations in line with other European countries. The effect will be profound. As noted above, starting in 1995 the importation of bottled quality white wine will no longer be controlled by quota. Although bulk wine imports will still be subject to regulation and tariffs, this revision will likely prove to be important. Competition for the lower/middle range of white wines will increase dramatically as tariffs come down over time. Some estimates are that the total sales of domestic wine could fall by 10%.

Reflecting the lesser economic importance of domestic red wine production, red wine imports in bottles have generally not been restricted. The tariff supplements of one franc per liter above the base tariff of 0.5 francs a liter on imports in excess of 150,000 hectoliters per year were removed when the new quota regulations were introduced in 1993. Previously, despite the restrictions and tariffs, 1.71 million hectoliters of wine was imported into Switzerland in 1990, a notable 55% of domestic consumption. Ninety percent of the imported wines were red.

Another Swiss curiosity has been the official designation of who may import. To begin with, import permits and quota entitlements are only allocated to "established" wine traders domiciled within Switzerland. Breaking into the system was difficult and the lack of transparency makes adjustments to changing circumstances equally challenging. The overall number of importers declined from 1,869 in 1933 to around 550 in 1991. Whereas the initial justification for government intervention in the wine sector was to protect small producers, the regulatory system now touches all segments of the wine industry.

In April 1990, a national referendum rejected a proposal to revise the national agricultural law *(Arrêté fédéral instituant des mesures en faveur de la viticulture)*, in particular, the regulations relating to the quality, importation and support system for wine. The initiative had sought to improve domestic quality and supply management, and would also have established a regular auction for the re-allocation of quota shares among importers. Although many believed that change was necessary, the proposals went too far for some and not far enough for others. There is, therefore, still no final resolution of the tension created by protection of domestic producers and the public demand for better access to less expensive wines. The conflicting interests of the many affected parties have made it extremely difficult to achieve a consensus.

Exports

It has unfortunately become a truism that Swiss wines do not travel. In the recent past this misconception was perhaps unwittingly encouraged by the Swiss themselves, who were quite prepared to supply their own protected but secure market without the need to worry about the sin and consequences of excess production. But in the recent cold economic winds, global competition may not be nearly so forgiving for the Swiss *vignerons*.

In 1992, just over one million litres of bottled wine was exported from Switzerland. An additional 100,000 litres of bulk wine was also exported, although the actual totals could be slightly less because of wine which is transshipped through Switzerland but registered as an export. The amount of white wine exported exceeds red wine shipments by more than two to one but interestingly, the total value of red wine exports is consistently higher than the total value of white wine exported. These figures are minuscule compared to French or Italian shipments and the volume comprises slightly less than one percent of total Swiss production. At the same time exports pump almost 20 million Swiss francs into the industry which is an amount that cannot be ignored.

Continental sales to Germany, and the Benelux countries have traditionally been the most important Swiss wine exports. Germany's market share in 1992 fell from 55% to 45%, although the shortfall was picked up through increases to France (up 35% over 1991), Belgium, United States and Japan. Some of the specialty wines in particular have an avid following among northern European consumers. Most of the official marketing efforts of the Swiss government and wine associations have concentrated on the German and Benelux markets, although promotional activities are increasingly taking place even farther afield in the UK and in the USA.

In 1992, the international markets for all Swiss wines were, actually, quite widely spread. According to the Swiss Wine Growers Association, the major importing countries, with the percentage of total market share, were as follows:

Germany	45%
France	13%
Belgium	12%
United States	6%
Japan	5%
Canada	3%
Sweden	3%
Others	13%

In France and Germany, many of the better restaurants near the Swiss border carry a limited number of Swiss bottles on their cartes des vins. As mentioned earlier, despite the Swiss origins of its founder, Paris's Hotel Ritz retains a classically French wine list. Fortunately, the wine shop Au Verger de la Madeleine in the center of Paris, just off the Place de Madeleine, usually carries several different Swiss white wines such as Féchy La Villardière and Fendant Les Murettes. Other French wine merchants, such as Fauchon and Nicholas, and various restaurateurs have undoubtedly been seduced by the better Swiss wines.

Sales to the UK remain modest, reflecting price sensitivity and the extremely competitive nature of the UK wine market. 60% of all wines sold in the UK are priced at under £3.00 per bottle and 80% at less than £4.00 per bottle. For Switzerland this is very stiff competition. Specialist importers dominate the wholesale market, although most of their clients are private customers, special orders or businesses, (e.g. restaurants with a Swiss connection). Wholesale sales from 1990 to 1994 have expanded considerably and the range of wines imported is actually quite extensive. Under the aegis of the Swiss Wine Growers Association, Swiss wine producers participated in the London Wine Trade Fair for the first time in 1993. The experience was repeated in 1994 and 1995.

In the London retail market, Harrod's department store in Knightsbridge often has perhaps the most extensive selection with up to a half dozen wines, mainly from Vaud and concentrating largely on the wines from the Ville de Lausanne. Their prices are not inexpensive. Harvey Nichols, the wine chain Nicholas and the specialty wine store Roberson's on Kensington High Street all stock a limited selection of Swiss wines such as Château Châtaignéréaz and Cave St. Pierre from the Vaudois shipper Schenk. Selfridge's restocked several different Swiss wines in the spring of 1994, including good selections from Dézaley and Hallau. In addition, the Swiss Center in Leicester Square carries a limited selection of wines from the Mövenpick hotel and restaurant chain. Basic export prices and exchange rate fluctuations continue to exert a strong influence on UK consumers. The rise of the Swiss franc makes securing export markets that much more difficult.

Even farther afield across the Atlantic, the consumer is ill-served because Swiss wines are not often encountered on wholesale lists from which most retail merchants purchase. However, a trade group, the Swiss Wine Information Council, is working to rectify the situation. In New York City, specialty fine wine shops do offer one or more Swiss wines, and the Swiss wine industry has done some promotional work along the eastern seaboard of the United States. A couple of years ago, Morell's, the well-known Madison Avenue wine store in New York, offered Epesses Coup de Go from Testuz for a not insignificant $21.00, describing the wine as "aromatic and pungent, ...burgundian breadth of flavour". Morell's actually listed a dozen different Swiss wines, largely from Valaisan and Vaudois producers such as Gilliard, Testuz and Badoux in addition to Château d' Auvernier from Neuchâtel. Other better merchants are willing to request Swiss wines from wholesalers if they sense the demand is evident.

Farther north, the large provincial monopolies in the Canadian provinces of Ontario and Quebec stock a limited selection in their fine wine specialty shops, from three to seven different types at any one time. These are usually bottles from some of the larger but still well-recognized producers. Annual purchases by Canada's two largest provincial liquor boards range between 500 and 1,000 cases. Quebec stocks in 1993 included a Dôle "Raccards" from Caves Orsat, and two Mont-sur-Rolle Châteaux, while Ontario listed several Provins wines from Valais along with Château d'Auvernier and the Domaine Château Vaumarcus Pinot Gris from Samuel Châtenay of Neuchâtel. Recently, the Ontario specialty list also included a rather surprising Thurgau Ittingener. According to the provincial buyers, consumer demand in Canada is largely concentrated on the wines of Valais and Neuchâtel. It is not a wide selection, but considering the competition, distance and trouble involved, the mere fact that these wines are available is encouraging.

Axel and Jean-François Maye of the firm of Simon Maye at St. Pierre-de-Clages, Valais. Their wines are always in great demand in Switzerland and abroad.

XIII

The Fête des Vignerons

The celebration of wine, especially following a successful harvest, remains a continuing feature of wine-making communities. Switzerland is no exception and in the grape growing areas around the country, the social and economic value of the grape is annually honoured. Some of these *fêtes* have become a tourist promotion exercise but they are, nonetheless, a genuine manifestation of both the importance of, and attachment to, an earlier, rural lifestyle.

The timing of these festivals is well-advertised in local papers. The inevitable parade includes the usual combination of floats, bands and firemen. Local wine makers open the doors to their cellars and the entire proceedings are accompanied by general good cheer and copious consumption of village wines and *moût* (fresh grape juice) from the just-harvested vintage. Most harvest festivals are extremely simple and casual affairs which give both producers and dignitaries an occasion to demonstrate their continuing mutual solidarity and the quality of the native products. Small *fêtes* are held annually in villages like Russin, just to the west of Satigny near Geneva, and in many other small towns with a wine-making tradition. Larger-scale festivals are held in late September/early October in Locarno and Lugano in Ticino, Neuchâtel, Zurich, and Morges in Vaud.

In addition to the local gatherings, the Comptoir suisse, a Swiss national fair, is held in September every year at the Palais Beaulieu in Lausanne. The fair attracts over one million visitors and has a small but important section dedicated to wines from across the country. Many of the larger negotiant houses are represented, and some of the smaller more experimental growers turn up from time to time. If one can brave the smoke and noise which permeates the hall, the Comptoir suisse affords a useful opportunity to talk directly to the growers about their wines and to experience a wide range of Swiss wines, although the focus is clearly on the French-speaking Suisse romande.

The fair also hosts the annual Jean-Louis competition, sponsored by the Office des vins vaudois (OVV), the best-known tasting competition in the country. For a small entrance fee, thousands of enthusiasts attempt to identify five selected wines which are served blind. Competition, not surprisingly, is particularly fierce and, although the task might at first glance seem impossible, every year there are winners who correctly identify all the wines. The winner's reward is a *Chapeau Noir* (Black cap) of the Vaud growers.

In an entirely different league from the local wine festivals is Vevey's *Fête des Vignerons*, described rightly in Alexis Lichine's *Encyclopedia of Wines and Spirits* as "the world's most important wine festival". The 1955 *fête* took five years to organize, and when it was last held in 1977 the celebration attracted more than 200,000 participants. This century the *Fête des Vignerons* has taken place only every quarter century, and the next full *fête* is not scheduled until after the year 2000.

The *Confrérie des vignerons de Vevey*, which stages the *Fête des Vignerons*, is just one of the many wine fraternities which enliven the Swiss wine world. It is, however, the oldest Swiss wine fraternity and has grown from thirty master-growers *(maître-vignerons)* at the beginning. But it occupies a very special position because of its unique responsibility to organize the Vevey celebration. The Confrérie was originally established with the noble objective of protecting the quality and reputation of the vines, wine and livelihood of its members, the *vignerons* of Vevey.

The vineyards of Vevey may no longer be as extensive as they once were but the *Confrérie des Vignerons* still maintains its counsel halls and museum in an ancient Vevey house. The origins of the Confrérie certainly predate the Bernois invasion of the Vaud in 1536. Although the oldest archives were destroyed in a 16th century fire, rare documents and artifacts attest to the activities of the Confrérie in the 16th, 17th and 18th centuries. Included in its momentos are faded but still recognizable flags from earlier *fêtes* dating back to 1744 and 1791.

The origins of the current Vevey festival are found in the annual processions the Confrérie made into the vineyards to confirm the state of the vines, dikes and terraces. Over time, as the number of participants grew, the simple annual procession through the vineyards became an increasingly elaborate event which eventually took on a life and budget of its own.

By the 18th century, the Confrérie's celebratory parades, organized around figures of Bacchus, had become quite frequent. From the latter part of the 18th century, the wine festival captured the growing spirit of naturalism, increasingly popular throughout Europe, and took on a new importance and stature. From 1783 the festival was held at six-year intervals to permit proper organization. Even the Vaudois revolution, which ended the rule of "Their Excellencies" from Berne, did not stop the festival. The Bernois, in any case, seemed to have had some serious misgivings about the *fête* at which "anti-foreign" sentiments had been expressed. After a short post-Napoleonic hiatus in the early 19th century, the festival was back, stronger than ever.

Beginning in 1819, the Confrérie staged four additional *Fêtes des Vignerons* during the 19th century: in 1833, 1851, 1865 and 1889. Organized around mythological themes, the festivals combined music, choral music, poetry and dance in an increasingly magnificent event. By 1865, an amphitheater had to be built in Vevey to accommodate 11,000 spectators. In 1889, despite the then-recent damage from phylloxera, oïdium and mildew, the festival was more grand than ever.

In the 20th century, the *Fêtes des Vignerons* has been held in 1905, 1927, 1955 and most recently 1977. The festival continued to grow in the magnificence of its colour and sound, and in the complexity of its staging. By 1955 it had become a spectacle involving some 4,000 participants who performed before an audience of 180,000. It still maintained its Greek mythological focus, alternating tales of

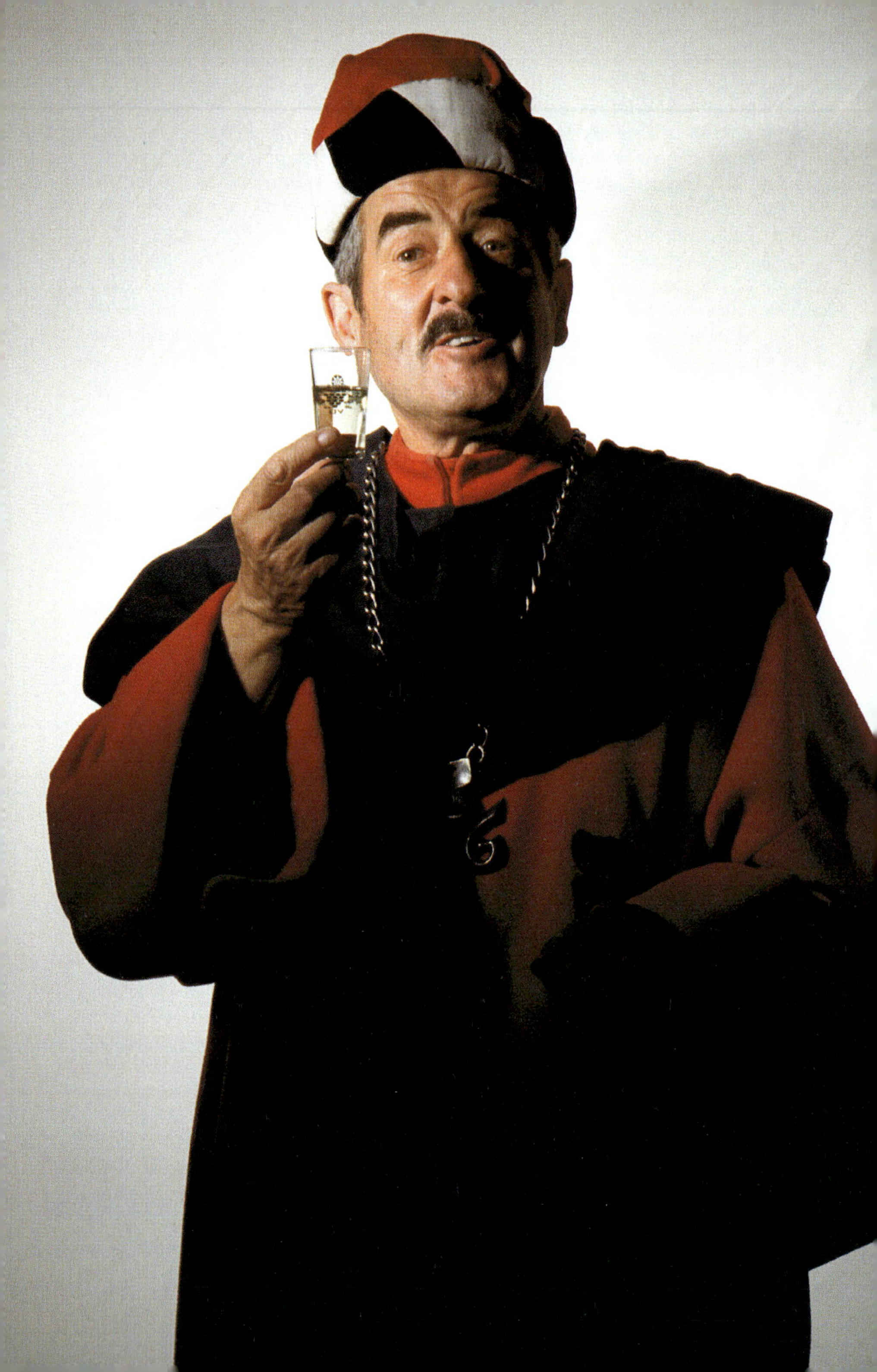

Bacchus with vignettes highlighting the importance of vines and wines throughout the seasons of the year. With several small nods in the direction of modernity and popular appeal, the 1977 festival again combined art, choreography, music, choral singing and poetry in a celebration of vines and wine. Over 40,000 persons participated in the 1977 event in front of crowds several times greater. Already the planning has begun for the next full *Fêtes des Vignerons* which will take place shortly after the turn of the century. This will be a major event, the planning for which will be tracked assiduously to see how close the *Confrérie des Vignerons de Vevey* remains loyal to the traditions and innovations of past festivals.

The direct link between the festival and the wines of Vevey may have weakened. Almost as if in compensation, the Confrérie now stages an international event that celebrates not only the wines of Switzerland but also wine-making throughout the world. This is an enviable legacy for a small group of local growers whose first revenues, often paid in wine, came from small fines levied against members for modest social transgressions.

Claude Massy, wine producer in Espesses, former member of the Swiss National Council, shown here in the robes of the Confrérie du Guillon.

XIV

Future Trends

The year 1991 was the 700th anniversary of the Swiss Confederation. The commemoration of the alliance of three cantons which became the Helvetic Confederation provided an opportunity for at least some national soul-searching and debate on where Switzerland should position itself in the structures of a gradually unifying Europe. Part of the answer was given in December 1992 when the Swiss voters decided to chart an independent course. A majority of voters, divided along linguistic lines, chose to stay outside an enlarged European Economic Area, preferring instead to maintain their time-honoured freedom of manoeuver. However, the political debate on Switzerland's role in a more focused Europe is far from over and will continue to influence the evolution of national institutions. This is equally true for the wine industry, especially as Switzerland is increasingly realigning its trade regime with the rest of Europe. It is interesting to note, however, that the strongest support for closer ties with Europe has consistently arisen in the French-speaking cantons.

Quite separately, wine producers used the early 1990s as an occasion for a more serious stock taking of the future of wine making in Switzerland. This introspection coincided with the implementation of the European Communities' single market; the conclusion of the GATT Uruguay Round on international trade; the debate in several cantons over the structure and the severity of the *appellation d'origine* regulations; and at least one national referendum attempting to reform the wine import system. In all, it was an appropriate time to take a hard look at the future.

Assessing the current Swiss wine industry, one must conclude that wine production will remain an important component of the national economy. Despite its small impact internationally, a sector of this size and depth provides ample opportunity for conscientious wine makers to diversify, experiment and improve. The country's affluence will support a competitive and creative domestic industry and even with the introduction of labour-saving technologies, the number of direct participants in wine business remains large, e.g., over 20,000 *vignerons* in the Valais alone. Their political clout cannot be ignored, nor can the sentimental links which bind many to a bucolic past and which still remain a very real part of the Swiss national psyche. Building on these economic and psychological factors, the wine industry has developed considerable standing in a country where change usually comes slowly and only after extensive consultations.

While the domestic support for wine production appears solid, Switzerland's international posture remains uncertain. Hence the pressing need to put the best foot forward. The significant role the wine industry plays in society will be increasingly important as the country confronts the fundamental economic, social and national identity challenges which are part of the current European landscape. Despite the important qualitative improvements during the latter part of the 20th century, the Swiss wine industry remains caught up in an ongoing cycle of change, adaptation, innovation and, where necessary, response to crisis. Even with the recent fall of land prices, the basic cost structure for wine producers will remain much higher in Switzerland than for her neighbours. Consequently, in purely economic terms, it will be a challenge to maintain a commercially viable and internationally competitive wine industry in an environment of reduced trade barriers. Continued high levels of restrictive regulations and government support will be contentious, both domestically and internationally.

In the years to come, the necessary movement towards higher quality wines will grow ever stronger because scarce and expensive land must be used to produce superior products. *Vignerons* must develop recognizable marketing niches for wines from identifiable high quality areas. The gradual but irresistible reduction of marginal land planted in vines will continue until a new equilibrium is established. Measures to preserve rural lifestyles and land for agricultural production will exert a moderating influence, but less-favoured vineyards on the edge of urban expansion cannot expect to survive indefinitely.

Complete rationalization of Switzerland's vineyards will not occur overnight. Traditional practices are just too entrenched. Gradual change will, however, inexorably continue, sparked by the work of the best of each new generation of *vignerons*. This process is unlikely to satisfy completely any of the competing interest groups. Nonetheless, the Swiss penchant for practical solutions will undoubtedly keep the system inching forward.

The evolution of the legal structure and the continued refinement of the basic regulations of the systems of *appellation d'origine contrôlée* will progress on both the federal and cantonal levels. Standards will continue to be raised, loopholes or gaps eliminated and some of the more questionable traditional practices, i.e., *coupage* and *ouillage*, will permanently fall out of favour. In time, consumers will have ever more precise expectations when faced with *appellations* such as Dôle, Calamin or Pinot Gris de Dardagny. These expectations will increasingly be backed up by legal strictures – which undoubtedly the Swiss authorities will ensure are enforced. This will not lead to a shallow homogeneity or "pasteurization" of Swiss wines, but rather will provide a more solid framework within which wine makers can experiment and grow. Controversies are bound to continue in sensitive areas such as the minimum levels of natural sugar required for certain higher quality wines, or maximum allowable levels of chaptalization, but these debates will evolve within certain already-agreed parameters.

The key will be greater restrictions on yields and the elimination of vineyards only capable of producing great quantities of low-quality grapes. Trends beyond their control will ensure that Swiss *vignerons* will eventually have considerable difficulty servicing the low end of their own domestic market. Unless continually subsidized, cheap Swiss wines will never underprice their French, Italian and Spanish competitors once the latter are freed from quota restrictions.

The salvation, therefore, is to produce better products for a higher real return. Many of the wine makers mentioned in this book prove daily that this can be done. The best wine makers do not have a problem selling their production. Quite the opposite. The best will have to keep up their standards, as they show every intention of doing. It is, however, the merely good, or the nearly good that are going to have to work that much harder for their share of a more competitive market.

The continuing quest for better quality, which is very genuine, will ensure that even in a high cost environment, the Swiss wine industry will flourish. Evolution and change, some of it rather fundamental, will be necessary. The commitment to the production of quality wine, however, remains undiminished among many dedicated Swiss wine makers. A steady domestic demand for their product will remain the foundation for their economic well-being; an increased international demand for the finer wines can only inspire an even greater search for the means, skill and art required to produce fine wines from this challenging environment.

Château Crans near Celigny in the La Côte region.

XV

A Final Word On Vintages

Although the vast majority of Swiss wines are still produced for consumption within one or two years after harvest, there are an increasing number of Swiss wines that will benefit from, if not require, laying down. Most notable are the reds of Valais (Dôle with a high ratio of Pinot Noir, pure Pinot Noir, Syrah and Humagne Rouge), the Merlot del Ticino, the finest Pinot Noir of Neuchâtel and Lake Bienne, the oak-aged Pinot Noir from the eastern cantons and the new Merlot and Cabernet Sauvignon from Geneva. The more concentrated single-vineyard wines of Vaud such as those from Dézaley, Epesses and St. Saphorin, the better-made varietal whites of Valais and the special wines of Grisons such as the Completer can also benefit from some aging.

In the chapter on Vaud, brief reference was made to white wines from the 1950s from Clos des Abbayes and Clos des Moines tasted in the early 1990s. Although drying out, these wines still had a full nutty nose and more than enough "fat" to last for several years without beginning to go downhill – solid proof that Swiss wines can age if well treated. It must, however, be stressed that for a Chasselas to survive successfully for 40 years it needs to be from a great site in a great year, enhanced by disciplined wine making.

For the other regions, current consumption has been a general, but not absolute, rule. It is occasionally possible to find older bottles on wine lists or in specialty shops and as more and more wines meant for aging are produced, older bottles should remain in circulation. Variation between vintages is important in Switzerland, especially as weaker vintages (e.g., 1987, 1991 (in some areas) and 1993) will magnify the faults of a wine suffering from the sins of overproduction.

In general, the vintages of Switzerland follow those of the neighbouring regions of France, Germany and Italy. A magnificent year in nearby Burgundy is likely to be at least a good year in Geneva, Vaud or Neuchâtel. Valais and the Bündner Herrschaft, in particular, are exceptions, given their relative isolation, the overall drier micro-climate and the influence of the *foehn*. The importance of this warm wind is such that late-harvest grapes can be excellent despite only average results from the regular harvest.

* * * * *

The table below is adapted loosely from the 1992 "Agenda Suisse des Vins" and is based on a one * (poor) to five ***** (outstanding) scale. It is meant to assist those who might be tempted to lay down a case or two of a Swiss wine or who might be lucky enough to discover a forgotten bottle on an extensive wine list. As always, the adage "there are no great vintages, only great bottles" should be borne in mind. For Valais, the marks are for the normal vintage only; the late-harvested wines which are affected by the *foehn* are not listed separately. The difference between the numerous cantons of eastern Switzerland unfortunately make a single vintage designation impractical.

Table XI: A Vintage Chart for Switzerland

Year	Vaud	Valais	Geneva	Neuchâtel
1966	*****	*****	****	***
1967	****	****	**	**
1968	*	**	*	*
1969	****	****	***	**
1970	**	**	***	**
1971	*****	*****	****	***
1972	**	***	**	*
1973	***	***	***	***
1974	***	***	**	**
1975	***	*****	***	**
1976	*****	*****	****	****
1977	*	**	**	*
1978	**	***	**	**
1979	****	****	****	****
1980	*	**	*	*
1981	***	****	****	****
1982	***	***	**	**
1983	****	***	***	***
1984	**	***	**	**
1985	****	****	****	****
1986	*****	*****	**	*****
1987	**	***	**	**
1988	****	*****	*****	*****
1989	****	****	****	****
1990	*****	*****	*****	*****
1991	***	***	***	***
1992	****	****	****	****
1993	***	***	***	***
1994	****	****(*)	****(*)	***
1995	****	****(*)	****	****

Measurements

Expressions of area and volume use the standard European measurements based on meters and litres. Given the small size of some Swiss vineyards, the area is often calculated in square meters or occasionally in "are" (one-hundredth of a hectare), rather than hectares. In general, however, areas are expressed in hectares, and volumes in hectoliters, although limited cross reference is made to acres and gallons to assist readers more used to these systems.

Area

100 square meters = 1 are
100 ares = 1 hectare
10,000 square meters = 1 hectare
1 hectare = 2.47 acres

Volume

1 hectoliter = 100 litres
1 liter = 2.11 pints
1 liter = 1.06 US quarts
1 hectoliter = 26.4 US gallons
1 hectoliter = 21.9 Imperial gallons

Weight
1 kilogram = 35.2 ounces
1 pound = 453.5 grams

Temperature

0° Centigrade = 32° Fahrenheit
10° Centigrade = 50° Fahrenheit
-10° Centigrade = 14° Fahrenheit

Glossary

alcoholic fermentation: The first or primary fermentation that converts sugar into ethyl alcohol and carbon dioxide.

bisses: The wooden or stone channels bringing water from the glaciers to irrigate the Rhône valley in Valais.

botrytis cinerea: *Pourriture noble* in French and noble rot in English. The fungus that causes the grapes to shrivel and dry out causing the juice to concentrate its sweetness.

chaptalization: The addition of sugar to the must to increase the alcoholic level and fullness of a wine.

cépage: French for grape variety.

chai: French for the place where the wine is stored, usually in barrels.

charmus: The thin arable strips in Vaud, especially the slopes of Dézaley where grapes are planted.

coulure: A poor fruit set in grapes caused by an imbalance of carbohydrates in the vines. Some varieties are more susceptible to coulure than others.

coupage: The term used for blending of different wines. It literally means "cutting" the wines.

flétrie: French for "shriveled" signifying a wine made from grapes that have dried out and therefore have greater sweetness. *Mi-flétrie* is also used for less sweet wines.

flor: A film forming yeast, most commonly found during the production of sherry.

foehn: The warm wind from the south that is particularly important in ripening grapes in Valais and in eastern Switzerland.

gradin: Terraces carved out in the Ticino region for planting grapes. Also known as *banquettes*.

hutin: A name commonly used in the Geneva region for pergolas upon which the grapes were grown.

maceration: Steeping the grapes (usually red) before or after fermentation to extract greater colour and body from the skins, seeds and stems.

malo-lactic fermentation: The secondary fermentation that turns malic acid into lactic acid in white wines. The wines softens in the process.

must: The grape juice produced after pressing the grapes.

oïdium: French term for powdery mildew, a fungal disease which attacks the green parts of the vine. *Oïdium* reduces yields and inhibits colouring.

ouillage: Normally the evaporation that takes place in the bottle after some years of storage. In Switzerland it also describes the addition of wines to made up for volume losses during the fermentation process.

phylloxera: A small yellow aphid that feeds off the roots of the vine. The phylloxera louse arrived in Europe from America in the 19th century. Today virtually all Swiss vines are grafted on to phylloxera-resistant American root stock.

rougeot: A fungal disease known as "red burn" which attacks the leaves, shoots and grape bunches of the vine.

spritz: The slight prickly sensation in wine caused by residual carbon dioxide. Not as strong as *petillant.*

tablars: The large vineyard terraces of Valais.

vin de paille: French for "straw wines", the sweet, luscious wines made from grapes dried on straw mats before fermentation.

vendage tardif: French for "late harvest". The wines from late-harvested grapes should be rich and sweet.

véraison: The point in the growing cycle where the grapes begin to take on a touch of colour. During véraison the berries soften, enlarge, increase in sugar content and decrease in acidity.

vitis labrusca: The vine species, originally from North America, which provides a "foxy" wine. Swiss plantings are limited to Ticino.

vitis silverius: The wild grape species which originally populated the Jura mountains and provided grapes for Switzerland's early inhabitants.

vitis vinifera: The "noble" vine species from which virtually all fine wines are produced.

Bibliography
Books:

Allen, H. Warren, A *Contemplation* of Wine, Michael Joseph, London 1951.

Allen, H. Warren, *White Wines* and *Cognac*, Constable and Co., London 1952.

Anex, Paul, *Les Routes du Vin en Suisse Romande*, Editions Hifach, Château de Malessert, Perroy (Vaud) 1991.

Carruzzo, Claude-Henri, *Cépages du Valais*, Ketty & Alexandre, Chappelle-sur-Moudon 1991.

Chatelain-Courtois, Martine, *Les mots du vin et de l'ivresse*, Belin, Paris 1984.

Craven, Jean, *Brévaire du Vigneron*, Imprimerie E. Schoechli, Sierre 1943.

Coutaz, Gilbert, *Les 450 Vendanges des Vignobles de la Ville de Lausanne*, Editions du Verseau, Lausanne 1987.

Dubois, Jacques, *Le Vigneron Vaudois et ses Vins*, Imprimerie Centrale, Lausanne 1944.

Editions de la Fédération suisse des cafitiers, restaurateurs et hôteliers, *Tour de Suisse des Vins*, Volume 8 Genève, Geneva 1987.

Editions du Grand-Pont, *Les Vins de la Ville de Lausanne*, Lausanne 1987.

Eggenberger, Dr. Walter et al., *Schweizer Weinatlas*, Pharos-Verlag Hansrudolf Schwabe AG, Basel 1977.

"Fêtes des Vignerons, Lausanne '91", June 28-30, 1991 Concert Program.

Gardaz, Massy, Anex, Romieux & Hammel, *Le Vin Vaudois*, Editions Vie Art Cité, Lausanne 1975.

Gay, Daniel, *Le Statut du Vin*, Editions Payot, Lausanne 1985.

Grival, Olivier, *Les Vignerons Suisses du Tsar*, Editions Ketty & Alexandre, Chappelle-sur-Moudon 1993.

Jackisch, Philip, *Modern Winemaking*, Cornell University Press, Ithaca 1985.

Jamieson, Ian, *German Wines*, Faber and Faber, London, 1991.

Jault, Yves, *Les Châteaux Viticoles du Pays de Vaud*, Editions 24 heures, Lausanne 1990.

Johnson, Hugh, *Vintage: The Story of Wine*, Simon and Schuster, New York 1989.

Johnston, Hugh, *The World Atlas of Wine*, 4th edition, Michell Beazley, London 1994.

Jordon, Michel, *Agenda Suisse du Vin* 1991, Promo Edition, Geneva 1990.

Jordon, Michel, *Agenda Suisse du Vin* 1992, Promo Edition, Geneva 1991.

Josephson, Matthew, *Jean-Jacques Rousseau*, Harcourt Brace and Company, New York 1931.

Keller, Andreas, *Wein Einkaufsführer* 1984, Hallwag Verlag, Bern, 1994.

Kümin, Walter, *Schweizer Weinführer*, AT Verlag, Arrau 1992.

Lichine, Alexis, *Alexis Lichine's New Encyclopedia of Wines and Spirits*, Alfred A. Knopf, New York 1987.

Loftus, Simon, *Puligny-Montrachet, Journal of a Village in Burgundy*, Ebury Press, London 1992.

Lubbock, Sir John, *The Scenery of Switzerland*, Macmillian, London 1986.

Marchand Leslie A., Editor, *So Late Into the Night*, Byron's Letters and Journals Volume 5 1816-1817, John Murray, 1976.

Mathews, Patrick Editor, *Christie's Wine Companion*, Salem House Publishers, 1987.

OFD communication et information + documentation, *Conaissance des Vins Suisses*, Genève, Editions Payot, Lausanne 1993.

OFD communication et information + documentation, *Guide des vignobles et des vins suisses*, Geneva 1994.

Office des vins vaudois, *Economie Viti-vinicole Vaudoise*, Lausanne 1991

Ordish, George, *The Great Wine Blight*, Sidgwick and Jackson, 1972 & London 1987.

Pillon, Gérard & Schlaepfer, Jean-Daniel, *Les Vins de Genève*, Editions Zoé, Geneva 1988 and 1993.

Renoy, Georges, *Les Etiquettes de Vin, Un monde merveilleux*, Rossel Edition, 1981.

Robinson, Jancis, *Vines, Grapes and Wines*, Mitchel Beazley, London 1986.

Robinson, Jancis, *The Oxford Companion to Wine*, Oxford University Press, Oxford 1994.

Rochaix et al., Vignes et Vins de Notre Pays, Editions Mondo, Vevey 1977.

Scheurer, Porret, Baillod, *Vins et Vignoble Neuchâtelois*, Centre d'arts graphiques, Neuchâtel 1975.

Seward, Desmond, *Monks and Wine*, Mitchel Beazley, London 1979.

Simon, Schwarzenbach, Mischler, Eggenberger & Koblet, *Viticulture*, Editions Payot, Lausanne 1977.

Style, Sue, *A Taste of Switzerland*, Pavillion, London 1992, and Bergli Books, Riehen, 1996.

Woutaz, Fernand, *Guide des Cépages d'Europe*, M.A. Editions, Paris 1990.

Periodicals:

Divo, Défense et Illustrations des Vins d'Origine, Divo SA, Lausannne.

Amphitrium, Magazine de la gastronomie, de l'hôtellerie et du tourisme, Amphitrium Magazine S.A., Genève.

Journal Vinicole Suisse.

Vinum, Vinum Verlags AG, Zurich.

Index

A

Aar 197, 207
Aargau cantonal wine museum 208
Abbaye de Mont 114, 131
Abbey of Bevaix 163, 167
Abbey of Cluny 13
Abbey of Haut Crêt 121
Abbey of Hauterive 117
Abbey of Joux 121
Abbey of Montheron 121
Abbey of Muri 13
Abbey of Salaz 105
Abbey of St. Peter and St. Paul 136
Académie du Cep 160
acidity 31, 37, 38, 40
Aesch 208, 218
Agno 181
agricultural research station 22, 29, 127
Aigle 13, 99, 103, 104, 105, 106, 107, 108, 110, 112, 114, 117, 139
alcohol levels 41, 54
alcoholic fermentation 54, 55, 238
Alemanni 10, 11, 13, 196
Alexander I, Russian Czar 21
Alicante 28
Aligoté 32, 33, 44, 56, 64, 75, 145, 148, 153, 156, 214
Allaman 114, 130
Allen, H. Warren 85, 109
alpine geography 27
Alsace 20, 34, 37, 38, 39, 149, 203
Altesse 44, 64, 75, 88, 95
Altstätten 210
Ambresin, Jean-Louis 104
American root-stock 20, 29, 31
Americano 49, 181, 184, 186
Amigne 32, 33, 40, 41, 61, 64, 72, 86, 87, 88, 90, 91
Ancellota 49, 64
Andelfingen 200
Angst, Mattias 200
Anières 158, 159
Anniviers valley 44
Antagnes 105
Aosta valley 48

appellation 8, 50, 52, 56, 57, 58, 65, 103, 146, 165, 221, 222, 223, 232, 233
Appenzell 190, 211
Aran 124
Ardon 66, 91, 94
Argovie 190, 192, 195, 207, 218
Arlesheim 208
Arnex 136
Arosa 198
Arve 142, 157, 158
Arvine 33
Association des organisations viticoles genevoise 146
Association genevoise des vignerons et encaveurs i 142
Association of wine makers of eastern Switzerland 224
Association Vinicole of Aigle 108
Association Viticole Aubonne 130
Au 198
Auberge au Raisin 126
Auberge de l'Onde 119
Aubonne 103, 128, 130
Augustinian monks 144
Australia 21, 58, 179, 197
Auvernier 168, 176, 223
Aux Trois Amis 174
Auxerrois 109
avalanches 61
Avenches 137
Avully 157, 158
Aymon of Savoie 112

B

Bacchus 10, 123, 201, 231
Bachtobel 203
Bad Osterfingen 202
Bad Ragaz 211
Baden 201
Badoux SA, Henri 106, 107, 110, 139, 227
Balavaud 91
Balgach 210
banquettes 181

243

Barbey, Roger 119, 140
Bardonnex 157
Barrault, Jean-Louis 93
barrel maturation 204
Basel x, 163, 171, 190, 191, 192, 208
Battle of Bribracte 11
Battle of Mortgarten 16
Baud, Pierre-André 108
Baumann, Max and Ruedi 202, 218
Bayard Tower 93
Beaujolais 46, 55, 66, 97, 149
Beaune 117
Beer 17
Beerliwein 212
Begnins 103, 128, 130, 133
Belgium 226
Bellerive 137
Bellinzona 180
Bender, Adrian 94
Béné, Edouard 159, 160
Benedictines 12, 13, 27, 137, 171, 196, 200
Bergwein 210
Beride 183, 187
Bernarde 64
Berne x, 4, 136, 138, 163, 164, 170, 190, 209
Berneck 210, 218
Berneck Weinbaugenossenschaft 210
Bernese Alps 174
Bernex 157, 158, 160
Besitzer, Josef 210
Besse, Gérald 95, 98
Bex 99, 103, 104, 105, 112
Biborne 132
Biollaz, Albert 91, 92
biological de-acidification 57
biological viticulture 155
bisses 28, 63, 72, 89, 238
Blanchard, Fernand 132
Blanchier 75, 80
Blauburgunder 6, 45, 191
Blenio 181
Blonay 114, 115
Bocquet-Thonney 158
bois ridé 73
Bôle 167
Bolle 129
Bon Père Germanier 90
Bonaduz 215
Bonarda 181
Bondola 32, 48, 129, 179, 184, 186, 192
Boner, Adolf 215, 218
Bonne Côte 128, 130
Bonvillars 100, 103, 135, 136, 137

Bonvin et Fils SA, Charles 87, 98
Bordeaux 28, 44, 61, 179, 183
Bossey 144
Bosshart, Bruno 211
botrytis cinerea 38, 69, 238
Boudry 165, 166, 168
Bougy-Villars 131
Bourdigny 150
Bovard, Antoine 126, 127
Bovard, Philip 126
Bovard SA, Louis 120, 122, 125
Bovier, François 76
Bovy, Bernard 119
Bramois 89
Branson 94
Breganzona 183, 187
Brig 61, 80, 217
Brigerbad 80
Briguet, Paul 93
Buchs 210
bunches per vine 31
Bündner Herrschaft 7, 189, 193, 195, 211, 213, 214, 215, 235
Burgundians 11, 12, 144, 172
Burgundy x, 1, 12, 37, 44, 56, 76, 128, 235
Burignon 119, 121
Bursinel 103, 128, 133
Buus 208
Byron, Lord 114

C

Cabernet Franc 64
Cabernet Sauvignon 32, 33, 47, 61, 89, 90, 145, 150, 152, 155, 165, 168, 181, 183, 185, 199, 215, 235
cadastre 104
Cademario 183
Caesar, Julius 10
Calamin 103, 124, 125, 233
California 20, 21, 37, 58, 61, 179, 184
Calvin, John 17
Canada 4, 36, 226, 227
Cantina Giubiasco 180, 183, 186, 187
Cantina Sociale Mendrisio 180, 187
Cantonal regulations 222
capsule dorée 96, 97
carbon bisulphide 20
carbon dioxide 55
Carre d'Aval 159
Carthaginians 10
Carthusians 13, 15
Castel di Morcote 185, 187
Castella, Hubert de 21

Castelrotto 185, 187
caterpillars 31
Caudaux 127
cave communale 37
Cave d'Anchettes 84
Cave de Beauvent 158, 160
Cave de Champ de Clos 140
Cave de Cimes 105
Cave de Genève, La 141, 144, 147, 150, 157, 161
Cave de la Bâtiaz 95
Cave de la Muscadelle 132
Cave de Liandaz 95
Cave de Lully, La 157
Cave de Mandement 152
Cave de Sézenove 158
Cave des Bossons 150, 155
Cave des Deux Crêtes 84
Cave des Viticulteurs de Bonvillars 136
Cave du Crépon 112
Cave du Mandement 145, 150
Cave du Signal, 129
Cave du Village 129
Cave St. Matthieu 86
Cave St. Pierre 93, 132, 226
Caveau de Salquenen 81, 82
Caves Châtenay 176
Caves d'Ayer 85, 86
Caves de Troub 165, 170
Caves des Côteaux 167
Caves des Places 86
Caves du Prieuré 139, 169
Caves Imesch 83, 85
Caves Orsat 95, 227
Céligny 159, 234
Celtic monks, tribes 10, 13
cépage 105, 238
Chablais 49, 100, 103, 104, 105, 106, 107, 108, 111, 112, 117, 133, 139
Chablis 15, 100
chai 238
Chalais 86
Chamonix 142
Chamoson 40, 66, 68, 82, 89, 91
Champagne 12, 37, 127, 136
Champlan 86
Changins 30, 127, 134, 171, 222
channe 59
Chanton, Josef-Marie 80
Chanton, Oskar 80, 98
Chapeau Noir (Black cap) 228
Chappaz, Marie-Thérèse 95
Chappuis, Alexandre 119
chaptalization 53, 55, 238

Chardonnay 5, 32, 33, 37, 47, 56, 61, 64, 71, 82, 84, 100, 113, 127, 131, 145, 148, 152, 153, 156, 159, 165, 168, 172, 174, 183, 196, 197, 199, 201, 203, 205, 211, 213, 215, 216
Chardonne 103, 116
Charlemagne 13, 196
Charles the Bold 17, 136, 164, 172
Charmont 45, 64, 75
charmus 120, 238
Chartreuse 15
Chasselas vii, 5, 6, 15, 19, 21, 30, 32, 33, 34, 37, 38, 43, 44, 45, 53, 54, 56, 61, 66, 69, 81, 83, 84, 89, 90, 92, 100, 104, 108, 109, 110, 112, 113, 115, 124, 127, 129, 131, 133, 137, 138, 141, 145, 146, 153, 155, 165, 166, 172, 173, 174, 179, 183, 208, 235
Châtaingneriaz 134
Château Barillet 152
Château Bothmar 214, 215
Château Châlon 15, 39
Château Crans 234
Château d'Aigle 106, 139
Château d'Allaman 130
Château Dardagny 150, 160
Château d'Auvernier 166, 167, 168
Château de Châtagnéréaz 132
Château de Châtelard 115
Château de Chillon 113, 114
Château de Coppet 115
Château de Cotterd 137
Château de Denens 129
Château de Fontainbleau 35
Château de la Bâtie 133
Château de Luins 132
Château de Mont 132
Château de Ripaille 34, 114
Château de Villa 83
Château d'Es Bons 130
Château du Crest 158, 159
Château du Rosey 133
Château Latour 155
Château Maison Blanche 110, 111, 132
Château Mouton Rothschild 215
Château Pavie 109
Château Petrus vii
Château Ravire 83, 84, 86, 98
Château Rochefort 114, 130
Châtelard 124
Châtenay SA, Samuel 165, 166, 168, 227
Chenin Blanc 44, 64, 75
Cheseaux, Jean-Luc 93

Chevalley, Albert 132
Chevalley SA, Auguste 127, 132, 140
Chevrier, Philippe 156
Chexbres 38, 106, 112, 117, 119, 124, 140, 153
Chiasso 180, 181, 184, 187
Chiésaz church 114
Chigny 129
Chile 37
Choulex 158
Chur 210, 211, 215, 216, 217
Cistercians 13, 15, 113, 117, 120, 121
Cîteaux 15
clairets 18
Clarens 114, 115
Clavadeltscher, Godi 7
Clavien, Gérald 83, 84, 98
Clavien, Jacques 83
Clavien, Michel 88, 98
Clavoz 89
Clevner 16, 45
climate 11, 27, 34, 36, 61, 103, 104, 112, 142, 167, 170, 177, 189, 191, 200
Clinton 181
Cloister of Engelberg 171
clones 49, 76
Clos Balavaud 92
Clos d'Anzier 90
Clos de Balavaud 93
Clos de Bèze 12
Clos de Bolombert 130
Clos de Céligny 159
Clos de Jérusalem 129
Clos de la Béguine 124
Clos de la Châtaigneraie 134
Clos de la Colombière 134
Clos de la Combaz 136
Clos de la Combettaz 84
Clos de la Fontaine 134
Clos de la George 110, 139
Clos de la Pompe 127
Clos de la République 124
Clos de la Roche 215
Clos de l'Abbaye 110
Clos de l'Eglise 136
Clos de Murci 158
Clos de St.-Amour 124
Clos de Villars 134
Clos de Vougeot 15, 64, 114
Clos des Abbayes 15, 47, 113, 114, 117, 121, 122, 127, 131, 235
Clos des Abbesses 129
Clos des Avaris 137
Clos des Barrettes 131

Clos des Berles 129
Clos des Burnettes 124
Clos des Combes 136
Clos des Crusilles 136
Clos des Epinettes 136
Clos des Grillières 136
Clos des Mangones 136
Clos des Moines 15, 114, 117, 121, 235
Clos des Murets 136
Clos des Pierres 136
Clos des Repingonnes 134
Clos des Secrétaires 136
Clos des Seigneurs 144
Clos des Treize-Vents 124
Clos des Truites d'Avaux 129
Clos des Vallaires 129
Clos des Verchères 134
Clos du Bochet 134
Clos du Château 133
Clos du Paradis 144
Clos du Rocher 110
Clos Dufour 136
Clos O(r)goz 117
closed cuvée method 55
Cluny 12, 137
Coderey et Fils, Paul 127
cold-climate strains 45
Coldrerio 181
Colli degli Ulivi 182
Colline de Géronde 83, 84
Collivo 185
Collonge-Bellerive 145, 158
Cologny 142, 158, 160
Colombier 129, 166, 168
Columban 13
Comby, François-Emmanuel 91
Commugny 134
Compagnie des vignerons de Neuchâtel 164, 168
Compesières 144
Completer 75, 80, 191, 193, 197, 211, 214, 215, 216, 235
Completerhalde 193, 215
Comptoir suisse 228
Comté of Valais 87
Concise 137, 164
Confrérie des vignerons de Vevey 110, 116, 229
Confrérie des Vignolans 139
Confrérie du Guillon 114, 139, 231
Confrérie du Tastevin 114
Confrérie St. Théodule 84, 93
Congress of Vienna 68, 164, 216
Conne, Bernard 153, 160

Conne, Jean-Michel 105, 117, 119, 140
Constance 205
Constantine 137
Constantinople 34
consumption 4, 17
consumption taxes 220
Contesse SA, Henri 120, 125
Conthey 40, 66, 90
Convention of Fribourg 106
Coopérative Center Ajoie 176
Cooperative of Schinznach 207
cooperatives 24, 144
Coppet 134
Corcelles 124, 137, 169
cordon de royat 30
corks 58
Cormondrèche 169
Cornalin 32, 33, 48, 61, 64, 78, 84, 86, 157, 186
Corot, Camille 150
Corseaux 116
Corsier 116, 158
Cortaillod 15, 75, 76, 166, 167, 172, 176
Corthay, Daniel 159
Corton 12, 123
Cossy, Maurice 119
Côte de Morges 128
Côte de Nyon 128, 134
Coteau de Lully 157
Coteau de Peissy 153
Coteau de Vincy 103, 128, 133
Coteaux de Dardagny 157
Coteaux de Planey 168
Coteaux du Châtelard 116
Côtes de l'Orbe 100, 103, 135
Côtes de Russin 156
coulure 34, 37, 78, 238
coupage 233, 238
Cramer, Roland 159
Crans-Montana 107
Crépy 34
Cressier 165, 170, 176
Cretegny, Phillipe 131
Crissier 89, 126
cross-breeds 21, 44, 49, 75
Crousaz, Jean-Charles 155, 160
Cruchon, Henri 129, 140
Cruchon-Muller family 129
Cruz, Bernard 158, 160
Cully x, 120, 122, 123, 125, 126, 140
Cure d'Attalens 116
Curzille 130
cutting (coupage) 55, 57, 223
Cybele 117

D

Danube 36
Darbellay, André 87
Dardagny 38, 44, 148, 150, 153, 156, 157, 160, 161
Deladoey, Jacques 109, 139
Delea, Angelo 184, 187
Delémont 176
density of planting 29
Desfayes-Crettenand, Edmund 90
Devayes, Ulrich 93
Dézaley x, 5, 15, 45, 90, 103, 110, 112, 113, 114, 116, 117, 120, 131, 226, 235
Dijon 61
Diolinoir 49, 64
Diolly 79, 185
Dionysus 10
disease-resistant clones 25
Dôle 6, 45, 76, 77, 81, 82, 88, 91, 96, 149, 223, 233, 235
Dôle Blanche 79, 87, 97
Domaine Brûlefer 87
Domaine Château Vaumarcus 166, 227
Domaine Clos du Château 87
Domaine de Chafalet 156, 161
Domaine de Charmigny 107
Domaine de Châteauvieux 156
Domaine de Chatroz 88, 98
Domaine de Famolens 132
Domaine de Fischer 131, 132
Domaine de la Brosse 169
Domaine de la Cotzette 87
Domaine de la Grille 127
Domaine de la Maison Blanche 125
Domaine de la Tour 159, 160
Domaine de la Tourelle 159
Domaine de la Treille 134
Domaine de la Tuilière 133
Domaine de la Ville de Berne 172
Domaine de l'Hôpital Pourtalès 170
Domaine de Lichen 81
Domaine de l'Ovaille 109, 139
Domaine de Martheray 132
Domaine de Montmollin 169
Domaine de Riencourt 132
Domaine des Balisiers 153, 155, 161
Domaine des Caillettes 104, 132
Domaine des Châbles 115
Domaine des Charmes 153
Domaine des Claives 95
Domaine des Curiades 158
Domaine des Esserts 156

Domaine des Faunes 156
Domaine des Hutins 160
Domaine des Rothis 153, 156, 157, 161
Domaine des Trois Etoiles 155
Domaine du Burignon 114, 117
Domaine du Centaure 156, 161
Domaine du Château de Rougemont 158, 160
Domaine du Crêtacombe 92
Domaine du Grand-Brûlé 93
Domaine du Mont d'Or 98
Domaine Grange Volet 106
Domaine Le Grand Clos 152, 160
Domaine Les Creuses 133
Domaine Les Hutins 156
Domaine Les Perrières 153
Domaine of Champréveyres 165
Domaine Plan Loggier 87
Domaines des Repaires 168
Donatsch, Thomas 215, 218
Doral 45
Dorin 34, 100, 108
Döttingen 207
Dubois Frères et Fils 126, 140
Duboux, Vincent and Blaise 127
Duc de Rohan 191, 212
Duc, Jules 86
Ducret et fils, Marius 116
Dufour, J.J. 21
Duillier 134
Duke of Burgundy 17
Dukes of Savoie 106, 114
Dupraz, Paul 158, 160
Durize 64
Dutruy, Jean-Jacques 134

E

Echandens 129
Echichens 129
Eclépens 135
Egli, Michel 167
Eglisau 200
égrappage 53
Eichholtz 210
Elbling 191, 192, 195, 207, 211
Eldegarde, Countess 144
Engel, Werner K. 174
Epesses 45, 103, 108, 113, 120, 123, 124, 125, 140, 231, 235
Erlach x, 172
Ermitage 33, 39, 51, 64, 69, 85, 86, 90, 97
erosion 25, 28
Essertines 150, 161

Etruscan 10
European Union 37, 85
exports 94, 132, 225
Eyholz 80

F

Faverges 117
Favre, Hanny 88
Favre, Les Fils de Charles 88
Favre, Maurice 91
Favre, René 91
Favre, Simon 83, 84
Favre-Caruzzo, Vincent 91
Favre-Philippoz, Jean-Claude 91
Féchy 103, 128, 131, 132, 140
Federal legislation on viticulture 24, 221
Federal Office of Agriculture 2
Federation of Neuchâtel vignerons 166
Federweiss 54, 192, 200, 201, 211, 212, 219
Fehr + Engeli 208, 218
Feldmeilen 197, 217
Felsberg 215
Fendant 6, 33, 65, 66, 83, 86, 87, 88, 89, 90, 91, 96, 100, 152, 166, 223, 226
fermentation 53, 107
fertilizers 25
fêtes des vignerons 123, 228, 229
filtering 54
Findling 45, 149, 153
Fläsch 213, 218
flétrie 6, 41, 52, 63, 69, 72, 74, 88, 238
flor 44, 238
Florence 28
Flurlingen 200, 217
foehn 60, 61, 73, 109, 189, 196, 199, 210, 213, 214, 235, 238
fog 103, 104, 112, 142, 201
fond vinicole 222
Fondation Pierre Gianadda 95
Fonjallaz, François 125
Fonjallaz, Jean-Daniel 125, 127
Fonjallaz, Michel 123
Fonjallaz, Patrick 125
Fonjallaz SA 108, 120, 124, 140
Food Products Ordinance (ODA) 56, 57
Formentin 43
Forstwein 210
Founex 134
France ix, x, 5, 58, 104, 226
Franche-Comté 76
François I, King 34
Frankfurt 28
Fratelli Valsangiacomo 183, 184, 187

Index

Frauenfeld 204
Freiburg 195
Freienbach 199
Freisa 181
Freisamer 45, 64, 195, 197, 205, 211
French Revolution 18
Fresens 166
Fribourg 4, 99, 117, 124, 136, 137
Fricktal 208
frost 29, 30, 31, 37, 63, 71, 103, 130, 196, 201
Fully 40, 49, 61, 69, 76, 94
future trends 25, 232

G

Gaillard, François 132
Gaja, Angelo 88
Gallay, Edmond and Jean-Daniel 132
Gallus 13
Gamaret 49, 64, 192, 201
Gamay 6, 18, 30, 32, 33, 45, 46, 49, 54, 55, 63, 64, 65, 66, 76, 77, 89, 95, 97, 100, 104, 105, 108, 110, 113, 115, 117, 122, 125, 129, 131, 136, 137, 145, 146, 149, 152, 153, 155, 156, 157, 158, 159, 176, 192
Gamay nouveau 46, 76, 149
Gantenbein, Daniel and Martha 213, 218
Garmet 157
Gaul 10
Gault Millau 123, 152
Gavillet, J.J. and P. 159
Gay, Madeleine 51
Gay, Maurice 93, 132
Geisenheim research station 22, 36
Geneva ix, 1, 4, 5, 6, 9, 12, 17, 19, 20, 28, 33, 35, 37, 38, 44, 45, 46, 47, 55, 61, 65, 103, 110, 128, 133, **141 - 162**, 164, 220, 223, 224, 228, 235, 236
Gerber, André 165
Germanier, Jacques 90
Germanier, Urbain 90
Germany 21, 22, 37, 39, 45, 64, 94, 193, 202, 226
Gevrey-Chambertin 66
Gewürztraminer 39, 53, 56, 64, 75, 131, 138, 145, 149, 173, 195, 196, 199, 203, 205, 208, 211, 216
Gex 150
Gex, Phillippe 110
Giez 136
Gilliard SA, Robert 87, 96, 98, 227
Giornico 13, 27

Girardet, Fredy 89, 92, 126
Glacial Express 217
Glacier d'Anniviers 85, 86
Glaris 190
gobelet 30, 191
gobelet sur échalas 29, 191
Godet, H.A. 169
Gollion 129, 135
Gombette, Law of 12
Gondebaud, King 12, 155
Gorgier 167
Goron 6, 77
Gouais 75
goût du terroir 109
gradin 238
Grand Chavalard 94
Grand Council of Vaud 103
Grand-Brûlé 79
Grande Arvine 41
Grandson 137, 164
Grandvaux 124, 127, 140
Grange Hermitage vii
Granges 86
Granoir 49, 176, 192, 201, 208
grape types 32, 64, 146
Grappa 181
Grauburgunder 38, 69
gray rot 28, 31
Greeks 10
Grilli, Groset 126
Grisoni, Jacques 170
Grisons x, 10, 38, 80, 189, 190, 192, 193, 198, 210, 211, 215, 235
Grône 86
Gros Rhin 36
Grosjean, Thierry 168, 176
Grumin 43
Grüner Veltliner 212
Gruyère 138
Gugelberg, Andreas von 213, 219
Gutedel 33
guyot 30, 146, 195
Gwäss 64, 75, 80
Gy 158

H

Hafnätscha 80
hail 29, 130, 201
Haldemann, Stefano 187
Hallau 191, 200, 202, 217, 226
Hammel SA 108, 111, 112, 131, 132, 140
Hapsburg 16, 207
Haraszthy, Count Agoston 20
Harrod's 226

249

Hartmann, Bruno 208
Hartmann, Emil 207
Hartmann-Saladin 208
Hasler, Hansueli 198, 217
Haubensak, Heini 210
Haug, Heinrich 199
Haussener et Fils, François 170, 176
Haussmann, Ulrich 204
Haut Crêt 117
Haut Valais 73, 76, 80
Haut-de-Cry 92
Haute Savoie 34, 40
Hauterive 165, 169
Hegg, Louis 125
Heida (Païen) 32, 39, 40, 43, 73, 74, 80
Helvetic Confederation 232
Helvetic Republic 19
Helvetii 9, 10, 11, 16
Hermance 158
Hermitage 88
Hertli, Heiner 200, 217
Herzog, Christian 210
Herzog, Hans 199, 217
Hibou 80
Himbertscha 64, 75, 80
Hôpital des Bourgeois 124, 172
Hospices de Beaune 125
Hospitaller, Knights 16
Hotel Metropole 159
Hotel Ritz 21, 226
Hubacher, Fritz Peter 174, 176
Huber, Daniel 183, 185, 187
Hug, Laurent 86
Huguenots 144
Humagne Blanc 32, 33, 40, 44, 73, 78, 84, 97
Humagne Rouge 6, 32, 33, 44, 48, 55, 61, 64, 72, 73, 78, 84, 91, 92, 97, 123, 129, 186, 235
humidity 29
Hungary 21
hutin 144, 239
Hutin, Jean and Pierre 156, 160
hybrids 21, 145, 146

I

Igis 215
Imhof, Hans 183
immigrant workers 20
import regulations 5, 224
imports 2, 20, 23, 24, 132
Indermühle, Pierre-Alain 105
industrialization 22
international markets 225

irrigation 28
Isabella 49, 181
Iselisberg 204
Isle St. Pierre 171, 172
Isoz, Claude 110
Italian Swiss Colony 21, 179
Italy 49, 64, 88, 179
Ittingen 204

J

Jackisch, Philip 50
Japan 226
Jefferson, Thomas 21
Jenins 213, 214, 215, 219
Jesuits 117
Johannisberg 36, 68, 81, 85, 87, 88, 90, 92, 96, 223
Johnson, Hugh 20, 48
Jomini, Jean-Louis 119, 140
joran 170
Joris, Alexis 76
Josephson, Matthew 173
Joyce, James 166
Jura 4, 9, 11, 13, 15, 39, 43, 87, 116, 137, 142, 164, 172, 174
Jussy 144, 150, 158, 159

K

Karthäuser wine 15
Kaufmann, Adriano 183, 187
Kerner 45, 156, 196, 201, 211
Kesselring, Hans-Ulrich 203, 218
Klausener, Erich and Fabienne 187
Klettgau 202, 203
Klevner 191
Klingnau 207
Kloster Sion 207, 218
Knights of Malta 81
Kümin, Gebrüder 199, 205, 211
Kuntzer et Fils, Jean-Claude 170, 176
Kuonen et Fils, Gregor 81, 82
Kursner, Willy 131
Küsnacht 16, 197
Kybourg family 207

L

La Côte 29, 103, 108, 114, 121, 128, 132, 141, 146, 159
La Lance 15
La Neuveville 172, 173
La Sarraz 135
La Souche cooperative 145, 158
La Tour de Pressy 159

Index

labour intensity 30
Laconnex 144
Lafnetscha 64, 75, 80, 193
Lagnaz, Henri 108
Lake Baldegg 209
Lake Bienne 45, 163, 164, 170, 174, 235
Lake Bienne Museum of the Vine 174
Lake Constance 10, 195, 203, 205, 210
Lake Geneva 10, 12, 13, 15, 27, 34, 36, 40, 76, 94, 95, 99, 103, 104, 112, 113, 115, 120, 125, 130, 134, 135, 158, 159
Lake Lucerne 209
Lake Lugano 184
Lake Maggiore 180
Lake Morat 103, 137
Lake Neuchâtel 10, 38, 103, 137, 163, 166
Lake Thun 209
Lake Walensee 199, 211
Lake Zurich 16, 40, 171, 189, 193, 195, 197, 198, 211
Lake Zurich Wine Museum 198
Lamone 182, 185, 187
Landquart 190, 191, 212
Lausanne x, 1, 15, 89, 103, 113, 121, 126, 127, 128, 139, 140, 228
Lavaux 23, 35, 37, 47, 60, 90, 100, 103, 104, 106, 107, 108, 112, 115, 116, 119, 128, 137, 141
Law on Agriculture 24, 221
Le Landeron 164, 170, 172
lees 54, 55
legislation governing wine production 24
Lens 86
Lentine 89
Lenzbourg 207
Leuk 81
Leventine 27, 181
Leytron v, 66, 69, 79, 91, 93
Leyvraz, Marc 123
Leyvraz, Pierre 120
Lichine, Alexis 229
Liechtenstein 212
Lienhard, Geri 200
Ligerz 171, 172, 173, 174
Limmat 40, 193, 196, 197, 199, 207
linguistic divisions 8, 11
Lion d'Or 159
Locarno 181, 228
Loire 44
London 124, 132, 150, 169, 202, 226
Louis XI x, 17
Louis XIII 191
Louis XV 214

low-alcohol wines 209
Lubbock, Sir John ix
Lucerne 190, 209
Lugano 28, 180, 186, 228
Luins 103, 128, 133
Lully 44, 129
Lutry 103, 124, 127
Lutzenberg 211
Luxembourg 22
Lyon 12, 28, 61

M

maceration 54, 55, 239
Mâcon 34
Magliocco, Daniel 92
Maienfeld 191, 211, 212, 213, 216, 219
Malans 7, 191, 193, 195, 213, 214, 215, 218, 219
Malanserrebe 193
Malbec 181
Malcantone 185, 187
malic acid 53
malo-lactic fermentation 54, 55, 239
Malvaglia 181
Malvasia x
Malvoisie 6, 38, 69, 84, 86, 87, 88, 90, 92, 95, 96
Mandement 142, 148, 156, 160
Marbach 210
marc (brandy) 53
Marcelin 129
Maréchal Foch 49
Mariafeld 191
Marienfeld 76
Marsanne 32, 39, 47, 69, 85, 87, 95
Marseilles 10
Marsens 121
Martigny x, 11, 12, 40, 49, 61, 63, 66, 72, 77, 94, 95
Marugg, Daniel 213
Massy et Fils, Claude 123, 125, 140, 231
Massy, Jean-François and Luc 124, 140
Matasci Fratelli 184
Mathier, Adrian 81, 82
Mathier, René 81, 82
Mathier-Kuchler 81, 98
Mathod 136
Matterhorn 73, 80
Maye, Léonide 93
Maye SA, Les Fils 93
Maye, Simon, Axel and Jean-François 91, 92, 98, 227
measurements 237
mechanization 24, 30, 31, 145, 181, 191

251

medieval military religious orders 15
medieval monastic orders 12
Medoc 47
Meier, Anton 207, 218
Meilen 16, 197, 198
Meinier 158, 159, 160
Mels 210
Mendrisio 180, 181, 185, 187
Merlot 32, 33, 46, 48, 54, 55, 64, 113, 122, 123, 145, 150, 152, 155, 177, 181, 184, 185, 187, 192, 199, 216
Merlot del Ticino 6, 179, 184, 223, 235
Mesolcina 211, 216
méthode champegnoise 55, 71
Metternich, Prince 68
Meyer, Michael 202, 218
Meylan, Roger 159, 160
mi(half)-flétrie 41
Michelet-Escher, Gabrielle 90
Micheli family 159
Miège 82, 83, 84
migration 20
mildew 22, 23, 28, 31
minimum natural sugar levels 56
Misox 46, 190, 192, 216
Mission Hill 34
Mistral-Monnier, G. & D. 156, 157, 160
Monastery of St. Gall 13
Monastery of St. George 203
Mondavi Reserve vii
Mont d'Or 63, 68, 69, 71, 74, 90
Mont d'Orge 89
Mont-sur-Rolle 103, 114, 128, 131, 132, 227
Montagny 136
Montaigne 18
Monteggio 183, 187
Monthey 95
Monti, Sergio and Ivo 183, 185, 187
Montreux 28, 61, 99, 103, 113, 114, 115
Morat 99, 138, 164
Morbio 181
Moren, Les Fils de François 90
Morges 103, 121, 128, 129, 131, 135, 228
Mosel 149
moût 228
Moutier-Grandval 13
Mövenpick 226
Müller, Franz 211
Müller, Josef 209
Müller-Thurgau 22, 35, 45
Müller-Thurgau, Hermann 21
Munot 201
Muraz 83

Muscat 15, 32, 33, 40, 43, 53, 56, 64, 71, 86, 87, 92, 96, 145, 172, 184, 197
Musée cantonal argovien de la vigne 217
Musée de la vigne au lac de Bienne 174
Musée de la vigne et du vin 83, 107, 168
Musée de la vigne et du vin de Schaffhouse 217
Musée de la vigne et du vin du lac de Zurich 217
Musée du vin et de la vigne 139
Musée valaisan de la vigne et du vin 97
Museum of the Vine and Wine 106, 107, 168

N

Naef, François 132
Napa Valley 21
Napoleon 19
Napoleon Bonaparte, Louis 205
Napoleon III 112
Napoleonic invasions 9
Nebbiolo 49, 64, 93, 216
Neftenbach 199, 217
Neolithic sites 163, 167, 168
Nestlé 116
Neuchâtel ix, x, 1, 4, 6, 9, 19, 28, 35, 37, 45, 75, 80, 91, 99, 109, 135, 149, **163 - 176**, 192, 223, 227, 228, 235, 236
Neuhausen 202
Neukom, Kurt 200, 217
neutrality 9, 17
Neuveville 172
New Helvetia 21
New South Wales 37
New York 36, 87, 108, 124, 150, 226
New Zealand 22, 36, 37
Niederwald 21
Nièvre 34
noble rot 38, 238
Nobling 45, 64, 75
Nostrano 48, 181
Novelle, Charles and Jean-Michel 152, 160
nuclear magnetic resonance spectrometers 56
number of bunches 30
Nussbaumer, Kurt 208, 218
Nyon 11, 103, 128, 133, 134

O

Oberflachs 207
Oberhallau 202

Oberland 210
Obermeilen 209
Oberstammhein 200
Obrecht, Christian 214, 219
Obrist 108, 110, 116, 132, 140
Octodure 72
Oechsle 31, 43, 50, 51, 56, 77, 90, 193, 196, 200, 212, 213
Oeil-de-Perdrix 6, 45, 54, 79, 82, 97, 127, 137, 163, 165, 167, 169, 170, 172, 173, 192, 223
Office de promotion des produits de l'agriculture 97
Office des vins de Neuchâtel 176
Office des Vins Vaudois (OVV) 139, 228
oïdium 22, 23, 31, 37, 239
Okanagan Valley 34
Ollon 86, 99, 103, 104, 105, 107, 112, 117, 127
Orbe 133, 136
Order of the Channe 83
Ordine dei Grancoppieri 186
Oregon 45
Oriou 78
Ortelli, Mauro 187
Osterfingen 202, 218
Ottenberg 203
Ottoberg 218
Oudinot, General 167
ouillage 57, 233, 239
Ovaille 108, 109
oxidization 54

P

Paccot, Raymond 131
Païen (Heida) 15, 64, 73
Palaz, Hoirie 125
parasites 31, 43
Paris 226
Parisod, Alain 127
pax romana 11
Payerne 124
pectins 53
Peissy 150, 153, 160, 161
Pelichet, Jacques 140
Peney 150, 153, 155, 161
percentage of alcohol 52
pergolas 80
Perlan 33, 141, 147, 150, 155
Perle du Lac 156
Perret, Les Fils de Arthur 169
Perroy 103, 128, 130
Peseux 169
pesticides 25

Petit Rhin 36
Petit-bourgogne 75
Petite Arvine 32, 38, 40, 41, 61, 64, 72, 87, 88, 90, 91, 92
Petite Dôle 75
Pfäffers 191, 210, 214
Pfister, Joe 185, 187
Phoenicians 10
phylloxera louse 20, 21, 22, 23, 31, 49, 93, 144, 239
Pillon, Gérard 155, 161
Pinget, Gérard 123
Pinot Blanc 38, 64, 74, 87, 88, 100, 145, 148, 155, 156, 157, 165, 184, 193, 201, 211, 213, 214, 215, 216
Pinot Gris 5, 6, 32, 38, 45, 56, 64, 69, 79, 85, 100, 113, 131, 132, 145, 148, 152, 153, 156, 165, 170, 172, 174, 176, 179, 183, 193, 195, 196, 197, 199, 200, 203, 205, 208, 211, 213, 215, 216, 223, 233
Pinot Noir vii, 6, 15, 16, 18, 32, 33, 45, 49, 54, 55, 56, 61, 63, 64, 65, 66, 75, 76, 77, 80, 81, 82, 84, 87, 88, 89, 93, 97, 100, 104, 105, 107, 108, 110, 113, 115, 117, 122, 129, 131, 136, 137, 145, 146, 152, 155, 157, 159, 165, 166, 168, 170, 172, 173, 174, 176, 181, 185, 186, 189, 191, 196, 197, 199, 203, 204, 205, 208, 212, 215, 216, 235
plant density 29
Plata d'en-Bas 75
pneumatic presses 53
Poire William 90
Pomerol 33, 184
Pompaples 135
Pont de la Morge 88, 98
Porret, Albert 167, 176
Posch-Jutz, Peter 174
Poschiavo 211, 216
Pouilly Fumé 34
Pouilly-sur-Loire 34
Pradier d'Agrain, Marquis 18
Prégny 20
Premploz 90
presses 53, 107
prices 5, 22, 23, 58, 224
production limits 65
protectionist economic and trade policies 23
Provence 72
Provins 24, 51, 57, 60, 63, 77, 96, 98, 227
PROVITI 186

pruning 30, 38, 46, 56
Prussia, King of 164
Puidoux 120, 124
Pully 127
Puplinge 159
Putallaz, Jean-Luc 90

Q

Quinten 199, 211
quotas 5, 23, 25, 92, 220

R

racking 54
Rafz 200, 217
Ragaz 191
rainfall 28, 63
Ramu, Claude 156, 161
Ramu et Fils, Edouard 156, 161
Ramu, Guy and Sylvie 156, 157, 161
Rapperswil 199, 211
Raron 73
Rätikon 213
Ratsstube of Grimentz 59
Räuschling 40, 138, 191, 193, 196, 197, 199, 205, 208, 216
Raymond & Fils, Marc and Gérard 91, 93, 98
Redding, Cyrus x
Reformation 17
Regensberg 199, 218
Registre du Conseil 17
Reichenau 219
Reichensteiner 49, 125, 176, 192
Relais de Chambésy 110
Remingen 208
Renaud, Madeleine 93
République lémanique 121
ressats 114
Restaurant Ochsen 215
Reuss 207
Reynard & Varone 89, 98
Rèze 32, 40, 43, 44, 61, 64, 73, 74, 80, 86
Rhaeti 10, 11
Rheinau 200, 203
Rheingau 68, 74
Rhin/Sylvaner 64
Rhine ix, x, 11, 99, 135, 189, 191, 196, 200, 202, 203, 207, 210, 217
Rhône ix, 10, 12, 13, 27, 28, 39, 44, 47, 61, 66, 74, 76, 80, 81, 86, 89, 91, 94, 95, 99, 100, 104, 106, 109, 112, 135, 142, 155, 157, 217
Richli, Jacob 202

Riddes 93
Riesling 22, 33, 36, 45, 64, 68, 74, 90, 166, 203, 213
Riesling x Sylvaner 22, 32, 33, 35, 40, 56, 64, 74, 100, 129, 135, 146, 149, 152, 153, 165, 176, 183, 189, 191, 192, 196, 197, 199, 203, 204, 205, 208, 212, 213, 215
Rieux 124
ripening conditions 30
Ritz, César 21
Rivaz 112, 117, 119, 120, 123
Rivera 181, 184, 187
Robinson, Jancis 48, 77, 213, 218
Rochaix, Bernard and Brigitte 153, 161
Roduit, Eloi and Gérard 94
Roh, Marc 90
Rolle 108, 111, 116, 132
Romainmôtier 133, 136
Romans 9, 10, 11, 12, 95, 119
Roncobello 187
root stocks 29, 80
rosés 54, 76, 79, 82, 95, 134, 201
Roter Ochsen 203
Rothlisberger, Jean-Pierre 156, 157, 161
Rothschild, Baron 20
Rouge, André 123
rouge de Diolly 49
rougeot 31, 239
Roussanne 95
Rousseau, Jean-Jacques 18, 86, 115, 172
Roussette 44, 75, 88
Route Joyeuse du Joli Vin de Neuchâtel 164
Rouvinez, Anita and Dominique 83, 84
Rouvinez, Bernard 83, 84, 98
Rudolphe III, King 87, 105
Ruedin, François 170
Ruedin, Jean-Paul 165, 176
Rüfenacht, Hans-Peter 174, 176
Ruländer 38, 69
Russia 20
Russin 150, 156, 228
Rutishauser, Walter 205
Rütli 16

S

Sacramento 21
Sager, André 115
Saillon 66, 91, 93, 94
Salève 142, 156
Salquenen 37, 76, 77, 81
Salvagnin 18, 46, 100, 108, 129, 132, 149
San Nicolau 13, 27

Index

Sargans 211
Sarraux 130
Sassicaia 155
Satigny 44, 144, 150, 153, 155, 156, 160, 161, 228
Saulieu 12
Saussure, Claude de 129
Sauvignon 44, 64, 152, 156, 172, 179, 183, 185, 199
Savagnin 15, 39, 43, 73
Savagnin Rosé Aromatique 39
Savièse 66, 89
Savioz, Jean 86
Savioz, Michel 83, 84
Savoie 44, 144, 150
Saxon 95
Schaffhouse 190, 197, 199, 200, 203, 218, 224
Schaffhouse Wine Museum 202
Schafis 172, 173, 176
Schenk, Anita and Jean 112
Schenk SA 93, 108, 110, 116, 132, 226
Schernelz 173, 176
Scherzingen 205
Schiller wine 54, 192, 195, 212, 219
Schinznach 207
Schlaepfer, Jean-Daniel 155, 161
Schlatter, Hans 202
Schloss Johannisberg 68
Schloss Reichenau 215
Schloss Salgenegg 213, 219
Schlossgut Bachtobel 203, 204, 218
Schmid, Jakob 218
Schmid, Tobias 210
Schmucker, Andreas 203
Schneider, Jürg 197, 217
Schwarzenbach, Hermann 197, 198, 209, 217
Schweizerischer Weinbauverein 217
Schwyz 16, 144, 190, 199, 205
screw top 58, 112, 117, 132
secondary fermentation 57
Seebach 203, 204
Seetal 209
Seibel 49
Semillon 44, 179, 183, 185
Sensine 90
Sézenove 157
Shelley, Mary 115
Siegrist, Marie-Hélène 85
Sierre 15, 43, 44, 49, 63, 66, 69, 82, 83
Sigismund, King 13
Simon, André 121
Simon, Olivier 119

Simplon 60
Sion 10, 28, 40, 49, 61, 66, 68, 69, 71, 73, 86, 87, 89
Société d'Emulation Patriotique 164
Société Vinicole de Perroy 130
soil 23, 25, 27, 28, 39, 61, 100, 104, 107, 109, 110, 113, 120, 131, 132, 137, 142, 165, 172, 174, 180, 189, 192, 200, 201, 215
Soleure 190, 209
Sonderbund War 19, 90
Sonnenberg 197, 210
Sopraceneri 48, 180, 186
Soral 157, 158, 160
Sottoceneri 184
sparkling wine 55
Spätburgunder 45
Spumante 179, 183
St. Aubin 166, 167
St. Benedict 12
St. Bernard Pass 40, 60, 95
St. Blaise 163, 164, 169, 176
St. Emilion 33, 155, 184
St. Gall x, 13, 190, 191, 197, 205, 209
St. Gottard Pass 13, 16
St. Jodern-Kellerei 73, 80, 98
St. Katharinethal 205
St. Léonard 66, 86, 87
St. Maurice 11, 12, 13, 95
St. Moritz 198, 217
St. Pierre-de-Clages 91, 92, 227
St. Prex 129
St. Saphorin 45, 103, 107, 112, 113, 114, 117, 119, 123, 129, 140, 235
St. Triphon 105
stabilization 54
Stabio 181
Staël, Madame de 134
Stäfa 197, 198
Stamm, Thomas 203
Stammhein 196
Stein-am-Rhein 203
Steiner, Charles 173, 176
Straub, Philippe 133
Stucky, Werner 184, 185, 187
subsidies 24
sugar 31, 38, 44, 50, 51, 55, 56, 65, 223
sulfur dioxide 53, 54
Süssdruck 192, 212
Sutter Home 21
Sutter, Johann August 21
Swiss Confederation 9, 16, 19, 136, 144, 164, 198, 221, 232
Swiss Cup 92

255

Swiss mercenaries 17
Swiss National Exhibition 72
Swiss Wine Growers Association 226
Swiss Wine Information Council 226
Swissair 82
Sylvaner 22, 32, 35, 36, 45, 63, 65, 68, 81, 85, 105, 165, 172, 195
Syrah 6, 32, 33, 47, 55, 61, 64, 65, 77, 79, 92, 93, 113, 122, 123, 152, 155, 185, 235

T

tablars 63, 239
Tain l'Hermitage 69
Tamborini, Claudio 185
Tamborini, Eredi Carlo 182, 185, 187
tariffs 5, 20, 25, 220
tartaric acid 53, 54
Tartegnin 103, 128, 132
Tavel 58
Tegerfelden 208, 217
Tell, William 16
temperature 27, 29
Templars 16
Tenuta Bally 183, 185, 187
terraces 28, 103, 113, 145
Terravin 100
Testuz SA, Jean and Pierre 119, 122, 126, 129, 140, 226
Teufen 200
Teutsch, Heinz 173, 176
Thal 210
Thalheim 207
thermovinification 55
Thirty Years War 164
Thoiry 157
Thonon 34, 104, 114
Thun 190
Thur 15, 204, 207
Thurgovie 15, 190, 197, 199, 203, 224
Ticino 4, 11, 13, 27, 29, 30, 33, 44, 45, 46, 48, 49, 129, 164, **177 - 188**, 192, 223, 228
Tille, Paul 108, 139
Tokay 38
trade restrictions 220
training the vines 29
Traminer 15, 39, 64
Traubenkocher 189
Trebbiano grape 72
treille du roi 35
trellises 79, 146, 191, 207, 213, 216
Treytorrens 122, 126
Trimmis 215

Troinex 157
Trollinger 45
Truttikon 199, 218
Tscharner, Gian-Battista von 215, 219
Tschugg 172
Tuscany 72
Tüscherz 172, 173, 174, 176
Twann 172, 173, 174, 176

U

Uekon 208, 218
Uerikon 198, 217
Uesslingen-Iselisberg 204
Ugni Blanc 72
UK wine market 4, 226
Unavins 130
United States 4, 45, 226
Unterland 197, 199, 200
Untersee 203, 205
Unterwald 16, 144
Uri 16, 144, 209
Uvrier 86, 89

V

Vaduz 212
Val d'Anniviers 84
Val d'Hérens 89
Val-de-Travers 169
Valais v, x, 4, 5, 6, 12, 19, 28, 29, 31, 32, 33, 35, 36, 37, 38, 39, 40, 43, 44, 46, 47, 48, 52, 55, **60 - 98**, 104, 129, 145, 149, 185, 186, 192, 193, 217, 223, 227, 232, 235, 236
Valeyres-sous-Montagny 136
Valeyres-sous-Rances 136
Vallamand-Dessous 137
Valle Maggia 181
Valley of the Virgin 73
Valorbe 133
Valsangiacomo, Cesare 183, 185
Vandoeuvres 159
Varen (Varonne) 81, 88
Varone, Dany 89
Varone Vins 87
Vaud ix, x, 4, 6, 12, 15, 18, 21, 23, 28, 29, 32, 35, 37, 45, 46, 47, 49, 58, 60, 93, **99 - 140**, 145, 149, 166, 223, 226, 228, 235, 236
Vaudois Federation of Vignerons 100
Vaudois Revolution 18, 107, 112, 125
Vaumarcus 164, 166
Veltliner 211
vendage tardif 239

Venthône 82, 83, 84
véraison 28, 239
Verbier 107
Vers-Chiez 105
Vétroz 41, 66, 73, 89, 90, 91
Vevey 21, 104, 108, 110, 114, 115, 116, 132
Veyras 82
Vienna, Congress of 19
Villa Diodati 115
Villard et Fils, Pierre 159
Ville de Lausanne 113, 117, 121, 130, 131, 140, 226
Villeneuve 103, 107, 112
Villette 103, 124, 127
Villigen 208
vin de paille 15, 239
Vin des Glaciers 6, 44, 59, 74, 85
Vin du Diable 167
vin gris 18
vin jaune d'Arbois 39
vin liquoreux 152
vin mêlés 18
Vin Union 24, 141, 144, 146, 159
Vinattieri Ticinesi 187
vineyard management 25
Vingelz 172, 173
vinification 50
vinification technology 24
vintage chart 236
Vinum 92, 155
Vinzel 103, 128, 133
Vionnaz 95
Visp 73, 80
Vispertermin 43, 61, 63, 73, 74, 80
VITI 182, 187, 223
vitis labrusca 21, 49, 179, 186, 239
vitis sylvestris 9
vitis vinifera 21, 34, 41, 44, 49, 239
Vocat, Joseph 83
Vogel, Jean 127, 140
Vogler, Peter 199
Volg Weinkellereien 214
Vouvry 95
Vufflens-le-Château 129
Vully 100, 103, 135, 137

W

Wädenswil 22, 45, 76, 135, 171, 173, 192, 198, 222
Walenstadt 210
Warth 204, 207
Weber, Eder 21
Wegelin, Peter and Elisabeth 214, 219

Weidmann, Thomas 199, 218
Weinbaumuseum zum Zürichsee 198
Weinfelden 203
Weingut zur Sonne 214, 219
Weiningen 199
Weinland 197, 199
Weissburgunder 38
Weissherbst 201
Werdenberg 210
Wheeler, Joe 166
White Zinfandel 21
Wil 200, 211
Wilchingen 202
wild yeasts 53, 54
wine festivals 156
Wine Museum 139
Wine Statute (Statut du vin) 24, 221
Winterthur 197, 199, 214, 217
Wuilloud, Dr. Henry 75, 79
Würenlingen 207, 218

Y

yeast 22, 54, 55
Yverdon 135, 136
Yvorne 13, 103, 104, 107, 108, 109, 110, 111, 112, 114, 132, 133, 139

Z

Zahner, Waldemar 199, 218, 219
Zermatt 73, 80, 107
Zinfandel 20, 21, 184
Zizers 215
Zufferey, Maurice 83, 98
Zug 190
Zumofen House 83
Zündel, Christian 187
Zurich 9, 17, 138, 189, 190, 191, 196, 199, 203, 205, 224, 228
Zwingli, Ulrich 17

Acknowledgments

This book would not have been possible without the kind, generous and informed assistance of numerous friends, colleagues and acquaintances. Special mention must be made of the members of the Swiss wine industry who gave considerable time and thought to answering basic, or even pointed, questions. Without their knowledge, patience and assistance many inaccuracies would have crept into the text.

Any book on wine will, of necessity, contain many judgments and assessments with which not all readers, especially those most directly affected, will agree. This book is no exception. While I make no apology for expressing my opinions or evaluations, throughout I have tried to remain as objective as possible. I, however, remain solely responsible for any mistakes of fact.

In particular I must acknowledge the contribution of my colleague, Eber Rice, who was critical in transforming a dense draft into readable prose. His was not an easy task but he rose to the challenge admirably. In addition, Richard Bastien and Thomas Feller, during his posting to the Swiss Embassy in Ottawa, provided encouragement and constructive observations as the text moved through its various drafts.

Edouard Graf of Ville de Lausanne, Axel Maye of Simon Maye et Fils, Sergio and Ivo Monti of Lugano, and Urs Giezendanner of Wädenswil all kindly commented on specific chapters in the book, although they can in no way be held accountable for the opinions expressed in final text. Michel Clavien of Domaine Chatroz in Sion offered his support for the project at a critical time. Gérard Pillon & Jean-Daniel Schlaepfer, vignerons at Les Balisiers in Geneva and authors of the book "Les Vins de Genève", were extremely generous with both their commentaries and expert insight. Allan Abel can claim credit for the title. All the above were instrumental in making this book a reality, and to them I give my sincere thanks.

I must finally offer a special thanks to my Swiss brother-in-law, Fredy Flühmann, of Lake Placid, New York who faithfully continues to carry on the best of Swiss traditions despite now living in America.

About the Author

John Sloan is a Canadian diplomat who first developed an interest in wine during his undergraduate studies at Stanford University in California. He subsequently obtained his Higher Certificate (with distinction) from the Wine and Spirit Education Trust while completing graduate work at the London School of Economics in the mid 1970s. He maintained his interest in wines after joining the Canadian Foreign Service in 1975 and throughout subsequent postings in Tokyo, Beijing and Geneva. The genesis for this book grew naturally out of his experiences and travel in Switzerland where he was Counsellor at the Permanent Mission of Canada to the United Nations from 1988 to 1992. In 1991, Mr. Sloan co-edited a book on the economic transformation in Eastern Europe, *La nouvelle europe de l'est, du plan au marché: les defis de la privatisation*, published by Editions Bruylant in Brussels. In the summer of 1993 he was appointed Counsellor (Finance) at the Canadian High Commission in London.

Bergli Books

publishes, promotes and distributes books in English that focus on intercultural issues of interest to people living in Switzerland and working with the Swiss:

Ticking Along with the Swiss, edited by Dianne Dicks, entertaining and informative personal experiences of many 'foreigners' living in Switzerland from all walks of life and many different countries. They record their impressions, wonder, perplexity and assimilation. Includes essays, poems, anecdotes, letters and an A – Z on customs and foibles. ISBN 3-9520002-4-8.

Ticking Along Too, edited by Dianne Dicks, has more personal experiences of authors of different nationalities who live in Switzerland. Their stories are a mix of social commentary, warm admiration and observations of getting along with the Swiss as friends, neighbors and business partners. ISBN 3-9520002-1-3.

Cupid's Wild Arrows; *intercultural romance and its consequences*, edited by Dianne Dicks, contains personal experiences of 55 authors of many different nationalities about living with two worlds in one partnership. These stories not only show the romance and excitement of such relationships but talk about the real-life challenges to be expected, the ups and downs, laughter, tears and peculiar situations. ISBN 3-9520002-2-1. German edition: *Amors wilde Pfeile.* ISBN 3-406-37410-7.

The Perpetual Tourist; in *Search of a Swiss Role*, by Paul N. Bilton, is an entertaining and light-hearted diary of an Englishman who lives and works in Zurich. Cultural values of the Swiss and the British have never been compared with such wit and insight. He reveals the pleasures and pitfalls of cross-cultural adaptation. Great for culture shock (getting it, not curing it). ISBN 3-9520002-3-X.

Soul Stripping; *autobiography of a go-go dancer*, by Paula Charles, is the touching story of this extraordinary woman who arrived in Switzerland with the wrong credentials, the wrong language, education, background and colour. She managed to stay true to herself in spite of the odds stacked against her. She takes you along on her journey to find a better life, love and approval and a way to stay out of the wrong corners. ISBN 3-9520002-5-6.

A Taste of Switzerland, by Sue Style, bears witness to the richness and diversity of Switzerland's gastronomic tradition and demonstrates the wealth of the local, regional and seasonal specialities which have evolved in Swiss kitchens over centuries. This beautifully illustrated book and its many recipes enable you to sample the food, folklore, history and traditions of this country of diverse cultures.The author takes you along on her visits to the country's best cheesemakers, vineyards, butchers, dairies, bakeries and chocolate factories. ISBN 3-9520002-7-2.

Dear Reader,

Your opinion can help us. We would like to know what you think of *The Surprising Wines of Switzerland*.

Where did you learn about this book?

Had you heard about Bergli Books before reading this book?

What did you enjoy about this book?

Any criticism?

Would you like to receive more information about the books we publish and distribute? If so, please give us your name and address:

Name:

Address:

City/Country

Cut out page, fold here, staple and mail to:

Bergli Books Ltd.
Aeussere Baselstrasse 204
CH-4125 Riehen/BS
Switzerland